The Musical Experience

THIRD EDITION

John J. Chiego
University of Memphis

Kendall Hunt
publishing company

Book Team

Chairman and Chief Executive Officer   Mark C. Falb
President and Chief Operating Officer   Chad M. Chandlee
Vice President, Higher Education   David L. Tart
Director of Publishing Partnerships   Paul B. Carty
Senior Editor   Lynnette Rogers
Vice President, Operations   Timothy J. Beitzel
Assistant Vice President, Production Services   Christine E. O'Brien
Senior Production Editor   Mary Melloy
Senior Permissions Coordinator   Caroline Kieler
Senior Cover Designer   Mallory Blondin

Kendall Hunt
publishing company

www.kendallhunt.com
Send all inquiries to:
4050 Westmark Drive
Dubuque, IA 52004-1840

Dedication

This book is dedicated to those who have taught me most of what I know about music, my students. Our conversations, arguments, and shared musical experiences have allowed my musical path to grow ever wider over the years. Because of my students, I have maintained an ever appreciative ear for the extraordinary variety of music in the world. They have reminded me time and time again that the musical experience is, and has always been, the human experience.

John J. Chiego

Brief Contents

Chapter 1   Introduction and Historical Overview   1

Chapter 2   Music of the Religious Experience   25

Chapter 3   Music for the Stage   61

Chapter 4   Music for Dancing   89

Chapter 5   Songs   117

Chapter 6   Music for Mourning   153

Chapter 7   Music for Celebration, Inspiration,
              and Commemoration   175

Chapter 8   Music for the Concert Hall   201

Chapter 9   Music for the Movies   245

Chapter 10   The Experience of Improvisation   273

Contents

Preface   xvii
New to the Third Edition   xix
Features of This Book   xxi
Acknowledgments   xxiii
About the Author   xxvii

Chapter 1

Introduction and Historical Overview   1
Focus Points   1
What Is Music?   1
Elements of Music   2
  Melody   2
  Harmony   3
  Rhythm   4
  Form   4
  Texture   5
  Timbre   5
What Makes Music—Musical Instruments:
  Ensembles   6
Historical Periods and Characteristics   6
  Medieval Period ca. AD 500–1450   7
    O Fortuna from the *Carmina Burana*   7
    Kyrie—Hildegard of Bingen   8
  Renaissance Period 1450–1600   8
    Ave Maria—Josquin des Prez   9
    Canzon XVII—Giovanni Gabrieli   10
  Baroque Period 1600–1750   10
    Canon a tre in D major—Johann Pachelbel   11
    Hallelujah Chorus from *Messiah*—
      George Frideric Handel   11
  Classical Period 1750–1825   11
    Eine Kleine Nachtmusik (A Little Night Music)—
      Wolfgang Amadeus Mozart   12
    Symphony #5 in C minor—1st movement—
      Ludwig van Beethoven   12

Biographical Spotlight: Ludwig van
  Beethoven   12
  Romantic Period 1825–1900   13
Perspective—Art and Music   14
    Symphony #4 in F minor, 4th movement—
      Peter Tchaikovsky   17
    Intermezzo in A major—Johannes Brahms   17
  Twentieth/Twenty-First Century 1900–Present   17
    The Rite of Spring (excerpt)—Igor Stravinsky   17
    Hoedown from *Rodeo*—Aaron Copland   17
Timeline of the Historical Periods   18
Listening Chart   19
    O Fortuna from *Carmina Burana (Songs from
      Benediktbeuern)*—Carl Orff   20
Summary   20
Suggested Further Listening   22
Question Assignment   23
Listening Exercises   24

Chapter 2

Music of the Religious Experience   25
Focus Points   25
Different Approaches to Common Elements
  of Music   26
  Rhythm   26
  Melody   27
  Harmony   27
  Verses and Choruses   28
  Timbre   28
Gregorian Chant   28
The Mass   29
  Early Monophonic Style   30
    Kyrie from *First Mass for Christmas*—
      Anonymous   30

Polyphonic Style—Renaissance and Baroque 30
  Gloria from *Missa Pange Lingua*—
    Josquin des Prez 31
  Credo (excerpt) from *Mass in B minor*—
    Johann Sebastian Bach 32
Classical Style 32
Biographical Spotlight: Wolfgang Amadeus
  Mozart 33
  Sanctus from *Requiem Mass*—
    Wolfgang Amadeus Mozart 34
Romantic Style 34
  Agnus Dei from *Messe di Gloria*—
    Giacomo Puccini 34
Timeline of Music of the Religious
  Experience 35
Psalms 36
  Chichester Psalms, 2nd movement—
    Leonard Bernstein 37
The Oratorio 37
Perspective—Religious Texts and Church
  Influence 38
  Characteristics of an Oratorio 39
  Messiah (excerpts)—
    George Frideric Handel 39
El Niño—A Modern Oratorio 40
  "Shake the Heavens" from *El Niño*—
    John Adams 41
Cantata 41
  "Allegro vivace" from *Gloria*—John Rutter 42
Hymns 42
  All Creatures of our God and King 43
  Veni, veni, Emmanuel 43
Spirituals and Gospel Music 44
  Brother Mosely Crossed (Smote) the Water—
    Traditional Spiritual sung by Andy
    Mosely 44
  Witness—Traditional Spiritual sung by
    Jubilant Sykes 44
  Clap Your Hands—John P. Kee 45
World Worship Music 46
  Ketjak 46
  The Ramayana Monkey Chant—
    Balinese Ketjak 47
  Tibetan Buddhist Monk Chant 47
  Invoking the Spirit of Kindness Through Sound—
    Tibetan Buddhist Monk Chant 48
  Muslim "Call to Prayer" 48
  Call to Prayer—Muslim Invitation to Pray 49
  Tuvan Throat Singing 49
  Kh mei—Performed by Hun-Huur-Tu 50

Contemporary Christian Pop and Rock 50
  Christian Pop Music 51
  El Shaddai—Words and music by
    Michael Card and John Thompson,
    sung by Amy Grant 51
What Makes Music—Musical Instruments:
  The Bowed String Family 51
  I Can Only Imagine—Bart Millard, performed by
    Mercy Me 52
  Christian Rock Music 52
  Alive—P.O.D. 52
  A Tower of Ashes—Theocracy 52
Other Types of Religious Music 52
  Motet 52
Listening Chart 53
  Magnificat 54
  Organum 54
  Stabat Mater 54
Summary 54
Suggested Further Listening 55
Additional Worship Music Texts 56
Question Assignment 59
Listening Exercises 60

Chapter 3

Music for the Stage 61
Focus Points 61
  Star Wars—Imperial March, Darth Vader's
    Theme 61
Early Dramatic Musical Composition 62
Biographical Spotlight: Hildegard of Bingen 62
  Ordo Virtutum excerpt—
    Hildegard of Bingen 63
Opera 64
  Early Opera 65
  Mozart and Classical Opera 66
    "Queen of the Night Aria"
      from Act II of *The Magic Flute*—
      Wolfgang Amadeus Mozart 67
  Romantic Opera 67
    "Vesti la giubba," Canio's Aria from *Pagliacci*—
      Ruggiero Leoncavallo 68
Perspective—Early Theatrical Forms 69
    "O mio babbino caro" from *Gianni Schicchi*—
      Giacomo Puccini 70
  Modern Opera 70
    "The New York Lights" from *A View from the
    Bridge*—William Bolcom 70

What Makes Music—Voices: Female Voices   71
Incidental Music   71
  L'Arlésienne   72
    "Farandole" from *L'Arlésienne*—
      Georges Bizet   72
The Musical   72
  Forerunners of the Musical   73
  Musical Songwriting Teams   73
  The Operatic vs. the Musical Vocal Style   73
  The Evolution of the Musical—50 Years of Song
    and Dance   74
  Tunes, Lyrics, Dialogue, and Dances   74
    I'm an Ordinary Man from *My Fair Lady*—
      Lerner and Loewe   75
    I Could Have Danced All Night from *My Fair
      Lady*—Lerner and Loewe   75
    Tonight—Quintet from *West Side Story*—
      Leonard Bernstein   76
  The Musical Overture   76
    Overture to *Candide*—Leonard Bernstein   76
  The Evolving Musical   76
A Musical Timeline   77
Music for the Stage Timeline   78
    The Phantom of the Opera from *Phantom of the
      Opera*—Andrew Lloyd Webber   79
    Stars from *Les Misérables*—
      Schönberg and Boublil   80
    Bring Him Home from *Les Misérables*—
      Schönberg and Boublil   80
The Modern Stage Spectacle   80
    "Alegria" title song from *Alegria* (a Cirque du
      Soleil show)—René Dupéré   81
    "Drumbone"—Blue Man Group   81
    "Riverdance"—Bill Whelan   81
    "Orinoco Flow"—Enya   81
World Musical Theatre Genres   81
  Kabuki Theatre   81
    Ozatsuma—Traditional Japanese shamisen
      music   82
    Kanjincho—Kabuki theatre music   82
  Chinese Opera   83
    The Story of the White Snake—
      Chinese opera aria   83
Listening Chart   84
Summary   85
Suggested Further Listening   86
Question Assignment   87
Listening Exercises   88

Chapter 4

Music for Dancing   89
Focus Points   89
Rhythm and Meter in Dance Music   89
Box: Time Signatures   90
Dance Music in the Western Tradition   91
  Medieval Dance—Estampie   91
    Estampie—Anonymous   92
  The Dancing Master of the Renaissance
    and Baroque Periods   92
  The Baroque Dance Suite   92
  The Orchestral Dance Suite   93
What Makes Music—Musical Instruments:
  The Woodwind Family   94
    Water Music (excerpts)—
      George Frideric Handel   95
    "Air" from *Orchestral Suite #3 in D major*—
      Johann Sebastian Bach   95
  Solo Instrumental Dance Suite   96
    Suite for Solo Cello in G major—
      Johann Sebastian Bach
        "Bourrées I & II"   96
Nineteenth-Century Waltzes   96
    *An der schönen blauen Donau
      (On the Beautiful Blue Danube)*—
      Johann Strauss II   97
The Full-Length Ballet   97
Timeline of Music for Dancing   98
  Swan Lake   99
    "Lake in the Moonlight" from *Swan Lake*—
      Peter Ilyich Tchaikovsky   99
Perspective—Ancient Dance References   100
Ballet Music of Remarkable Significance   100
  The Rite of Spring   100
Biographical Spotlight: Igor Stravinsky   101
    The Rite of Spring (two excerpts)—
      Igor Stravinsky
        "Auguries of Spring"
          (Dances of the Young Girls)   103
        "Sacrificial Dance"
          (The Chosen One)   103
Thoroughly American Ballet   103
  Rodeo   104
    Rodeo (two excerpts)—Aaron Copland
      "Corral Nocturne"   105
      "Hoe Down"   105

Folk Dance Music from Around the World 105
Balinese Gamelan Music 105
  Gamelan Angklung—
    Balinese Gamelan Music 106
Tibetan Buddhist Monk Dancing 106
  Dance of the Skeleton—
    Tibetan Buddhist Monks 107
Italian Tarantella and Saltarello 107
  Saltarello—Traditional Italian Folk Dance 108
  Symphony #4—Felix Mendelssohn
    "4th Movement" (Saltarello) 108
West African Folk Dance Music 108
  Peul's Dance—Senegal 109
  Acrobatic Dance of the Youths—Liberia 109
  Initiation Dance—Togo 110
Celtic Reels 110
  Three Reels (played without pause)—
    Traditional Celtic Dance Music
      "The Boys of the Lough" 111
      "Over the Bog Road" 111
      "The Merry Harriers" 111
The American Square Dance 111
  Bob Wills Square Dance #1—
    Bob Wills and His Texas Playboys 111
Listening Chart 112
Summary 113
Suggested Further Listening 113
Question Assignment 115
Listening Exercises 116

Chapter 5

Songs 117
Focus Points 117
Folk Songs, Art Songs, and Popular Songs 118
Representative Folk Songs 119
English Folk Songs 119
  Greensleeves—Traditional English Folk Song
    (poss. Henry VIII of England, 1500s) 120
  Blow the Man Down—
    Traditional English Sea Chantey 120
African Folk Songs 120
  Gumbukumbu—
    Traditional African Folk Song 121
  Kumbaya—
    Traditional African Folk Song 122
What Makes Music—Voices: Male Voices 123
American Folk Songs 123
Folk Song Inspired by War 123
  The Cruel War—Traditional Folk Song 124

Folk Song Born of Slavery 124
  All the Pretty Little Horses—
    Traditional Folk Song 125
Folk Song to Accompany Work 125
  John Henry—
    Traditional American Work Song 125
Box: A Unique Type of Folk Song 126
  Pilentze Pee (Little Bird)—
    Traditional Bulgarian Folk Song.
    Translated by Milena Albrecht 127
Art Songs in the Western Historical
  Periods 127
A Medieval Troubadour Song 128
  Ahi! Amours (Alas Love)—
    Conon de Bethune, ca. 1150–1220 128
A Renaissance Lute Song 129
  I Care Not for These Ladies—
    Thomas Campion, 1567–1620 129
A Classical/Romantic Art Song 130
Biographical Spotlight: Franz Schubert 131
  Erlkönig (The Erlking)—Franz Schubert 132
Art Songs with Orchestral Accompaniment 133
  "The Drunkard in Spring" from *Das Lied Von
    Der Erde*—Gustav Mahler 133
The Emergence of Popular Song 134
Stephen Foster 134
Perspective—Words in Song 135
Timeline of Songs 136
  Jeanie with the Light Brown Hair—
    Stephen Foster 137
The Blues 137
Twelve-Bar Blues Chord Progression 137
Chord Names 138
  Every Day (I Have the Blues)—B. B. King 138
Tin Pan Alley 138
  Puttin' on the Ritz—Irving Berlin 139
Jazz Songs 139
  Blue Skies—Irving Berlin 139
  Strange Fruit—Lewis Allan
    (Abel Meeropol) 139
Rock and Roll 140
  Good Golly Miss Molly—Little Richard 140
  Roll Over Beethoven—Chuck Berry 141
  Rock Around the Clock—
    Bill Haley and the Comets 141
The Impact of Rock and Roll 141
Box: Rock and Roll Icons 141
  Blue Suede Shoes—Elvis Presley 142
  (I Can't Get No) Satisfaction—
    The Rolling Stones 142

Other Popular Styles   142
 Urban Folk   142
  The Times They Are a' Changin—
   Bob Dylan   143
 R&B/Motown   143
  My Girl—The Temptations   143
 Blues/Rock   143
  Crossroads—Robert Johnson,
   performed by Cream   143
 Heavy Metal   144
  Metal Meltdown—Judas Priest   144
 Country   144
  Folsom Prison Blues—Johnny Cash   145
 Pop Music   145
  Candle in the Wind—Elton John,
   lyrics by Bernie Taupin   145
 Alternative Rock   145
  Jeremy—Pearl Jam   145
Listening Chart   146
  Higher Ground—
   The Red Hot Chili Peppers   147
 Rap/Hip-Hop   147
  Hard Times—Run-D.M.C.   147
  Lose Yourself—Eminem   147
  Swagga Like Us—
   T.I., Jay-Z, L'il Wayne   148
Summary   148
Suggested Further Listening   149
Question Assignment   151
Listening Exercises   152

Chapter 6

Music for Mourning   153
Focus Points   153
The Requiem Mass   154
Biographical Spotlight: Giuseppe Verdi   155
 The Dies Irae   156
  Sequence (Dies Irae excerpt)
   from *Requiem Mass in D minor*—
   Wolfgang Amadeus Mozart   157
  Sequence (Dies Irae excerpt) from *Messa da Requiem*—Giuseppe Verdi   158
What Makes Music—Musical Instruments:
 The Brass Family   159
 A Requiem without the Dies Irae   159
  In Paradisum from *Requiem in D minor*—
   Gabriel Fauré   160
Songs of Mourning   160
  Tears in Heaven—Eric Clapton   161

"Nun will die Sonn . . . " Movement I from
   Kindertotenlieder—Gustav Mahler (Now the
   sun will rise . . .)   161
 Instrumental Music of Mourning   161
Perspective—*On the Transmigration of Souls*
 by John Adams   162
 The Funeral March   163
  3rd Movement "Funeral March" from
   Piano Sonata #2 in B-flat minor—
   Frederic Chopin   163
  2nd Movement "Marcia Funebre" from
   Symphony #3 in E-flat major—
   Ludwig van Beethoven   164
Threnody   164
  Threnody to the Victims of Hiroshima—
   Krzysztof Penderecki   164
 The *Adagio for Strings*   164
Timeline of Music for Mourning   165
  Adagio for Strings—Samuel Barber   166
 Dogon Funeral Music   166
  Dogon Funeral Music   167
 The New Orleans Jazz Funeral   167
  Just a Closer Walk with Thee—
   Jazz Funeral Dirge   168
  When the Saints Go Marching In—
   Traditional   168
 Native American Funeral Music   168
  Funeral Song—Watapai (Walapai)   168
Listening Chart   169
  Warrior Death Song (for Sitting Bull)—
   Assinboine (Assiniboine)   170
Summary   170
Suggested Further Listening   171
Question Assignment   173
Listening Exercises   174

Chapter 7

Music for Celebration, Inspiration, and Commemoration   175
Focus Points   175
Music for Celebration   176
  Happy Birthday   176
  Auld Lang Syne   177
  Auld Lang Syne—Traditional Scottish Folk Song
   performed by Guy Lombardo's
   Orchestra   178
  The *Wedding March* from *A Midsummer Night's
   Dream*   178

Wedding March from *A Midsummer Night's Dream*—Felix Mendelssohn   179
Jewish Wedding Music   179
Hava Nagila (Come Let Us Be Glad)—Traditional Jewish Folk Dance   179
Wedding Dance—Traditional Jewish Klezmer Music   180
Mexican Hat Dance   180
Jarabe Tapatío—Jesús Rubio   181
Music of Inspiration   181
Fanfares   181
Hail to the Chief—Ceremonial Fanfare   181
Olympic Fanfare (opening flourish)—John Williams   182
Olympic Fanfare (entire composition)—John Williams   182
Fanfare for the Common Man—Aaron Copland   182
National Anthems   182
What Makes Music—Musical Instruments: The Percussion Family   183
The Star Spangled Banner (verses 1 and 4)—words by Francis Scott Key, music by John Stafford Smith   184
Marches   184
The Stars and Stripes Forever—John Philip Sousa   185
Music of Commemoration   185
The Concert Overture   185
Festive Overture—Dmitri Shostakovich   186
The *1812 Overture*   186
Timeline of Music for Celebration, Inspiration, and Commemoration   187
Perspective—Monuments and Memorials   188
Biographical Spotlight: Peter Ilyich Tchaikovsky   190
1812 Overture—Peter Ilyich Tchaikovsky   192
Lincoln Portrait   193
Lincoln Portrait—Aaron Copland   193
A Song of Celebration, Inspiration, and Commemoration   194
Listening Chart   195
We Shall Overcome—Pete Seeger, Guy Carawan, and Frank Hamilton   196
Summary   196
Suggested Further Listening   197
Question Assignment   199
Listening Exercises   200

Chapter **8**

Music for the Concert Hall   201

Focus Points   201
Development of the Concert Tradition   201
Box: Musical Experiences before the Twentieth Century 203
Music for the Concert Hall—Historical Periods, Common Genres, and Composers   203
Baroque Period, 1600–1750   203
Style and Characteristics   203
Musical Elements   204
Baroque Instruments   204
Box: The Baroque Orchestra   205
The Basso Continuo   205
Baroque Instrumental Genres   205
Concerto Grosso   206
Brandenburg Concerto #2, 1st movement—Johann Sebastian Bach   206
Concerto   207
Lute Concerto in D major, 2nd movement—Antonio Vivaldi   207
The Fugue   207
What Makes Music—Musical Instruments: Keyboards   207
Little Organ Fugue in G minor—Johann Sebastian Bach   208
Little Organ Fugue in G minor—Johann Sebastian Bach   208
Little Fugue in G minor (orchestrated)—Johann Sebastian Bach   209
Biographical Spotlight: Johann Sebastian Bach   209
The Trio Sonata and the Sonata   210
Sonata, Opus 1 #3, Presto—Arcangelo Corelli   211
Box: Italian Terms   211
Classical Period, 1750–1825   211
Style and Characteristics   211
Perspective—Baroque to the Twenty-First Century (Part 1)   212
Musical Elements   213
Single-Movement Forms of the Classical Period   214
Sonata Form   215
Classical Instrumental Genres   216
The Symphony   216
Box: The Classical Orchestra 217

Symphony #5 in C minor, 1st movement—
Ludwig van Beethoven 218
The String Quartet 218
String Quartet in D minor, 2nd movement
(*Andante con moto*)—Franz Schubert 218
Box: Composition 219
The Concerto 219
Concerto for Trumpet and Orchestra, 1st
movement—Franz Joseph Haydn 219
The Sonata 219
Piano Sonata, Opus 13, 2nd movement—
Ludwig van Beethoven 220
Romantic Period, 1825–1900 220
Style and Characteristics 220
Timeline of Music for the Concert Hall 221
Musical Elements 222
Box: The Romantic Orchestra 223
The Romantic Piano 223
Ballade in G minor—Frederic Chopin 223
Romantic Period Instrumental Genres 224
Program Music, Nationalism, and
Impressionism 224
Program Music 224
*Til Eulenspiegel's Lustige Streiche
(Til Eulenspiegel's Merry Pranks)*—
Richard Strauss 225
Nationalism 225
Night on Bald Mountain—Modest Mussorgsky,
revised by Nicolai Rimsky-Korsakov 226
Impressionism 226
*L'Apres-midi d'un faun (The Afternoon of a
Faun)*—Claude Debussy 227
The Romantic Symphony 227
The New World Symphony 227
Symphony #9, 2nd movement, Largo—
excerpt Antonin Dvořák 228
Goin' Home—Melody composed by
Antonin Dvořák, words by William Arms
Fisher 228
Symphony #9, 4th movement, Allegro con fuoco
(Fast with fire)—Antonin Dvořák 228
Twentieth/Twenty-First Century 1900–
Present 228
Style and Characteristics 228
Perspective—Baroque to the Twenty-First
Century (Part 2) 229
A New Musical Language—Re-Evaluating Common
Practices 230
Serialism 231
Expressionism 231

Five Piano Pieces, two movements—
Arnold Schoenberg 232
Langsam (Slowly) 232
Sehr rasch (very quickly) 232
Primitivism 232
The Rite of Spring, excerpt "Adoration of the
Earth"—Igor Stravinsky 232
Neoclassicism 232
Pulcinella, Overture and Allegro—
Igor Stravinsky 233
Avant-garde: Experiments in Modern
Music 233
The Banshee—Henry Cowell 234
Traditionalism 234
Twentieth/Twenty-First Century Tonality-Based
Compositions 235
Rhapsody in Blue 235
Rhapsody in Blue—George Gershwin 235
Afro-American Symphony 235
Afro-American Symphony, 3rd movement
"Animato"—William Grant Still 236
Symphony #2, Mysterious Mountain 236
Symphony #2, Mysterious Mountain, double fugue
excerpt—Alan Hovhannes 236
In C 236
In C—Terry Riley 236
Symphony #3, 4th movement—Philip Glass 237
Crossover Music 237
Blackberry Winter, 3rd movement—
Conni Ellisor 238
"Vivace" from *Concerto Suite for Electric Guitar
and Orchestra*—Yngwie Malmsteen with
David Rosenthal 238
Listening Chart 239
Summary 240
Suggested Further Listening 241
Question Assignment 243
Listening Exercises 244

Chapter **9**

Music for the Movies 245
Focus Points 245
Early Years of Movie Music 246
The Jazz Singer 246
Toot, Toot, Tootsie, Goodbye—Gus Kahn,
Ernie Erdman, Dan Russo 247
Kol Nidre—Jewish Prayer 247

Orchestral Scores 247
  King Kong, Main Title Sequence—
    Max Steiner 248
  The Sea Hawk, Main Title Sequence—
    Erich Wolfgang Korngold 248
  Gone with the Wind, Main Title Sequence—
    Max Steiner 248
  Alexander Nevsky—A Milestone in Movie
    Music 249
  Alexander Nevsky, "Battle on the Ice"—
    Sergei Prokofiev, Two excerpts 250
Songs in Film 250
  Somewhere, Over the Rainbow—music by Harold
    Arlen, lyrics by E.Y. Harburg 251
  As Time Goes By from *Casablanca*—
    Herman Hupfield 251
An Evolving View of the Role of Music
  in Movies 251
  "Circus Music" from *The Red Pony*—
    Aaron Copland 253
Musical Performances as Pivotal Scenes 253
  Die Wacht am Rhein/La Marseillaise from
    Casablanca 253
  The Storm Cloud Cantata—Arthur Benjamin,
    from *The Man Who Knew Too Much* 253
  Wild Signals from *Close Encounters of the Third
    Kind*—John Williams 254
Staged Musical Adaptations 254
What Makes Music—The Conductor 255
  "Dat's Love" from *Carmen Jones*—
    lyrics by Oscar Hammerstein,
    music by Georges Bizet 256
Classical Compositions That Appear
  in Movies 256
Musical Biopics 256
Timeline of Music for Movies 257
Music for Animated Movies and Cartoons 258
  Cartoon Shorts 259
  Powerhouse—Raymond Scott 259
  House Hunting Mice 259
  William Tell Overture—
    Gioacchino Rossini 260
Electronic Scores 260
Perspective 1—Music on Radio and
  Television 261
Perspective 2—Music For Video Games 262
  Forbidden Planet, Main Title Sequence—
    Louis and Bebe Barron 263
  Forbidden Planet, "Battle with Invisible
    Monster"—Louis and Bebe Barron 263

Chariots of Fire, Main Title Sequence—
    Vangelis 264
  The Day the Earth Stood Still, "Prelude"—
    Bernard Herrmann 264
The Influence of the Director 264
  "Ride of the Valkyries" from *Die Walküre*—
    Richard Wagner 265
Prominent Composers of Movie Music 265
  "Murder" (Shower Scene from *Psycho*)—
    Bernard Herrmann 265
  The Good, The Bad and The Ugly—
    Main Theme—Ennio Morricone 265
  Gabriel's Oboe from *The Mission*—
    Ennio Morricone 265
  Dr. No, "James Bond Theme"—John Barry 266
Biographical Spotlight: John Williams 267
Listening Chart 268
  Jaws, "Main Title and First Victim"—
    John Williams 269
  Star Wars, "Main Title Sequence"—
    John Williams 269
Summary 269
Suggested Further Listening/Watching 270
Question Assignment 271
Listening Exercises 272

Chapter 10

The Experience of Improvisation 273
Focus Points 273
Improvisation, A Uniquely Musical
  Experience 273
  The Improvisatory Framework 274
  Improvisation in Western Art Music 274
    Lute Concerto in D major, 2nd movement—
      Antonio Vivaldi 275
    Piano Concerto #1 in C major, 1st movement—
      Ludwig van Beethoven 275
  Improvisation in the Contemporary "Classical"
    Context 275
    A Night in Tunisia—Dizzy Gillespie, performed
      by the Turtle Island String Quartet 276
    Muir Woods Suite, "Phase 5"—
      George Duke 276
  Improvisation in Jazz 276
    When the Saints Go Marching In—
      performed by Louis Armstrong 277
    West End Blues—
      Louis Armstrong and His Hot Five 277

Biographical Spotlight: Louis Armstrong 277
    One O'Clock Jump—
        Count Basie and His Orchestra 279
    Take the "A" Train—Billy Strayhorn, performed
        by the Duke Ellington Orchestra 279
    In the Mood—Glenn Miller Big Band 279
    Straight No Chaser—Thelonious Monk 280
    A Night in Tunisia—Dizzy Gillespie 280
    Yvette—Stan Getz 280
    So What—Miles Davis 280
    Bitches Brew—Miles Davis 281
   Improvisation in Rock Music 281
    Good Golly Miss Molly—Little Richard 281
    Roll Over Beethoven—Chuck Berry 281
The Experience of Improvisation
   Timeline 282
Perspective—Improvisation in Theatre
   and Dance 283
    Rock Around the Clock—
        Bill Haley and the Comets 284
    Spoonful—Willie Dixon, performed
        by Cream 284
    You Enjoy Myself—Trey Anastasio,
        performed by Phish 285

Improvisation in Non-Western Music 285
    Maqam Kurd—Traditional Arabic
        Improvisation 287
What Makes Music—Musical Instruments:
   Plucked Strings 287
    Raga: Tilik Shayam—Performed by
        Ravi Shankar 288
Listening Chart 289
Summary 290
Suggested Further Listening 291
Question Assignment 293
Listening Exercises 294

Glossary of Key Terms 295
Glossary of Key People
   and Compositions 307
Appendix 315
Index of Key Terms 317
Index of Key People and Compositions 327

Preface

Do you need a textbook to "appreciate" music? Of course not. You listen to music, you decide if you like it, and choose whether or not to listen to it again. That is the wonder of music in the twenty-first century, having the ability to listen to music whenever you want, choose only the music that you like, and never have to listen to anything you don't.

That is also the tragedy of music in the modern age. We can choose to ignore centuries of inspired music that can still touch us today, even though it was written long ago. We can spend an entire lifetime listening only to the music we already know we want to hear. We can tune our radios to the stations that play just the right style of music to fit our mood at any given moment and we fill our MP3 players with just the music that makes us happy. While that control over our musical experience can be enjoyable, it can also be very limited and confining. This book will most likely introduce you to some types of music that you have never experienced before. If you use this book as both a resource for information about music and also as a guidebook to a wider world of musical experiences then it will have served its purpose, to foster an "appreciation" of all music, regardless of when or where it originated.

This book is unlike most books of its type in that while it is about music there is no musical notation anywhere in the text. Most introductory books about music spend a good deal of time trying to teach the student how to read music. Those books then attempt to apply that knowledge to understanding the underlying music theory that defines music from different eras and cultures. That is a task that is best undertaken over a much longer period of time than one semester or quarter. If a working knowledge of written notation is desired there are a number of links on the Web site that accompanies this text that can teach the student the fundamentals of reading music.

Music Appreciation textbooks are usually organized chronologically according to the art music of the Western world. Music that does not fit into that style or the chronological sequence, such as World Music, Jazz, Rock and Roll, etc, is given a separate chapter. This book takes a different approach. It assumes that music is often best discussed according to how and why it is experienced rather than how it is constructed or when it was written. In the course of that discussion the history of music is certainly covered when it is appropriate to the particular topic, such as in the discussion of music for the concert hall, and the structure of the music is examined when that is fitting.

People listen to music in a variety of settings, for a variety of reasons. Music is experienced through religious observance, song, dance, celebration, mourning, etc. It is the author's belief that examining music from a variety of eras and cultures within each of these experiential categories elicits a true appreciation of the power and beauty of music. It is the author's hope that after completing this course the student will more readily include a wider diversity of musical styles from all historical eras in their choice of listening than he or she did before taking the class. In writing this book it has been the author's desire to present material that truly represents one of the most remarkable and rewarding of human endeavors, the musical experience.

New to the Third Edition

The Third Edition of *The Musical Experience* contains a number of new features, some of which are gradable components that can be completed by the student on an ongoing basis throughout the semester so as not to rely solely on test results for the semester grade. Each chapter now contains four components that expand upon the chapter content or add a new dimension to it. The four new components in each chapter are Biographical Spotlights, Listening Exercises, Chapter Question Assignments, and What Makes Music.

The Biographical Spotlights feature a more in-depth look at a composer discussed in the chapter. There is also a gradable assignment at the end of each Spotlight that requires the student to compare material in the Spotlight to another biographical sketch of the composer, ensuring a fairly thorough understanding of the composer's life and contributions.

Each chapter also has several Listening Exercise questions intended to guide the student in a directed way toward identifying certain aspects of selected musical examples.

Chapter Question Assignments also appear in each chapter and direct the student toward a solid understanding of an important concept or set of facts found in that chapter.

And finally, each chapter also contains a feature called "What Makes Music," which looks at an individual instrument family, a type of voice, musical ensembles, etc., anything that makes music.

As you explore the extraordinary breadth and variety of music from yesterday and today, and cultures familiar and exotic, it is my hope that these additions further enrich your own musical experience.

John J. Chiego

Features of This Book

Welcome to *The Musical Experience*. To help you get the most out of this course I have included a short description of the main features of the text.

𝄞♪ ONLINE MUSIC LIBRARY

Musical examples for *The Musical Experience* are provided through an optional online music library. The examples referenced in the text will be available in a chapter playlist in the Music Library on the accompanying website. This library contains over three million musical selections. Each textbook contains an access code that entitles the user to a free four-month subscription to this library with unlimited access to all available music. Instructors can stream this music in real-time in the classroom through a computer or play it from an MP3 player. When streaming music live via computer the instructor can access any of the available music selections instantly, providing a level of flexibility in classroom presentation heretofore not possible.

LISTENING CHARTS

Each chapter's comprehensive Listening Chart includes all of the musical examples presented in that chapter. The charts serve as practical tools for chapter test preparation. They are not second-by-second descriptions of individual pieces. The charts provide logical listening cues that will help the student zero in on the pertinent information instructors usually ask for on tests, such as: historical period, genre, likely composer, and any other unique aspect of individual compositions. These listening charts are also included online to allow the student to study even if they don't have their textbook handy.

TIMELINES

Timelines found in each chapter relate the pertinent information presented in that chapter in a clearly-presented visual snapshot. The genres, styles of music, influences, and composers are included in the Timelines, which serve as visual study guides for the chapter material in preparation for chapter tests. These timelines are interactive on the web to aid the student in studying.

PERSPECTIVES

A Perspective is a short essay on a subject related to, or that serves as supporting material for, chapter content. Topics include *Art and Music* in conjunction with the elements of music and the historical overview in Chapter 1, *Religious Texts* as supporting material for genres, such as the Mass, in Chapter 2; and *Words and Music* in Chapter 5. The Perspectives can also be found online.

SUGGESTED FURTHER LISTENING

One of the advantages of using the Online Music Library as the music delivery system for *The Musical Experience* is the ability to go far beyond the playlists to explore the widest possible range of recorded music. Suggested Further Listening lists provide the student with musical options beyond the examples discussed in the text for projects and papers and afford the instructor easy access to additional supporting examples for chapter topics.

 ## WEB COMPONENT

Interactive Chapter Timelines

Students can sort by composers, genres, styles, etc. within the timeline and when clicking on an item a brief description appears.

Practice Quizzes

Students can take practice quizzes to gauge their mastery of the chapter material. Each quiz is composed of randomly selected questions. These quizzes can be taken as often as the student wants to prepare for chapter tests.

Chapter Tests

The instructor can choose to administer tests online and have them automatically graded and entered into an electronic grade book. This allows the student immediate test results.

PowerPoint Presentations

Students can access PowerPoint presentations of classroom material to reinforce and confirm their note taking.

Drop Box

Students can submit papers online by placing them in the provided Drop Box.

Listening Charts

Students can listen to examples from the playlists and follow the Listening Charts online at the same time.

Acknowledgments

The author wishes to thank and acknowledge those whose support, encouragement, thoughtful contributions and corrections made this text possible: The University of Memphis, Richard R. Ranta, Dean of the College of Communication and Fine Arts, Patricia Hoy, Randal Rushing, Lecolion Washington, Tim Goodwin, Konnie Saliba, Leonard Schranze, Peter Spurbeck, David Williams, David Spencer, Robert Elliott, Laura Feo-Fernandez, my sons Christopher, Andrew, and Peter and my wife Sara.

The author also gratefully acknowledges the helpful feedback of the following reviewers who provided suggestions for individual chapters of this text.

Dan Allcott
Tennessee Technological University

Beth Aracena
Eastern Mennonite University

Carol Ayres
Iowa Lakes Community College

James Bankhead
California State University, Chico

Philippe Baugh
Tarrant County Jr. College—NE

Mark Berry
Western Kentucky University

Ira Bigelow
University of Colorado—Denver

LaWanda Blakeney
Louisiana State University, Shreveport

William Braun
Wisconsin Lutheran College

Rina Bristol
Alabama State University

Debra Brown
Johnson County Community College

Michael Brown
Mississippi State University

Phillipa Burgess
Ohio Dominican University

Robert Busan
San Francisco State University

Ken Cardillo
Chattanooga State Technical
    Community College

Walter Carr
Portland Community College

Marianne Chaudoir
Marian College of Fond du Lac

Jackie Chooi-Theng Lewis
Salisbury University

John Christian
Patrick Henry Community College

Christy Colburn
Itawamba Junior College

Carmelo Comberiati
Manhattanville College

Richard Condit
McNeese State University

Carolyn Conners
Wor-Wic Community College

Timothy Crain
Indiana State University

Norval Crews
Midwestern State University

Scott Davis
Broward Community College

Seth Davis
Kingwood College and Alamo District

Kevin Delgado
San Diego State University

Maria DiPalma
Simpson College

Dr. Carmen Dominguez
Saddleback College

Gavin Douglas
University of North Carolina
  at Greensboro

Rebecca Dunnell
Northwest Missouri State University

Linda Durham
Virginia Western Community College

Judith Failoni
Fontbonne University

Beth Farber
Southern Polytechnic State University

Angelo Favis
Illinois State University

Stephen Feldman
University of Central Arkansas

William Folger
Salisbury University

Gloria Frank
Austin Peay State University

Roger Franklin
Richard Bland College

Brad Fugate
University of North Carolina
  at Greensboro

Richard Gardzina
New England College

Alan Goldspiel
Louisiana Tech University

Todd Guy
Indiana Wesleyan University

George Halsell
College of Southern Idaho

Brian Hamilton
Long Beach City College

Curt Hamlett
Louisiana College

Rachel Harris
Louisiana State University

Judy Hedberg
Portland Community College

Craig Hembree
Atlanta Christian College

Earl Henry
Webster University

Matthew Herman
Montgomery County Community
  College and West Chester University

Mark Hertica
Cuyamaca Community College

John Hildreth
Augustana College

Jeanette Hinkeldey
Buena Vista University

Bill Hinkle
Seminole Community College

Mark Hollingsworth
East Central University

Martha Horst
East Carolina University and Illinois
  State University

Debra Inglefield
Indiana University South Bend

Chuck Iwanusa
CS Mott Community College

Sarah Jamison
Broward Community College

Peter Janson
University of Massachusetts, Boston

David Kassler
Fort Hays State University

John Keene
Xavier University

Robert Kehle
Pittsburgh State University

Robert Kehrberg
Western Carolina University

Yvonne Kendall
University of Houston, Downtown

Donna King
Lipscomb University

James Kirkwood
SUNY Geneseo

Carey Kleiman
Broward Community College

David Knowles
Mississippi Gulf Coast Community
    College

Tama Kott
West Liberty State College

Tim Krueger
Metropolitan St. College, Denver

Susan Kynkor
Palm Beach Community College

Mark Latham
Butte College

Maria Letona
Barry University

Gary Lewis
Midwestern State University

John Little
James Madison University

Jannine Livingston
Rio Hondo College

Don Malone
Roosevelt University

James A. Martin
Webster University

David Mathew
Georgia Southern University (retired)

Sbeth May
Northwest Vista College

Byron McGilvray
Trinity Valley Community College

Greg McLean
Georgia Perimeter College

Mikylah Myers McTeer
Fort Lewis College

Dr. Valerie Meidinger
Marian College

Charlotte Meuller
Lee College

Carole Miklos
Indiana University Northwest

Ruth Morrow
Midwestern State University

Eric Moseley
Trinity Valley Community College

Laurel Moser
Kirkwood Community College

Dave Moskowitz
University of South Dakota, Vermillion

Paul Mosteller
University of Alabama, Birmingham

Jocelyn Nelson
East Carolina University

Deborah Nemko
Bridgewater State College

Laura New
Johnson County Community College

Paul North
Ivy Tech Community College

John Norton
Moraine Valley Community College

Steven Raisor
College of the Albemarle

Sister Philomene Reiland
Sauk Valley Community College

Carla Reisch
Irvine Valley College

Dennis Renfroe
John Wesley College

Vaughn Roste
Andrew College

Dr. Clark Roush
York College

Elise Schowalter
Northern Kentucky University

Jan Scott
NcNeese State University

Catherine Seifert
Providence College

Pat Setzer
Cuyamaca College

James Shearer
New Mexico State University

Deborah Simmons
Manchester Community College

Joseph Skillen
Louisiana State University, Baton Rouge

Alan Smith
Bowling Green State University

David Smith
Neosho County Community College

James Starr
Emporia State University

Georgea (Tony) Steve
Jacksonville University

Pamela Stover
Southern Illinois University

Vicki Stroeher
Marshall University

Karla Stroman
North Hennepin Community College

Michael Tausig
Mt. San Jacinto College

Gary Thomasson
Grays Harbor College

Andrew Tomasello
Baruch College

Susan Treacy
Ave Maria University

Andrea Trent
Tyler Junior College

Susan Tusing
Andrew College

Sarah Tyrrell
Johnson County Community College

Christopher Ulffers
East Carolina University

Jane Viemeister
Bridgewater State College

Thomas Vozzella
Sterling College

Lori Wacker
East Carolina University

Hsin-yi Wang
Tarrant County Junior College, South

Dennis Weber
Shasta College

Dr. Stephen Weber
University of Science and Arts
of Oklahoma

Mary Whartenby
Wytheville Community College

Craig Whittaker
Guilford College

Richard Yaklich
Florida Memorial University

Robin Zemp
College of Charleston

Thomas Zirkle
St. Louis Community College

Shanon Zusman
Pasadena City College

About the Author

John J. Chiego is Professor of Music in the Rudi E. Scheidt School of Music at the University of Memphis. He is an active performer, educator, and clinician with a wide variety of experience in both classical and popular music. He has held positions as the Principal Bassist of the Nashville Chamber Orchestra, Mentor and Principal Bassist of the Hot Springs Music Festival, Principal Bassist of the Memphis Symphony, the bassist for touring Broadway productions at the Orpheum Theatre in Memphis, Tennessee, and has taught at a number of summer music festivals including the Brevard Music Center. Mr. Chiego has performed solo recitals and given Master Classes across the US and Europe and at *The International Society of Bassists* worldwide conventions. His solo CD, *It's A Bass Thing!*, was released in 1997. Mr. Chiego has taught Music Appreciation since 1979 when he joined the faculty at the University of Memphis. The breadth of his educational and performing experience has enabled him to bring a fresh approach to the writing of *The Musical Experience*.

Photo courtesy of the University of Memphis, Rhonda Cosentino photographer.

Introduction and Historical Overview

FOCUS POINTS

The Elements	Historical Periods
Melody	Medieval
Harmony	Renaissance
Rhythm	Baroque
Form	Classical
Texture	Romantic
Timbre	Twentieth/Twenty-First Century

WHAT IS MUSIC?

Do you think your answer to that question will be the same as that of the person sitting next to you in class? How about the answer a parent or grandparent might give? Would their definition of music be different from yours? What about someone who lived a hundred years ago, or even a thousand years ago?

No doubt the music from past eras sounded different because the instruments used in earlier times were not the same as those used today. But what about the music itself? What about the things that make music meaningful for us? The things that touch us on a level and in a way that no other form of communication can? Are those things really so different today than they were a hundred or a thousand years ago?

What about music from other countries? Do people from other cultures listen to music for the same reasons we do? Do they listen for the same things in the music? Do they react the same as we do to different types of music?

Our experience of music is linked to the time and place from which the music comes and our own time and place during which it is heard. When we hear music today that was written a hundred years ago it is helpful to understand the time during which it was written, what the accepted norms were for music of that time, and how people of that time might have experienced the music. For even though the sounds from different historical eras and different cultures may be unusual for us listening to them today, they were the norm for the time and place from which they originated.

Etruscan wall painting, fifth century BC. Corel

But back to our original question. What is music? We know music is sound. On that we can probably all agree. But beyond that we run into problems defining music. The words we use to define and describe music include terms like melody, harmony, rhythm, form, texture, and timbre (tim'bər). Some of these words are probably familiar to you in reference to music, such as melody, harmony, and rhythm. Form and texture are words you most likely know but are unsure how they refer to music. And timbre is probably a new term for you. Let's look at each term briefly.

ELEMENTS OF MUSIC

Melody

The Fifer, Edouard Manet (1832–1883). Corel

Melody refers to the tune of a piece of music, the thing we would most likely whistle or sing after we've heard a piece. Melodies are made up of pitches, sounds that have a certain frequency of vibration that determines whether the sound is perceived as sounding high or low to us. The pitches used for melodies come from scales, a kind of basic alphabet that is used as the basis of a piece of music.

Focusing on the melody is an important part of listening to musical compositions and can greatly add to our enjoyment of all types of music. Many pieces of music are organized by how the melody is used so it is useful to be able to discern it in different types of settings. Most music we hear today has the melody in the vocal line. Listen to the following example. It will start with a short introduction in which we hear instruments that are not playing the melody but serve to set the "feel" of the song. The melody is easily distinguished when the voice enters. After the song is over you can recreate the melody by singing it yourself with little effort.

 I Heard it Through the Grapevine—
Written by Norman Whitfield and Barrett Strong, performed by Marvin Gaye

When we listen to instrumental music, that is music played only by instruments with no vocal part, we sometimes have to listen a little more attentively to pick out the melody. In the next example it is still fairly easy to hear the melody. It is played by a solo violin with the other instruments playing an accompaniment that is clearly less prominent than the melody.

 "Winter," Concerto for Violin and Orchestra, 2nd movement—
Antonio Vivaldi

Sometimes the music has many things going on at the same time and we have to listen with an even greater level of attention to pick out the melody from all of the other sounds. In the following example the melody is sometimes played by many instruments very loudly, so it is easy to hear, and sometimes it is played softly and shared among several instruments. That is a bit more difficult to hear clearly. Try to allow your ear to wander from instrument to instrument as the melody is played by different parts of the orchestra.

Lohengrin, prelude to Act 3—
Richard Wagner

Harmony

Harmony is all of the pitches that aren't the melody. We commonly refer to harmony in terms of chords. Chords are three or more pitches played simultaneously. Harmony has the ability to make us "feel" certain ways when we hear different types of harmonies. While any particular combination of pitches contains no inherent emotional quality, major chords are often described as having a bright, triumphant sound. Minor chords frequently sound brooding and somber. The emotional reactions we have when we hear these types of harmonies add richness to the musical experience.

While our ears tend to gravitate toward the melody we can't help but react, even subconsciously, to the harmony. The two most common types of harmonies, major and minor, are often taken to imply the emotional states of happy versus sad or something similar, such as confident versus fearful, triumph versus defeat, etc. In the following example there will be a series of three full orchestral outbursts. Each one will occur after a three-note trumpet statement. The first orchestral outburst is a major harmony followed quickly by a minor harmony, as if to imply confidence followed by fear. The second orchestral statement is the reverse, a minor harmony followed by a major harmony. You might interpret this as a confident feeling triumphing over that fear. The third orchestral entrance consists of two major harmonies one after the other, reinforcing the positive feeling of the previous statement. The music that follows that third statement strengthens the overall feeling of confidence, triumph and happiness. This interpretation of the opening few moments of this piece is reflective of the opening pages of the philosophical novel, *Also Sprach Zarathustra (Thus Spake Zarathustra)* by the German author Frederich Nietzche, on which the composition is based.

Thus Spake Zarathustra, Introduction—
Richard Strauss

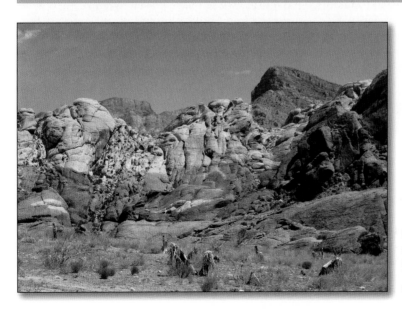

In this image the layering of colors creates a richer visual component than any one of the colors could if viewed individually. That is similar to the effect of simultaneous sounding pitches that create harmony.

Rhythm

Rhythm is the aspect of music that animates it, makes it feel like it's alive and vibrant. It's the element of music that we "feel," not in the emotional sense but in the physical. We tap our feet to the **beat**, the basic, underlying pulse of the music. Beats are often felt in groups of two, three, or four beats at a time, with the first note of a group being accented and the rest unaccented. That's called **meter**. Triple meter is when three beats are grouped together, duple meter is when two beats are grouped together. Beyond the beat and the meter we perceive rhythmic patterns in music, successions of pulses that create distinct rhythmic characteristics that can be as memorable as melodies.

Before we can clearly hear the melody or emotionally respond to the harmony in a piece of music we often "feel" the rhythm. That rhythmic pulse can have characteristics typical of a certain type of music that allows us to immediately identify the style of the music. It would be difficult to not know the following example is some kind of Latin/salsa music. The rhythm is typical of a Latin dance called the mambo which we have all heard many times and associate that "feel" with Latin/salsa music.

 Mambozooka—
Tito Puente

Meter, as mentioned above, is the grouping of beats into regularly recurring numbers of beats. Can you tell what the grouping of beats is in the following example?

 Take Five—
Paul Desmond performed by the Dave Brubeck Quintet

The even spacing of the trees in this image is similar to the beat, the basic underlying pulse of musical compositions, which occurs at regular intervals in time. © 2009 Chip Pankey Photography. All rights reserved.

Form

Music exists in time. It has a beginning and an end. How the time is organized is the **form** of the music. Just as the spaces we occupy in buildings and in cities are organized in understandable layouts, the organization of the time during which music occurs allows us to make sense out of that as well. There are many different types of forms in music, but most require only the understanding of the composer rather than the listener. What is helpful for the listener to understand about form is that most forms depend on a balance of repetition and contrast to achieve an organization of time. Most often understanding the details of a specific form are not necessary for the listener to enjoy the music, but sometimes perceiving the details of a specific form are helpful in hearing more in a piece of music than first meets the ear.

Repeating a melody at certain times throughout a composition gives us a feeling of continuity and familiarity. Putting something different in between repetitions of the melody provides contrast. Beginning and ending a piece with the same melody provides a sense of completeness to a composition. Listen to the following example and take note of the melody played by the flutes at the beginning. That melody, with a "major" sound, will disappear in the middle of the piece when the underlying harmony changes to "minor" and trumpets briefly take over the melody. The flutes then return to play the melody heard at the beginning again to give the piece a sense of closure. This is a type of form we call A-B-A form.

 "Dance of the Reed Flutes" from *The Nutcracker Ballet*—
Peter Ilyich Tchaikovsky

Texture

The term texture in music is used to describe the relative complexity of the combination of sounds in a composition. Some music has a relatively transparent, simple sound while other music sounds thick and complicated. This is the texture of the music. Some specific kinds of textures are:

monophonic texture—one melodic line with nothing else going on

homophonic texture—one melodic line with some kind of accompaniment

polyphonic texture—several melodic lines occurring simultaneously

Timbre

The timbre of music is the quality of sound that allows us to perceive differences between instruments and voices. It is often called the "tone color" of a sound. Just as our eyes can detect differences between different colors as well as subtle shades of the same color so can our ears perceive differences between instruments, voices, and even one voice from another or one violin from another. In a larger sense we can readily tell the difference between a rock band, a jazz band, an orchestra, or any instrumental or vocal ensemble by the timbre the combination of sounds create. When we scan stations on our car radio looking for something we like we need only a second or two to recognize the "sound" we want to hear. When we do that we are relying on our perception of timbre to guide us.

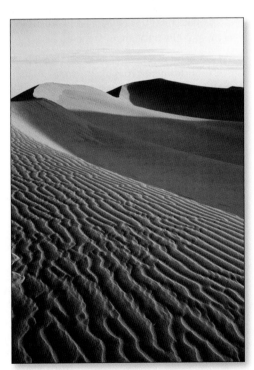

We see textural differences in the world around us, such as in the image above. In this case there are two contrasting textures in one scene. In music we often perceive changing degrees of musical complexity, textures, within one composition but sometimes the texture remains the same throughout an entire piece. © 2009 Chip Pankey Photography. All rights reserved.

What Makes Music—Musical Instruments

Ensembles

In Western art music some of the most common ensembles include the Orchestra, Band, Choir, and Chamber Ensembles.

Orchestra—The orchestra is an ensemble that came into being during the Baroque period, grew in both size and importance through the Romantic era, where it came to be referred to as a symphony orchestra, and has continued to be the most significant instrumental ensemble in the Western art music tradition. Comprised of instruments from all of the individual families of instruments, strings, woodwinds, brass, and percussion, along with instruments such as the harp and piano, the orchestra is the most diverse and adaptable ensemble through which to express a composer's ideas. Initially an ensemble expressing only European composers' musical ideas, the orchestra is now a universally accepted ensemble with orchestras found in schools from elementary to college level and professional orchestras which can be found in virtually every major city throughout the world.

Band—A band is similar to an orchestra in that it is comprised of instruments from many of the individual families of instruments but it does not contain instruments of the string family, which is the most important family of instruments in an orchestra. Bands are often found in schools from elementary through college level and in the military. While many communities support amateur bands it is not common for bands to be "professional" ensembles; that is, with paid members who perform in the ensemble for a living.

Choir—A choir is an ensemble made up of mixed voices: usually soprano, alto, tenor, and bass, that performs both as a stand-alone ensemble, giving concerts of vocal music, and in conjunction with orchestras to perform large-scale works such as oratorios and other works for choir and orchestra. Choirs can be found in most Christian churches, in schools from the middle-school level through college, and in communities as amateur ensembles often associated with professional symphony orchestras.

Chamber Ensembles—Chamber ensembles are any small grouping of instruments where each player plays an individual part. In orchestras and bands many of the instrumentalists play in "sections." A section is a group of players who all play the same instrument and who all play the same music at the same time. For example, the "bass section" of a modern orchestra is comprised of anywhere from 6–9 players and each of them plays exactly the same music. In contrast to this a string quartet is made up of two violinists, one violist, and a cellist. Each of them plays a different part, including the two violinists who are referred to as a first violinist and a second violinist. Common chamber ensembles include the string quartet, woodwind and brass quintets, and the percussion ensemble, but in reality any combination of instruments can constitute a chamber ensemble.

HISTORICAL PERIODS AND CHARACTERISTICS

When discussing the history of art music in the Western world, also commonly referred to as "classical music," we often describe the music in terms of the historical period from which it comes. Why do we use this method to discuss the music from the Western world and not use it to describe music from other cultures? Because the story of music in the Western world is the story of its *evolution*. It evolved in ways that transcended the cultural conventions of the time from which it came and linked it to both the preceding and the following historical periods. This connection to the music before and after it lends the music of the Western world especially well to this kind of examination. While music from other cultures has also changed over time, this music is often inextricably linked to the *preservation* of the characteristics of the culture from which it came, which is very different from Western music. As we go through the chapters in this book, it will become more apparent why we discuss Western music in terms of historical periods and music from other cultures in a variety of ways.

Singing monks. Copyright ©
Scala/Art Resource, NY

Medieval Period ca. AD 500–1450

Most preserved music from the Medieval period is from the Catholic Church and was written down by monks in monasteries. During the first 500 years of this period the predominant type of music is referred to as Gregorian Chant, a monophonic vocal music sung in the church. The remainder of the period saw a gradually evolving complexity in the music from chant consisting of a single melodic line to two-part writing called organum, and finally to polyphonic sacred (religiously based) compositions called motets (often settings of prayers) and masses (settings of certain texts from the ritual celebration of the Mass). Most of the music written during this time was composed by monks serving the church. Secular (non-religious) music such as music for dancing and music for singing was common, but far less of it was written down. The songs of the Troubadours and Trouveres, French noblemen who wrote poetry and music, are a major source of secular music during this time. Major centers of music making existed in Italy and France.

Medieval vielle player, organist, and singer.
Copyright © Scala/Art Resource, NY

MEDIEVAL PERIOD

Major Composers

Hildegard of Bingen—1098–1179
Leonin—ca. 1163–1190
Perotin—flourished ca. 1200
Guillaume de Machaut—1300–1377

The following two examples exhibit the characteristics of both the secular and sacred music of this time.

O Fortuna—
Secular song from the *Carmina Burana*
(Songs from Benediktbeuern), anonymous

O Fortuna	O Fortune,
velut luna	like the moon
statu variabilis,	you are changeable,
semper crescis	ever waxing
aut decrescis;	and waning;
vita detestabilis	hateful life
nunc obdurat	first oppresses
et tunc curat	and then soothes
ludo mentis aciem,	as fancy takes it;
egestatem,	poverty
potestatem	and power
dissolvit ut glaciem.	it melts them like ice.
Sors immanis	Fate—monstrous
et inanis,	and empty,
rota tu volubilis,	you whirling wheel,
status malus,	you are malevolent,
vana salus	well-being is vain
semper dissolubilis,	and always fades to nothing,

(continued)

obumbrata	shadowed
et velata	and veiled
michi quoque niteris;	you plague me too;
nunc per ludum	now through the game
dorsum nudum	I bring my bare back
fero tui sceleris.	to your villainy.
Sors salutis	Fate is against me
et virtutis	in health
michi nunc contraria,	and virtue,
est affectus	driven on
et defectus	and weighted down,
semper in angaria.	always enslaved.
Hac in hora	So at this hour
sine mora	without delay
corde pulsum tangite;	pluck the vibrating strings;
quod per sortem	since Fate
sternit fortem,	strikes down the strong man,
mecum omnes plangite!	everyone weep with me!

Kyrie— Hildegard of Bingen

Kyrie, eleison	Lord, have mercy on us
Christie, eleison	Christ, have mercy on us
Kyrie, eleison	Lord, have mercy on us

Pieter Brueghel the Elder (ca. 1525–1569). *Peasants' Dance,* 1568. Corel

Renaissance Period 1450–1600

The **Renaissance** period saw a continuation of the polyphonic writing style of the late Medieval but with an eye toward developing a systematic harmonic language, a logical way to use harmony. Composers realized toward the end of the Medieval period that certain combinations of pitches could elicit emotional reactions in the listener. The

Renaissance saw an increasing awareness on the part of composers of the importance of harmony. The polyphony of this era is clearer and easier to perceive than polyphony of the Medieval in that the Renaissance style was more of an imitative polyphony. This is a compositional technique whereby each voice imitates the melody of the previously heard voice. This was especially true in a cappella, or unaccompanied, vocal music of the time. The Renaissance also gave rise to ever more important genres of instrumental music, such as the ricercar and canzon, though most of the instruments in use at the time were not in the form we know them today. Most composers during this time worked for churches as choir masters with a much smaller number employed as court musicians for aristocratic households. The Protestant Reformation and the Catholic Counter Reformation were major influencing factors in church music of the Renaissance. Italy and the Netherlands were major centers of musical activity and progress.

 RENAISSANCE PERIOD

Major Composers

Josquin des Prez—ca. 1440–1521
Giovanni Perluigi da Palestrina—1525–1594
Giovanni Gabrieli—ca. 1555–1613

The following two examples exhibit the characteristics of the sacred vocal music of this time and a typical instrumental work for brass instruments.

 Ave Maria—
Josquin des Prez

Ave Maria, gratia plena, dominus tecum, virgo serena.	Hail Mary, full of grace, the Lord is with thee, serene Virgin.
Ave, cuius conceptio, solemni plena gaudio, coelestia terrestrial nova replet laetitia.	Hail, whose conception, full of great jubilation, fills Heaven and Earth with new joy.
Ave, cuius nativitas nostra fuit solemnitas, ut lucifer lux oriens verum solem praeveniens.	Hail, whose birth brought us joy, as Lucifer, the morning star, went before the true sun.
Ave, pia humilitas, sine viro fecunditas, cuius annuntiatio nostra fuit salvatio.	Hail, pious humility, fruitful without a man, whose Annunciation brought us salvation.
Ave, vera virginitas, immaculata castitas, cuius purificatio nostra fuit purgatio.	Hail, true virginity, immaculate chastity, whose purification brought our cleansing.

La Gioconda, commonly known as the Mona Lisa, by Leonardo Da Vinci (1452–1519) ca. 1505.
Corel

(continued)

| Ave, praeclara omnibus
angelicis virtutibus,
cuius assumptio
nostra glorificatio.

O mater Dei,
memento mei. Amen. | Hail, glorious one
in all angelic virtues,
whose Assumption
was our glorification.

O Mother of God,
remember me. Amen. |

 Canzon XVII—
Giovanni Gabrieli

The lute was a popular instrument during the Renaissance and Baroque periods. Corel

Baroque Period 1600–1750

During the Baroque period many of the concepts and ideals we take for granted in music today were firmly established, including the harmonic language that is one of the defining elements of Western art music. In vocal music a homophonic texture, such as a solo voice singing the melody with an instrumental accompaniment, became the norm. The combination of a low-pitched instrument such as the cello, bass, or bassoon, paired with a keyboard instrument such as the harpsichord or the organ, created the "basso continuo." This instrumental ideal was the centerpiece of almost all music during this period. It provided a firm harmonic foundation (the keyboard) with a moving bass line (the cello, bass, or bassoon) and a regular rhythmic pulse (the combination of the two). This is the basic concept of the rhythm section of modern day bands without the drums to propel the rhythm. Melodies tended to be played by the highest pitched instruments, harmony was provided by the other instruments, and a bass line moved underneath it all. This is very similar to the way most popular music is played today. The violin family of instruments reached their present day form during this period and became the foundation of the modern orchestra. Emotion in music was highly valued and opera was developed during this time. Improvisation became a valued performing ability during this time as well. During the Baroque period composers were fairly evenly divided between working for churches or at court. Germany, England, and Italy are at the forefront of musical activity during the Baroque period.

The Five Senses: Hearing, by Abraham Bosse (1602–1676). Copyright © Reunion des Musees Nationaux/Art Resource, NY

BAROQUE PERIOD

Major Composers

Claudio Monteverdi—1567–1643
Antonio Vivaldi—1678–1741
Johann Sebastian Bach—1685–1750
George Frideric Handel—1685–1759

The following examples are two of the most frequently performed works from this historical period.

 Canon a tre in D major—
Johann Pachelbel

 Hallelujah Chorus from *Messiah—*
George Frideric Handel

Hallelujah! Hallelujah!
Hallelujah! Hallelujah! Hallelujah! etc.

For the Lord God omnipotent reigneth.
Hallelujah, Hallelujah, Hallelujah, Hallelujah!
For the Lord God omnipotent reigneth.
Hallelujah, Hallelujah, Hallelujah, Hallelujah! etc.

The kingdom of this world is become,
The kingdom of our Lord, and of His Christ, and of His Christ.
And He shall reign forever and ever. etc.

King of Kings! Forever and ever. Hallelujah, Hallelujah!
And Lord of Lords! Forever and ever. Hallelujah, Hallelujah!
King of Kings! Forever and ever. Hallelujah, Hallelujah!
And Lord of Lords! Forever and ever. Hallelujah, Hallelujah!
King of Kings! Forever and ever. Hallelujah, Hallelujah!
And Lord of Lords! King of Kings and Lord of Lords! etc.

Classical Period 1750–1825

During the Classical period the music reflected a general philosophical outlook that valued reason, balance, symmetry, and elegance. It also reflected the tastes of the wealthy ruling class that paid for it. Most music was composed according to established forms (sonata form, rondo, ternary, theme and variations) and conventions (question and answer melodies, static bass lines, slowly changing harmonies). In the first half of this period much of the music was simple and decorative, good background music for social occasions. The second half of this era saw the rise in importance of music that emphasized thematic development, the logical manipulation of melodies for the sheer intellectual enjoyment of exploring the possibilities inherent in a tune. Symphonies, concertos, and string quartets became important instrumental genres, all based on the concept of thematic development. Opera spread from Italy throughout all of Europe and took on an increasingly important role in the conflict between the classes. While most composers worked at court during this time, the undercurrents of revolutionary change both in America and in France propelled music in a new direction aimed at the masses rather than the aristocracy. Germany and Austria were the center of the musical world during this time.

Louis de Carmontelle (1717–1806). Leopold Mozart and his children Wolfgang Amadeus and Maria Anna. Copyright © Erich Lessing/Art Resource, NY

CLASSICAL PERIOD

Major Composers

Franz Joseph Haydn—1732–1809
Wolfgang Amadeus Mozart—1756–1791
Ludwig van Beethoven—1770–1827 (major figure in the trend toward Romantic music)
Franz Schubert—1797–1828 (often considered a Romantic period composer)

Here are two examples of Classical period music with very familiar tunes.

Eine Kleine Nachtmusik (A Little Night Music), 1st movement—Wolfgang Amadeus Mozart

Symphony #5 in C minor, 1st movement—Ludwig van Beethoven

Biographical Spotlight

Ludwig van Beethoven.
© 2013, Nicku, Shutterstock, Inc.

Ludwig van Beethoven

If there is one name of a classical music composer that most people know, it is the name Beethoven. Ludwig van Beethoven was born on December 16, 1770, in the city of Bonn, in what is today, Germany. While a young man he moved to Vienna, the center of musical activity at that time. There he established himself as a musical force to be reckoned with and where he would exert an influence over the course of music perhaps unparalleled in the history of Western art music.

Beethoven was the son of Johann van Beethoven, a prominent musician in Bonn. The social status of the Beethoven family as commoners would cause recurring difficulties for Ludwig, including disappointments in his love-life and in legal proceedings. He exhibited a talent for music at an early age and was given instruction in piano, violin, viola, and composition. He found success in Vienna writing in a style similar to other Classical period composers such as Wolfgang Amadeus Mozart and Joseph Haydn. This time, up until 1802, during which he imitated the style of established composers, is known as his *Early Period.* At the age of 26 Beethoven learned that he was losing his hearing. He fought profound depression over an extended period of time with the realization that he was destined to lose the one faculty indispensable to his art. At the direction of a doctor he moved to a small village outside of Vienna, Heiligenstadt, in hopes he might better deal with his growing despair away from the pressures of the city. It was there that Beethoven came to terms with his encroaching deafness and wrote a moving letter to his brothers, Carl and Johann, describing the hopelessness that brought him to the brink of suicide but also his resolve to live for the sake of his art. In this *Heiligenstadt Testament,* as it has come to be known, Beethoven wrote, "*. . . what a humiliation when one stood beside me and heard a flute in the distance and I heard nothing, or . . . the shepherd singing and again I heard nothing, such incidents brought me to the verge of despair, but little more and I would have put an end to my life—only art it was that withheld me, ah it seemed impossible to leave the world until I had produced all that I felt called upon me to produce, and so I endured this wretched existence.*"

Beethoven returned to Vienna from Heiligenstadt with a renewed vigor and approach to his music. The works from this time, beginning with his *Symphony #3 in E flat major*, the *"Eroica" (Heroic)* symphony, show a marked departure from other Classical period composers. The works from this *Middle Period, 1803–1814*, are longer, more complex, infused with more emotional power than anything previously heard, and reveal a more authoritative musical voice with which Beethoven was now speaking. His *Symphony #5 in C minor* is perhaps his best known work and the most representative of this *Middle Period*. He was a changed man as he confronted his diminished hearing, and his music reflected his determination not to let it diminish him.

Beethoven never married but had several significant relationships with prominent women. A love letter written to his *"Immortal Beloved"* has fueled speculation as to the identity of the intended recipient, but no definitive answer as to whom she might have been has been universally accepted. *Immortal Beloved* was the name of a highly speculative 1994 movie about the search for her identity. Beethoven was involved in protracted legal proceedings to gain custody of his deceased brother Carl's son, Karl. He eventually prevailed in court and Karl's care was entrusted to Beethoven, but the drain on his energy, coupled with recurring illnesses of an undiagnosed nature, reduced his composing output significantly.

The music from Beethoven's *Late Period, 1815* until his death in 1827, is characterized by extensive explorations into ever more creative realms, sometimes to the point of challenging the listener's ability to understand it. But it is during this time that Beethoven's *Symphony #9 in D minor* is written, which many have called the greatest piece of music ever written. Beethoven breaks with tradition in adding vocal soloists and a chorus to the traditional orchestra in the final movement of the symphony. The text is the *Ode to Joy*, a poem written by Friedrich Schiller in 1785, along with additions made by Beethoven. The theme of the symphony is the brotherhood of all people.

Beethoven lived during a time of political upheaval and social turmoil. He was challenged by personal loss and a society segregated by class. His music is overwhelmingly uplifting and triumphant, but often tinged with melancholy, much as his own life was. Beethoven died on March 26, 1827, a revered composer whose funeral procession saw some 20,000 people line the streets of Vienna to pay their final respects.

Biographical Spotlight Exercise

Instructions: Log in to the textbook web site and click on the **Assignments** tab. Click on **Chapter 1** and scroll to the **Biographical Spotlight area**. Answer the question based on the information in the biography above.

Which of the following is a true statement?

1. Beethoven's music is written in essentially the same style throughout all periods of his life.
2. Beethoven wrote a letter, the *Heiligenstadt Testament*, to his brothers Carl and Johann describing the despair he felt at the knowledge that he was losing his hearing.
3. Beethoven died unknown and unappreciated.

Romantic Period 1825–1900

The Romantic period was the antithesis of the Classical. If the Classical period outlook was basically objective, then the Romantic was patently subjective. To understand how this difference in outlook might manifest itself, consider the statements, "I am going to write *a* symphony" and "I am going to write *my* symphony." One views a symphony objectively, the other subjectively. That is a simple illustration of the opposing approaches one finds in these contrasting periods. Form in Romantic period music was not as important as in the Classical, free expression was. Romantic period music was emotional and dramatic. It's not surprising that this period was a time of much operatic writing. Composers experimented with new forms and genres. Defying convention was valued more than following it. Composers were more influenced by the world around them than at any other time. Fascination with exotic places, exoticism, was widespread.

PERSPECTIVE—ART AND MUSIC

When discussing Western art music it is common to categorize music according to the historical eras from which it originates. The same is true when discussing works of art. Paintings or sculptures tend to share certain characteristics when their creation falls within certain parameters of time. The historical periods that are commonly referred to when discussing music, Medieval, Renaissance, Baroque, Classical and Twentieth/Twenty-First Century, have their counterparts in the realm of visual art. The dates commonly used to define each musical period are fairly close to those used when discussing art.

The Medieval period in art is frequently described as being from approximately 200 AD to the middle of the fifteenth century. The Renaissance is dated from the fifteenth to the seventeenth century. The Baroque period spans the seventeenth century up to approximately 1730. The term Neo-Classical is used when discussing art instead of the term "Classical" that is used when discussing music. That era in art closely mirrors the comparable era in music from approximately 1750 to 1830. The Romantic era is often described as being from the late eighteenth through the nineteenth century. The term Modern Art is used to describe art works from the later nineteenth century up to approximately 1970 and Contemporary Art is the designation for works from 1970 onward. It is more common when describing historical periods in art to have a somewhat more flexible approach to dating the beginnings and endings of eras than it is in music. Perhaps because creating works of art is not dependent on others to perform the creation,

Renaissance: *Self Portrait*—Albrecht Durer (1471–1528). Corel

as is the case in music, that movement in certain artistic directions is initially apparent in fewer individuals. That would make the beginnings of the artistic qualities associated with each period more difficult to pinpoint in art than in music.

The musical elements, melody, harmony, rhythm, form, timbre and texture, have counterparts in the realm of the visual arts. Line, color, space, form, value, texture and shape are all common elements in art. Line can be seen as analogous to melody, color as a counterpart to harmony. The use of space can be a manifestation of a rhythmic sense and form is how these parts are organized and fit together. Value, a measure of the intensity of color, reflects the concept of timbre or tone color in

Medieval: *The Black Madonna of Częstochowa*—Anonymous. Corel

Baroque: *Aristotle Contemplating the Bust of Homer*—Rembrandt van Rijn (1606–1669). Corel

PERSPECTIVE—ART AND MUSIC

music, and texture is a measure of the relative complexity of a musical sound or an artistic surface. Space, another artistic element, is a result of how lines are connected. A musical equivalent is a musical "phrase," the result of how a melodic line unfolds.

The characteristics that are generally associated with the historical periods in music have their complements in art. Medieval art may seem flat and one-dimensional to our modern eyes, not truly representative of the real world. Medieval music can sound thin and one-dimensional as well since the concept of harmony was in the formative stages. In art the concept of perspective that provides a realistic depiction of depth wouldn't be fully incorporated into painting until the Renaissance.

Modern/Contemporary: *Gypsy Woman with Baby*—Amedeo Modigliani (1884–1920). Corel

Classical: *The Roman Forum*—Giovanni Pannini (1691–1765). Corel

The Renaissance in music explored the possibilities in the harmonic element, the combination of pitches that created a richer, more complex texture, due to the

Romantic: *Peace—Burial at Sea*—Joseph Mallord William Turner (1775–1851).
Tate London/Art Resource, NY

interaction of the melodic lines. Similarly in art the works of the Renaissance artists displayed a richer palette of color along with a more realistic representation of depth. This can be seen as the equivalent of the "depth" created by harmony in music.

The Baroque period in both music and art exhibits characteristics of energy and movement. In music this is often depicted by many notes played in quick succession. In art the scene portrayed is often one of action with the subjects engaged in a physically significant moment.

Music from the Classical period often is governed by a strict adherence to formal structure. Art from the comparable Neo-classic period displays a similar concern for a clear layout of the images depicted.

The Romantic period in music is one of high emotional content and a freer (than the Classical period) handling of all musical elements. Romantic era art is similarly more highly charged emotionally and very personal in its outlook. Both composers and artists of this time were more concerned with presenting their own views of the world rather than a preconceived notion of structure and emotional content.

Twentieth/Twenty-First century music and modern/contemporary art explore their respective disciplines with an ever more adventurous and questioning approach. The elements of both music and art are manipulated in heretofore unimagined ways and composers and artists question the basic tenets of their arts, fundamentally asking the question, "What is art/music?"

Julius Schmid (1854–1935). Franz Schubert at the piano during a "Schubert Evening" in a Viennese salon, 1897. Copyright © Erich Lessing/ Art Resource, NY

Music that was based on, or reflected, a composer's national or ethnic heritage, **nationalism**, was common. While music in previous eras generally emphasized "pleasant" qualities and was generally pleasing to the ear, composers in the Romantic period began to explore the disreputable side of the human character, which often resulted in music that was somewhat harsh and often frightening. Compositions dealing with death, murder, the occult, and other nefarious topics were fairly common. The Romantic period was all about extremes. While many composers explored the dark side of life, others exulted in the grandeur of it and created works of unsurpassed beauty and joy. All of the instruments that are common today, except electronic ones, were in use during the Romantic period. Composers attempted to find their own unique musical voice rather than fit in with someone else's preconceptions of what made good music. Composers rarely worked for churches or courts during this time, instead becoming entrepreneurial artists who supported themselves through concert performances, teaching, and publication of their works.

Peter Ilyich Tchaikovsky (1840–1893)—a Russian composer of the Romantic era. Copyright © Ann Ronan Picture Library/ HIP/Art Resource, NY

ROMANTIC PERIOD

Major Composers

Hector Berlioz—1803–1869
Felix Mendelssohn—1809–1847
Frederick Chopin—1810–1849
Giuseppe Verdi—1813–1901
Richard Wagner—1813–1883

Bedrich Smetana—1824–1884
Johannes Brahms—1833–1897
Peter Tchaikovsky—1840–1893
Antonin Dvorak—1841–1904

(Post Romantic)

Giacomo Puccini—1858–1924
Gustav Mahler—1860–1911
Claude Debussy—1862–1918
Maurice Ravel—1875–1937

Here are two contrasting examples of Romantic period music, one for a full orchestra and the other for a solo piano.

Symphony #4 in F minor, 4th movement—
Peter Tchaikovsky

 Intermezzo in A major—
Johannes Brahms

Twentieth/Twenty-First Century 1900–Present

The twentieth century was the most eclectic of the historical periods. More styles existed side-by-side during this time than during any other. Radically new approaches to writing music developed and were widely adopted. The acceptance by composers of dissonance as a desirable quality in music led to the abandonment by many listeners of serious music in favor of more popular styles. Throughout history dissonance in music almost invariably resolved to consonance. Dissonant sounds, which sounded harsh and tended to grate on the ear, created an unstable feeling for the listener which necessitated a move to a more stable, pleasant sound, a consonant sound. That is how dissonance had been handled for centuries. Twentieth-century composers used dissonance freely without feeling the need to soften its effect by resolving it to a consonant sound. While many composers adopted the new atonal style of writing, many others rejected it and continued composing in more or less traditional ways. Some explored Baroque and Classical ideals with a twentieth-century outlook, neoclassicism, and others wrote in a modified Romantic style reminiscent of the previous century, neoromanticism. The United States became a major musical force during the twentieth century with many composers emigrating there to flee oppression in their European homelands. Composers continued working as free artists, selling their compositions for publication and performance, but they also began taking advantage of the growing number of available university teaching positions that afforded them a comfortable living while composing.

TWENTIETH/TWENTY-FIRST CENTURY

Major Composers

Arnold Schoenberg—1874–1951	Dmitri Shostakovich—1906–1975
Bela Bartok—1881–1945	Samuel Barber—1910–1981
Igor Stravinsky—1882–1971	Leonard Bernstein—1918–1990
Aaron Copland—1900–1990	Philip Glass—b. 1937

The following three examples of twentieth-century music are just a small sampling of the extraordinary variety of music from this interesting time.

 The Rite of Spring (excerpt)—
Igor Stravinsky

 Hoedown from *Rodeo*—
Aaron Copland

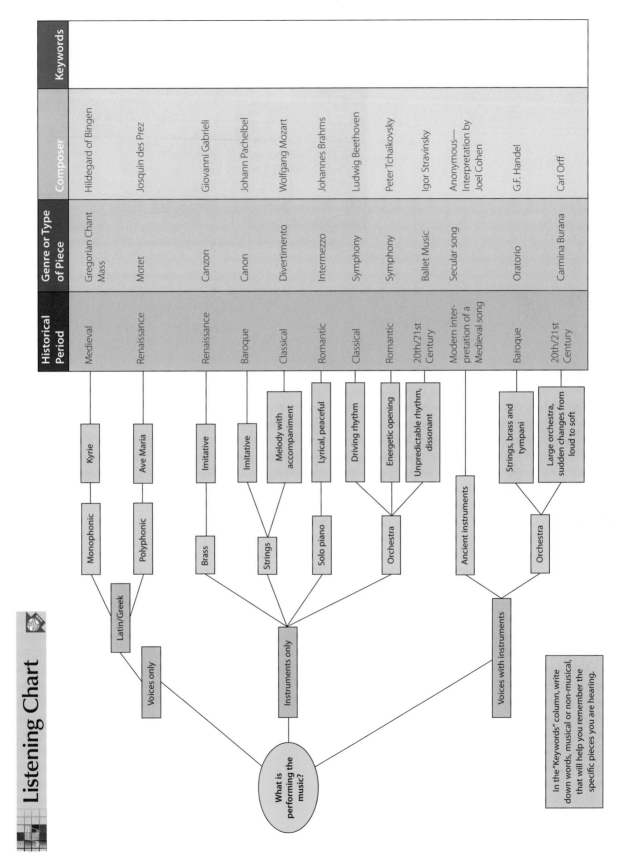

Listening Chart

Historical Period	Genre or Type of Piece	Composer	Keywords
Medieval	Gregorian Chant Mass	Hildegard of Bingen	
Renaissance	Motet	Josquin des Prez	
Renaissance	Canzon	Giovanni Gabrieli	
Baroque	Canon	Johann Pachelbel	
Classical	Divertimento	Wolfgang Mozart	
Romantic	Intermezzo	Johannes Brahms	
Classical	Symphony	Ludwig Beethoven	
Romantic	Symphony	Peter Tchaikovsky	
20th/21st Century	Ballet Music	Igor Stravinsky	
Modern interpretation of a Medieval song	Secular song	Anonymous—Interpretation by Joel Cohen	
Baroque	Oratorio	G.F. Handel	
20th/21st Century	Carmina Burana	Carl Orff	

What is performing the music?

- Voices only
  - Latin/Greek
    - Monophonic — Kyrie
    - Polyphonic — Ave Maria
- Instruments only
  - Brass — Imitative
  - Strings — Imitative / Melody with accompaniment
  - Solo piano — Lyrical, peaceful
  - Orchestra — Driving rhythm / Energetic opening / Unpredictable rhythm, dissonant
- Voices with instruments
  - Ancient instruments
  - Orchestra — Strings, brass and tympani / Large orchestra, sudden changes from loud to soft

In the "Keywords" column, write down words, musical or non-musical, that will help you remember the specific pieces you are hearing.

Stage design for Igor Stravinsky's Ballet
Petrouchka by Alexandre Nikolaevich Benois
(1870–1960). Copyright © Erich Lessing/Art
Resource, NY

 O Fortuna from *Carmina Burana (Songs from Benediktbeuern)*—
Carl Orff

This is a twentieth-century expression of the Medieval song heard
earlier. See page 7.

SUMMARY

All music is a combination, to varying degrees, of the basic elements: melody, harmony, rhythm, form, timbre, and texture. Melody is the tune, the thing we sing or
whistle. The melody is a collection of pitches, in a certain sequence, and with specific
rhythmic qualities, that identify it as unique and differentiates it from other melodies.
Harmony consists of the other pitches that we hear in a piece of music that are not
part of the melody. The harmony notes enhance the sound of the music, especially
when used as chords. Chords are certain combinations of pitches that have unique
characteristics, two of which are referred to as major (happy, triumphant, grand) and
minor (melancholy, fearful, introverted). Rhythm animates the music, makes it feel
like it is moving, going somewhere. We "feel" the rhythm of a piece of music as well as
hear it. We discern the basic pulse of the music, the beat, and often organize those
beats into regularly recurring groups of beats we call meter. Form in music allows us
to make sense out of the music as it occurs in time. Often this is done by repeating
melodic ideas enough to relate music separated by some span of time to music that
occurs later in a composition. Contrasting melodic ideas are interspersed between
repetitions to keep the music from becoming boring. Texture in music refers to the

relative complexity of the music, especially as it relates to the use of melodies. A piece with one melody and nothing else is called monophonic. A piece with a melody plus some kind of accompaniment is called homophonic. A piece in which two or more melodic ideas share a more or less equal level of importance is called polyphonic. Timbre is the tone color or quality that we perceive in a musical sound. It's what makes a trumpet sound different from a violin or allows us to differentiate one human voice from another. The unique timbre of instruments comes from the different materials used to make them and by the different ways vibrations are produced on those instruments.

Western art music is usually discussed in terms of historical periods, spans of time during which similar characteristics are evident across many types of music. The Medieval period, 500–1450, is by far the longest. It is a time dominated by the influence of the Catholic Church. During this time sacred, religious music evolves from monophonic Gregorian Chant to polyphonic sacred works such as motets and masses. Secular, non-religious music such as dances and songs, are represented by the music of the Troubadours. The Renaissance, 1450–1600, is a time when the polyphonic style became more refined, with an emphasis on using the simultaneously sounding melodic lines in a more harmonically conceived manner. Imitative polyphony, where each melodic line imitates a previously heard melody, was the predominant style in both instrumental and vocal works. The Baroque period, 1600–1750, saw the harmonic basis of Western art music firmly established. Many of the characteristics of modern music were developed during this time. The basso continuo provided a bass line, the harmony, and a rhythmic regularity that we have come to expect in today's music. The Classical period, 1750–1825, is a time when concepts such as reason, symmetry, balance, and elegance are in evidence. A clearly defined form in all musical compositions is highly valued during this time. The practice of thematic development, taking a melodic idea and exploring the possibilities inherent in it, becomes of paramount importance to composers. The music of the Romantic period, 1825–1900, is more emotional and dramatic than that of the Classical. Form and thematic development are not as important to composers as is finding a unique way to express themselves. Nationalism, an emphasis on one's national, cultural, or ethnic heritage, is prevalent in many works. The Twentieth/Twenty-First Century 1900–The Present, is a time of extraordinary variety in music, with many distinct styles occurring simultaneously. Dissonance becomes an accepted quality by many composers, which challenges the expectations of audiences, turning many from "classical music" to the emerging popular styles.

The story of music in the Western world is a tale of musical evolution. Music evolved from simple compositions consisting of a single melodic line to multi-part works with a complex harmonic language. The evolution of harmony led to the development of standard forms, longer, more complicated compositions, and an increasingly rich harmonic language. Eventually many composers abandoned the tonal, harmonically-based, approach to composition and explored music without a tonal center, while others retained a more traditional style. The twentieth century also saw the emergence of popular music as the predominant style of music in the Western world.

SUGGESTED FURTHER LISTENING

Videmus stellam—Gregorian Chant

Lo' how a Rose e're blooming—Michael Praetorius

Come Again—John Dowland, performed by Sting

Cantata #140 "Wachet auf," 4th movement—Johann Sebastian Bach

The Water Music—George Frideric Handel

Symphony #40 in G minor, 1st movement—Wolfgang Amadeus Mozart

Symphony #94 in G major, 2nd movement—Franz Joseph Haydn

Pathetique Sonata, 1st movement—Ludwig van Beethoven

Symphony #8, 1st movement—Franz Schubert

Symphonie Fantastique, 4th and 5th movements—Hector Berlioz

Academic Festival Overture—Johannes Brahms

Five Pieces for Orchestra—Arnold Schoenberg

Appalachian Spring—Aaron Copland

Rainbows in Curved Air—Terry Riley

QUESTION ASSIGNMENT

Instructions: Log in to the textbook web site and click on the ASSIGNMENTS tab. In the Chapter Question Assignment area read the instructions and answer the question(s) or provide the asked for information. Be sure to click the SUBMIT THIS FORM button after you complete the Assignment.

Give the name and dates for each of the six historical periods. Provide the names of two composers from each era along with a description of two qualities of the music from each period. An example of a mythical historical era with the equally mythical required information is provided on the site.

Historical Period Name:

Historical Period Dates:

Historical Period Composers:

Historical Period Musical Characteristics:

Historical Period Name:

Historical Period Dates:

Historical Period Composers:

Historical Period Musical Characteristics:

Historical Period Name:

Historical Period Dates:

Historical Period Composers:

Historical Period Musical Characteristics:

Historical Period Name:

Historical Period Dates:

Historical Period Composers:

Historical Period Musical Characteristics:

Historical Period Name:

Historical Period Dates:

Historical Period Composers:

Historical Period Musical Characteristics:

Historical Period Name:

Historical Period Dates:

Historical Period Composers:

Historical Period Musical Characteristics:

LISTENING EXERCISES

Instructions: Log in to the textbook web site and click on the ASSIGNMENTS tab. In the Listening Exercises area click on the links to the musical examples for each question and answer the questions. Be sure to click the SUBMIT button after you answer all of the questions.

Listen to each of the musical examples below from the Chapter 1 Playlist while noting the appropriate descriptive prompt on the Listening Chart for Chapter 1 and determine the best answer to each question.

1. *Ave Maria* by Josquin des Prez—This piece, sung in Latin, is written in a polyphonic style called imitative polyphony. In this type of texture each musical "voice" imitates what a previous voice has already stated. Listen to the beginning of this composition and determine which timing represents when the fourth statement of the words "Ave Maria" begins.

    a. 15 seconds
    b. 25 seconds
    c. 35 seconds

2. First Movement, Allegro from *Eine Kleine Nachtmusik* by Wolfgang Amadeus Mozart—This piece begins with all of the instruments, the strings from the orchestra, playing the main theme (melody) together. Listen to the beginning of this composition and determine which timing represents when the texture separates into the melody with accompaniment.

    a. 3 seconds
    b. 8 seconds
    c. 22 seconds

3. "O Fortuna" from *Carmina Burana* by Carl Orff (Please use the last musical example on the playlist for this question. That is the version of "O Fortuna" for orchestra and chorus)—Listen to this composition for voices with instruments and determine which timing below represents when the sudden change from loud to soft occurs.

    a. 10 seconds
    b. 26 seconds
    c. 55 seconds

Chapter 2

Music of the Religious Experience

FOCUS POINTS

Western Religious Genres
Gregorian Chant
Mass
Psalms
Oratorio
Cantata

World Religious Genres
Balinese Ketjak
Islamic Call to Prayer
Tibetan Buddhist Monk Chant
Tuvan Throat Singing

Popular Genres
Spirituals
Gospel
Christian Pop
Christian Rock

Perhaps the most universal experience people have with music is hearing it in conjunction with religious worship and beliefs. This experience transcends historical eras, national boundaries, and cultural perspectives. As we begin our discussion of musical experiences by examining religiously inspired music, we should briefly discuss how and where this music has been heard and some of the factors that influence our reaction to it.

Tibetan Buddhist monks playing long horns.
Corel

Many people today experience music of worship within a "sacred space," such as a church or a temple, during a religious ritual or gathering. It is a time when people of like mind gather to share their faith in a communal setting. This shared experience based on a common belief intensifies the effect of the music. This is no different from the way music has been heard for centuries. Most of the religious music we will listen to in this chapter was intended to be performed within similar spaces. Sometimes the music was incorporated into the religious service. At other times it was heard in a separate experience, a concert presented in a church for example.

Our experience of religious music today may be similar to older, traditional settings or it might be quite different. Concerts of religious music are frequently presented in churches but just as often they are produced in concert halls, out of the religious setting. This can dramatically affect our perception of the music. Many in the audience may be there simply because they like the music of that composer and want to hear as much of it as they can. They may not share the religious beliefs that are the basis of the music. This can also affect the shared experience of worship music. Look at the images of the concert hall and the church interior. In which space do you think

Orchestra Hall—Home of the Berlin Philharmonic.
© 2010, JupiterImages Corporation

one would have a more meaningful experience of religious music?

We can also listen to religious music today separate from any particular space. Our modern expectation is that we can hear music anywhere and anytime. We can listen to any kind of music, even worship music, while grocery shopping or working out at the gym. Does this enhance the experience or diminish it?

Being inside a "sacred space" may not be the way some worship music was intended in the first place. There are some examples of religious music meant for the concert hall, or the open air such as Balinese Ketjak, Tibetan Buddhist monk chanting or the call to worship of the "muezzin" in Muslim countries. Should we have to recreate those settings in order to fully experience this music? It would be very impractical to do so. But understanding that the music was intended for a particular setting helps with our understanding and appreciation of it. An outdoor setting requires a different kind of emphasis on the vocal quality than music intended for an enclosed, resonant space. Outdoor performance necessitates a more forceful kind of vocal style, while an indoor performance might take advantage of the resonance possible in a large hall. One kind of vocal style would not work for the other.

The interior of a gothic cathedral.
Corel

DIFFERENT APPROACHES TO COMMON ELEMENTS OF MUSIC

The experience of religious music today may be quite different from the practices and settings in which similar music was heard in earlier eras. Additionally, some of the musical elements common in ages past or other cultures will affect our reaction to the music. Our concepts of rhythm, melody, harmony, form, and timbre (tone color) may or may not be shared by previous eras or other cultures. A brief look at some of the diverse concepts concerning the shared elements of music may be helpful in understanding why some music sounds the way it does.

The onion-shaped cupolas of a Russian orthodox church are interspersed in a visually rhythmic pattern. Corel

Rhythm

One of the characteristics that we expect to hear in music today is a strong rhythmic quality, a beat. We usually hear the rhythm expressed through drums setting the beat with accents on certain beats at regular intervals. This rhythmic characteristic is called meter. Meter underlies virtually all music we hear today. We feel the beat of the music and tap our feet. We snap our fingers. We move our bodies to the feel of the beat. Just as we do not read individual words in a sentence separately from the words preceding and following them, but rather take them in within the context of the words surrounding them, we feel the beats in the music in groups of beats. Marches come in groups of two beats at a time:

one-two, one-two, one-two, one-two

Waltzes come in groups of three beats:

    one-two-three, **one**-two-three, **one**-two-three, **one**-two-three

Notice that when you read these metrical representations you naturally emphasize the bold faced words in a rhythm that groups the beats in regularly recurring groups of two or three beats. That's meter. If you were to listen to an example of worship music from Europe from between the years 500–1100 AD you would be hard pressed to feel any meter in the music, perhaps not even a basic beat. Does this lack of a rhythmic quality, common in our own time, make this music less valid? No, but it does require us to listen to it on a different set of terms than our music today. We cannot expect it to have the same rhythmic feel of today's music simply because that was not a consideration of the time in which it was written.

Rhythm is motion, an unseen force that animates music. The bending of the stalks in this image tells us the wind is blowing, moving things forward, even though it is an unseen force. © 2009 Chip Pankey Photography. All rights reserved.

Melody

Melody is another element of music that we expect to perceive in music today. Melody is the "tune" that we often remember from a song or piece of music. It consists of **pitches** drawn from the **scale** on which the music is based. But if we listen to music of certain time periods or certain cultures we might find it difficult to recognize a "tune" as we know it. The music of the late Medieval period in Western music commonly has several melodies occurring simultaneously, none of which is particularly distinctive to our ears. This makes it extremely difficult to pick out the "melody." One of our expectations of a melody is that we should be able to perceive it easily and remember it. It also helps our perception of melody if we can sing or whistle it after we hear it. We would find it difficult to do this with

The contour of the Sydney Opera House can be seen as a visual representation of melody. © 2013, Shutterstock, Inc.

much early music. The same is true for some other types of religious music from other cultures. The chanting of Tibetan Buddhist monks has no melody as we would define it, just a low, monotonous incantation. Not having a repeatable tune to carry with us after hearing something makes the music difficult for us to remember or fully enjoy.

Harmony

Harmony is also something we take for granted in music today. When pitches are combined to create harmony, or **chords**, particular combinations of pitches can give the music an upbeat or triumphant sound (**major** chords). Other combinations can contribute to a somber or melancholy mood (**minor** chords). Still other combinations of pitches can sound suspenseful or relaxed, rich or plain. The use of harmony can be quite complex or it can be extremely simple. Some styles of music don't even have harmony as a common element. The music exists as a single melodic line, unadorned with any additional sounds. Gregorian Chant from the early Medieval period is an example of that. Some music has **consonant** sounding harmonies that impart a stable, predictable kind of feeling in the music. Harmony can create **dissonant** sounds that create tension and in extreme cases grate on our nerves. Much non-Western music

Harmony, similar to the layers of this rooftop, is created by stacking pitches on top of each other. © 2010, JupiterImages Corporation

makes use of a kind of harmony called a drone, a constant unchanging pitch or combination of pitches in the background to a melody. Much of the music from India makes use of a drone harmonic accompaniment to melodies.

Verses and Choruses

Another quality of music that we expect to hear in music today is repetition of sections of music as the words change. These changing words to repeated musical sections are called verses or stanzas. Each verse has essentially the same musical content (melody, rhythm, etc.) while the words change from verse to verse. Sometimes both the musical content and the words are repeated in a section of music. That is what we call a chorus. Much of the worship music we will listen to in this chapter does not have this kind of structure. Does that make the music less interesting, less valid? No. Just different, and we must accept that as the custom of that time and/or place for that music or it cannot have any meaning for us.

Timbre

Today's music has a sound that we find quite normal because we are accustomed to hearing it every day. Electronically amplified instruments and voices, guitars, basses, drums, keyboards, etc. are all common. These instruments create the timbre, or tone color, of our music, and it seems very logical to us that music should sound this way. However, in times past and cultures far from our own, the basic sound of the music has been quite different. Acoustic instruments are the norm in all music more than 50 years old. Un-amplified voices require a very different kind of tonal ideal than amplified voices. Without amplification the human voice must adopt either a very nasal or very robust tone quality in order to be heard, especially above instrumental accompaniment. Consequently, the basic sound or the tone color, timbre, of most music from earlier times or other cultures differs considerably from the norm today. If we expect this music to conform to our preconceptions based on today's music, we will always find the music lacking in some way and uninteresting. If we open our ears to the incredible range of tonal possibilities explored throughout the world and across the expanse of time, we will find an art form of infinite beauty and expression that truly mirrors the breadth and depth of the human experience.

GREGORIAN CHANT

In Medieval (500–1450) Europe the Roman Catholic Church was the primary religious institution. Music was an integral part of the Roman Catholic Church service, though the music was radically different from church music we are used to hearing today. The church music common between 500 and 1000 AD is commonly called Gregorian Chant, a monophonic (single melodic line) vocal music sung by the monks in the churches and monasteries. The name Gregorian Chant is used in reference to Pope Gregory I, who was long thought to have decreed this style of music acceptable for inclusion in the church service. These chants have a freely flowing rhythm that doesn't have a perceptible beat. Rather, the music unfolds in a leisurely manner, unhurried, without a strong rhythmic pulse. This rhythmic quality is reflective of the text-driven nature of this music. The melody itself doesn't have a catchy "tune" that is easily sung by the listener after hearing it. Also, there is no harmony (pitches other than the melody) complementing the melody as we expect to hear in music today. So if there is no memorable melody, no rhythmic pulse, and no harmony, what is there?

To answer that question you need to understand why the music was written and what role it served in the church. If you heard this music in the ninth century you wouldn't be listening to it in order to understand anything about the music itself. The music contributed to the worshipful atmosphere, and it was a way for the sacred texts of the church to be shared with the congregants. Music was as much a part of the religious experience as the soaring ceilings of the cathedral reaching upward to heaven and the stained glass windows depicting angels and scenes from the Bible. The music was simply another aspect of the experience, as important as the prayers you spoke or the words you heard the priests intone. Seen in this context the unusual sound of Gregorian Chant is perfectly appropriate to enhance the worshipful atmosphere that the church wanted to set for the faithful as they stepped into that holy space.

THE MASS

One of the most significant sacred genres in Western music is the **Mass**. When we use that term in a musical sense we are not referring to the traditional ritual of the Catholic Church in which the celebrant reenacts the transformation of the bread and wine into the body and blood of Jesus. A musical mass is a setting of some of the traditional texts found within that religious ritual including the:

Kyrie—Lord have mercy, Christ have mercy, Lord have mercy

Gloria—Glory to God in the highest . . .

Credo—I believe in one God the Father almighty . . .

Sanctus—Holy, holy, holy, Lord God of hosts . . .

Agnus Dei—Lamb of God who taketh away the sins of the world have mercy on us.

These five specific texts are called the **ordinary** of the Mass. They are present in virtually all masses throughout the year in the Catholic Church. This is in contrast to the **proper** of the Mass, those texts that are appropriate for specific feast days and specific masses such as the mass for the dead, or **Requiem** Mass. The texts listed above are

A Roman Catholic priest celebrates mass. Corel

what we call "movements" in the musical context. A movement is a self-contained piece of music, with a beginning and an end, but it is only a part of a larger composition. In this instance the larger composition, the Mass, would consist of five movements, each dedicated to a specific text from the ritual of the Mass.

Since the Medieval era composers have written masses reflective of both their individual styles and the prevailing musical characteristics of their time and location. By comparing several masses we can see the timelessness of the message presented through an ever evolving musical language.

Early Monophonic Style

As was discussed above, during the early to middle Medieval period (500–1000) the predominant style of sacred vocal music was Gregorian Chant. This music typically consisted of a single melodic line without any accompanying pitches. Gregorian Chant has a very consonant (pleasing, stable, soothing) sound free of all dissonance (clashing, harsh, abrasive).

Listen to the first movement of a Mass that comes from that time period. The first part of a musical mass is usually a setting of the words, "Kyrie, eleison" (Lord, have mercy), "Christe, eleison" (Christ, have mercy), "Kyrie, eleison" (Lord, have mercy). Note that the music sounds a certain way during the entire first section of the piece when the words "Kyrie, eleison" are sung. Notice what changes in the music during the second section when the words, "Christe, eleison" are sung. Can you guess what happens when the words "Kyrie, eleison" return?

Kyrie from *First Mass for Christmas*—Anonymous

Kyrie, eleison	Lord, have mercy
Christie, eleison	Christ, have mercy
Kyrie, eleison	Lord, have mercy

What is your reaction to this music? Does it sound simple? Complicated? What is the overall mood of the music? Does this music set the words in an appropriate manner? What images do you create in your mind as you listen to this?

Polyphonic Style—Renaissance and Baroque

As time went on additional melodic lines were added to the music that was heard in the church. By the end of the fifteenth century it was common to have sacred compositions with four and five distinct melodic lines occurring simultaneously. This is referred to as polyphony, or polyphonic music. With simultaneously sounding pitches a whole new world of possibilities opened up. Combinations of pitches created a new kind of reaction in the listener. Notes had to be considered in relation to each other, not just as isolated pitches. When speaking of two pitches the term interval is used to describe their relationship to each other. Two pitches played in sequence are considered a melodic interval, while two pitches played simultaneously are called a harmonic interval. Three or more simultaneously sounding pitches create chords. This time period was the beginning of the development of harmony, the concept that would set Western art music apart from so much of the world's music.

The increased complexity of writing for several melodic lines challenged composers to explore the characteristics of the new harmonic ideas. It also required a new compositional approach to organizing the more complex textures. The relative density of the sound is what we refer to as texture. One of the novel ways composers organized the music was to have each voice imitate what other voices were doing. This technique is called imitative polyphony. This gave the music a sense of continuity in that it allowed the listener to follow something relatively simple, one melodic idea, through the complex maze of voices. When we listen to music we try to sort through the different sounds we hear in order to make sense of it. Imitative polyphony accomplished just that.

Josquin des Prez was a Flemish composer who lived from 1450–1521, during the historical period called the Renaissance (1440–1600). The Renaissance was noted for increasingly complex textures in music. Josquin used a pre-existing Gregorian chant as the basis of this composition to which he added several other melodic lines. The result is a polyphonic texture. Listen to how the music changes from thick to thinner textures throughout the piece and how the voices sometimes imitate each other when they enter to keep the piece interesting, and to illuminate the words more expressively. Josquin is regarded as one of the foremost composers in the polyphonic style of the Renaissance.

IOSQVINVS PRATENSIS.

Josquin des Prez (ca. 1440–1521). Josquin was one of the greatest composers of the Renaissance. Copyright © Bridgeman-Giraudon/Art Resource, NY

🎼 *Gloria* from *Missa Pange Lingua*— Josquin des Prez

Gloria in excelsis Deo et in terra pax hominibus bonae voluntatis.	Glory to God in the highest, and on earth peace to men of good will.
Laudamus te, benedicimus te, adoramus te, glorificamus te, gratias agimus tibi propter magnam gloriam tuam, Domine Deus, Rex caelestis, Deus Pater omnipotens.	We praise Thee, we bless Thee, we adore Thee, we glorify Thee, we give thanks to Thee for Thy great glory, Lord God, heavenly King, almighty God the Father.
Domine Fili unigenite, Iesu Christe, Domine Deus, Agnus Dei, Filius Patris, qui tollis peccata mundi, miserere nobis; qui tollis peccata mundi, suscipe deprecationem nostram. Qui sedes ad dexteram Patris, miserere nobis.	Lord Jesus Christ, only begotten Son, Lord God, Lamb of God, Son of the Father, Thou who takest away the sins of the world, have mercy on us; Thou who takest away the sins of the world, hear our prayers. Thou who sittest at the right hand of the Father, have mercy upon us.
Quoniam tu solus Sanctus, tu solus Dominus, tu solus Altissimus, Iesu Christe, cum Sancto Spiritu in gloria Dei Patris. Amen.	For Thou art the only Holy One, the only Lord, the only Most High, Jesus Christ, with the Holy Spirit in the glory of God the Father, Amen.

Does this richness of texture allow you to perceive a wider range of emotions than a single line of music, or is it simply more complicated and cluttered? Does this thicker texture allow the meaning of the words to be expressed more clearly, or does it obscure the words?

The previous examples illustrate how the number of melodic vocal lines increased from the eleventh through the fifteenth centuries. Later composers used multiple vocal lines, polyphonic writing, in conjunction with orchestral accompaniment to explore the expressive possibilities of the same texts.

Johann Sebastian Bach, a German composer of the latter seventeenth and early eighteenth centuries is often considered the master of the Baroque polyphonic style. Bach wrote music for several churches during his career. One of his most significant compositions is the *Mass in B minor*. Though this piece was composed while he was

Johann Sebastian Bach
(1685–1750). Copyright
© Erich Lessing/Art Resource,
NY

employed at St. Thomas church in Leipzig, Bach may not have had a specific performance planned when he wrote it. The Mass was composed over a fifteen-year period from 1733–1748 and is an excellent example of the style typical of the Baroque period (1600–1750). The Baroque period is characterized by harmonies that changed frequently, a bass line serving both as the foundation of the harmony and as a rhythmic pulse (the basso continuo) and the use of highly embellished melodies. The *Credo* movement from this mass shows the use of the basso continuo and the highly imitative vocal style that had evolved over several centuries.

 Credo (excerpt) from *Mass in B minor*—
Johann Sebastian Bach

Credo in unum Deum	I believe in one God
Credo in unum Deum	I believe in one God
Patrem omnipotentem	the Father almighty
Factorem coeli at terrae,	maker of heaven and earth,
Visibilium omnium nat invisibilium.	all that is visible and invisible.

Does this music affect you differently from the previous examples? Does it sound more like music you are familiar with today than the music from earlier eras? If you said yes, it's probably because by the time the *Mass in B minor* was written the same musical elements we expect to hear in music today were firmly in place. There was a clearly defined melody. There was a definite harmony supporting that melody. There was a bass line. In this example there are instruments accompanying the vocal lines. That was not the case in the previous examples. The fact that the instruments are very similar to the instruments we use today adds to the modern sound of this music. In fact most of the concepts we take for granted in music today found their first expression in music of the Baroque period.

The *Credo* is an expression of faith. As such it assumes the listener shares that faith. Can this music be listened to by someone of a different religion and still be enjoyed and appreciated? Does one need to share the faith expressed through a religious musical composition in order to fully understand the music?

Classical Style

Posthumous portrait
done ca. 1819 of
Wolfgang Amadeus
Mozart (1756–1791).
Copyright © Erich Lessing/
Art Resource, NY

Wolfgang Amadeus Mozart, an Austrian composer of the eighteenth century was not employed by a church when he wrote a mass. The trend in the mid-eighteenth century was that fewer composers were employed by churches to provide music for their congregations while more composers were employed by aristocratic households. Most patronage, the financial support of a composer, came from these aristocratic families in order to provide entertainment for their social activities. Composers were often employed by these families on similar terms as other household servants. Churches were more likely to commission a specific work from a composer for a special occasion rather than employ him full time.

Mozart lived during what is called the Classical period (1750–1825), a time when the characteristics of music included a simpler approach to harmony (the harmonies in a piece didn't change as frequently as in the preceding Baroque period), and the melodies had more of a singable, predictable nature about them. Listen to the *Sanctus* movement from this mass by Mozart and compare it to the Bach movement. Is it easier to hear what is going on in this? If so, how does that affect your reaction to the music? Do you enjoy it more or less? Which do you think expresses the words better?

Biographical Spotlight

Wolfgang Amade Mozart.

© 2013, Nicku, Shutterstock, Inc.

Wolfgang Amadeus Mozart

Wolfgang Amadeus Mozart was born on January 27, 1756, in the city of Salzburg, in what is now Austria. His father, Leopold, was a fairly successful composer himself who taught the young Wolfgang the clavier (a forerunner of the modern piano) and gave him his early lessons in composition. Mozart and his older sister, Maria Anna (nicknamed Nannerl), along with their father, toured Europe extensively over a period of eleven years from 1762–1773, giving performances before the royal courts. During these trips Mozart met many of the leading composers of his day and he incorporated into his own writing many of the stylistic characteristics found throughout Europe at the time. Leopold hoped that the result of these trips would be an appointment as a court composer for the young Wolfgang but no offer was forthcoming. Mozart's father would play a continuing and important role throughout Mozart's life, in both personal and professional circumstances.

Returning to Salzburg in 1773 Mozart was appointed to a minor position at the court where he continued to develop as a composer. He stayed in Salzburg until 1781, except for a year-long excursion to Paris, again seeking a better court appointment, but returned to Salzburg when a better paying appointment was offered there, courtesy of his father's arrangements.

In 1781 Mozart moved to Vienna where he could fulfill his desire to compose operas. He took up residence with a family, the Webers, who had also recently moved to Vienna. Mozart was quite familiar with the Webers as he had fallen in love with one of the Weber daughters, Aloysia, while visiting the city of Mannheim. Upon his settling in Vienna, Mozart became enamored of the third daughter in the Weber family, Constanze, whom he would eventually marry.

In Vienna Mozart's reputation grew with successful performances of concerts given at his own expense for the presentation of his newest compositions. Mozart was the featured piano soloist in performances of his Piano Concertos, and these performances solidified his reputation as perhaps the greatest keyboard player of his time. He also wrote some of his most celebrated operas while living in Vienna, including *Abduction from the Seraglio, The Marriage of Figaro,* and *Don Giovanni.* Despite the enormous success he found in Vienna Mozart never did achieve the one thing he desired the most, a prestigious appointment as court composer to the Emperor. He did accept a part-time appointment at the court at a modest salary, but it was not enough to finance the lavish lifestyle he and Constanze had indulged in. Mozart moved out of Vienna in 1788 when his financial situation was no longer viable and he began borrowing large sums of money from friends.

Mozart composed some of his greatest works during the final year of his life. *The Magic Flute,* his last opera, exhibiting the strong influence of Freemasonry, which he joined in 1784, the *Clarinet Concerto,* and the sketches that became his final composition, the *Requiem,* were all products of his last year, 1791. His death on December 5 of that year from a severe fever brought to a close one of the most intensely productive musical careers ever to be seen. He composed over 600 works, many considered the highpoint of their genre, in just 35 short years.

Mozart was a product, and the apex, of the Classical period. His extensive travels as a child exposed him to all of what was best in the music of the Classical period. He took the qualities he heard in others' music, added his own touch of genius, and melded them into a musical style that is unquestionably greater than the sum of its parts.

Biographical Spotlight Exercise

Instructions: Log in to the textbook web site and click on the **Assignments** tab. Click on **Chapter 2** and scroll to the **Biographical Spotlight area**. Answer the question based on the information in the biography above.

(continued)

Which of the following is a true statement?

1. Mozart had no siblings.
2. Mozart never married.
3. Mozart became a Freemason, which heavily influenced the writing of his final opera, *The Magic Flute*.

 Sanctus from *Requiem Mass*—
Wolfgang Amadeus Mozart

Sanctus, Sanctus, Sanctus,	Holy, Holy, Holy,
Domine Deus Sabaoth	Lord God of Hosts;
pleni sunt coeli	Heaven and earth
et terra gloria tua	are full of Thy glory.
Hosanna in excelsis	Hosanna in the highest.

Romantic Style

Photo-portrait of Giacomo Puccini, an Italian composer of operas from the late Romantic period.
Copyright © Snark/Art Resource, NY

Giacomo Puccini, an Italian composer of the latter nineteenth and early twentieth centuries, was the epitome of the Romantic period (1825–1900) composer. His music has a wonderfully lyrical quality that practically invites the listener to sing along with the vocal lines. The emotional impact of both the story and the music is the prime focus of his work. Puccini specialized in writing operas, especially tragic love stories. *La Boheme, Tosca,* and *Madame Butterfly* are a few of the operas by Puccini which end tragically for the lead female character. The *Messe di Gloria (Mass of Glory)*, was Puccini's final composition as a student, his final exam, so to speak. After its initial performance it lay quietly dormant while Puccini pursued his goal of writing operas. It was rediscovered in 1951 and a performance was mounted in Chicago in 1952. Its operatic lyricism foreshadows the style that was to be Puccini's trademark. The final movement, *Agnus Dei*, captures the pleading for mercy of the supplicant seeking eternal rest.

Agnus Dei from *Messe di Gloria*—
Giacomo Puccini

Agnus Dei	Lamb of God
Qui tollis peccata mundi	who takest away the sins of the world
Miserere nobis.	Have mercy on us.
Agnus Dei	Lamb of God
Qui tollis peccata mundi	who takest away the sins of the world
Miserere nobis.	Have mercy on us.
Agnus Dei	Lamb of God
Qui tollis peccata mundi	who takest away the sins of the world
Dona nobis pacem.	Grant us peace.

Jewish faithful praying at the Wailing Wall in Jerusalem. Corel

Having now listened to each movement of the Mass individually it might be an interesting exercise to listen to all five movements in sequence, experiencing approximately 1,000 years of musical styles within the context of a single genre. Keep in mind the listening experience of those for whom the music was written and the context in which it was first heard. While the movements from the Medieval and Renaissance periods may have been heard during an actual celebration of the Mass, the other examples probably were heard in concert, separate from the ritual. Regardless of this difference, the intent of the music was the same, to worship and glorify God.

We are listening to these examples from our own perspective many years after they were written. We are used to hearing many different styles of music every day. When each of these pieces were written there was only one predominant style of music. There were no recordings to compare that music to earlier styles and approaches. The relative sophistication of our musical experience today allows us to listen, compare, and make judgments on how effective each approach is in conveying the meaning of the text. In earlier times this was not even a consideration. While we are often concerned with music in its historical context, we must remember that the reason for this music was to express a deeply held belief, to worship God. As we explore different types of music throughout this text, it would be best to keep in mind why the music was written and how it was experienced by the listener. In this way we can achieve a true understanding of the musical experience for each piece we hear.

PSALMS

The Mass is an ancient genre through which we can hear a variety of approaches to setting traditional texts of the Catholic Church. Similar texts, with a much older lineage can be examined in the same way. The Psalms have been a source of inspiration for many composers, both Christian and Jewish. While the mass texts are primarily statements of faith made on behalf of the church, many of the Psalms are personal statements made by individuals. The 23rd Psalm, with its familiar opening words,

Leonard Bernstein ca. 1960. Courtesy of Photofest, NY

"The Lord is *my* Shepherd . . ." is the affirmation of one person professing their faith in God.

Leonard Bernstein, a twentieth-century American composer, conductor, and author used the 23rd Psalm in his *Chichester Psalms*, a modern setting of several Psalms written to commemorate the anniversary of Chichester Cathedral in England. Many composers in the twentieth century used irregular and unpredictable rhythms, unusual scale systems, dissonant harmonies, and unique combinations of instruments to write music of extraordinary variety and expressive range. All of these characteristics are apparent in Bernstein's work. Does the inclusion of these qualities detract from a religious work? Can you hear any of the characteristics described in the earlier works in the *Chichester Psalms*?

Chichester Psalms, 2nd movement—
Leonard Bernstein

Psalm 23

Adonai ro-i, lo echsar.
Bin'ot deshe yarbitseini,
Al mei m'nuchot y'nachaleini,
Naf'shi y'shovev,
Yan'cheini b'ma'aglei tsedek,
L'ma'an sh'mo.
Gam ki eilech
B'gei tsalmavet,
Lo ira ra,
Ki Atah imadi.
Shiv't'cha umishan'techa
Hemah y'nachamuni.

Ta'aroch l'fanai shulchan,
Neged tsor'rai
Dishanta vashemen roshi
Cosi r'vayah.
Ach tov vachesed
Yird'funi kol y'mei chayai,
V'shav'ti b'veit Adonai
L'orech yamim.

Psalm 2, verses 1–4

Lamah rag'shu goyim
Ul'umim yeh'gu rik?
Yit'yats'vu malchei erets,
V'roznim nos'du yachad
Al Adonai v'al m'shicho.

N'natkah et mos'roteimo,
V'nashlichah mimenu avoteimo.
Yoshev bashamayim
Yis'chak, Adonai
Yil'ag lamo!

Psalm 23

The Lord is my shepherd;
I shall not want.
He maketh me to lie down in green pastures:
He leadeth me beside the still waters.
He restoreth my soul:
He leadeth me in the paths of righteousness
for his name's sake.
Yea, though I walk through the valley
of the shadow of death,

I will fear no evil:
for thou art with me;
Thy rod and thy staff they comfort me.
Thou preparest a table before me
in the presence of mine enemies:
Thou anointest my head with oil;
My cup runneth over.
Surely goodness and mercy shall follow me
all the days of my life:
And I will dwell in the house of the Lord
for ever.

Psalm 2, verses 1–4

Why do the heathen rage,
and the people imagine a vain thing?
The kings of the earth set themselves,
and the rulers take counsel together,
against the Lord,

and against his anointed, saying,
Let us break their bands asunder,
and cast away their cords from us.
He that sitteth in the heavens shall laugh:
the Lord shall have them in derision.

Some of the qualities heard in the previous examples include imitation, repetition, and contrast. Are those characteristics present in this music? What characteristics make this music sound like it comes from the twentieth century and not from another?

THE ORATORIO

The **oratorio** is a sacred vocal genre that was popular during the **Baroque period**. **George Frideric Handel**, the most prominent composer of oratorios, was German by birth but spent most of his professional career in England. He had his own theatre where he produced operas and was a favorite of both the aristocracy and the common people.

George Frideric Handel (1685–1759). German composer who lived in England for most of his career. He wrote the famous oratorio *Messiah*.
Copyright © Scala/Art Resource, NY

PERSPECTIVE—RELIGIOUS TEXTS AND CHURCH INFLUENCE

The texts that are the basis of some religious musical genres are often traditional prayers or words that are part of the spoken rituals of a particular religious order. Many of these texts have remained unchanged for centuries. Some, like the Psalms from the Old Testament of the Bible, are thousands of years old.

Psalm 23, which is the majority of the text for Leonard Bernstein's *Chichester Psalms*, is attributed to King David (ca. 1011 bc–971 bc), the Hebrew leader of the united nation of Israel. David is credited with writing most of the Psalms. These "songs" have been included not only in the Old Testament of the Bible shared by both Christians and Jews, but in the Zabur, an Islamic holy book. The Zabur is a collection of songs that predates the Qur'an.

The texts of the musical mass are all Latin in origin except for the "Kyrie" which is from the Greek. All of the texts of the musical mass are components of the spoken mass, the most important ritual of the Roman Catholic Church. Some of these texts are shared by Protestant denominations and some are not. The "Kyrie" was incorporated into the mass ritual somewhere around the fifth century. The "Gloria" was originally a hymn of praise and included in early masses only on celebratory occasions. The "Credo" is the only one of the mass texts that is in the first person. It is not used during weekday masses but is reserved for masses celebrated on Sundays and special occasions. The "Sanctus" text comes from Isaiah 6:3, "Holy, holy, holy, is the Lord of hosts: the whole earth is full of His glory" and is spoken/sung during the consecration of the bread and wine toward the end of the mass. The "Agnus Dei" was in common usage in Catholic areas of the Middle East until those areas became predominantly Muslim. It was added to the mass ritual in the seventh century when brought to Europe by Catholic priests fleeing those lands.

Individual texts from the mass have also been used as the basis of other musical compositions. Settings of the "Gloria" that have become staples of the choral/orchestral repertory were composed by Antonio Vivaldi and Francis Poulenc (1959). The "Kyrie" and "Agnus Dei" have been given modern renditions by the pop group Mr. Mister (1985) and the contemporary Christian artist Michael W. Smith (1991) respectively.

It is difficult to measure the effect exerted on Western music by the Roman Catholic Church. The codification of all aspects of the church, including music, in the sixth and seventh centuries put in place one type of music, Gregorian Chant, that remained unchanged for nearly 500 years. How music would have evolved without that constraint is impossible to say, but it is fair to conjecture that the development of a harmonic system similar to the Renaissance concept of harmony would have occurred much earlier than it did. Would the course of Western music history have been different if the widespread use of harmony became common hundreds of years earlier, during a time still governed primarily by the church rather than during the emerging secular society of the sixteenth and seventeenth centuries? Might church music, written in a more "dramatic" musical language, have been more widely mirrored in secular music? Would that have changed the course of the development of music in Western society?

There is no way to know how music would have evolved if this had happened. But it is safe to say that music evolved in the way it did because the Roman Catholic Church directed the early course of music in the west and as such has been the single most important influence on it.

Handel was born in 1685 in Halle, Germany, and died in London in 1759. Handel moved to England in 1710 and for 30 years was the most popular composer of operas in England. After 1740 he turned his attention to writing oratorios. In 1741 Handel received a letter from Charles Jennens, a wealthy Englishman, that contained scriptural passages that Handel immediately decided he must set to music in an oratorio.

Characteristics of an Oratorio

The oratorio form consists of a series of short individual movements of vocal music called recitatives, arias, and choruses. These three types of vocal styles have distinct characteristics. The chorus is a piece of music for a large group of voices consisting of sopranos, altos, tenors, and basses, the traditional divisions of the human voice, accompanied by an orchestra. The aria is a lyrical solo piece for one voice with orchestral accompaniment. The recitative is a somewhat less lyrical piece for solo voice with orchestral accompaniment, but it is not as regular in its rhythmic qualities as the aria and is subject to dramatic changes in mood, tempo, and dynamics depending on the meaning of the words. An orchestral introduction called an overture usually precedes the vocal movements. Oratorios can be very long compositions, lasting upwards of two and a half to three hours in length. The oratorio that Handel wrote based on the scriptural passages sent to him by Charles Jennens is called *Messiah*.

Messiah is by far the most frequently performed oratorio of all time. This work is divided into three large sections concerning the birth, redemption, and resurrection of Jesus. The entire composition was completed in 30 days, a remarkable achievement by any measure. The first performance of *Messiah* took place in 1742 and was a benefit for a hospital and an infirmary in Dublin, Ireland. The piece became quite successful in England, and Handel continued to conduct performances of it for seventeen years up until his death in 1759.

Oratorios, though religious compositions, are not usually performed during a church service. They are intended as concert pieces to be performed either in a church or in a concert hall. While most oratorios are dramatic works that tell a story, they are not usually acted out on stage with costumes or scenery. They are presented in concert form, which means that all of the performers, the solo singers, chorus, and orchestra are on stage. The orchestra is not in an orchestra pit in front of and below stage level as would be common in an operatic performance.

In the *Messiah* excerpts below, listen for the following:

"Behold I Tell You a Mystery"—Absence of a truly lyrical melody and regular rhythmic pulse. Change of mood on the words, "In a moment, in the twinkling of an eye."

"The Trumpet Shall Sound"—Use of the trumpet as the primary melodic instrument in the introduction and as a complementary melodic line to the solo bass voice. The piece is in a three part, A-B-A, form. In the A sections the solo voice, trumpet, and full orchestra engage in a wonderful polyphonic interplay of lines supported by the basso continuo. In the B section the texture is reduced to just the solo voice and the basso continuo.

"Hallelujah"—Change of textures throughout piece. Monophonic or homophonic textures whenever new words are presented, polyphonic texture to repeat and emphasize words that have already been presented.

Messiah (excerpts)—
George Frideric Handel

Behold I Tell You a Mystery—Recitative
Behold, I tell you a mystery.
We shall not all sleep,
But we shall all be changed,
In a moment,
In the twinkling of an eye,
At the last trumpet.

(continued)

The Trumpet Shall Sound—Aria
A section: Solo trumpet, solo voice, full orchestra, basso continuo.
The trumpet shall sound and the dead shall be raised,
And the dead shall be raised incorruptible.
The trumpet shall sound, and the dead shall be raised,
Be raised incorruptible, be raised incorruptible,
And we shall be changed, and we shall be changed.

The trumpet shall sound, the trumpet shall sound,
And the dead shall be raised,
Be raised incorruptible, be raised incorruptible,
And we shall be changed, we shall be changed,
And we shall be changed.
And we shall be changed,
We shall be changed, and we shall be changed,
And we shall be changed, and we shall be changed,
We shall be changed, and we shall be changed,
We shall be changed. (Second time end here)

B section: Solo voice, bass continuo.
For this corruptible must put on incorruption,
For this corruptible must put on, must put on, must put on,
Must put on incorruption.

And this mortal must put on immortality.
And this mortal must put on immortality, immortality.

Back to beginning (Da Capo)

Hallelujah—Chorus
Hallelujah! Hallelujah!
Hallelujah! Hallelujah! Hallelujah! etc.

For the Lord God omnipotent reigneth.
Hallelujah, Hallelujah, Hallelujah, Hallelujah!
For the Lord God omnipotent reigneth.
Hallelujah, Hallelujah, Hallelujah, Hallelujah! etc.

The Kingdom of this world is become,
The kingdom of our Lord, and of His Christ, and of His Christ.
And He shall reign forever and ever. etc.

King of Kings! Forever and ever. Hallelujah, Hallelujah!
And Lord of Lords! Forever and ever. Hallelujah, Hallelujah!
King of Kings! Forever and ever. Hallelujah, Hallelujah!
And Lord of Lords! Forever and ever. Hallelujah, Hallelujah!
King of Kings! Forever and ever. Hallelujah, Hallelujah!
And Lord of Lords! King of Kings and Lord of Lords! etc.

El Niño—A Modern Oratorio

A modern oratorio counterpart to *Messiah* is *El Niño (The Child)* by **John Adams** with **Peter Sellars**. This work, which premiered in 2000, is most often called an oratorio but it is sometimes also included in discussions of opera. It is a work that reflects the content of the first two parts of *Messiah* in that it deals with the birth of Jesus. While *El Niño* pays homage to Handel's masterwork in the subject matter, Adams draws on a wider variety of texts beyond biblical passages, including the Gnostic Gospels, writings of Hildegard of Bingen and several modern Hispanic poets. Some similarities with traditional oratorios include the performing forces, which consists of vocal soloists, a choir, and an orchestra. Differences include the instrumentation of the orchestra, Adams uses a full symphony orchestra (with two steel guitars) as opposed to the small number of strings plus minimal winds and percussion of Handel, as well as the variety of voices which includes three countertenors, exceptionally high-pitched male voices and a children's choir. Perhaps the most striking difference is the inclusion of an audiovisual component which projects images on a large screen above and behind the performers on the stage throughout the performance. Also included in this element of the performance are dancing and staging for the choir and solo singers. Adams is often classified as a minimalist composer. That twentieth/twenty-first-century style is often characterized by repetition of short rhythmic and melodic patterns and slow changing harmonies.

The following example, which shares much of the text with a recitative from Handel's *Messiah*, features a solo bass voice accompanied by the orchestra. The chorus interjects forcefully slightly after the mid-point, after which the three countertenor voices enter. Their section of the movement is characterized by harmonies that alternate between the traditional and the dissonantly modern.

 "Shake the Heavens" from *El Niño*— John Adams

Bass Soloist

Thus saith the Lord, at once it is a little while and I will shake the heavens. For thus saith the Lord. I will shake the heavens, and the Earth . . ., I will shake the sea, I will shake the dry land, and I will shake the heavens . . ., and the Earth and the sea and the dry land. It is a little while and I will shake the heavens, and I will shake the dry land, and I will shake the Earth . . . etc.

And the desire of all the nations, and the desire of all the nations shall come.

I will shake . . . at once it is a little while and I will shake the heavens.

Chorus

And I will fill this house with glory, and in this place I will give peace.

Countertenors

In Judea to Bethlehem, they were three miles distant and Joseph turned and saw Mary, and Joseph turned and saw Mary, weeping, and he said, "Probably that which is in her is distressing her." Once again Joseph, Joseph, turned and saw her laughing, and he said, "Mary, how is it that I see your face at one moment laughing and at another time weeping"? She said to Joseph, "It is because I see two people with my heart, the one with him and one he, he loved more rejoicing and glad."

Cantata

The cantata is a genre that had its origins in the Baroque period. The Baroque cantata was primarily associated with the Lutheran church and the composer Johann Sebastian Bach. Bach wrote over two hundred cantatas for use during worship services. This was one of the distinguishing features of the cantata, it was often an integral part of the worship service. A cantata might consist of anywhere from six to fifteen movements of music performed at intervals throughout the service. Each movement might be approximately six or seven minutes in length, sometimes shorter, sometimes longer. The individual movements that constituted a cantata were recitatives, arias, and choruses, similar to the oratorios of that time. The entire composition might be thirty minutes to over an hour in length, in contrast to an oratorio which was two and a half to three hours long. The cantatas were frequently based on melodies that were already familiar to the congregation, and the final movement, played at the end of the service, was sometimes a simple four-part harmonization of the familiar melody. This allowed the congregation to join in the singing and bring the service to a satisfying conclusion.

Cantatas are still written today but in a format somewhat different from the Baroque period. Today's cantatas employ contemporary instruments, modern song forms, and frequently a spoken narration. They often tell a biblical story and some are acted out with costumes and scenery. In this way the modern church cantata is a hybrid, drawing on older genres such as the oratorio, opera, and its namesake, the Baroque era cantata.

The excerpt below by contemporary English composer John Rutter (b. 1945) is from his cantata *Gloria*, which premiered in 1974. Rutter is known for his choral works and his numerous settings of Christmas-related songs and music. The text is the same as that used from the Gloria movement of the mass discussed earlier in this chapter.

 "Allegro vivace" from *Gloria*— John Rutter

HYMNS

The term hymn can refer to any religious song intended for the express purpose of praising God. In that regard it can be an ancient song of any religion used to glorify the deity of that people. In more common usage it refers to the types of songs frequently sung during Christian worship services in which the congregation often participates in the singing. This tradition had its beginning in the Protestant Reformation. Indeed, many of the most famous hymns were written by prominent religious figures of that movement. Martin Luther (1483–1546) was the central figure in the early days of the Reformation and his teachings led to the establishment of the Lutheran denomination. Luther wrote, among others, the familiar hymn *A Mighty Fortress is our God*. Later, influential religious figures such as John Wesley (1703–1791) used hymns as a means to teach their denominations the central tenets of their faith. Wesley's *A Collection of Hymns for the use of the People Called Methodists* was just such an instructional instrument.

Hymns are often organized by themes such as seasonal celebrations, holy days, the purpose of faith, redemption, etc. in collections called hymnals which are made available in the church pews for use by members of the congregation. Hymns are frequently presented in four-part harmony for the common divisions of the voice, soprano and alto for the female voices, and tenor and bass for the male. In practice most members of the congregation sing only the hymn tune, which is usually presented in the soprano line. Members of the choir, along with the more musically inclined congregants, usually fill in the other three harmony parts. Some hymns, the older ones in particular, are in a simple strophic form, meaning they are a series of verses or stanzas in which the melody remains the same for each repetition while the words change with each subsequent stanza. In more modern hymns a chorus is sometimes incorporated between verses in which both the words and the melody remain the same for each repetition. Hymns are sometimes a compilation of words from one source, melody from another, and even a third contributor for the harmony. The words of the following example, *All Creatures of our God and King*, were written by Saint Francis of Assisi in the thirteenth century. The melody was the creation of a German composer, Peter von Brachel, in the seventeenth century, and the harmony most frequently used today was added by the English composer Ralph Vaughn Williams in the early twentieth century.

 All Creatures of our God and King

One particular type of hymn, the **Christmas carol**, has transcended the worship service and become a common musical fixture in modern society. Christmas carols are songs based on the Christmas story or related ideas. They have been sung in church services since the mid-nineteenth century but many can trace their melodies back to the Medieval era. Today Christmas carols are sung not only during church services but can be heard during all types of Christmas and winter seasonal observances both sacred and secular. As such, Christmas carols lend themselves to an unusually wide variety of interpretations. Listen to the following traditional rendition of *Veni, veni, Emmanuel (O come, o come, Emmanuel)*, author unknown. The melody of this hymn comes from a fifteenth-century French march. The tune is first presented with no accompanying harmony after which subsequent verses add varying harmonic richness. The second version of the hymn below incorporates contemporary instruments along with the traditional melody to provide a setting probably never envisioned by the early creators of this seasonal favorite.

Veni, veni, Emmanuel

Veni, veni, Emmanuel
captivum solve Israel,
qui gemit in exsilio,
privatus Dei Filio.

Gaude, gaude, Emmanuel
Nascetur pro te, Israel.

Veni, O Jesse virgula,
ex hostis tuos ungula,
de spectu tuos tartari
educ et antro barathri.

Gaude, gaude Emmanuel
Nascetur pro te, Israel.

Veni, veni O Oriens,
solare nos adveniens,
noctis depelle nebulas,
dirasque mortis tenebras.

Gaude, gaude Emmanuel
Nascetur pro te Israel.

Come, O come, Emmanuel,
and ransom captive Israel,
that morns in lonely exile here
until the Son of God appear.

Rejoice! Rejoice!
Emmanuel shall come to thee, O Israel!

O come, Thou Rod of Jesse's stem,
from ev'ry foe deliver them
that trust Thy mighty power to save,
and give them vict'ry o'er the grave.

Rejoice! Rejoice!
Emmanuel shall come to thee, O Israel!

O come, Thou Dayspring from on high,
and cheer us by thy drawing nigh;
disperse the gloomy clouds of night
and death's dark shadow put to flight.

Rejoice! Rejoice!
Emmanuel shall come to thee, O Israel!

(continued)

Veni, Clavis Davidica,	O come, Thou Key of David, come,
regna reclude caelica,	and open wide our heav'nly home,
fac iter tutum superum,	make safe the way that leads on high,
et claude vias inferum.	that we no more have cause to sigh.
Gaude, gaude Emmanuel	Rejoice! Rejoice!
Nascetur pro te Israel.	Emmanuel shall come to thee, O Israel!
Gaude, gaude Emmanuel	Rejoice! Rejoice!
Nascetur pro te Israel.	Emmanuel shall come to thee, O Israel!

SPIRITUALS AND GOSPEL MUSIC

At the Greater St. Stephens Baptist Church, a predominately African-American church in New Orleans, the religious experience is celebrated with spirituals and gospel music. © Bob Sacha/Corbis

A kind of intense, high-energy, worship music found in the United States is the music known as **gospel music**. Gospel music can be heard in any number of predominantly African-American churches throughout the country. It has its roots in the "**spirituals**" of southern African-American slaves and the folk and country music of rural Christian whites in the southern United States. Spirituals are songs that often have their basis in Bible stories and in the slaves' yearning for freedom that couldn't openly be expressed in other ways. These songs were sung in the fields while working, in church, or in other settings where the overseers of the slaves were not likely to be. Spirituals often mask the literal meaning of the words through references to biblical stories concerning freedom from worldly bonds. Much music originating in the slave culture of the formative United States reflects the yearning for freedom from oppression often found in biblical stories of the Jewish people from the Old Testament.

In the performance of spirituals one is likely to hear several idiomatic characteristics strongly associated with this kind of music. A simple rhythmic accompaniment is common. Since the slaves had few if any worldly possessions, including musical instruments, rhythmic accompaniments could be provided by virtually any material that could be struck or scraped to make a sound. Hand clapping and finger snapping in the performance of this music is also frequently heard. Additionally, the use of **microtones**, bending the pitch from one note to another, can often be heard in spirituals. The use of **verse** and **chorus** form is also common in this music, as it is in much folk music.

 Brother Mosely Crossed (Smote) the Water
Traditional Spiritual sung by Andy Mosely

 Witness
Traditional Spiritual sung by Jubilant Sykes

Oh lord what man is this?
All the nations in him are blessed,
All things are done by his will,
He spoke to the sea and the sea stood still.

Now aint that a witness for my Lord?
Aint that a witness for my Lord?
Aint that a witness for my Lord?
My soul is a witness for my Lord.

There was a man of the Pharisees,
His name was Nicodemus and he did not believe.
But the same came to Christ by night,
He wanted to be born on a human sight.
Christ told Nicodemus as a friend
"Man, you must be born again."
He said, "More than that man if you want to be wise,
Repent, believe and be baptized."

Then you'll be a witness for my Lord.
You'll be a witness for my Lord.
You'll be a witness for my Lord.
My soul is a witness for my Lord.

You read about Samson from his birth,
Strongest man that ever lived on Earth.
Way back yonder in ancient times,
He killed ten thousand of the Philistines.
Then old Samson went wandering about,
Samson's strength was never found out.
Til his wife she said upon her knees,
She said, "Tell me where your strength lies if you please?"
Samson's wife she talked so fair.
Samson said, "Cut off my hair
Shave my head, just as clean as your hand,
and my strength will come like a natural man."

Oh Samson was a witness for my Lord.
Samson was a witness for my Lord.
Samson was a witness for my Lord.
My soul is a witness for my Lord.

And there's another witness,
Oh there's another witness,
Oh there's another witness,
My soul is a witness for my Lord.

Much African-American gospel music consists of verses and choruses, sung by large choirs, often in unison, with occasional sections of harmony. It's common for some sections of these pieces to be repeated many times with increased energy each time. Instead of the reflective restraint often found in other kinds of sacred music this music adopts a joyous, exhilarating style, emphasizing the jubilation of salvation over the fear of damnation. An accompanying band consisting of a keyboard (piano, organ, or synthesizer), bass, drums, guitar, and a horn section is common. This music frequently features vocal soloists, instrumental solos, and spoken/sung exhortations to praise or join in the singing.

♪ *Clap Your Hands—*
John P. Kee

In the case of spirituals and gospel music the shared beliefs of the faith are but a part of the musical experience. There is something beyond the music and the faith that energizes these styles. Based as they are in the slave experience of African-Americans, spirituals and gospel music recall the struggle for freedom against enormous odds that the slaves faced, just as the Jewish people of the Bible did thousands of years ago.

WORLD WORSHIP MUSIC

Ketjak

We can look at religious music from societies very different from our own and see commonalities, no matter how different the music may sound on first hearing. One of the most strikingly different kinds of religious music you may ever hear is a kind of rhythmic chanting from the southern Indonesian island of Bali, called Ketjak. While this may not be everyone's idea of worshipful music, there is no denying the powerful belief the Balinese islanders have in the ability of this chanting to drive out the influence of evil forces. The example we will hear is called *The Ramayana Monkey Chant,* a re-enactment of a battle between the people of Bali and an invading group of competing tribes from another island. As legend has it, the Balinese were about to be defeated in battle when hordes of monkeys from the mountains descended into the villages driving the invaders out. Since then monkeys have been revered as sacred animals. The chant is an extraordinary display of precise polyrhythmic chanting. Small groups of men chant simple rhythms that combine with other simple rhythmic patterns other groups are chanting. This creates an overlapping rhythmic texture similar to the interacting melodic lines, polyphony, of late Medieval and Renaissance vocal music. Over this rhythmic pulse a leader, sitting in the center of the assembled, tells the story. At certain points in the story the tempo will increase, half of the group will wave their hands at the opposing group imitating the attack while the other half lays back on the ground succumbing to the onslaught. At times a repetitive melodic line takes over as the most prominent feature only to be overtaken by the rhythmic chant that is driving out the evil spirits, exorcising the demons.

Ketjak dancers from Bali, Indonesia. © Bernard
Annebicque/Corbis Sygma

The Ramayana Monkey Chant—
Balinese Ketjak

Tibetan Buddhist Monk Chant

As opposite from the Balinese chanting in its rhythmic qualities as music can be, the chanting of Tibetan Buddhist monks evokes an otherworldly calm and peacefulness as deep as the valleys in the Himalayas from which it originates. The low intonations of the monks are a restatement of prayers uttered by one of their members while in a hypnotic, trancelike state. The prayers are "received" by the monk in a trance while the other monks write down what he says. That becomes a prayer shared by all. There is no melody, at least not one as we would normally expect a melody to sound like, there is no harmony, just a very low-pitched incantation of the received prayer. The

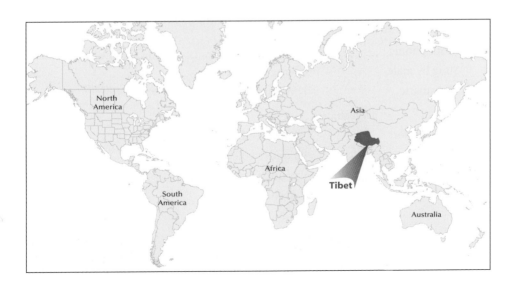

low-pitched chant may be preceded by, as in the example below, or punctuated by bells, gongs, and low-pitched mountain horns. There is an extremely rare kind of vocalization that some of the monks can perform called "**multiphonics**." This is the ability to "sing" more than one pitch at a time. While producing one tone intentionally, one or two sympathetic tones are produced simultaneously through the resonating sinus, throat, or chest cavity. The production of multiphonics is extremely difficult and requires a very pronounced physical effort to accomplish. Shepherds from an area known as Tuva are also known for their ability to produce multiphonics. Their unique type of vocal music is discussed below.

Invoking the Spirit of Kindness Through Sound—
Tibetan Buddhist Monk Chant

Muslim "Call to Prayer"

The muezzin calls the Muslim faithful to prayer. © David Rubinger/Corbis

From ancient times to the present, Muslims the world over have been called to prayer five times a day by the "muezzin," the man designated in each community to climb the minaret of the mosque to call the faithful to face Mecca and pray. This "**Call to Prayer**" is similar to the Medieval **Gregorian Chant** in that it is monophonic, sung by a male voice, and often requires the singer to sing many notes to one syllable of the text. This style of vocalization, where many notes are sung to one syllable, is called "**melismatic**." The "Call to Prayer" is sung outdoors in a loud projecting voice and is not an actual prayer. Gregorian Chant is usually a prayer of some kind, sung indoors in a reverberant church in a voice that is not as loud and forceful, and always sung in Latin, the official language of the Catholic Church. The call to prayer is in Arabic. Just as the chant sets the worshipful mood inside the church, the call to prayer exhorts the Muslim faithful to put aside the daily concerns of living and focus on God throughout the day. Listen to the example included and listen for other similarities or differences between the Muslim "Call to Prayer" and the Christian Gregorian Chant.

Gregorian Chant	Call to Prayer
Similarities	
Monophonic	Monophonic
Sung by male	Sung by male
Melismatic	Melismatic
Differences	
Sung indoors	Sung outdoors
Softer voice	Louder voice
Is often a prayer	Is not a prayer
Latin	Arabic

Call to Prayer—
Muslim Invitation to Pray

EZAN—The Muslim Call to Prayer

Allahu Akbar, Allahu Akbar.	Allah is the Greatest, Allah is the Greatest.
Allahu Akbar, Allahu Akbar.	Allah is the Greatest, Allah is the Greatest.
Ash-hadu alla ilaha illa-llah.	I bear witness that there is none worthy of worship but Allah.
Ash-hadu alla ilaha illa-llah.	I bear witness that there is none worthy of worship but Allah.
Ash-hadu anna Muhammadar-Rasulullah.	I bear witness that Muhammad is the Messenger of Allah
Ash-hadu anna Muhammadar-Rasulullah.	I bear witness that Muhammad is the Messenger of Allah
Hayya 'ala-s-Salah, hayya 'ala-s-Salah.	Hasten to the Prayer, hasten to the Prayer.
Hayya 'ala-l-falah, hayya 'ala-l-falah.	Hasten to real success, hasten to real success
Allahu Akbar, Allahu Akbar.	Allah is the Greatest, Allah is the Greatest.
La ilaha illa-llah	There is none worthy of worship but Allah.

Tuvan Throat Singing

Tuva is an autonomous republic belonging to the Russian Federation in central Asia, situated next to Mongolia on the Chinese and Russian border. The population is mostly rural with many of the inhabitants making their meager living tending sheep on the plains. The capital, Kyzyl, is home to a third of the 300,000 people who call themselves Tuvans. In this remote area many of the activities engaged in by the people are often related to the land, which is the source of their livelihood. Musical activities are mostly relegated to individual performances by everyday citizens, not professional musicians. Concerts, as such, are not performed. Music is a folk tradition performed by amateur practitioners.

It is in this less than ideal atmosphere for musical engagement that one of the more interesting performance traditions has developed. Tuvan throat singing, as it is known, is the practice of singing one pitch while allowing the naturally occurring overtones inherent in all musical pitches to be amplified by the singer, so as to create melodies above a droning low tone. This vocal style is similar to the mulitiphonic

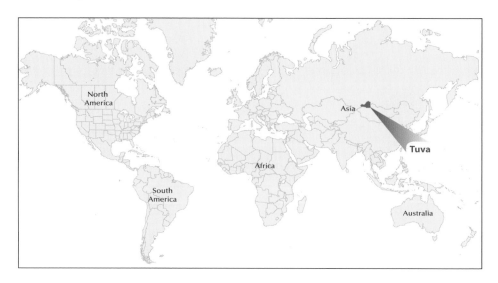

singing of the Tibetan Buddhist monks. But rather than be performed as part of formal religious observances the Tuvan throat singers practice their art as a way to interact with the spirits of the world that they believe reside in the mountains surrounding Tuva.

Tuvan throat singing is often accompanied by instruments and the songs frequently evoke some aspect of the land or animals that are such an integral part of Tuvan life. Songs that imitate the sounds of horses' hooves, birds singing, or the wind blowing, are common. The following example, however, is an instance of pure throat singing. The name of the song, *Kh mei*, is simply the Tuvan name for throat singing. It would be performed outside, probably in the mountains, as a way to communicate with the spirits of the land.

Kh mei—
Performed by Hun-Huur-Tu

Amy Grant, Christian pop superstar. © John Atashian/ Corbis

CONTEMPORARY CHRISTIAN POP AND ROCK

One of the biggest changes in contemporary music over the last 20–30 years has been the emergence of Christian-based popular and rock music. Historically most rock and roll and popular music have been strongly secular in their appeal. The songs have been mostly devoted to topics such as love, sex, and rebellion and appealed primarily to an adolescent audience. The rise in popularity of religiously-based music with the same basic "sound" as other types of popular music has been one of the more interesting developments in popular music in recent history.

Most pop/rock music has been based on the verse/chorus/bridge song structure. In this form there is a series of verses of text set to a catchy tune where the words change each time the music repeats. There is also a chorus that is based on a different melodic idea. The chorus melody usually appears several times during a song with both the same music *and* words. The third part of this kind of song form is the bridge, a short section of music that is different from the verse and chorus and serves to connect one to the other.

Christian Pop Music

One of the first superstars on the contemporary Christian music scene was Amy Grant. From the late 1970s until today, Grant's music has transcended the adolescent pop music audience that defined popular music. One of her early hits, *El Shaddai* (God Almighty), blends the sound of the pop music medium with traditional Hebrew words of praise. The Hebrew portion of the text is:

El Shaddai, El Shaddai, (God Almighty, God Almighty)
El- Elyon Na Adonai, (God Most High O Lord)

El Shaddai, El Shaddai,
Erkamka Na Adonai, (We Will Love You O Lord)

 El Shaddai—
Words and music by Michael Card and John Thompson,
sung by Amy Grant

What Makes Music—Musical Instruments

The Bowed String Family

Instruments of the orchestra are grouped into four families according to certain characteristics. All of the instruments in this family are made of wood, usually spruce and maple. All have four strings. All are played with a bow. The bow is most frequently made out of Pernambuco wood, found only in Brazil, and horsehair.

Violin—This is the smallest and highest pitched of the bowed string instruments and is held under the chin while it is played. There are usually more violins in an orchestra than any other instrument.

Viola—The viola looks like a violin, and is also held under the chin, but is slightly larger. It usually plays lower notes than a violin and also usually plays harmony rather than melody.

Cello (Violoncello)—The cello is not held under chin like the violin and the viola but is held between the legs while sitting.

Bass (Double Bass, Contra Bass, Bass Fiddle)—The bass is played standing up or sitting on a stool. It is the largest and lowest pitched of the bowed string instruments. It is often played pizzicato; that is, plucked with the fingers rather than stroked with a bow. This is especially common when playing jazz.

Bassist Tim Goodwin playing pizzicato; that is, with the fingers instead of using a bow. Photo courtesy of Heather Goodwin

There is a standard performing ensemble for the stringed instruments called a String Quartet, which consists of two violins, a viola, and a cello. There is no bass in a string quartet.

View the video of English composer Benjamin Britten's *Young Person's Guide to the Orchestra* performed by the YouTube Symphony Orchestra on the chapter video playlist.

The string family of instruments is featured from 1:16– 1:32, and each of the strings is featured individually beginning at the 5:06 mark.

The Ceruti String Quartet, Timothy Shiu and Soh-Hyun Altino, violins; Leonardo Altino, cello; and Lenny Schranze, viola. Photo courtesy of Ana Lucia Garcia Altino

I Can Only Imagine

The following song by the contemporary Christian pop group Mercy Me is a straightforward pop style song that gives a first-person testament of the singer's faith. An initial minimal accompaniment grows to include all of the instruments typical of a modern pop song, keyboards, guitars, bass and drums, along with the full-sounding string section of violins, violas, and cellos.

I Can Only Imagine—
Bart Millard, performed by Mercy Me

Christian Rock Music

Contemporary Christian music, unlike sacred music of earlier eras, is not experienced only in a church. In fact it's most likely to be heard on the radio, through recorded performances on CD, in MP3 format, in concert, on television, or at any number of other locations. One of the biggest differences in sacred music from today and from the past is how and where it is heard. We can just as easily hear religious music driving in our cars as we can attending a church service. Does hearing the music outside of the "sacred places" change our perception of it? If so, how? Does it make the experience less or more powerful? Consider the next example performed by a Christian rock band, P.O.D. (Payable on Death). This band's music is grounded in the hard rock style and appeals to a younger audience. Still, the music has the same basic components—verse, chorus, and bridge—found in most pop/rock music and carries the Christian message through that medium.

Alive—
P.O.D.

A Tower of Ashes

The Christian metal band Theocracy was initially a single-handed creation of Matt Smith, the band's founder. Now a three-man group, their style has similarities to progressive metal bands such as DragonForce and Dream Theater. The epic atmosphere and extended forms, coupled with virtuosic instrumentals, reveal a desire to create something on a larger scale than simple songs.

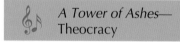

A Tower of Ashes—
Theocracy

OTHER TYPES OF RELIGIOUS MUSIC

Some other examples of religious music are worth noting.

Motet

The motet is a sacred, choral composition, dating from the late thirteenth to the eighteenth century that is based on a Latin text.

Listening Chart

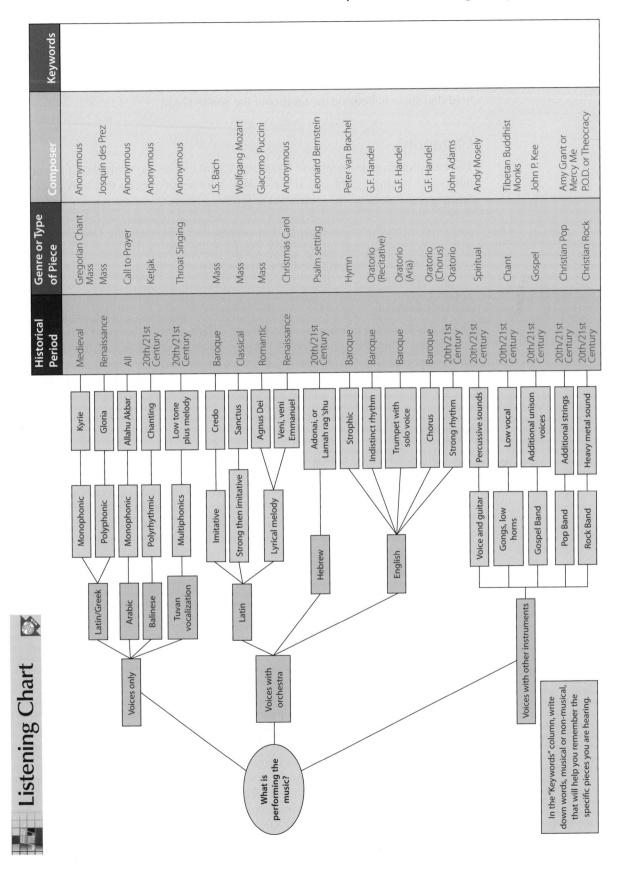

Historical Period	Genre or Type of Piece	Composer	Keywords
Medieval	Gregorian Chant Mass	Anonymous	
Renaissance	Mass	Josquin des Prez	
All	Call to Prayer	Anonymous	
20th/21st Century	Ketjak	Anonymous	
20th/21st Century	Throat Singing	Anonymous	
Baroque	Mass	J.S. Bach	
Classical	Mass	Wolfgang Mozart	
Romantic	Mass	Giacomo Puccini	
Renaissance	Christmas Carol	Anonymous	
20th/21st Century	Psalm setting	Leonard Bernstein	
Baroque	Hymn	Peter van Brachel	
Baroque	Oratorio (Recitative)	G.F. Handel	
Baroque	Oratorio (Aria)	G.F. Handel	
Baroque	Oratorio (Chorus)	G.F. Handel	
20th/21st Century	Oratorio	John Adams	
20th/21st Century	Spiritual	Andy Mosely	
20th/21st Century	Chant	Tibetan Buddhist Monks	
20th/21st Century	Gospel	John P. Kee	
20th/21st Century	Christian Pop	Amy Grant or Mercy Me	
20th/21st Century	Christian Rock	P.O.D. or Theocracy	

In the "Keywords" column, write down words, musical or non-musical, that will help you remember the specific pieces you are hearing.

Magnificat

The Magnificat is a prayer from the Catholic Church that has been set to music by many composers throughout the centuries. The most famous is the Magnificat by Johann Sebastian Bach. The Magnificat is Mary's response when told by the Angel Gabriel that she is to become the mother of the Son of God.

Organum

The evolution from monophonic Gregorian Chant to four-part polyphonic music was not a quick or single giant step. It was a slow, incremental process that took place over several centuries. From the twelfth to the fourteenth centuries additional melodic lines were added to pre-existing Gregorian Chant melodies to create two- and then three-part pieces. Organum was a genre that consisted of a pre-existing Gregorian Chant with an additional vocal melodic line. Occasionally, a third line might be added that could be played by an instrument instead of a voice.

Stabat Mater

The Stabat Mater is a thirteenth century hymn describing Mary's sorrow at the crucifixion of Jesus. Many composers have set this traditional text to music, including Renaissance composer Giovanni Palestrina, Classical period composer Franz Joseph Haydn, and Romantic composers Giuseppe Verdi, Franz Schubert, and Antonin Dvorak.

SUMMARY

In this chapter we have seen how ancient religious texts have been used by composers across the centuries in music for worship services and for concert performances. The Roman Catholic Mass texts have been the basis of the musical genre of the mass throughout all historical periods, and the Jewish and Christian psalm texts have been used in musical psalm settings as well. The individual texts for the ordinary of the Mass, Kyrie, Gloria, Credo, Sanctus, and Agnus Dei, lend themselves well to the multi-movement structure of an extended musical genre such as the mass. Many of the greatest composers throughout history, such as Johann Sebastian Bach and Wolfgang Amadeus Mozart in addition to many others, have set the Mass texts to music whether they were members of the Catholic Church or some other Christian denomination.

The Christian faiths have also seen other religious texts set in significant musical genres such as George Frideric Handel's use of Biblical texts in his oratorios, such as *Messiah*, and Bach in his cantatas. Both the oratorio and the cantata share the use of three types of vocal styles: the recitative, the aria, and the chorus, in combination with orchestral accompaniment. Both of these composers, flourishing as they did during the Baroque period, made significant use of the basso continuo in these compositions. The oratorio and cantata have both maintained their place in composers' output up to the present day with changes of style appropriate to today's music.

Hymns, religious songs intended for the express purpose of praising God, have figured prominently in the Christian denominations since the Protestant Reformation of the sixteenth century. A specific type of hymn, the Christmas carol, which refers to the Christmas story of Jesus' birth and related ideas, has transcended the worship service and become part of the cultural fabric of Western society. Spirituals and gospel music, both closely associated with African-American churches in the United States, have also become part of modern culture. Spirituals have their genesis in Biblical stories, especially those relating to the Jewish peoples' enslavement and eventual release from Egyptian imprisonment. Gospel music tends to have a more modern, popular sound, using as it does instrumental accompaniment found in other types of popular music.

Religious music from non-Western cultures takes on many varied forms. Vocal, rhythmic chanting of Balinese Ketjak, low, sustained chanting of Tibetan Buddhist monks, melismatic vocalizations of Muslim muezzin, and multiphonic throat singing of Tuvan shepherds are just some of the variety of musical forms used to praise God throughout the world.

In this chapter we have heard music that transcends time and place. The Mass texts have survived for centuries, presented in different ways depending on the musical language of the unique point in time during which a piece was written. Hearing musical settings of the ordinary of the Mass from different historical periods is an unusual way of experiencing these ancient texts, but by doing so we can see that the role of music has always been to illuminate the words, regardless of when the music was written. And that is the importance of this music, to bring the words to life in a way that the words alone cannot. Music for worship fills a need within people of many faiths, a need borne of mystery, faith, and hope. This music, these words, must be shared.

So, why does the Tibetan monk intone his unchanging drone? Why set the ancient Biblical Psalms to new music thousands of years after they were first penned? Why would Bach write a piece that might never be performed? For Bach it was his ultimate statement of faith. A statement made with the musical language of his time, the language he adopted, and adapted, to profess his faith through music. For Bernstein, the Psalms were timeless expressions of belief in the benevolence of a loving, protective God. For the Buddhist monk it is being the vessel that carries the word of God into the world. Powerful expressions all, of music of the religious experience.

SUGGESTED FURTHER LISTENING

L'homme armé Mass (The Armed Man Mass)—Guillaume Dufay

Ave Maria—Josquin des Prez

Stabat Mater—Giovanni de Palestrina

Magnificat—Johann Sebastian Bach

Cantata #140—Johann Sebastian Bach

"Credo" from *Mass in G major*—Franz Schubert

Missa Solemnis—Ludwig van Beethoven

Quatro Pezzi Sacri (Four Sacred Songs)—Giuseppe Verdi

Sacred Service—Ernest Bloch

"Overture" and "Pastorale Symphony" from *Messiah*—George Frideric Handel

Mass—Leonard Bernstein

Ev'ry Time I Feel The Spirit—Traditional Spiritual

Agnus Dei—Michael W. Smith

With Arms Wide Open—Creed

ADDITIONAL WORSHIP MUSIC TEXTS

Magnificat

My soul magnifies the Lord,
And my spirit rejoices in God my Savior.
For He has regarded the low estate of His handmaiden,
For behold, henceforth all generations shall call me
    blessed.
For He who is mighty has done great things for me, and
    holy is His name. And His mercy is on those who fear
    Him from generation to generation.
He has shown strength with His arm:
He has scattered the proud in the imagination of their
    hearts.
He has put down the mighty from their thrones,
and exalted those of low degree.
He has filled the hungry with good things;
and the rich He has sent empty away.
He has helped His servant Israel, in remembrance of His
    mercy;
As He spoke to our fathers, to Abraham and to His
    posterity forever.

Magnificat anima mea Dominum;

Et exultavit spiritus meus in Deo salutari meo,
Quia respexit humilitatem ancillae suae; ecce enim ex
    hoc beatam me dicent omnes generationes.
Quia fecit mihi magna qui potens est, et sanctum
    nomen ejus,
Et misericordia ejus a progenie in progenies
    timentibus eum.
Fecit potentiam brachio suo;
Dispersit superbos mente cordis sui.
Deposuit potentes de sede, et exaltavit humiles.
Esurientes implevit bonis, et divites dimisit inanes.
Sucepit Israel, puerum suum, recordatus
    misericordiae suae,
Sicut locutus est ad patres nostros, Abraham et semeni
    ejus in saecula.

Stabat Mater

At the cross her station keeping,
Mary stood in sorrow weeping
When her Son was crucified.

While she waited in her anguish,
Seeing Christ in torment languish,
Bitter sorrow pierced her heart.

With what pain and desolation,
With what noble resignation,
Mary watched her dying Son.

Ever-patient in her yearning
Though her tear-filled eyes were burning,
Mary gazed upon her Son.

Who, that sorrow contemplating,
On that passion meditating,
Would not share the Virgin's grief?

Christ she saw, for our salvation,
Scourged with cruel acclamation,
Bruised and beaten by the rod.

Christ she saw with life-blood failing,
All her anguish unavailing,
Saw him breathe his very last.

Mary, fount of love's devotion,
Let me share with true emotion
All the sorrow you endured.

Stabat Mater

Stabat Mater dolorósa
Juxta Crucem lacrimósa,
Dum pendébat Filius.

Cujus ánimam geméntem,
Contristátam et doléntem,
Pertransivit gladius.

O quam tristis et afflicta
Fuit illa benedicta
Mater Unigéniti!

Quae maerébat, et dolébat,
Pia Mater, dum vidébat
Nati poenas inclyti.

Quis est homo, qui non fleret,
Matrem Christi si vidéret
In tanto supplicio?

Quis non posset contristári,
Christi Matrem contemplári
Doléntem cum Filio?

Pro peccátis suae gentis
Vidit Jesum in torméntis,
Et flagéllis súbditum.

Vidit suum dulcem natum
Moriéndo desolátum,
Dum emisit spíritum.

Virgin, ever interceding,
Hear me in my fervent pleading:
Fire me with your love of Christ.

Mother, may this prayer be granted:
That Christ's love may be implanted
In the depths of my poor soul.

At the cross, your sorrow sharing,
All your grief and torment bearing,
Let me stand and mourn with you.

Fairest maid of all creation,
Queen of hope and consolation,
Let me feel your grief sublime.

Virgin, in your love befriend me,
At the Judgment Day defend me.
Help me by your constant prayer.

Savior, when my life shall leave me,
Through your mother's prayers receive me
With the fruits of victory.

Virgin of all virgins blest!
Listen to my fond request:
Let me share your grief divine.

Let me, to my latest breath,
In my body bear the death
Of your dying Son divine.

Wounded with His every wound,
Steep my soul till it has swooned
In His very Blood away.

Be to me, O Virgin, nigh,
Lest in flames I burn and die,
In His awe-full judgment day.

Savior, when my life shall leave me,
Through your mother's prayers receive me
With the fruits of victory.

While my body here decays
May my soul your goodness praise,
Safe in heaven eternally. Amen. Alleluia.

Eja mater, fons amóris,
Me sentíre vim dolóris
Fac, ut tecum lúgeam.

Fac, ut ürdeat cor meum
In amándo Christum Deum,
Ut sibi compláceam.

Sancta Mater, istud agas
Crucifixi fige plagas
Cordi meo válide.

Tui nati vulneráti,
Tam dignáti pro me pati,
Poenas mecum dívide.

Fac me tecum pie flere,
Crucifixo condolére,
Donec ego víxero.

Juxta Crucem tecum stare,
Et me tibi sociáre
In planctu desídero.

Virgo vírginum praeclára,
Mihi jam non sis amára:
Fac me tecum plángere.

Fac, ut portem Christi mortem,
Passiónis fac consórtem,
Et plagas recólere.

Fac me plagis vulnerári,
Fac me Cruce inebriári,
Et cruó re Fílii.

Flammis ne urar succénsus,
Per te, Virgo, sim defénsus
In die judícii.

Christe, cum sit hinc exíre
Da per Matrem me veníre
Ad palmam victóriae.

Quando corpus moriétur,
Fac, ut ánimae donétur
Paradísi glória. Amen. Allelúja.

QUESTION ASSIGNMENT

Instructions: Log in to the textbook web site and click on the ASSIGNMENTS tab. In the Chapter Question Assignment area read the instructions and answer the question(s) or provide the asked for information. Be sure to click the SUBMIT THIS FORM button after you complete the Assignment.

Listen to a musical example from the Western tradition (pages 30–44) and a musical example from the World Music section of Chapter 2 (pages 47–50) and cite three differences between the two.

Western Tradition Example: _____

World Music Example: _____

Difference #1: _____

Difference #2: _____

Difference #3: _____

LISTENING EXERCISES

Instructions: Log in to the textbook web site and click on the ASSIGNMENTS tab. In the Listening Exercises area click on the links to the musical examples for each question and answer the questions. Be sure to click the SUBMIT button after you answer all of the questions.

Listen to each of the musical examples below from the Chapter 2 Playlist while noting the appropriate descriptive prompt on the Listening Chart for Chapter 2 and determine the best answer to each question.

1. "Sanctus" from *Requiem Mass* by Wolfgang Amadeus Mozart—This piece for voices with orchestra begins with the choir, singing in Latin, and the orchestra playing music with a strong, stately rhythmic feel, which is followed by a quicker section that has the imitative quality often found in the polyphonic style. Choose the timing below that represents when the character of the music exhibits the change from strong then imitative.

    a.   15 seconds
    b.   30 seconds
    c.   49 seconds

2. "The Trumpet Shall Sound" from *Messiah* by George Frideric Handel—This piece for voices with orchestra begins with the orchestra and the solo trumpet playing an extended introduction before the bass voice enters singing the text, which is in English. Listen to this composition and determine which timing represents when the trumpet with solo voice begin to alternately share the melodic line.

    a.   15 seconds
    b.   38 seconds
    c.   60 seconds

3. *El Shaddai* by Michael Card and John Thompson, sung by Amy Grant—This song for voice with other instruments begins with the voice accompanied by the piano for the first verse. As a method of adding interest to the second verse, violins, violas, and cellos, are added. Choose the timing below that indicates when the additional strings first enter.

    a.   10 seconds
    b.   50 seconds
    c.   60 seconds

Chapter 3

Music for the Stage

 FOCUS POINTS

Western Art Music Stage Genres	**World Music Stage Genres**
Morality Play	Japanese Kabuki Theatre
Opera	Chinese Opera
Musical	
Modern Stage Spectacle	

A story unfolds on a stage. We follow it through the words that are spoken and the action that takes place. That should be sufficient to tell the story, shouldn't it? After all, don't the words and the actions comprise all we need to experience the story and the range of emotions associated with it? Perhaps not, since the addition of music to dramatic productions has been a common practice since the ancient Greeks formulated the basic concepts that still comprise modern theatre. Greek theatre, renowned for its exploration of the breadth and depth of the human experience, incorporated music to enhance the theatrical presentation. The addition of music, in varying degrees, has been commonplace in theatre for as long as people have stepped onto a stage.

Let's see how music can enhance our experience of something dramatic on the modern extension of the stage, the movie theatre screen. Think about the well-known character from the *Star Wars* movies, Darth Vader. When you picture this character in your mind, do you "hear" the music that often accompanies his presence on the screen?

A scene from Nashville Opera's production of *Turandot,* an opera by Giacomo Puccini. Courtesy of the Nashville Opera

 Star Wars—
Imperial March, Darth Vader's Theme

This ominous music, full of dread and foreboding, would never be used to represent a hero. The sound of this music represents "The Dark

Side." While Darth Vader's visual presence is intimidating without music, associating a specific musical **motive** with this character gives us an additional cue to fire our imaginations about the evil he represents. This kind of musical enhancement of dramatic productions has been common throughout the history of music in the West and in cultures around the world.

EARLY DRAMATIC MUSICAL COMPOSITION

The ancient Greeks were one of the first civilizations to develop a significant theatrical art form. Their plays often employed the use of masks with music being an essential component. Corel

The earliest surviving example of a staged musical composition in the West is the **morality play**, *Ordo Virtutum (Play of the Virtues)*, composed by **Hildegard of Bingen**. Hildegard was born in 1098 and established a convent at Rupertsburg near Bingen, Germany, ca. 1146. *Ordo Virtutum* was written for the dedication of the convent. This composition is similar in style to other sacred music from the time period, which was monophonic vocal music, but it is different in that it is sung for the most part by women's voices. The role of the Devil is played by a man. This work was meant not as worship music for a church service but as a dedicatory piece for a public event. It probably had a minimal instrumental accompaniment in some form even though the specifics of that instrumentation are not indicated in the score. *Ordo Virtutum* recounts the struggle of the "Soul" against the temptations of the world. The Devil lures the Soul away from the Virtues but the Soul eventually repents and is accepted back into God's grace.

Biographical Spotlight

© 2013, Zvonimir Atletic, Shutterstock, Inc.

Hildegard of Bingen

Hildegard of Bingen was born, it is believed, in 1098 and died on September 17, 1179. From an early age she experienced "visions" that she interpreted as revelations as to the true meaning of Christian doctrine. Her parents committed her to a life of religious study, recognizing in her an individual with a rare gift that needed to be protected and encouraged. She was entered into the service of the Church at a monastery in Disibodenberg, Germany, along with another young woman who also experienced "visions," named Jutta. They were constant companions for many years, sharing their monastic life and "visions" with each other. At the encouragement of a monk named Volmar, who became her teacher and close confidant, Hildegard began writing down her accounts of the "visions" in a book she called *Scivias (Know the Ways [of God])*. When Jutta died in 1136 Hildegard was elected the leader of her order which resulted in their eventual move from the relative comfort of the Disibodenberg monastery to the more primitive Rupertsburg monastery where they were granted more autonomy for their order. Hildegard's writings about her "visions" where brought to the attention of Pope Eugenius III who proclaimed them divinely inspired. The Papal stamp of approval quieted rising criticism of Hildegard's interpretation of Church doctrine.

The above facts, while interesting, were not especially unusual for a young woman dedicated to the religious life at the time and who claimed to have God-inspired "visions." It's what Hildegard did during her long tenure at Rupertsburg, and subsequently at Eibingen (another monastery that she founded), which separates her from the other women of her time. She wrote hundreds of letters to many of the religious and political leaders of the time, not hesitating to offer her interpretation of political events and religious doctrine. In doing so she gained immense respect for her thoughts and insights among both the sacred and secular authorities. She wrote three large volumes, the above-mentioned *Scivias, Liber Vitae Meritorum (Book of Life's Merits)*, and *Liber Divinorum Operum (Book of the Divine Works)* which cover virtually every aspect of religious life and belief. She wrote two comprehensive books on medicine, *Liber Simplicis Medicinae (Book of Simple Medicine)*, and the *Causae et Curae (Causes and Cures)*. These writings on medicine are based on her vast knowledge of the medicinal qualities found in herbal substances and her observations of the many sick and infirm that found their way to the monastery for help.

These books are only the most impressive writings among a long list of less extensive efforts. She wrote much poetry. She invented her own alphabet/language that she used on occasion in some of her musical compositions. She composed numerous pieces revealing her own unique musical voice, often employing a more melodic variation of the Gregorian Chant style common at the time. She even undertook several preaching tours beyond the confines of the monastery, publicly engaging in the kind of learned discourse reserved only for men at the time.

It is important to understand that Hildegard never regarded or spoke of herself as an educated person qualified to speak on such a broad range of issues, especially matters relating to the Church. She only related what God wanted her to share. Her influence on Church teachings and doctrine has been profound. In October of 2012 she was declared a *Doctor of the Church*, a designation reserved only for those Saints who have had an especially significant impact on Church teachings. She is only the 35th person ever to be so designated.

Biographical Spotlight Exercise

Instructions: Log in to the textbook web site and click on the **Assignments** tab. Click on **Chapter 3** and scroll to the **Biographical Spotlight area.** Answer the question based on the information in the biography above.

Hildegard frequently offered her interpretations of political events and religious doctrine to:

1. Artists and musicians
2. Religious and political leaders
3. University students

 Ordo Virtutum excerpt—
Hildegard of Bingen

Sed, gravata, Anima conqueritur:	*Soul turns to sadness:*
O gravis labor, et o durum pondus quod habeo in vesto huius vite, quia nimis grave michi est contra carnem pugnare.	Oh heavy toil, oh harsh weight that I bear in the dress of this life: it is too heavy for me to fight against my body.
Virtutes ad Animam illam:	*Virtues to Soul:*
O Anima, voluntate dei constituta, et o felix instrumentum, quare tam flebilis es contra hoc quod deus contrivit in virginea natura? Tu debes in nobis superare diabolum.	Anima, you that were given your place by the will of God, you instrument of bliss, why are you so tearful in the face of the evil God crushed in a maidenly being? You must overcome the devil in our midst.
Anima illa:	*Soul:*
Succurrite michi, adiuvando, ut possim stare!	Support me, help me to stand firm!
Scientia Dei ad Animam illam:	*Knowledge-of-God to Soul:*
Vide quid illud sit quo es induta, filia salvationis et esto stabilis, et numquam cades.	See the dress you are wearing, daughter of salvation: be steadfast and you will never fall.

(continued)

Infelix, Anima:
O nescio quid faciam, aut ubi fugiam! O ve michi, non possum perficere hoc quod sum induta. Certe illud volo abicere!

Virtutes:
O infelix conscientia, o misera Anima, quare abscondis faciem tuam coram creatore tuo?

Scientia Dei:
Tu nescis, nec vides, nec sapis illum qui te constituit.

Anima illa:
Deus creavit mundum: non facio illi iniuriam sed volo uti illo!

Strepitus Diaboli ad Animam illam:
Fatue, fatue quid prodest tibi laborare? Respice mundum, et amplectetur te magno honore.

Virtutes:
O plangens vox est hec maximi doloris! Ach, ach, quedam mirabilis victoria in mirabili desiderio dei surrexit, in qua delectatio camis se latenter abscondit, heu, heu, ubi voluntas crimina nescivit et ubi desiderium hominis lasciviam fugit. Luge, luge ergo in his, Innocentia, que in pudore bono integritatem non amisisti, et que avariciam gutturis antiqui serpentis ibi non devorasti.

Diabolus:
Que est hec Potestas, quod nullus sit preter deum? Ego autem dico, qui voluerit me et voluntatem meam sequi, dabo illi omnia. Tu vero, tuis sequacibus nichil habes quod dare possis, quia etiam vos omnes nescitis quid sitis.

Humilitas:
Ego cum meis sodalibus bene scio quod tu es ille antiquus dracho qui super summum volare voluisti— sed ipse deus in abyssum proiecit te.

Virtutes:
Nos autem omnes in excelsis habitamus.

Soul, sadly:
I don't know what to do or where to flee Woe is me, I cannot perfect this dress I have put on! Indeed I want to cast it off!

Virtues:
Unhappy state of mind, oh poor Anima, why do you hide your face in the presence of your Creator?

Knowledge of God:
You do not know or see or taste the One who has set you here.

Soul:
God created the world: I'm doing him no injury—I only want to enjoy it!

Devil, shouting at Soul:
What use to you is toiling foolishly? Look to the world: it will embrace you with great honor.

Virtues:
Is this not a plangent voice of the greatest sorrow? Ah, a certain marvelous victory already rose in that Soul, in her wondrous longing for God, in which a sensual delight was secretly hidden, alas, where previously the will had known no guilt and the desire fled man's wantonness. Mourn for this, mourn. Innocence, you who lost no perfection in your fair modesty, who did not devour greedily, with the belly of the serpent of old.

Devil:
What is this Power—as if there were no one but God? I say, whoever wants to follow me and do my will, I'll give him everything. As for you, Humility, you have nothing that you can give your followers: none of you even know what you are!

Humility:
My comrades and I know very well that you are the ancient dragon who wanted to fly higher than the highest one: but God himself hurled you in the abyss.

Virtues:
As for us, we dwell in the heights.

http://www.oxfordgirlschoir.co.uk/hildegard/ordovirtutumtext.html

Morality plays became a common form of dramatic presentation through the remainder of the Medieval period and into the Renaissance. As such they played a significant role in the move toward the development of the secular dramatic genre that became opera.

OPERA

The term opera conjures up more preconceptions than any other classical music genre. Just about everyone born within the last 50 years has seen Saturday morning

The interior of the Theater La Scala di Milano during a performance. Copyright © Alinari/Art Resource, NY

cartoons lampooning opera with outrageous characters and melodramatic story lines. Bugs Bunny, Daffy Duck, and Elmer Fudd singing melodies from some of the world's most famous operas have been the first exposure to operatic music that many people have had. What exactly is this genre called opera that lends itself to such caricature?

Early Opera

Technically speaking, opera is a dramatic stage production incorporating singing, instrumental music, costumes, scenery, and sometimes dancing. It is performed on a stage with the orchestra out of sight in an orchestra pit, in front of, and below, the stage. The genre developed during the Baroque period in Italy and has continued to be popular to this day in various incarnations. When operas first appeared the predominant type was opera seria, serious opera. During the eighteenth century a lighter style became accepted called opera buffa, comic opera. This distinction mirrored the two traditional types of theatre dating back to the ancient Greeks, tragedy and comedy. An influential group of Baroque era musicians and intellectuals from Florence, Italy, called the Camerata, sought a return to a more easily understood vocal style than had been common in the Renaissance. They held the ideals of the ancient Greeks in great regard and the resultant monodic vocal style and the similarity between early operas and Greek theatre was their legacy.

Opera Seria by Pietro Longhi (1702–1785). Copyright © Scala/Art Resource, NY

The audiences for the two types of opera were distinctly different. Comic opera was usually performed in a public theatre for anyone wishing to pay the admission price. That was usually the lower classes. Comic operas frequently featured common people as the central characters, and it was not unusual for them to display personal characteristics of a higher caliber than the aristocratic characters in the story. Often these stories were generally not well received by the wealthier classes. Opera seria was often performed in privately owned theatres on the estates of wealthy patrons. These works were written by composers employed by wealthy individuals, and the audiences for these performances were often invited guests. Serious opera story lines dealt with mythological characters, royal personages, and, in general, themes of lofty ideals.

Mozart and Classical Opera

It took a composer of enormous imagination and skill to combine the different qualities of these two operatic sub-genres into a new and more vibrant kind of theatre. That composer was Wolfgang Amadeus Mozart (1756–1791). Mozart inherited the tradition of operas buffa and seria, and he is often regarded as the greatest composer of these types of operas. But he went beyond the restrictions of both to create a new type of opera, one that incorporated aspects of the comic and the serious. That hybrid type of opera is often called a dramma giocoso, a jolly drama. *Don Giovanni,* an opera based on the legendary Spanish nobleman, Don Juan, is an example of that type of work.

Mozart lived in Austria during a time when most successful composers were employed by wealthy patrons. They composed music for household or court events such as dinners, dances, and other social gatherings as well as for concert presentations of instrumental music and for dramatic presentations such as operas. Mozart sought, but was never granted, a permanent appointment of that sort and spent most of his life writing commissioned works for individuals and churches, teaching students, and staging concerts of his own in order to support himself and his family.

The Magic Flute

One excerpt from one opera by Mozart cannot adequately display the breadth and depth of his operatic genius, but it can give a sense of why many consider him the greatest of the Classical period opera composers. *The Magic Flute* (*Die Zauberflöte*), written in 1791, was the last opera penned by Mozart. This work combines serious themes with comic scenes while telling a complicated story of treachery, love, faithfulness, and virtue. Tamino, a young man, searches for the woman he loves, Pamina, who has been captured by a powerful wizard named Sarastro. Aided by the powers of a magic flute given to him by three minions of the Queen of the Night, a powerful but evil woman, Tamino sets off to find Pamina accompanied by a strange, feathered bird-catcher named Pappageno (the comic relief of the story). When Mozart wrote this opera he had recently been exposed to the ideas and ideals of Freemasonry which emphasized self-determination, individuality, the importance of wisdom, and an appreciation of beauty. These themes are woven into the fabric of the story.

A production of Mozart's *Magic Flute* by the Vienna State Opera in Austria.
Copyright © Erich Lessing/Art Resource, NY

The following excerpt is from Act II of *The Magic Flute.* It is an aria sung by the Queen of the Night after her daughter, Pamina, tells her that Tamino has decided to join Sarastro's Brotherhood, a group of men not unlike the Masons. The Queen swears revenge on Sarastro for imprisoning Pamina and gives her a knife with which to kill him. This aria is for a coloratura soprano, a voice of extraordinarily high range and agility. While obviously written to show off the vocal virtuosity of the singer, the aria also is a dramatic focal point of the story.

🎼 "Queen of the Night Aria" from Act II of *The Magic Flute*— Wolfgang Amadeus Mozart

Der Hölle Rache kocht in meinem Herzen	Hells Revenge cooks in my heart,
Tot und Verzweiflung flammet um mich her!	Death and despair flame about me!
Fühlt nicht durch dich Sarastro	If Sarastro does not through you feel
Todesschmerzen,	The pain of death,
So bist du meine Tochter nimmermehr.	Then you will be my daughter nevermore.
So bist du meine Tochter nimmermehr	Then you will be my daughter nevermore.
	(virtuosic vocalizations)
Verstoβen sei auf ewig,	Disowned may you be forever,
Verlassen sei auf ewig,	Abandoned may you be forever,
Zertrümmert sei'n auf ewig	Destroyed be forever
Alle Bande der Natur	All the bonds of nature,
	(virtuosic vocalizations)
Alle Bande der Natur	All the bonds of nature,
Wenn nicht durch dich	If not through you
Sarastro wird erblassen!	Sarastro becomes pale!
Hört, Rachegötter,	Hear, Gods of Revenge,
Hoert der Mutter Schwur!	Hear a mother's oath!

Romantic Opera

Baroque and Classical period operas consisted of varying combinations of arias, recitatives, and choruses as independent musical compositions sometimes linked by spoken dialogue. The idea of a continuous musical drama, uninterrupted by the spoken word, had not developed fully at that time. It was to be a contribution of Romantic period (1825–1900) composers to weave a seamless tapestry of the musical and dramatic materials into a continuous stage presentation. Another development in the Romantic period was the adaptation for the musical stage of an Italian literary style called verismo. Emphasizing everyday people in real-life situations, while reveling in passion and violence, the story lines of operas written in the verismo style often sound like modern soap operas.

Pagliacci

A representative example of the verismo style of late nineteenth century Italian opera is *Pagliacci (The Clowns)* written by Ruggiero Leoncavallo (1858–1919). In the opera life imitates art (and vice versa) as a traveling troupe of actors and clowns unwittingly recreates on stage a drama unfolding amongst them. Canio, the leader of the troupe, suspects Nedda, his wife, of having an affair. He nearly catches her with her lover (Silvio) just

Nashville Opera's production of *Pagliacci,* an opera by Ruggiero Leoncavallo. Courtesy of the Nashville Opera

before the troupe is about to perform a comedy about a jealous husband. Canio demands to know who the other man is, but Nedda refuses to tell him. At this point in the opera Canio sings his famous aria, "Vesti la Giubba" ("Put on the costume"), in which he sings about having to go on stage to make people laugh as his own heart is breaking. The troupe performs that evening as planned, but the performance turns violent as Canio is increasingly unable to distinguish between the drama he is part of on the stage and the real-life drama unfolding around him. He stabs Nedda and her lover Silvio to the horror of the audience and is left on stage to utter the last words of the opera, "The comedy is finished."

🎼 "Vesti la giubba," Canio's Aria from *Pagliacci*— Ruggiero Leoncavallo

Recitar! Mentre preso dal delirio,	To recite! While gripped with delirium,
non so più quel che dico,	I do not know what to say,
e quel che faccio!	and what I am doing!
Eppur è d'uopo, sforzati!	And yet it is necessary, force yourself!
Bah! sei tu forse un uom?	Bah! Are you not a man?
Tu se' Pagliaccio!	You are "Pagliaccio?"
Vesti la giubba,	Put on your costume,
e la faccia in farina.	and the face in flour (white powder).
La gente paga, e rider vuole qua.	The people pay, and they want to laugh.
E se Arlecchin t'invola Colombina,	and if Harlequin steals Colombina
ridi, Pagliaccio, e ognun applaudirà!	laugh, Pagliaccio, and everyone will applaud!
Tramuta in lazzi lo spasmo ed il pianto;	Change into laughs the spasms of pain;
in una smorfia il singhiozzo	into a grimace the tears of pain, Ah!
il dolor, Ah!	
Ridi, Pagliaccio,	Laugh, Pagliaccio,
sul tuo amore infranto!	at your broken love!
Ridi del duol, che t'avvelena il cor!	Laugh at the grief that poisons your heart!

Gianni Schicchi

Giacomo Puccini (1858–1924), was another Italian composer known mostly for his tragic operas in the verismo style. His operas, *La Boheme, Tosca*, and *Madame Butterfly* are some of the most frequently performed works in the genre today. The enormous popularity of Puccini's stories has resulted in two of these works having modern adaptations for the Broadway stage. *La Boheme* was the basis of the musical *Rent*, and *Madame Butterfly* inspired *Miss Saigon*, two of the most popular musicals of the past twenty years. Many of Puccini's operas are tragic stories in which the leading female character dies at the end. Puccini wrote one comic opera, *Gianni Schicchi*, a brief, one-act opera buffa-inspired work based on a purportedly true story from thirteenth century Florence. The title character was supposedly so notorious that Dante referred to him and his suffering in the 8th circle of Hell in *The Divine Comedy*. The real-life Schicchi's crime was having forged the will of a deceased man, Buoso Donati. In the opera, at the behest of relatives furious to learn that Donati was leaving his fortune to a monastery, Schicchi agrees to impersonate the dead man and dictate a new will to a lawyer before anyone outside of the family is aware of his death. Schicchi does this but changes the will to benefit himself far more than anyone else and the family is powerless to stop this fraudulent charade lest they be considered accomplices.

PERSPECTIVE—EARLY THEATRICAL FORMS

Early theatrical forms, on which the staged musical genres were based, developed in several areas of the world independently of one another. Ancient theatrical traditions were established in China (1500 BC), India (500 BC), and Greece (600 BC). Early Chinese theatre incorporated a great deal of puppetry and seems to have always had a musical component. Indian theatre was reflective of religious ideals of the time and the depiction of the types of situations that people dealt with in everyday life. It too is believed to have had a significant musical element. An early Indian writer named Bharata Muni wrote a book on theatrical practices, including the use of music. Greek theatre explored the timeless questions of morality, mortality, and the weaknesses of the human spirit. Greek theatre typically employed a "chorus," a group of actors who sang or spoke in unison. The chorus interacted with the individuals on stage, which usually numbered no more than three, and commented on and directed the action. The first Greek plays were songs, poems, and dances offered to the God Dionysus in rural areas outside of the city.

Characteristics of Greek theatre were the model for important aspects of staged musical presentations in the Western tradition. While there is no continuous line from ancient Greek theatre to the rise of opera in Europe 2,000 years later, certain influences can certainly be seen. Early Greek plays were either tragedies or comedies, as were early European theatrical presentations and operas. A third type of Greek play later developed called a satyr play, which was a comic parody of mythological subjects. William Shakespeare, the great English playwright of the late sixteenth and early seventeenth centuries, imbued some of his most tragic plays with comic elements as well. The darkly comic scene from *Hamlet* in which Hamlet says, "Alas poor Yorick, I knew him Horatio" is one example. Hamlet says these words while holding the deceased court jester Yorick's skull in his hands. Mozart's opera *Don Giovanni* contains comic moments such as the pivotal scene in the graveyard. In this scene Don Giovanni holds a conversation with a statue of the man he killed at the beginning of the opera and invites him to dine with him. Other composers followed Mozart's lead and many later tragic operas contained lighter moments as well. Giacomo Puccini's *La Boheme* is one of many examples of this.

The themes of the tragic Greek plays were mirrored by the early opera composers who chose subject matter often based on Greek mythology. Another similarity is the practice of using recitatives and arias, which were performed by solitary characters, as well as choruses sung by a large group. The early operas also featured characters of importance rather than everyday people.

A number of terms that we associate with the theatre today have Greek origins. The word "thespian" comes from the name Thespis. A thespian is an actor or an actress. Thespis is reputed to have been the creator of the Greek tragedy. The term "theatre" itself comes from the Greek "theatron" which originally designated the place from which a play was observed by the audience.

The following aria from *Gianni Schicchi* is sung by Lauretta (a soprano), Schicchi's daughter, who is in love with the dead man's son, Rinuccio. If she and Rinuccio are to be married the will must provide adequately for them so she pleads with her father to ensure their financial, and amorous, future or she will throw herself into the Arno River. This aria is an excellent example of the fluid, melodic writing of Puccini where the voice is often doubled by instruments in the orchestra. This rich, melodic writing style has endeared Puccini to generations of opera audiences.

"O mio babbino caro" from *Gianni Schicchi*—
Giacomo Puccini

O mio babbino caro,	Oh my dear daddy
Mi piace, e bello bello,	I love him, he is so handsome
Vo andare in Porta Rossa	I want to go to Porta Rossa
A comperar l anello!	to buy the ring!
Si,si ci voglio andare	Yes, yes, I mean it
e se l amassi indarno	And if my love were in vain
andrei sui Ponte Vecchio	I would go to Ponte Vecchio
ma per buttaarmi in Arno!	and throw myself in the Arno!
Mi struggo e mi tormento!	I fret and suffer torments!
O Dio, vorrei morir!	Oh God, I would rather die!
Babbo, pieta, pieta!	Daddy, have pity, have pity!
Babbo, pieta, pieta!	Daddy, have pity, have pity!

Modern Opera

Operas continue to be written and performed today. Though their path to public recognition is more difficult than ever, having to compete with popular genres such as the musical and movies, composers today continue to explore the depth and breadth of human emotion and experience through this intensely dramatic genre. John Adams (b. 1947) (*Nixon in China, Doctor Atomic*), Philip Glass (b. 1937) (*Einstein on the Beach*), and William Bolcom (b. 1938) (*A View from the Bridge*) are some of the modern composers creating operas in a thoroughly contemporary style.

Most opera composers today do not try to emulate the flowery lyricism of Romantic era works or emphasize the virtuosic capabilities of the voice as had been common since the advent of the genre. More often than not each composer brings their own unique style to the genre branding it with their signature sound. Adams' and Glass' minimalism, and Bolcom's eclectic breadth are evident within each of their works.

In the following excerpt from Bolcom's *A View from the Bridge* the recent Italian immigrant, Eddie Carbone, sings of his home in Italy with wistful nostalgia. But even those strong memories cannot compare to his enchantment with his new life in the New World, in New York.

"The New York Lights" from *A View from the Bridge*—
William Bolcom

The "Queen of the Night" aria showcases the sound and quality of the soprano voice at its most dramatic. The soprano has historically been the female voice of choice when it comes to starring operatic roles. "O mio babbino caro" displays the gloriously lyric aspect of that voice along with the ever popular writing style of Puccini. The tenor has been the more prominent of the male voices in operatic roles as well. "Vesti la guibba" shows the passionate intensity that the tenor can evoke in the verismo operas of the nineteenth century and "The New York Lights" features the tenor voice in the more restrained style of modern opera. The lower-pitched voices have not had as many starring roles as the higher voices, but there have been more significant roles for the bass than for the alto. Perhaps because the need for a "bad guy" in many operas gives the bass voice an advantage over the alto.

What Makes Music—Voices

Female Voices

The human voice is the most basic instrument. It is generally divided into four main types according to register (relative highness or lowness) and gender (male or female).

There are two commonly recognized female voices.

Soprano—The higher-pitched female voice.

Alto (Contralto)—The lower-pitched female voice.

There is another female voice, the mezzo-soprano, whose pitch range lies between an alto and a soprano. A more rare and quite remarkable female voice is the coloratura soprano. This is a soprano voice that is extremely high and also quite agile in that it can jump from one note to another in the very highest register.

The mature female voices, in order from highest to lowest:

Coloratura Soprano
Soprano
Mezzo-Soprano
Alto

Margaret McMurray and Trisha Phillips Huntley in a scene from the University of Memphis production of Robert Ward's *The Crucible*. Photo courtesy of Steve Roberts

So, back to the question that began this section on opera, "What exactly is this genre called opera that lends itself to such (cartoonish) caricature?" Historically, it has been the equivalent of television, the movies, radio, and the Internet of today. It provided entertainment, information, and an opportunity for communal experience of stories with moral and ethical lessons, and it gave life to ideas that would otherwise be merely intellectual concepts without form and substance. Opera was the foremost vehicle for public entertainment for centuries as it explored the frailties of human beings at the limit of their emotional endurance. It is a genre that pokes fun at the curiosities of our foibles and is the musical incarnation of who and what we are as human beings.

INCIDENTAL MUSIC

Incidental music is composed to accompany a stage production such as a play. It differs from the music for an opera in that there is usually no singing involved in incidental music, it is most often instrumental music. Incidental music occurs in the background while the drama unfolds and during breaks in the action, as in between acts. Incidental music can also be heard before and after the drama is performed, such as in an overture before the curtain goes up or as a final piece of music to bring the drama to an appropriate conclusion. Incidental music is similar to much music experienced today, such as music heard while watching movies or television. Our experience of the drama is greatly enhanced by the addition of appropriate music. A tense scene can be made spine tingling in its effect by the use of music that can literally make you sit on the edge of your seat. A love scene can be made more touching through the accompaniment of lyrical violin music. Even before the advent of sound in movies, music was used to augment the action on the screen by the use of a piano, providing appropriate musical accompaniment to what was being presented dramatically on the screen.

The writing of incidental music for plays is not as common today as it was in eras past. Movies and television provide the incidental music of today. It is a curious fact about incidental music, however, that we know and listen to much incidental music from the past but the plays which were the inspiration for their creation are very infrequently performed today.

L'Arlésienne—portrait of Madame Ginoux, the proprietor of the Café de la Gare in Arles—by Vincent Van Gogh.
Copyright © Erich Lessing/Art Resource, NY

L'Arlésienne

L'Arlésienne (The Woman from Arles) was a tragic play written by the nineteenth-century French playwright, Alphonse Daudet. Georges Bizet (1838–1874) composed incidental music for the play. This music has become a staple of the orchestral repertory, not through performances of the music in its original form, accompanying the play, but through two suites that Bizet put together afterward. These orchestral suites are most frequently heard in concert form today, not in the context of the drama that inspired them.

The excerpt from *L'Arlésienne* included here is the Farandole, a traditional French dance, which contrasts two themes, one stern and melodramatic, the other playful and light. Listen to the theme presented at the beginning of the piece. It is a straightforward march-like tune. After it is played in its entirety the second theme is heard, one that is more playful and happy. The two themes are presented alternately several times before finally being played simultaneously, which leads to a rousing conclusion. The relatively simple homophonic treatment of the themes in the first part of the piece evolves into an effective climax by placing both themes before the listener in a polyphonic texture. The polyphonic texture sounds logical and uncomplicated since both of the themes have been heard previously by themselves. A clever compositional device leads to a very satisfying musical experience for the listener.

Is this understanding of the compositional technique employed by the composer important to know in order to enjoy the music? Not necessarily, but it does allow the listener a somewhat deeper understanding of what musical conventions make music interesting. It also allows us to regard a composer's work through a more knowledgeable scrutiny instead of uninformed opinion.

 "Farandole" from *L'Arlésienne*—
Georges Bizet

THE MUSICAL

One of the most popular contemporary theatrical genres is the musical. A musical is a story that is presented on stage through solo and ensemble vocal pieces, musical interludes, and dance numbers with orchestral accompaniment. In some musicals the music component is a continuous presence throughout the production. In others it is used only intermittently to enhance the story. This genre is frequently referred to as the "Broadway Musical" due to its rise in prominence in theatres on Broadway in New York in the early and middle twentieth century. Most early musicals were based on rather lighthearted stories with fairly simple melodies sung by the principal characters. Unobtrusive arrangements in the accompanying orchestra enhanced the vocals, dance numbers, and interludes. An overture was usually played by the orchestra before the show began and was frequently a compilation of tunes the audience would hear throughout the production.

Forerunners of the Musical

The basic format of the musical dates back to the previously discussed early form of opera known as opera buffa and operetta. Opera buffa was a kind of comic opera prominent in Italy in the seventeenth and eighteenth centuries. Similar versions of comic opera were common in other countries as well at this time such as the Singspiel in Germany and the Opéra Comique in France. Operetta was a popular genre in nineteenth-century Austria and England as represented by the works of Johann Strauss and the songwriting team of (William Schwenck) Gilbert and (Arthur) Sullivan. These pieces, lighter and often less complex than opera, were immensely popular among the middle class. Operettas also differed from operas in that operas were generally based on serious subjects such as tragic love stories, the lives of important people both real and mythological, honor, and betrayal. Operettas, on the other hand, were frequently comedies based on mistaken identities and lighthearted love stories. Operettas were often shorter than operas and incorporated spoken dialogue.

American singer and actress, Lillian Russell, was well known for her comic opera roles with the Weber and Fields Burlesque Company. © Bettmann/Corbis

The Broadway Musical had some immediate forerunners in the United States in two genres called vaudeville and the revue. Vaudeville shows consisted of a string of musical and non-musical acts presented one after the other throughout the evening. A singer might be followed by a comedian, who might be followed by a dancer or a dance troupe, who might be followed by an animal act or a magician. The revue was similar to vaudeville shows but the acts in revues were organized around a common theme such as patriotism for the 4th of July or holiday themes like Christmas and New Years. It was a small step from these popular genres to the telling of one story through singing, acting, and dancing and the Broadway Musical.

Musical Songwriting Teams

One of the curious differences between operas and musicals is the practice of acknowledging both the musical composer and the lyricist, the person who wrote the words to the songs, in musicals. When an opera by Mozart is performed it is billed as an opera by Mozart, even though he only wrote the music and not the words. The same is true for the vast majority of operatic composers, the writer of the music gets star billing and the writer of the words is mentioned in much smaller print further down in the credits. Not so in musicals. Most people have heard of Rodgers and Hammerstein, the great songwriting team of many of the most popular musicals of all time such as *South Pacific, The King and I, The Sound of Music,* and many more. Richard Rodgers wrote the music and Oscar Hammerstein wrote the words. Both get equal billing. The team of Lerner and Loewe wrote *My Fair Lady, Brigadoon, Paint Your Wagon,* and *Camelot.* Frederick Loewe wrote the music but the words are just as memorable, and Alan Jay Lerner gets equal recognition. Why is this common in musicals and not in operas? Perhaps it is because the style of singing in musicals puts more emphasis on clarity of diction and less emphasis on volume and tone production than operas do, which results in a more natural vocal style, one in which it is easier to understand the words.

The Operatic vs. the Musical Vocal Style

The operatic vocal style developed by necessity in order for the voice to be heard over the orchestral accompaniment. Producing the volume and tone necessary to do this happened at the expense of clarity of pronunciation. As a result the operatic vocal style developed to emphasize volume and tone, the musical quality of the voice, as opposed to clear diction. When you listen to an opera, even if you understand the language in which it is sung, it is often difficult to understand the words. It is even common practice in operatic performances to have a written libretto (the words and translation of the opera in pamphlet form) available for the audience to understand what is being sung. Many modern opera productions use supertitles (also called surtitles), a system of projecting the text on a narrow screen above the stage. In musicals no such listening aid is provided, and the audience must understand what is said on first hearing, otherwise the meaning of the story will be diluted. As musicals entered the electronic age, the voice became amplified. The emphasis on producing a strong vocal sound capable of being heard over the orchestral accompaniment became even less of a consideration.

A brief look at representative musicals of the last 50 years will give us a good idea of what the musical is, how it has changed, and why it has been a consistently popular genre.

The Evolution of the Musical—50 Years of Song and Dance

As mentioned previously, the Broadway Musical evolved during the first half of the twentieth century from vaudeville to the revue to the musical. However, most people today have difficulty readily naming a musical from before 1940. It is the Broadway Musicals of the 1940s and 1950s, as represented by the works of Rodgers and Hammerstein and Lerner and Loewe, that people know and love. Their works are a mix of singable tunes with memorable lyrics, big production dance numbers, and clever dialogue. The combination of dialogue, musical numbers, and relatively easy orchestral parts has made musicals a favorite among high school drama departments. That is where people have often had their first contact with musicals and it is an impression that lasts a lifetime. People who participate in high school, college, and community theatre productions of musicals frequently have no intention of pursuing a professional career in music or the theatre, but their intimate familiarity with these works fosters a lifelong love of the genre.

Tunes, Lyrics, Dialogue, and Dances

Listen to the following example of a song from the Lerner and Loewe classic, *My Fair Lady,* based on the play *Pygmalion* by George Bernard Shaw. The story concerns the transformation of a common flower girl into a sophisticated woman at the hands of an elocution (diction) professor. In this song Professor Henry Higgins, a speech expert, is complaining about how exasperating women are to him. Higgins has made a bet with a friend, Pickering, that he can turn the rather rough flower girl, Eliza, into a woman of distinction simply through the acquisition of polished speech. Part of the charm of this show is watching the tension between Higgins and Eliza as they wrestle with Eliza's low-class cockney accent and we wonder if the tension could possibly turn into . . . love? If not true love, then perhaps a deep affection.

Listen to how the music reflects the character of the words in this song. There are two sections of music, a calm one and a frantic one, that alternate throughout the song. The music is calm, reflective, and confident when Higgins is speaking about himself but it gets louder, faster, and more frantic when he speaks about how difficult life becomes once you "let a woman in your life." The tempo and

Dame Evlyn Laye in *My Fair Lady.* Courtesy of Photofest, NY

mood of the piece change frequently to reflect the contrasting meaning of the words. The song emerges seamlessly from the dialogue that precedes it and is an inventive combination of clever words and contrasting themes used to represent the character's changing emotions. It builds to a climax with Higgins's frustrations evident as he turns on multiple recordings of Eliza's voice that he has made, as if he is overwhelmed by her presence.

 I'm An Ordinary Man from *My Fair Lady*—
Lerner and Loewe

In contrast to this is another song from the same musical, *I Could Have Danced All Night*, sung by Eliza after her first successful attempt to speak without her cockney accent. Thrilled with her unexpected breakthrough and buoyed by the prospect that she might be able to pull off her unlikely transformation, Eliza exudes confidence and the restrained hope that her new persona may bring her the affection of Higgins. This joyous song, in which Eliza is joined briefly by the household staff, allows the vocal ability of the female lead to be shown to excellent advantage. A verse and chorus format is used in this song. That is a form in which changing verses of text are sung to one melody which alternates with the chorus, a different melody using the same words for each repetition.

Listen to how the composer presents the first verse very simply, just the solo voice with orchestral accompaniment. The second verse adds a second melodic line in other voices (the household staff), adding interest without becoming too complicated.

 I Could Have Danced All Night from *My Fair Lady*—
Lerner and Loewe

West Side Story

While most of the popular shows during the 1950s were light-hearted love stories, perhaps the most important musical of the decade was *West Side Story*, music by Leonard Bernstein with lyrics by Stephen Sondheim. *West Side Story* is an updated version of Shakespeare's *Romeo and Juliet* set on the upper west side of Manhattan in the late 1950s. Instead of Romeo and Juliet the main characters are Tony and Maria. Instead of the feuding Montague and Capulet families there are the Sharks and the Jets, rival street gangs. Tony is the former leader of the Jets, the white gang, and Maria is the sister of the leader of the Puerto Rican gang, the Sharks. This musical set the bar rather high for all future musicals in its more serious subject matter and musical complexity.

Three members of "The Sharks" gang from *West Side Story*; music by Leonard Bernstein. Courtesy of Photofest, NY

The following example shows Bernstein's use of music to portray two different themes from the story through different musical melodies. The musical themes are first presented alternately and then combined at the end just as the dramatic themes from the story converge in the fight between the gangs.

First theme—The impending "rumble," tension between the gangs

Second theme—Tony and Maria's love theme, *Tonight*

Combined themes—Musically they become intertwined just as the love of Tony and Maria will become entangled with the clash of the gangs.

The entire love story of Romeo and Juliet takes place in the shadow of the inevitable tragedy that is just over the horizon. Bernstein recreates that tension but adds a new dimension through the addition of musical themes handled in parallel ways to the dramatic themes.

 Tonight—Quintet from *West Side Story*—
Leonard Bernstein

The Musical Overture

While it has been fairly common for overtures to operas to take on a concert life of their own, separate from the drama for which they were written, it has been very rare for overtures to musicals to become established concert pieces. Musicals have such memorable tunes that it would seem a natural extension to their stage life for them to exist as unique compositions in the orchestral repertory. But such is not the case except in a few instances. One of those instances is the overture to the musical *Candide*, by Leonard Bernstein. *Candide*, based on the short eighteenth-century novel by Voltaire, was first staged in 1956 and went on to numerous revisions and productions. The musical itself has never quite caught on with the public, but the overture has become one of the most popular overtures in the concert repertory. The witty, rhythmically intricate work is very short, very fast, and lots of fun.

Try to perceive the structure of this work while listening to it. Listen for the different melodies or moods in the music and try to determine the sequence of events that the composer has laid out.

 Overture to *Candide*—
Leonard Bernstein

The Evolving Musical

As popular music styles changed from the 1950s through the 1960s, especially as the widespread acceptance of rock and roll became commonplace, some musicals adopted that style in a successful reaching out to an entirely new generation of audience members. The move away from the traditional pit orchestra-based genre to a current, trendy, hip style of musical theatre kept musicals alive and vibrant as traditional classical music continued in popular decline. The rock musical *Hair* in 1968 was a breakthrough event that propelled the then current rock style to the forefront of musical theatre. In 1971 *Jesus Christ Superstar*, the "rock opera" by Andrew Lloyd Webber and Tim Rice hit the stage in New York. Though the first short version of *Joseph and the Amazing Technicolor Dreamcoat*, also by Webber and Rice, was performed in 1968 in England, the full version didn't reach the United States until 1976. In 1981 *Dreamgirls* brought the Motown sound of Detroit to Broadway. By this time the "sound" of the musical had changed in fundamental ways. Amplified guitars, bass, and keyboards were common and a synthesis between the older, classical music-based pit orchestra and the modern rock band was accepted as the norm.

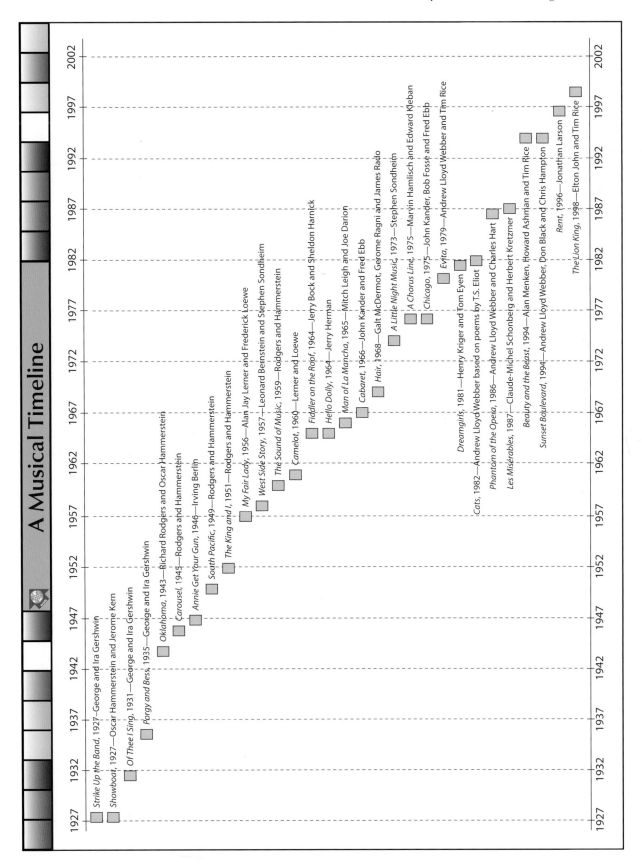

A Musical Timeline

Strike Up the Band, 1927—George and Ira Gershwin
Showboat, 1927—Oscar Hammerstein and Jerome Kern
Of Thee I Sing, 1931—George and Ira Gershwin
Porgy and Bess, 1935—George and Ira Gershwin
Oklahoma, 1943—Richard Rodgers and Oscar Hammerstein
Carousel, 1945—Rodgers and Hammerstein
Annie Get Your Gun, 1946—Irving Berlin
South Pacific, 1949—Rodgers and Hammerstein
The King and I, 1951—Rodgers and Hammerstein
My Fair Lady, 1956—Alan Jay Lerner and Frederick Loewe
West Side Story, 1957—Leonard Beinstein and Stephen Sondheim
The Sound of Music, 1959—Rodgers and Hammerstein
Camelot, 1960—Lerner and Loewe
Fiddler on the Roof, 1964—Jerry Bock and Sheldon Harnick
Hello Dolly, 1964—Jerry Herman
Man of La Mancha, 1965—Mitch Leigh and Joe Darion
Cabaret, 1966—John Kander and Fred Ebb
Hair, 1968—Galt McDermot, Gerome Ragni and James Rado
A Little Night Music, 1973—Stephen Sondheim
A Chorus Line, 1975—Marvin Hamlisch and Edward Kleban
Chicago, 1975—John Kander, Bob Fosse and Fred Ebb
Evita, 1979—Andrew Lloyd Webber and Tim Rice
Dreamgirls, 1981—Henry Kriger and Tom Eyen
Cats, 1982—Andrew Lloyd Webber based on poems by T.S. Eliot
Phantom of the Opera, 1986—Andrew Lloyd Webber and Charles Hart
Les Misérables, 1987—Claude-Michel Schonberg and Herbert Kretzmer
Beauty and the Beast, 1994—Alan Menken, Howard Ashman and Tim Rice
Sunset Boulevard, 1994—Andrew Lloyd Webber, Don Black and Chris Hampton
Rent, 1996—Jonathan Larson
The Lion King, 1998—Elton John and Tim Rice

1927 1932 1937 1942 1947 1952 1957 1962 1967 1972 1977 1982 1987 1992 1997 2002

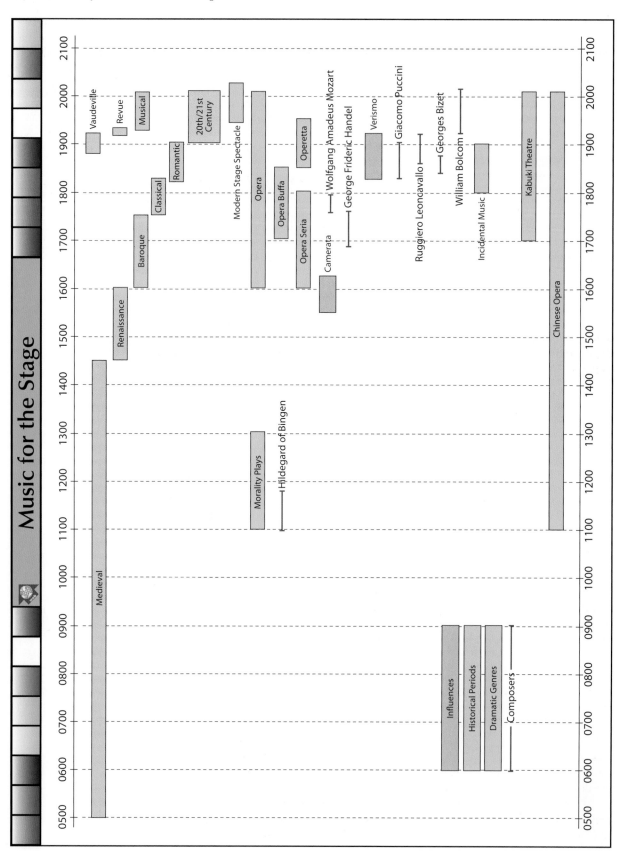

Phantom of the Opera

Without question, the most significant force in musical theatre since the 1970s has been Andrew Lloyd Webber (b. 1948) of England. The list of successful musicals penned by Webber include *Phantom of the Opera, Cats, Evita, Jesus Christ Superstar, Joseph and the Amazing Technicolor Dreamcoat,* and *Sunset Boulevard,* among others. Webber has often teamed with Tim Rice as lyricist but has collaborated with other writers as well. His style is at once wonderfully lyrical and dramatic. Webber's melodies are some of the most unforgettable in the history of musical theatre.

In 1986 *Phantom of the Opera* premiered in London. Based on a novel by Gaston Leroux, "*Phantom*" tells the story of a deformed man, the Phantom, hiding in the caverns under the Paris Opera House obsessed with a beautiful rising star named Christine. The Phantom holds sway over Christine because she believes he is the key to her success. Christine's love for another man, Raul, is threatened by the Phantom's obsession with her and her dependence on him. The story is reminiscent of traditional operas in its dark undercurrents, intense emotional and dramatic impact, and inevitably tragic ending.

The following example shows the dramatic yet lyrical quality of Webber's writing. In this example Christine and the Phantom sing about his mysterious hold over her while he brings her to his lair under the Opera House. The unforgettable musical theme that begins and underlies much of this song sets the tone for the entire musical.

The Phantom of the Opera.
Courtesy of Photofest, NY

> 🎼 *The Phantom of the Opera* from *Phantom of the Opera—*
> Andrew Lloyd Webber

Les Misérables

Les Misérables, based on the Victor Hugo novel of the same name, premiered in 1987. In many ways this work by Claude-Michel Schönberg and Claude Boublil brought the musical as a genre full circle with its ancient forerunners. The gripping tale of Jean Valjean, the desperate man imprisoned for stealing a loaf of bread, and the relentless Inspector Javert, who stalks him throughout his life after he is freed from prison, *Les Misérables* is more opera than musical in telling its heroic story. Valjean, after leaving prison, makes an honorable life for himself, becoming both wealthy and respected. However, his success is made possible by one indiscretion which haunts him forever. Penniless and destitute after leaving prison, Valjean is given refuge for a night by a kindly priest. Valjean steals silver candlesticks from the priest and disappears. Intent on returning Valjean to prison, Javert tracks Valjean relentlessly only to find him years later a successful businessman and mayor of the town in which he lives. Valjean agrees to return to prison but he requests a one-day reprieve so as to arrange for the support of a young girl, Cosette, who has been in his care. Javert refuses and there is a brief struggle during which Valjean has an opportunity to kill Javert but doesn't. Javert, unable to understand why Valjean didn't kill him when he had the chance, sees his life as a failure and throws himself into the river, committing suicide. All of this plays against the backdrop of the French Revolution contrasting the personal and societal themes of freedom, justice, honor, and duty.

There is no dialogue in this work, and dancing is limited to one tavern scene, which makes it more operatic than musical. Also, much of *Les Misérables* is sung in the style of operatic recitative, the semi-melodic singing discussed earlier. So which is it, a musical or an opera? It can be argued both ways, but in truth it is something slightly different from, yet similar to, both. It is the staged musical of today, not quite fitting the definitions of either the musical or opera. Perhaps a new term needs to be coined to describe this genre.

The following example is sung by Javert when he is vowing to find Valjean no matter what it takes. Javert is convinced that as the appointed arm of the law he is right in returning Valjean to prison. This song is Javert's statement of his life's philosophy, unyielding and unquestioning in his obligation to duty.

 Stars from *Les Misérables—*
Schönberg and Boublil

In contrast to Javert's hard-hearted quest for "justice" is the following plea by Valjean in which he begs God for the safe return from battle of the man Cosette loves. Valjean is about to go looking for him in the remains of a battle and bring him back to the woman who loves him. How stark a contrast this paints with Javert's reasons for bringing Valjean back.

 Bring Him Home from *Les Misérables—*
Schönberg and Boublil

THE MODERN STAGE SPECTACLE

Throughout the twentieth century there have been a variety of stage presentations that were some combination of singing, dancing, comedy, and storytelling. Vaudeville, the revue, and the musical have been discussed earlier in this chapter and they represent this type of stage entertainment. In more recent years new variations of these older genres have appeared and become enormously popular. *Cirque du Soleil (Circus of the Sun)* was the first of these new stage presentations, premiering in 1984. It was conceived by Guy Laliberté and Daniel Gauthier, two Canadian street performers, and emphasized athletic- and gymnastics-inspired movement coupled with fantastic settings. There have been a number of unique Cirque du Soleil shows, each with a different underlying theme. From the beginning composer Benoit Jutras provided much of the music that established this group's signature, world music-inspired, sound. René Dupéré composed the music for one of their most successful productions, *Alegria*, and one of the most recent and theatrically extravagant Cirque du Soleil shows, *KA*. *Blue Man Group*, with their unique use of costuming, first presented the expressionless Blue Men in 1988 as wide-eyed explorers of themes both great and small, accompanied by rock music and their nearly ever-present drumming. Founded by Phil Stanton, Chris Wink, and Matt Goldman, Blue Man Group's stage presentation is a kind of updated vaudeville-type entertainment incorporating music, comedy, juggling, mime and video. Both Blue Man Group and Cirque du Soleil's use of music is more atmospheric; that is, it sets a mood for a particular scene in a show, rather than serving as a plot-advancing device as is common in opera and the musical. They also share an affinity for the importance of the rhythmic element in their music, though it is manifested in different ways. Cirque du Soleil frequently uses an asymmetrical meter as the basic rhythmic foundation. An asymmetrical meter is one in which the number of grouped pulses felt by the listener changes instead of remaining constant. Blue Man Group prefers a more basic rock beat which usually has a meter with repeating four-beat groupings. *Riverdance*, the Irish dance-based production, premiered in 1994. *Riverdance* featured songs evocative of the culture and ambiance of countries such as Spain, the United States, and Ireland. Large-screen videos of scenes from nature and spectacularly choreographed dances for both solo dancers and a large ensemble comprised the visual component. The Celtic music-based musical score by Bill Whelan and traditional Irish step dancing tied everything together.

Two productions, *The Three Tenors* and *Celtic Woman*, have stressed the musical component rather than the theatrical, which was the essence of the above-mentioned shows. *The Three Tenors* premiered in 1990 and featured Placido Domingo, Jose Carreras, and Luciano Pavarotti, the three most prominent representatives of the tenor voice of their era, singing operatic arias and popular songs. These performances were so well-received that they were sometimes performed in sports stadiums to accommodate the demand for tickets. More recently in 2004 the first performance of *Celtic Woman* was produced which revived the *Riverdance*-inspired popularity of Celtic music through songs, sung by an all-female cast, and fiddling of the Scottish and Irish traditions.

Each of these shows brings its own unique perspective to the stage spectacle and each uses music as an integral component. Listen to the following representative excerpts from these shows and compare them to the music previously heard from operas and musicals. In what ways are they different and in what ways are they similar?

 "Alegria" title song from *Alegria* (a Cirque du Soleil show)— René Dupéré

 "Drumbone" (this is both the name of the piece and the unique instrument, constructed of varying lengths of PVC pipe, on which it is played)— Blue Man Group

 "Riverdance"— Bill Whelan

 "Orinoco Flow"— Enya

WORLD MUSICAL THEATRE GENRES

Kabuki Theatre

Japanese Kabuki theatre is a traditional theatrical genre employing elaborate costumes, equally elaborate make-up, dance, stylized movement, and music. Dating from the seventeenth century this type of theatre was initially developed by a young woman, so it is ironic that all roles are now played by men. Men who specialize in playing women's roles in Kabuki theatre are called "onnagata." The stories of Kabuki theatre range from themes of great personages and events to everyday people in everyday situations, just as Western opera spans the same expanse of themes.

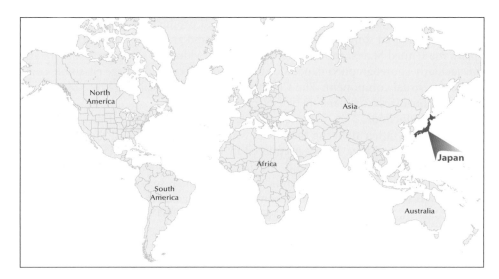

The music in Kabuki theatre is not as extensive or complex as the music in operas or musicals, but it serves essentially the same purpose, to enhance the dramatic presentation. It is more akin to incidental music than the full-fledged musical component of operas and musicals. There are a limited number of instruments used in Kabuki, the shamisen (a stringed instrument and the most important instrument in Kabuki), the odaiko (a drum used for sound effects), the tsuzumi (a drum played with the hands), and the shime-daiko (a drum played with sticks) which signals the beginning and the end of the presentation. In Kabuki theatre the instruments may be used to accompany singing, begin and end scenes, as background music to the drama, and during interludes.

One of the more unusual aspects of Kabuki theatre is the practice of calling out actors' names during the performances, called "kakegoe." Similar to the enthusiasm expressed by fans at sporting events, this practice can be a bit unnerving to the uninitiated audience member!

 Ozatsuma—Traditional Japanese shamisen music
Kanjincho—Kabuki theatre music

Japanese Kabuki Theatre. © Pierre Perrin/Sygma/Corbis

Chinese Opera

Typical costume from Chinese Opera. Corel

Chinese opera traces its heritage back as far as the twelfth century. Throughout this time a number of distinct styles have developed and flourished, which to the uninitiated Western listener sound fairly similar. A listener unfamiliar with Chinese opera may be expecting to hear "opera" as it is commonly practiced in Western cultures, that is, a dramatic genre based on the resonant projection of the singing voice. But the sound qualities of Chinese opera are quite different and can be a formidable challenge for anyone not accustomed to the animated sound of this unique genre. This music is full of history, tradition, and beauty. Incorporating music, dance, mime, and acrobatics, Chinese opera is a complete form of stage entertainment. The actor/singer's gestures are highly stylized, the costumes and makeup are significant in that they often communicate a character's relative importance through details of color and style, and the stage scenery is often minimal.

Chinese opera differs most noticeably from Western opera in the melodic content of the music. Western opera has been devoted almost exclusively to the presentation of the human voice in its most resonant and powerful incarnation. This has partially been driven by the need for the voice to project over an accompanying symphony orchestra. However, that approach to projecting the human voice has not been universally adopted. An alternate technique to achieving vocal projection has been to implement a somewhat nasal quality when singing, which cuts through just about any accompanying sounds to achieve the same effect. That is the approach most non-Western cultures took, including Chinese opera, and the effect is striking to the Western ear.

Chinese opera is accepted by rich and poor alike. It is a kind of **folk art** that transcends social and economic status. As such, it is treasured by the Chinese people, not just as a musical genre but one of cultural and historical significance.

The Story of the White Snake—
Chinese opera aria

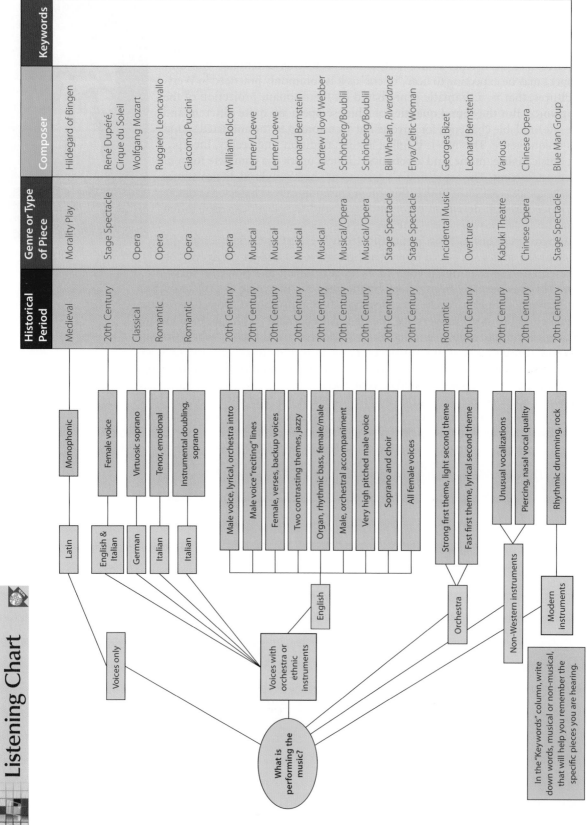

Listening Chart

Historical Period	Genre or Type of Piece	Composer	Keywords
Medieval	Morality Play	Hildegard of Bingen	
20th Century	Stage Spectacle	René Dupéré, Cirque du Soleil	
Classical	Opera	Wolfgang Mozart	
Romantic	Opera	Ruggiero Leoncavallo	
Romantic	Opera	Giacomo Puccini	
20th Century	Opera	William Bolcom	
20th Century	Musical	Lerner/Loewe	
20th Century	Musical	Lerner/Loewe	
20th Century	Musical	Leonard Bernstein	
20th Century	Musical	Andrew Lloyd Webber	
20th Century	Musical/Opera	Schönberg/Boublil	
20th Century	Musical/Opera	Schönberg/Boublil	
20th Century	Stage Spectacle	Bill Whelan, *Riverdance*	
20th Century	Stage Spectacle	Erya/Celtic Woman	
Romantic	Incidental Music	Georges Bizet	
20th Century	Overture	Leonard Bernstein	
20th Century	Kabuki Theatre	Various	
20th Century	Chinese Opera	Chinese Opera	
20th Century	Stage Spectacle	Blue Man Group	

What is performing the music?

- Voices only
  - Latin
    - Monophonic
  - English & Italian
    - Female voice
  - German
    - Virtuosic soprano
  - Italian
    - Tenor, emotional
  - Italian
    - Instrumental doubling, soprano
- Voices with orchestra or ethnic instruments
  - English
    - Male voice, lyrical, orchestra intro
    - Male voice "reciting" lines
    - Female, verses, backup voices
    - Two contrasting themes, jazzy
    - Organ, rhythmic bass, female/male
    - Male, orchestral accompaniment
    - Very high pitched male voice
    - Soprano and choir
    - All female voices
- Orchestra
  - Strong first theme, light second theme
  - Fast first theme, lyrical second theme
- Non-Western instruments
  - Unusual vocalizations
  - Piercing, nasal vocal quality
- Modern instruments
  - Rhythmic drumming, rock

In the "Keywords" column, write down words, musical or non-musical, that will help you remember the specific pieces you are hearing.

SUMMARY

The history of staged musical genres in Western music begins with the morality plays of the Medieval period, religiously based presentations intended to instruct the faithful on Church teachings. Hildegard of Bingen was an important composer in this genre. As secular music became increasingly prominent through the Renaissance and into the Baroque period, opera developed in Italy and became the most significant staged musical genre. Two distinct types of opera: opera buffa and opera seria (comic and serious opera), dominated the Baroque period and remained prominent through most of the Classical period. Wolfgang Amadeus Mozart was the greatest of the Classical period opera composers. During the Romantic period an Italian literary style called verismo was adapted to operatic storytelling. This approach, which emphasized portraying everyday characters in real-life situations, especially amorous ones, became extraordinarily popular in Italy and throughout the world. Ruggiero Leoncavallo and Giacomo Puccini were especially known for their operas written in this style. While operas have continued to be written throughout the twentieth and into the twenty-first century, those of John Adams, Philip Glass, and William Bolcom being especially significant, the musical eclipsed opera as the most popular staged musical genre.

Incidental music, music that accompanies a dramatic play, has been a relatively minor component of staged musical productions. But it is one that has still produced some wonderful music that has lived on long after the plays for which they were written have gone out of fashion. George Bizet's incidental music for *L'Arlésienne* is a notable example of this type of music.

The musical as a genre came into being during the twentieth century but was preceded by opera buffa, operetta, vaudeville, and the revue, all genres that contributed various aspects to the musical. Musicals often have been written by song writing teams that get equal billing, Rodgers and Hammerstein and Lerner and Loewe for example, rather than the common practice of emphasizing the composer of the music in operas. Musicals evolved throughout the latter decades of the twentieth century in both sophistication of the musical element and in the incorporation of popular styles, which kept the genre current in the face of changing public tastes. Significant composers of musicals have included Rodgers and Hammerstein, Lerner and Loewe, Leonard Bernstein with Stephen Sondheim, and Andrew Lloyd Webber, often with Tim Rice.

The last thirty years have seen the rise of more varied staged musical presentations such as *Cirque du Soleil, Riverdance, Blue Man Group, The Three Tenors,* and *Celtic Woman.* These are often musicals without a storyline but having a common thread or a theme that runs through them. In these productions the visuals are often just as important, if not more so, as the musical element. These productions are in some ways similar to earlier genres such as vaudeville and the revue, which often did not tell a story.

Non-Western staged musical presentations have significant traditions in Japan, Kabuki theatre, and in China, Chinese opera. Both of these genres exhibit a heavy emphasis on elaborate costumes and have an appeal across all classes of society. Kabuki theatre makes use of music more in the sense of incidental music, while Chinese opera is a fully musical genre emphasizing the story-telling aspect through singing.

The *shared* experience of an art form that communicates the variety and range of the *human* experience has made staged musical productions the most popular type of *concert* experience throughout history. The themes of all great theatre transcend cultural and ethnic boundaries, historical eras, and stylistic characteristics. The need to experience, in a theatrical setting, the triumphs, tragedies, and comic absurdities of our individual lives seems to be a constant across historical periods and geographical distances.

SUGGESTED FURTHER LISTENING

"Tu se morta," recitative from *Orfeo*—Claudio Monteverdi

"Verdi prati" from *Alcina*—George Frideric Handel

"I Rage, I Melt, I Burn" from *Alcis and Galatea*—George Frideric Handel

"Final Scene" from *Don Giovanni*—Wolfgang Amadeus Mozart

Egmont Overture—Ludwig van Beethoven

"Che gelida manina" from *La Boheme*—Giacomo Puccini

"Chorus of the Hebrew Slaves" from *Nabucco*—Giuseppe Verdi

"Coronation Scene" from *Boris Godunov*—Modest Mussorgsky

"Major General" song from *The Pirates of Penzance*—Gilbert and Sullivan

Summertime from *Porgy and Bess*—George Gershwin

Do, re, mi from *The Sound of Music*—Rodgers and Hammerstein

Aquarius from *Hair*—James Rado, Gerome Ragni, and Galt McDermot

One from *A Chorus Line*—Marvin Hamlisch and Edward Kleban

Circle of Life from *The Lion King*—Elton John and Tim Rice

QUESTION ASSIGNMENT

Instructions: Log in to the textbook web site and click on the ASSIGNMENTS tab. In the Chapter Question Assignment area read the instructions and answer the question(s) or provide the asked for information. Be sure to click the SUBMIT THIS FORM button after you complete the Assignment.

Listen to five musical compositions from this chapter that feature a singer. Name the composition from which the song comes, the composer of the piece, and the character from the opera or musical singing the example in the text.

1. Composition Name: _____

   Composer's Name: _____

   Character Singing the Example: _____

2. Composition Name: _____

   Composer's Name: _____

   Character Singing the Example: _____

3. Composition Name: _____

   Composer's Name: _____

   Character Singing the Example: _____

4. Composition Name: _____

   Composer's Name: _____

   Character Singing the Example: _____

5. Composition Name: _____

   Composer's Name: _____

   Character Singing the Example: _____

LISTENING EXERCISES

Instructions: Log in to the textbook web site and click on the ASSIGNMENTS tab. In the Listening Exercises area click on the links to the musical examples for each question and answer the questions. Be sure to click the SUBMIT button after you answer all of the questions.

Listen to each of the musical examples below from the Chapter 3 Playlist while noting the appropriate descriptive prompt on the Listening Chart for Chapter 3 and determine the best answer to each question.

1. "Queen of the Night" aria from *The Magic Flute* by Wolfgang Amadeus Mozart—This aria for voice and orchestra is sung in German with the soprano character of the Queen singing of her desire for vengeance against Sarastro. Her opening words are followed by a series of virtuosic vocalizations designed to show off the singer's abilities. Choose the timing below that represents when the virtuosic soprano first exhibits these extraordinary vocal capabilities.

   a. 20 seconds
   b. 30 seconds
   c. 40 seconds

2. "I Could Have Danced All Night" from *My Fair Lady* by Lerner and Loewe—This song for voice with orchestra is sung by the female character Eliza. It begins with the orchestra and the singer performing a short introduction before the first verse is sung at the 21 second mark. At what point does the second verse begin with backup voices added for additional interest?

   a. 35 seconds
   b. 60 seconds
   c. 1:39 seconds

3. "Farandole" from *L'Arlésienne* by Georges Bizet—This orchestra piece makes use of two contrasting melodic themes, a strong first theme followed by a light second theme. They alternate throughout the piece until they are presented simultaneously near the end. Choose the timing when that happens.

   a. 1:10 seconds
   b. 1:40 seconds
   c. 2:15 seconds

Music for Dancing

Chapter

4

FOCUS POINTS

Western Dance Music	*World Dance Music*
Estampie	Balinese Gamelan
Dance Suite	Tibetan Buddhist Skeleton Dance
Waltz	Italian Saltarello
Ballet	African Ritual Dances
Square Dance	Celtic Reel

Dance, the art form that finds its expression through bodily movement, has been an inspiration for music from ancient times to the present. Whether music was the catalyst for dance or whether dance existed before music is a question that may never be answered definitively, but since such a large portion of the music in existence is dance music it deserves our attention and a thoughtful examination.

The written record of dance is not as old as the written record of music. The earliest descriptive texts on dance date from the fifteenth century. Understandable manuscripts of music date from nearly a thousand years earlier. References to dance are as old as Old Testament Bible stories and the ancient Greeks wrote of dance, but what the movements that constituted those dances looked like is lost to us. Understanding what the dances looked like or how they were performed is not our purpose in studying them in a music class, rather, we will be examining dance music for its musical content, such as its form and rhythmic characteristics, and its purpose in a social context.

RHYTHM AND METER IN DANCE MUSIC

Any discussion of dance must begin with **rhythm** since that musical element is the foundation of dance. As was mentioned in Chapter 1, rhythm is the aspect of music that animates it, makes it feel like it is alive and vibrant. We tap our feet to the **beat**, the basic, underlying pulse of the music. Beats are often felt in groups of two, three, or four beats at a time. Feeling groupings of beats is called **meter**. **Duple meter** is when two beats are grouped together; **triple meter**

Girls performing acrobatic dances. Corel

The Dance Class by Edgar Degas (1834–1917). Corel

is when three beats are grouped together. Those are the two most basic meters. Other commonly used meters include quadruple meter, groupings of four beats at a time, and compound meter, felt as duple or triple meter with each beat consisting of three pulses. Less common are asymmetrical meters in which the number of grouped pulses changes instead of remaining constant.

The last term we need to know regarding rhythm is tempo. Tempo simply refers to the speed at which we feel the beats. For example, you can have two pieces of music in duple meter that feel completely different depending on how fast the tempo is of each piece. Count out loud a duple meter beat as if it were a march. Now count the same duple meter but wait longer between each beat. Now it no longer sounds like a march, well, maybe a funeral march, but not a sprightly piece to instill pride and courage. That's the difference tempo can make in a piece.

Time Signatures

The term **time signature** refers to the meter of a piece and is usually expressed as a fraction such as 2/4, 3/4, 4/4, or 6/8, which is written at the beginning of a line of music. The numbers refer to how many beats are felt in each measure/bar of music. A measure, or bar, the terms are interchangeable, is a small unit of time in a piece of music that contains a certain number of beats. The number of beats in a bar is expressed by the top number in the time signature. For example, the time signature 2/4 indicates that there are 2 (the top number) quarter notes (the bottom number) in each measure of music. A quarter note generally receives one beat in most music. So, counting four measures of music in 2/4 time would feel like this:

| **1** 2 | **1** 2 | **1** 2 | **1** 2 |

The vertical lines are called bar lines. The space between each of the vertical lines is called a measure or bar. Within each measure there are two beats with the first one, in bold face, emphasized. This is duple meter. The time signature would be 2/4.

Triple meter, with a 3/4 time signature, would be felt with three beats within each measure.

| **1** 2 3 | **1** 2 3 | **1** 2 3 | **1** 2 3 |

Quadruple meter, with a time signature of 4/4, or just the letter "C" denoting common time, would be felt like this:

| **1** 2 3 4 | **1** 2 3 4 | **1** 2 3 4 | **1** 2 3 4 |

Whereas quarter notes receive one beat each, eighth notes each receive one half of a beat. That is a difficult concept to think of in the abstract so think of eighth notes in terms of how they relate to quarter notes. Two eighth notes equal the time during which one quarter note is played. Count out loud the quadruple meter example above. Now, in the example below count the numbers at the same speed as you did above but add the word "and" in between each of the numbers. In this example each number and the following "and" constitute two eighth notes. They fill the same space of time as the "number" beat alone, but now there are two pulses, two eighth notes, filling the same amount of time.

| **1** & 2 & 3 & 4 & | **1** & 2 & 3 & 4 & | **1** & 2 & 3 & 4 & | **1** & 2 & 3 & 4 & |

The other time signature mentioned above, 6/8 time, is based on eighth notes rather than quarter notes. Each measure in 6/8 time contains six eighth notes, but you don't usually feel all six beats in each measure of a piece with this time signature. What you usually feel are two main beats with each one having three subdivisions within them. Here is the duple meter example from above. Say it out loud fairly slowly.

| **1** 2 | **1** 2 | **1** 2 | **1** 2 |

Now say the main beats again at the same speed but after each number say the words "and a." In this example you still have a duple meter pulse but there are actually six beats played in two groups of three beats each.

| **1** & a 2 & a | **1** & a 2 & a | **1** & a 2 & a | **1** & a 2 & a |

These are the most common time signatures. Understanding them allows us to discuss dance music with a bit more authority and detail.

DANCE MUSIC IN THE WESTERN TRADITION

From Medieval times to the present, dance music has been an important part of the musical experience. A discussion of dance music from each of the historical periods can show us not only what the music was like at different times throughout history but also illuminate some of the characteristics of the societies from which it arose.

Medieval Dance—Estampie

The physical movements of dances from the Medieval (500–1450) period are shrouded in mystery and conjecture, but we can still enjoy the music for its own sake. A fair amount of secular music from that time has survived until the present and a significant portion of it is dance music. The **estampie**, a quick, triple meter dance from the Medieval period, reveals that the secular music of the Middle Ages could be just as upbeat and energetic as any dance music heard today. Decisions as to how to perform this music are based on notated manuscripts of the melodies, paintings, illustrations in books that depict instruments used at that time, and literary references that describe the dances. From these sources we can infer that it was common to play percussion instruments along with melodic instruments during this time period, even though the music exists in written form as melodies only, without any accompanying parts. The entire range of instruments in use at the time was employed in the performance of dance music. Some of these instruments include the tambourine, drum, shawm (forerunner of the modern oboe), rebec (forerunner of the violin), bagpipes, lutes, and trumpets. The estampie was a dance believed to have employed a signature stomping motion.

Dance in the Medieval era was often accompanied by instruments such as the lute and the vielle.

Copyright © Erich Lessing/Art Resource, NY

Dance music from the Medieval period usually consisted of a melody that was repeated numerous times with different sections of music serving as endings to each of the repetitions. Sometimes one type of dance might be paired with another to create a small **suite** of dances, but during this time there was no agreed upon sequence of pairings. During the later Renaissance (1450–1600) and Baroque (1600–1750) periods consistent sequences of dances became established and the dance suite became an established genre.

Estampie—
Anonymous

The Dancing Master of the Renaissance and Baroque Periods

During the late Renaissance (1450–1600) and Baroque (1600–1750) historical periods it became commonplace for wealthy noblemen and aristocrats to employ a large household staff to provide for the everyday tasks of cooking, cleaning, gardening, etc. as well as the artistic, musical, and dance requirements of the nobleman and his family. While the artistic members of the staff were generally treated well, they did not hold a place of especially high rank within the staff, but served and lived much as the other servants. An artist would provide paintings, sculptures, and other adornments to visually enhance the home. A musician, usually an accomplished performer on some instrument in addition to being a composer, would write music, rehearse ensembles, oversee performances, and give instruction on instruments or the voice for the master of the house, his family, and guests. It was also not unusual for the household to employ a **dancing master**. This person gave performances of dances that may have been too difficult or intricate for the members of the household to perform themselves, and he was expected to teach the master, his family, and their guests the intricate steps of popular dances. These duties were analogous to what was expected of the musician in that the musician performed music, even though the master was often a musician of some accomplishment, and instructed other musicians as well as the family on whatever instruments they wanted to learn.

Some of the dances from the Renaissance that were common at court included slow, stately dances, such as the **bassadance** and **pavane**, and fast dances such as the **galliard**.

Country Festival by Pieter Brueghel the Younger (1564–1636). Corel

The Baroque Dance Suite

The presence of the dancing master at court coupled with a generally high level of dance ability within royal and aristocratic households contributed to the development of a refined style of courtly dance, more restrained than the earthy dances of the peasants. Some of the dances that were popular at court and became established within the genre of the dance suite were:

Courante—French, fast, triple meter

Allemande—German, fast, quadruple meter

Sarabanda—Spanish, slow, triple meter

Minuet—French, moderate, triple meter

Bourrée—French, moderate, duple meter

Gigue—English, fast, triple meter

Hornpipe—English, fast, triple meter

During the Renaissance dance music was intended to be danced to by the aristocrats for whom it was written. But during the Baroque period it became fashionable for composers to write dance suites, consisting of movements of music based on the popular dances of the time, without expecting anyone to actually dance to them. The suites were inspired by the contemporary dances that were in vogue, but the music itself was performed at locations and during events which would have made dancing to the music impracticable. These stylized dance suites became very popular at large public gatherings where entertaining music came to be expected. This type of dance suite was usually composed for large ensembles of brass, wind, percussion, and stringed instruments, basically large bands or orchestras. Other dance suites were written for solo instruments, including the harpsichord, violin, and cello, which were performed in more intimate indoor settings.

A ball in the Baroque era.
Copyright © Erich Lessing/Art Resource, NY

The Orchestral Dance Suite

The Baroque period was the time when the orchestra as we know it became a common instrumental ensemble. An orchestra is a performing ensemble consisting of string, woodwind, brass, and percussion instruments. The orchestra of the Baroque period was smaller in scope than our modern orchestra, which can have as many as 100 players. The Baroque orchestra typically had the full complement of string instruments from the violin family, violin, viola, cello, and contrabass; woodwind instruments such as the flute, oboe, and bassoon; brass instruments, primarily the trumpet and French horn; and tympani from the percussion family. Woodwind and brass instruments were often used singly or in pairs while multiple strings might be distributed as follows:

1st violins 4–6

2nd violins 4–6

Violas 2–4

Cellos 2–4

Basses 1–2

Orchestral dance suites could vary greatly in the number of movements they contained depending on the occasion for which they were written. A typical suite might contain 5–7 movements, while unusually long compositions might have twice as many or even more.

What Makes Music—Musical Instruments

The Woodwind Family

Instruments of the orchestra are grouped into four families according to certain characteristics. Originally these instruments were all made out of wood, but today some are made out of various of metals. The instruments in this family, unlike the strings, make their sounds in many different ways.

Flute—The flute is made out of silver, gold, or platinum. Its sound is produced by blowing air over an open hole, much like when you make a sound by blowing over the top of a soda bottle. There is a smaller version of the flute called a Piccolo. Since it is smaller it plays higher notes.

Oboe—This is an example of a double-reed instrument. Two pieces of cane are shaved very thin and tied together, then air is forced between the pieces and this produces a sound which is often characterized as nasal. There is a larger version called the English horn. It is lower in pitch because of its larger size.

Clarinet—This is a single-reed instrument. It has one piece of cane pressed tightly against a piece of plastic or glass.

Air forced between these makes a very pure tone. The size and shape of the instrument give it its characteristically mellow quality.

There are larger and smaller versions of the Clarinet. The larger version is called the Bass Clarinet and sounds lower. The smaller one is called the E-flat Clarinet and sounds higher in pitch.

Bassoon—This is the largest member of the Woodwind family and sounds the lowest. It is a double-reed instrument like the Oboe and English horn. There is a large version of the bassoon called the Contra Bassoon, which sounds even lower. It is so large it is held up by an endpin that rests on the floor.

Saxophones—Saxophones are only sometimes found in orchestras, but as members of the woodwind family, should be mentioned here. Saxophones are made out of brass but use a mouthpiece similar to the clarinet, a single-reed mouthpiece. The saxophones come in a number of sizes and their names are taken from the names for the voices: Soprano Sax, Alto Sax, Tenor Sax, and Baritone Sax.

There is a standard performing ensemble for the Woodwind family called the Woodwind Quintet. It consists of one flute, one oboe, one clarinet, one bassoon, and a member borrowed from the Brass family called the French horn.

View the video of English composer Benjamin Britten's *Young Person's Guide to the Orchestra* performed by the YouTube Symphony Orchestra on the chapter video playlist.

The woodwind family of instruments is featured from :33–:56 and each of the woodwinds is featured individually beginning at the 2:10 mark.

The University of Memphis Woodwind Quintet: Dan Phillips, French horn; Michelle Vigneau, oboe; Bruce Erskine, flute; Lecolion Washington, bassoon; Carina Washington, clarinet.
Photo courtesy of Chris Hill

The *Water Music*

George Frideric Handel (1685–1759), a German born composer living in England, was noted for his writing of dance suites. Two in particular have had a lasting popularity among concert audiences, the *Music for the Royal Fireworks,* written in 1749 for a fireworks display in London celebrating the end of the War of the Austrian Succession, and the *Water Music,* written in 1717 to accompany King George I on a barge trip on the Thames River. The *Water Music* is an especially long composition consisting of dozens of movements arranged in three separate suites. In addition to the standard dances of the time, suites frequently included an overture preceding the dance movements and airs, leisurely paced lyrical movements, interspersed among the faster movements.

The following two movements from the *Water Music* provide an interesting view of two dances of the time, the menuet (minuet) and the hornpipe, both of which share essentially the same definition but vary slightly in execution. The hornpipe, as it was performed in England from this time period, was a dance in triple meter in A-B-A form. The second section of the piece, the "B" section, was usually calmer with fewer instruments playing than in the more energetic "A" sections that began and ended the movement. The menuet was a dance in triple meter and A-B-A form as well, with the "B" section contrasting with the "A" sections both melodically and in mood. What was the difference? The hornpipe was characterized by a syncopated accent on the second half, or "and," of beat one. A syncopated rhythm is one where the emphasis is placed on unexpected beats or offbeats. A small difference in definition but a significant one in the mood the piece sets. The syncopation makes the hornpipe bouncier and more jovial in character than the more restrained menuet. Both of these movements were well suited for outdoor performance making use of the full orchestra of the time. Also note how short sections of music are repeated, often with a different group of instruments playing the repeated section, in order to provide contrast and timbral interest. Listen for the three distinct sections, A-B-A, in each of these excerpts from the *Water Music.* This is one of the most common forms used in music from all time periods. It is sometimes called ternary form or three-part form.

Water Music (excerpts)—
George Frideric Handel
"Menuet"
"Alla Hornpipe"

In order to provide contrast to the upbeat dances of the time, composers often included airs to provide peaceful, lyrical movements within the suites. One of the most famous of these airs is from an orchestral suite, the *Orchestral Suite in D major,* by Johann Sebastian Bach (1685–1750), another German composer. The beautiful melody in the violins is supported by the basso continuo with the other strings providing a simple harmonic accompaniment.

"Air" from *Orchestral Suite #3 in D major*—
Johann Sebastian Bach

Solo Instrumental Dance Suite

The dance suite for solo instruments is far less common than the orchestral dance suite, but can be even more captivating since it is always performed in a small venue for a relatively small audience. This intimacy can impart a level of energy difficult to duplicate in a large space. Solo dance suites generally consisted of stylized interpretations of the dances. That is, they were not actually meant to be danced to but rather to elicit the mood and characteristics of a dance in concert music. Johann Sebastian Bach wrote solo instrumental suites for harpsichord, violin, and cello. The following excerpt from the *Suite for Solo Cello in G major* shows the typical structure of the **bourrée** dance. A typical dance suite might actually contain two bourrées of contrasting character. The first is built of two halves with each half repeated. Then the second bourrée is played the same way, two halves, each repeated. You can tell when the second bourrée starts because there will be a distinct change of mood as well as melody. After the second bourrée is completed, the player returns to the first bourrée again and it is played without repeats. Below is a diagram of how a bourrée movement is usually performed.

Bourrée I— | first part, played twice | second part, played twice |

Bourrée II— | first part, played twice | second part, played twice |
(contrasting character)

Bourrée I— | first part, played once | second part, played once |

The result is that the listener will perceive an overall A-B-A form. This kind of **performance practice** relating to the form of this type of dance applies to the performance of most minuet movements as well.

Suite for Solo Cello in G major—
Johann Sebastian Bach
"Bourrées I & II"

Couples dancing a waltz at the Palais Auersperg, Vienna. Copyright © Erich Lessing/Art Resource, NY

NINETEENTH-CENTURY WALTZES

Over the course of time from the Baroque through the Romantic periods dance music became incorporated into other musical genres such as the **symphony** and opera. The minuet became the standard third movement in four-movement symphonies, and dance sequences in operas became integral parts of the story instead of pleasant diversions. Dance suites were relegated to a less prominent place in composers' output. The complexity of Baroque era dances gradually gave way to simpler, more easily learned dances such as the **waltz**. The shift away from relatively difficult dances reduced the aristocracy's reliance on dancing masters for instruction and contributed to participation in public dance by a wider segment of the population. The most influential dance in this transformation was the waltz.

The waltz is a dance in triple meter with an emphasis on the first beat and incorporates a characteristic turning motion. Developed in and around Vienna, Austria, from the late seventeenth into the nineteenth century, this dance was first popular among peasants and gradually gained prominence in public dance halls and among a wide range of the social spectrum. The rather slow acceptance of the waltz is often attributed to its being the first "forbidden dance" due to the close hold of the dancing partners. The burgeoning middle class of the nineteenth century propelled this dance to the forefront as the most popular dance of the century.

Johann Strauss II (1825–1899) was known as "The Waltz King" for his numerous compositions in this genre. Strauss not only composed an enormous number of waltzes, but he wrote many other types of pieces as well including the famous operetta, *Die Fledermaus (The Bat)*. He toured extensively with his own orchestra performing his compositions across Europe and in his native Vienna. While originally composed for dancing, performances of Strauss waltzes today often reflect a more stylized performance practice with many rhythmic irregularities, such as extensive ritardandos (a temporary slowing down of the tempo) and drastic tempo changes between sections of music that make them inappropriate for dancing. These pieces were usually composed using several different waltz tunes, with each being treated fairly extensively. These individual waltzes would be strung together to create an extended composition with several changes of mood.

Strauss' most famous waltz is *An der schönen blauen Donau (On the Beautiful Blue Danube)*. This piece was written in 1867 and the first performance was not quite the success Strauss hoped it would be. Perhaps that was due to the inclusion of less than inspiring lyrics sung to the main tune. In subsequent all-instrumental performances, the work was enthusiastically received and has remained a staple of the orchestral repertory ever since. Today the piece is frequently referred to as *The Blue Danube Waltz*.

This composition is in triple meter and takes approximately 10 minutes to play. As you listen to it you will note that there are a number of different sections to the piece. Can you perceive how the piece is structured? How does the composer tie it all together? What concepts does the composer employ to keep you interested for ten minutes?

 An der schönen blauen Donau (On the Beautiful Blue Danube)— Johann Strauss II

THE FULL-LENGTH BALLET

The waltzes of Johann Strauss were relatively significant musical compositions. Each had a number of large sections in contrasting moods, compared to the relatively short dance movements, each in one characteristic mood, of earlier suites. The nineteenth century saw dance music evolve further into full-length ballets telling a continuous story over the course of an entire evening's entertainment. Ballet was a type of dance with a rigorous set of movements and techniques by which to execute those movements. Ballet had been in existence since the late sixteenth century at the royal courts throughout Europe. Early ballets consisted of sequences of scenes that were based more around a central idea than actually telling a complete story. But in the nineteenth century ballet came to be the highest expression of the art of dramatic movement, vying to be the dance equivalent of opera in its story telling ability and dramatic effect. The music written for ballets was initially not very distinguished, serving merely as a decorative time-keeping device for the dancers, but it eventually became the genre for which some of the most interesting, provocative, and forward-looking music ever written was created.

The Orchestra by Edgar Degas (1834–1917). Copyright © Erich Lessing/Art Resource, NY

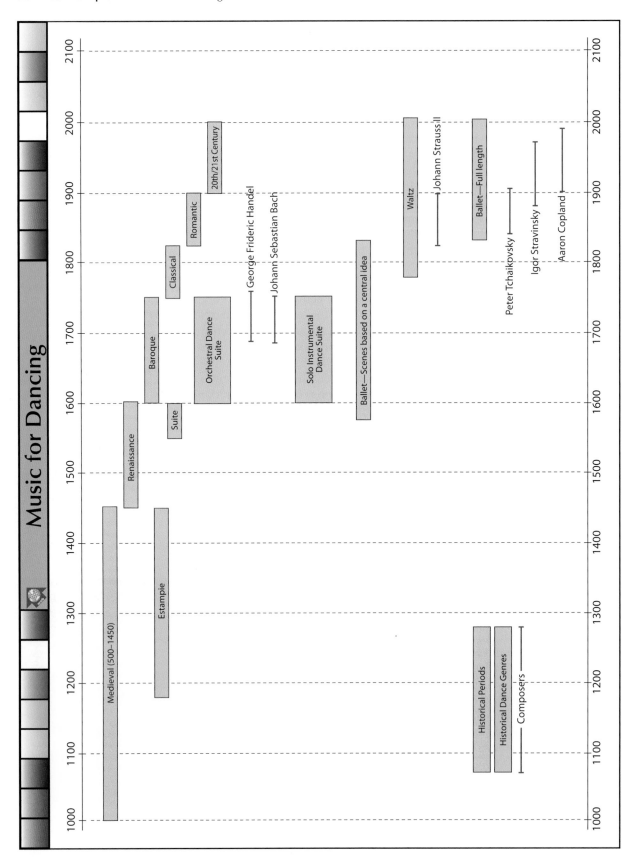

Music for Dancing

Historical Periods

Historical Dance Genres

Composers

Medieval (500–1450)

Renaissance

Estampie

Suite

Baroque

Classical

Romantic

20th/21st Century

Orchestral Dance Suite

Solo Instrumental Dance Suite

Ballet—Scenes based on a central idea

Ballet—Full length

Waltz

George Frideric Handel

Johann Sebastian Bach

Johann Strauss II

Peter Tchaikovsky

Igor Stravinsky

Aaron Copland

The word ballet brings to mind images of rows of ballerinas in tutus dancing on the tips of their toes, "on pointe," in seeming defiance of gravity. That stereotype of ballet was born in the nineteenth century when the role of the male dancer had diminished, following the decline of the dancing master, and ballet was centered around the prima ballerina. The male dancer was relegated to a largely supporting role. Fascination with contrasting the mortal and the immortal was an enduring theme in Romantic ballet beginning with the first full-length story ballet, *La Sylphide*, in 1832. This recurring idea is the basis for what is perhaps the epitome of Romantic ballet, *Swan Lake*.

Swan Lake

Swan Lake was written by Russian composer Peter Ilyich Tchaikovsky (1840–1893), and choreographed by Marius Petipa and Lev Ivanov. It germinated from inception to the version we know today over a period of twenty years. When the "final" version was performed in 1895 Tchaikovsky had been dead for two years. In nineteenth-century ballet, composers often worked almost independently from the choreographer in composing the music. They were given the basic story, how many dances were required for how many dancers, and expected to have it done by a certain date. *Swan Lake,* was the first ballet that Tchaikovsky composed and he brought to it a fresh approach that was fundamentally different from ballet music of that time. Until *Swan Lake,* ballet music was almost suite-like in its intermittent character. Tchaikovsky brought a more symphonic approach to the writing of *Swan Lake.* Many of the individual musical pieces within the ballet are longer, more complex, and more musically related than earlier compositions for the ballet. Tchaikovsky elevated the writing of ballet music to a level not previously attained and in so doing opened the door for other significant composers to follow suit.

In *Swan Lake* Prince Siegfried happens upon a group of beautiful swan maidens by the shores of an enchanted lake led by their queen, who is really a mortal princess named Odette. They have been turned into swans by an evil sorcerer named Rothbart. The swan maidens return to human form each night from midnight until dawn. The spell can only be broken by someone pledging eternal love, which Siegfried does for Odette. Later Siegfried mistakenly claims Rothbart's evil daughter, Odile, who is an exact double of Odette, as his bride. Realizing his mistake, Siegfried rushes to the lake where he finds Odette dying of sadness. As Siegfried tosses her tiara into the lake the waters engulf the tragic lovers and their spirits rise to heaven.

The scene depicted in this example is of the lake in the moonlight. It contains the haunting melody that represents the swan princess and is synonymous with this ballet. It is heard played first by the oboe and subsequently by the rest of the orchestra. This theme returns several times in differing moods throughout the ballet, imparting a sense of symphonic continuity over the length of the performance.

Danseuse sur Scene by Edgar Degas (1834–1917). Corel

 "Lake in the Moonlight" from *Swan Lake*— Peter Ilyich Tchaikovsky

PERSPECTIVE—ANCIENT DANCE REFERENCES

The presence of dance in ancient cultures is often inferred from pictorial representations in works of art, figures painted on or carved into buildings, and literary allusions. Since dance, like music, does not leave physical evidence of its presence we must be satisfied with an incomplete picture of it when discussing it in its earliest forms. While we know dance has been an integral part of virtually every society since ancient times, the exact manifestation of it, how it was performed, is often no more than an educated guess.

One of the few descriptions of actual dance movements from ancient times exists in a literary work from India. Bharata Muni, an Indian writer who lived, as best as can be determined, between 500 BC and 200 BC wrote a detailed textbook on theatre, music, and dance called the *Natya Shastra*. Bharata gave clear descriptions of movements appropriate to different types of dances as well as portray the various dances in the appropriate social context. Other references to dance from approximately the same era come from the nearby island nation of Sri Lanka off the southeastern coast of India. In the *Mahavamsa* (*The Great Chronicle* of early Sri Lankan society), dance is often referred to in relation to royal society. For example, ". . . and having gods and men dance before him, the king took his pleasure, in joyous and merry wise," and "The king . . . surrounded by many dancers . . ." The *Mahavamsa*, while written by a Buddhist monk named Mahanama in approximately 500 AD, describes Sri Lankan society from 500–200 BC and is based on fragmentary writings from that time.

Another ancient culture that developed dance to a sophisticated level was ancient Greece. The Greek philosopher Aristotle (384–322 BC) spoke eloquently in his *Poetics* of the expressive qualities of dancers, ". . . for by means of rhythmical gestures they represent both character and experiences and actions." The Greek poet Homer (ca. 750 BC) refers many times to dance in Book XIII of the *Iliad*. For example, "All things pall after awhile, sleep, love, sweet song, and stately dance . . ." and "Heaven has made one man an excellent soldier; of another it has made a dancer or a singer and player on the lyre . . ."

Biblical references to dance are numerous with perhaps the oldest being from the second book of the Old Testament, *Exodus*, believed to have been written ca. 650 BC. Chapter 15, verse 20 states, "Then Miriam, the prophetess, Aaron's sister, took a tambourine in her hand, and all the women followed her, with tambourines and dancing." Perhaps the most familiar biblical reference to dance comes from the book of *Ecclesiastes*, chapter 3, verse 4, ". . . a time to weep and a time to laugh, a time to mourn and a time to dance."

Ancient Egyptian dance is known mostly through pictorial representations of dance found in tombs. The earliest scenes come from the era known as The Old Kingdom, approximately 2650–2150 BC. Dances from this time were apparently performed by members of the same sex, women with women or men with men. Men and women are never shown dancing together. The dances often seem to be acrobatic in nature with synchronized motions being common.

BALLET MUSIC OF REMARKABLE SIGNIFICANCE

The Rite of Spring

The symphonic treatment of the musical score for *Swan Lake* really didn't break any new ground in the musical sense. It simply brought the existing standards for extended musical compositions of the Romantic period into the realm of ballet. But a composition for the ballet, *Le Sacre du Printemps* (*The Rite of Spring*), by Russian composer Igor Stravinsky, had profound effects on all dance and concert music that came after it.

Igor Stravinsky (1882–1971) had already composed two major ballets, *The Firebird* in 1910 and *Petrushka* in 1911, when he undertook the composing of a new full-length ballet, *The Rite of Spring*, for Serge Diaghilev's Ballets Russes in Paris in 1912. Diaghilev was a major force in the music and dance world of the late nineteenth and

Biographical Spotlight

Igor Stravinsky

© 2013, Brendan Howard, Shutterstock, Inc.

Igor Stravinsky

Igor Stravinsky was born on June 17, 1882, and died on April 6, 1971. He was a Russian-born composer who later spent significant time in both France and the United States where his reputation as one of the leading composers of the twentieth century was established and reaffirmed through several significant stylistic changes. He studied music as a youngster but attended law school at the behest of his parents. He was an indifferent student, spending more time in his musical pursuits than studying law. At the age of twenty he met the highly regarded Russian composer Nicolai Rimsky-Korsakov, who took him under his wing and gave him lessons in composition until Rimsky-Korsakov died three years later. Stravinsky was married in 1905 to a cousin with whom he eventually had four children.

In 1909, at the age of twenty-seven, a performance of Stravinsky's music was heard by Serge Diaghilev, a Russian living in Paris who was about to begin producing operas and ballets in the French capital. Diaghilev commissioned Stravinsky to write the music for a planned ballet called *The Firebird*, which was to be performed the following year by his dance troupe, *The Ballet Russe (The Russian Ballet)*. The success of *The Firebird* led to commissions for *Petrouchka, The Rite of Spring*, and *Pulcinella*, all ballets produced by Diaghilev's company. These compositions, especially the radically different *The Rite of Spring*, established Stravinsky as the leading figure in the move away from the Romantic style.

For several years after the premiere of *The Rite of Spring* Stravinsky's family split their time between Russia and Switzerland. They moved to Paris in 1920 and stayed there until 1939, becoming French citizens. This time, after the end of World War I and prior to the beginning of World War II, saw a radical change in Stravinsky's compositional style. He moved away from the large-scale compositions that had secured his reputation as a major figure in the world of music and gravitated toward a more austere style that came to be known as "neo-classicism." Stravinsky supported his family through astute business arrangements with a player-piano manufacturer, royalties from performances of his music, and commissions for new compositions. He, his wife, and a daughter all contracted tuberculosis in 1938 from which only he survived. Stravinsky moved to the United States in 1939 at the outbreak of World War II. He settled briefly in Boston where he married Vera de Bossett, with whom he had carried on a long-standing affair since they first met in Paris in 1921. They remained married for the remainder of his life, and she was at his bedside when he died in 1971.

In 1945 Stravinsky became a United States citizen. His composing style would change radically one more time in the mid-1950s when he gradually adopted the serial techniques of composing, which many of his contemporaries from earlier in the century had done years before. This move toward a predominantly dissonant style remained Stravinsky's approach for his remaining years. He moved to New York City in 1969 and died there on April 6, 1971. He was buried according to his wishes in Venice, Italy, near his long-time friend Serge Diaghilev, with whom he had changed the course of music history.

Biographical Spotlight Exercise

Instructions: Log in to the textbook web site and click on the **Assignments** tab. Click on **Chapter 4** and scroll to the **Biographical Spotlight area**. Answer the question based on the information in the biography above.

Which of the following is a true statement?

1. Stravinsky never studied with any known composers.
2. Stravinsky wrote his most important works in collaboration with a fellow Russian working in Paris name Serge Diaghilev.
3. Stravinsky maintained his style of writing large-scale compositions after World War I.

early twentieth centuries. An impresario of enormous talent, Diaghilev commissioned provocative works by the most forward-looking composers. He promoted adventurous choreographers, like Vaslav Nijinsky, choreographer for *The Rite of Spring,* who were not afraid to break with the conventions of the past.

The Rite of Spring had its premier in 1913 in Paris and created an immediate uproar due to the radical nature of both the music and the dance. The story was based on Stravinsky's images of the pagan rituals that would accompany the coming of spring in prehistoric Russia. In fact the work was subtitled, "Scenes from Pagan Russia." A disturbance at the premiere, and it was a virtual riot, was caused by a combination of factors. The music was not at all what the audience expected, dissonant, rhythmically unpredictable, and extraordinarily loud at times. This combination of musical qualities is often referred to as primitivism, *The Rite of Spring* being the most renowned musical example of that style. The expanded brass, woodwind, and percussion sections of the orchestra were not common in ballet orchestras of the time and were something of a shock to the Parisian audience. The two previous ballets by Stravinsky, *The Firebird* and *Petrushka,* had been written in a forward-looking late-Romantic style but gave no hint as to the radical departure represented by *The Rite of Spring.*

The dancing was a second shock to the system for the audience. Expecting traditional, elegant ballet moves, they were puzzled to see angular, jagged-shaped movements. The dancers frequently engaged in downward movements to the floor rather than the upward extensions of line for which ballet was noted. Gliding effortlessly over the floor gave way to short, staccato steps of a harsh, primitive nature. The story line did little to endear the work to the audience either. It was a story of human sacrifice to propitiate the gods of springtime, resulting in the sacrificial dance of a young girl.

In this work Stravinsky used short, motive-like melodies, reminiscent of the folk melodies he imagined would have been common long ago. Harmony in this piece was noteworthy for its characteristic use of unresolved dissonances. Composers had always used dissonant sounds to create tension. That tension was relieved by resolving the dissonant sounds to consonant ones. Whatever the historical period, the resolution of dissonance to consonance had been a universal concept. Not so with *The Rite of Spring.* Unresolved dissonance became a signature sound for this piece, and composers after Stravinsky adopted that as an acceptable harmonic concept.

Rhythmically, *The Rite of Spring* was ground breaking as well. Until that time the overwhelming majority of music in the Western world had utilized a repeating meter

Royal Ballet's production the *Rite of Spring* by Igor Stravinsky, at the Royal Opera House, Covent Garden, London. © Robbie Jack/Corbis

as the rhythmic engine of musical compositions, especially music for dancing. Meter that stayed constant provided a stable point of reference for the listener, making it easy to anticipate the flow of a melodic phrase or the pacing of a section of music. Composers might change the meter on occasion, or alternate between different meters for a short time within a composition, but it was always done as an unusual event. Changing meters provided temporary rhythmic diversions; it was not the norm. In contrast to this accepted practice, great sections of *The Rite of Spring* were written in constantly shifting asymmetrical meters, giving an unpredictable, almost out-of-control, feeling to the music. In addition, Stravinsky used many unusual meters in the piece, ensuring that even if played for an extended period of time those meters alone would provide an unsettled metrical basis for the work.

These compositional innovations were difficult for the audience to passively accept at that first performance. However, other composers heard in Stravinsky's writing elements of a new musical language that many were eager to adopt and adapt to their own compositional styles. The harmonic and rhythmic innovations heard in *The Rite of Spring* soon became the norm for much Western art music. Today we listen to this music almost disbelieving that it could have caused such a commotion. To our ears it sounds like exciting or scary music we hear every day in movies. That may be the greatest testament to Stravinsky's vision for this music. He intended it to be visually linked to the action on the stage, just as music for the movies is linked to the action on the screen. So when we hear the music today, even when played in a "concert performance" without dancers, we have no trouble conjuring up images that fit the music.

The two excerpts below highlight the primitivistic qualities associated with this piece. The first excerpt, "Auguries of Spring (Dances of the Young Girls)," is the first scene the audience saw in the original production as the curtain went up following the rather atmospheric introduction. The dissonant repeating chords, accented at unpredictable intervals, completely masked any metrical order. The lack of a discernable melody until well into this scene further confused and alienated the audience. And when a melody was heard it was a very short one never to be heard again in the piece.

The second excerpt, "Sacrificial Dance (The Chosen One)," is the final scene of the ballet during which the young girl is forced to dance herself to death. Continually shifting meters with interjected melodic motives create a relentless urgency toward the final frenzied atmosphere of the sacrifice. Even though the music is notated in exacting detail, the effect for the listener is a kind of compelling rhythmic anarchy, at once rhythmically strong and powerful while being totally unpredictable. *Swan Lake* this is not.

 The Rite of Spring (two excerpts)—
Igor Stravinsky
 "Auguries of Spring" (Dances of the Young Girls)
 "Sacrificial Dance" (The Chosen One)

THOROUGHLY AMERICAN BALLET

Aaron Copland (1900–1990) was an American composer who consciously decided to create a uniquely "American" sound in his music. Early in his career Copland was strongly influenced by the trends that were gaining in popularity among composers of the time, such as harsh dissonance and rhythmic complexity. But he saw in the audience reaction to his works a reluctance to fully accept those challenging concepts. That led him to adopt a less adventuresome compositional style, one that incorporated all of the revolutionary concepts but in a more constrained way. In addition Copland wrote music that had an "open" quality about it, suggestive of the openness and freedom of the American spirit. This atmospheric, open quality was created by the use of harmonies with wider intervals between the pitches and by orchestrations that refrained from close groupings of notes in the lower-pitched instruments. And while Copland did use dissonance and rhythmic complexity in his pieces, the restraint with which he handled these characteristics added a charm and attractiveness to the music that the more heavy-handed use of these same qualities did not. Think of it this way, in cooking, adding just the right amount of various spices to a recipe can create a wonderful flavor, whereas an overabundance of those same spices can make the food unpalatable.

Copland also made his music attractive to the listener by writing beautifully lyrical and memorable melodies, some of which were actual folk tunes of primarily American origin. The use of the Shaker hymn tune *Simple Gifts* in the ballet *Appalachian Spring* is the most frequently recognized traditional melody used by Copland. His use of recognizable melodies is in stark contrast to many of his contemporaries who often eschewed writing melodies in the traditional sense. The importance of the melody in Copland's music cannot be overemphasized. It is the first thing the ear is attracted to, and his tunes linger in the memory long after the music has ended.

All of the aforementioned characteristics were used by Copland in music that was written for the ballet. Just as Stravinsky had made a name for himself in this genre, so did Copland. His association with two of the great choreographers of the twentieth century, Agnes DeMille (*Rodeo*) and Martha Graham (*Appalachian Spring*), brought Copland to the forefront of both the musical and dance worlds. Beginning with the music for the ballet *Billy the Kid* in 1938, Copland's name became synonymous with a signature American style of music and dance. Some of the works by Copland with a distinctly American flavor include *Quiet City* (1940), *Fanfare for the Common Man* (1942), *Lincoln Portrait* (1942), *Rodeo* (1942), and *Appalachian Spring* (1944). These works ensured Copland's reputation as the most distinctly American voice among the significant composers of that era.

Rodeo

The two excerpts from *Rodeo* below illustrate the unique attributes of Copland's writing, evocative mood setting, and attractive use of both melody and rhythm. *Rodeo* is the story of a young Cowgirl in the American West who has a crush on the Head Wrangler of the ranch. The Head Wrangler wants nothing to do with the tomboyish Cowgirl, preferring the prettier rancher's daughter. At the big Saturday night dance the Cowgirl exchanges her cowhand clothes and hard-edged appearance for a more feminine look. Immediately she catches the attention of the Head Wrangler but she rebuffs him in favor of the Champion Roper who had always been kind to her, regardless of how she looked.

The first excerpt, "Corral Nocturne," reflects the sadness and loneliness of the Cowgirl as the Head Wrangler and the other men find the women from town more to their liking. The second excerpt, "Hoe Down," is the culminating scene of the ballet taking place at the Saturday night dance. The original tune from "Hoe Down," is variously known as *Bonaparte's Retreat*, *Bonaparte's Farewell*, or *Bonyparte*.

The ballet *Rodeo* (1942). Music by Aaron Copland, choreography by Agnes de Mille. Courtesy of Photofest, NY

> *Rodeo* (two excerpts)—
> Aaron Copland
>   "Corral Nocturne"
>   "Hoe Down"

How is the dance music from the Medieval and Baroque periods different from later dance music? Do you think the waltz by Strauss would make a good ballet? Why or why not? Do you think the ballet music you've listened to would be enjoyable if you did not know the story behind the music?

FOLK DANCE MUSIC FROM AROUND THE WORLD

Balinese Gamelan Music

Bali Temple Dance. © Bettmann/Corbis

A **gamelan** is a collection of instruments played as an ensemble that is found throughout the Indonesian islands, particularly in Java and Bali. The instruments are predominately "metallophones," percussion instruments consisting of a series of differently sized metal bars that are struck with hard sticks. Gongs, cymbals, and flutes are also commonly found in gamelans. Gamelan music takes several different forms, including **gamelan gong**, for a large group of instruments, **gamelan angklung**, for a smaller group of instruments, and **gamelan beleganjur**, with a somewhat different variety of portable instruments more suited to playing while walking during rituals and ceremonies.

Gamelan gong and angklung often accompany dancing. The dancing typically tells a story from Balinese history or religion through elegant movements done in elaborate costumes. Dancing in Bali is not restricted to professionally trained dancers but is an activity shared by people of all ages and ability levels. The gamelan music that

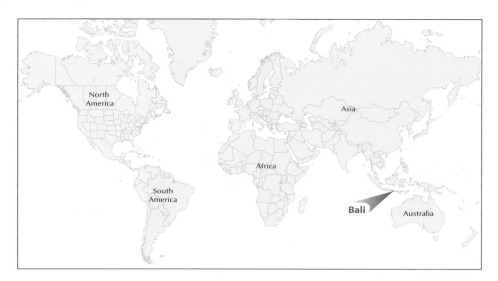

accompanies Balinese dancing can be fast and energetic, gamelan gong kebjar, or more restrained and elegant, gamelan angklung.

Gamelan music is based on two different types of scales, slendro, a pentatonic (five-note) scale and pelog, a seven note scale where only five of the pitches are usually used. It is important to understand that the pitches of these scales, and the way the instruments of the gamelan are tuned, do not mirror the concepts of pitch common in Western music. Balinese gamelan music has a characteristic, shimmering, and wavering sound quality that is the result of the instruments actually being slightly out of tune in the Western concept of pitch. The music often consists of very short melodic ideas split up and shared by several instruments and repeated numerous times.

🎼 *Gamelan Angklung—*
Balinese Gamelan Music

Can you imagine dancing to this music? What is the meter? Is this the kind of music you would dance to with a friend?

Tibetan Buddhist Monk Dancing

The *Dance of the Skeleton (Skeleton Dance)* is performed by Tibetan Buddhist monks wearing skeleton costumes. The costumes suggest the temporal aspect of life and serve as a way of warding off evil spirits. The *Skeleton Dance* is a type of sacred dance, Cham, danced by the monks in Tibetan Buddhism that is performed during religious rituals and ceremonies. Another type of Tibetan dance, Achi Llama, is a kind of folk dance, danced by the people outside of the monasteries for the purpose of preserving and retelling historical facts, legends, and myths of their culture.

In the sacred *Skeleton Dance* percussion instruments and low-pitched horns accompany the guttural vocal chanting of the monks, creating an eerie sound that is at once exotic and mesmerizing. The sustained vocalizations sometimes result in the production of multiphonics, the singing of two or more pitches at one time by a single performer.

Tibetan Monk in ritual dance. The symbolism of the sword is to cut the attachment we have for things, wealth, people, etc. © Tiziana and Gianni Baldizzone/Corbis

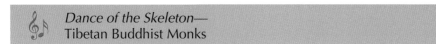

Dance of the Skeleton—
Tibetan Buddhist Monks

Can you imagine dancing to *this* music? Never mind trying to figure out the meter to this music, what about the basic beat? Can you feel one? Is there a basic beat? Do you need a beat or meter to dance?

Italian Tarantella and Saltarello

The Italian tarantella, a kind of song as well as a dance, takes its name from a legend that originated in Taranto, Italy, in the sixteenth century. The legend reportedly recounted numerous instances of people descending into trances characterized by constant vigorous dancing after having suffered the bite of the tarantula spider. Townspeople would play various types of increasingly faster dance music until the person, usually a woman, was cured of the poison. The tarantella is a fast dance in duple compound meter.

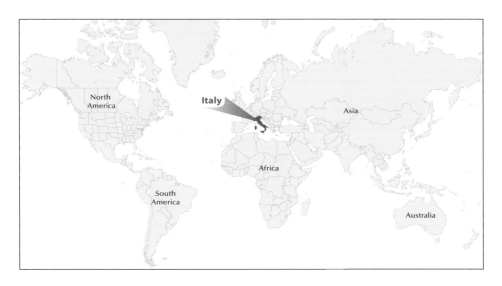

A similar dance, the saltarello, is a fast triple meter dance that incorporates a jumping motion from which the name is derived. Saltare is the Italian word meaning "to jump." This traditional folk dance was heard by the German composer Felix Mendelssohn on a visit to Italy in 1831 who was inspired to include a saltarello as the final movement of his *Symphony #4,* subtitled the "Italian Symphony."

Saltarello—
Traditional Italian Folk Dance

Symphony #4—
Felix Mendelssohn
    "4th Movement" (Saltarello)

Contrast this music with the previous two examples. How is rhythm used in this music as opposed to the two previous examples? Does this music seem more like dance music as you understand it? Can you feel the three-note pulses within each beat?

African ceremonial dancer.
Courtesy of Marcus Hurt &
DeWayne Hambrick

West African Folk Dance Music

Despite differences in certain characteristics, such as instruments used and the names and occasions for specific dances, the traditional folk dance music of western Africa is based first and foremost on drumming. Music from countries such as Senegal, Liberia, and Togo utilizes a complex practice of drumming based on the simultaneous playing of multiple rhythmic meters and/or rhythmic patterns. This type of music is called polyrhythmic.

Dance music from western Africa, like much folk music from around the world, is not music that you would find in a concert hall. It is music that accompanies ceremonies, rituals, celebrations, and events important to the culture. Marriage ceremonies, religious rituals and rites of passage are always accompanied by music and that music is almost always for the purpose of dancing. This dance music might include vocalizations such as shouts, chants, and call and response sequences, as well as other instruments, but the emphasis is always on the rhythmic drumming.

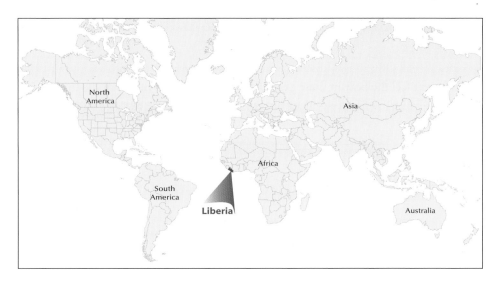

A common format for the performance of this type of music is for a basic rhythmic pattern to be established at the beginning of the dance. That pattern is then transformed by the addition of layers of rhythmic patterns that can either modify the established pattern or change it entirely into a new metrical pulse. Any number of transformations can take place during a piece depending on the length of the performance.

In the following three examples, listen for the rhythmic changes that take place and decide whether they change the entire rhythmic pulse of the music or just modify the existing rhythmic feel.

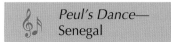
Peul's Dance—
Senegal

Acrobatic Dance of the Youths—
Liberia

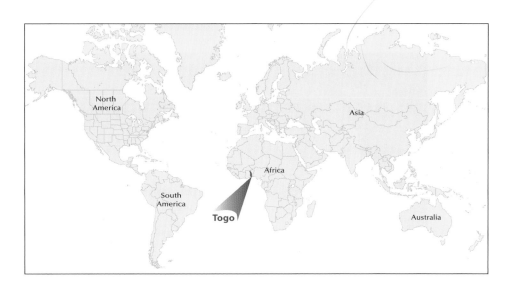

♪♪ *Initiation Dance—*
Togo

Can you feel the beat in these examples? Can you figure out what the meter is? Is the concept of rhythm different in this music from the previous example? If so, in what ways?

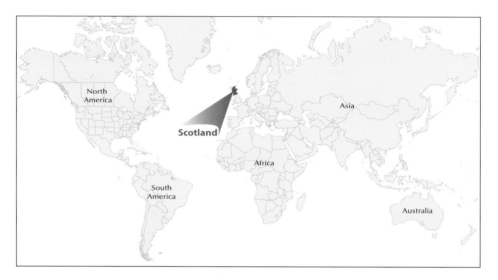

Celtic Reels

The term "Celtic" is most commonly used when referring to the people and cultures of Ireland, Scotland, and Wales. The people of these areas share a common ancestral culture and language and many of the characteristics of their respective styles of music and dance are indistinguishable. Some of the dances associated with Celtic culture are the reel, hornpipe, and jig. The hornpipe and jig (gigue) were discussed earlier in reference to dance suites of the Renaissance and Baroque periods, their influence being felt far beyond their geographical roots. The Irish reel was the model for the dance music that would become the American square dance. There are two basic types of dance in Celtic culture, the set dance and the step dance. The set dance is performed by four couples while the step dance is primarily a solo dance. The reel is a type of set dance.

Celtic reels.
© Berry Lewis/
Corbis

A set dance is composed of a sequence of sections danced first by the entire group of four couples, then repeated by individual couples. The set dance form fits well with the repeating nature of the music. Celtic reels are in quadruple meter and the traditional instruments used include the pipes, flute, Celtic harp, and bagpipes. In the following examples can you tell how many measures of quadruple meter constitute a repeating phrase?

Three Reels (played without pause)—
Traditional Celtic Dance Music
  "The Boys of the Lough"
  "Over the Bog Road"
  "The Merry Harriers"

This music is obviously very consistent in its beat and in its use of meter. Is this more to your liking than some of the previous examples?

The American Square Dance

The square dance consists of four couples starting from a position in which each couple faces inward forming one side of a square. This is essentially the same as the starting position for a reel. The entire group, as well as each couple within the group, performs a series of moves that are directed to them by a "caller." The caller literally calls out what moves they are to do next. The dance ends when the caller decides it is over. Square dances originated in Europe and became popular with the settlers of America. The music for a square dance could readily be played by a single fiddle player. A fiddle is essentially a violin. With room for a minimum of extras, such as musical instruments, the fiddle became a favorite instrument of the American settlers as they moved west.

The music for square dances is similar to reels in the repetitive nature of the music. It is constructed in phrases of eight bars (measures) with two sub-phrases of four bars each, providing a kind of question and answer format. The eight-bar phrases are often repeated. Any number of eight bar phrases might constitute the entire piece.

The square dance is still a popular dance in America with numerous square dance clubs and organizations dedicated to its propagation. The square dance might have gone the way of most of the dances that the early settlers brought with them, disappearing gradually with time, if not for three men whose interest in the dance sustained and spread its practice well beyond the realm of transitory immigrants. Henry Ford, the inventor of the automobile, took an interest in the dance and together with a master square dance caller, Benjamin Lovett, published a book entitled *Good Morning,* which was an enthusiastic endorsement of the square dance. A school superintendent in Colorado named Lloyd Shaw read the book and was inspired to collect as much information about the dance as he could. His book, *Cowboy Dances,* chronicled the square dance in more detail than anyone had until that point. Through a combination of writing, holding summer classes, and his limitless enthusiasm for the square dance, Shaw rekindled interest in the square dance that spread throughout the west.

Bob Wills Square Dance #1—
Bob Wills and His Texas Playboys

Listening Chart

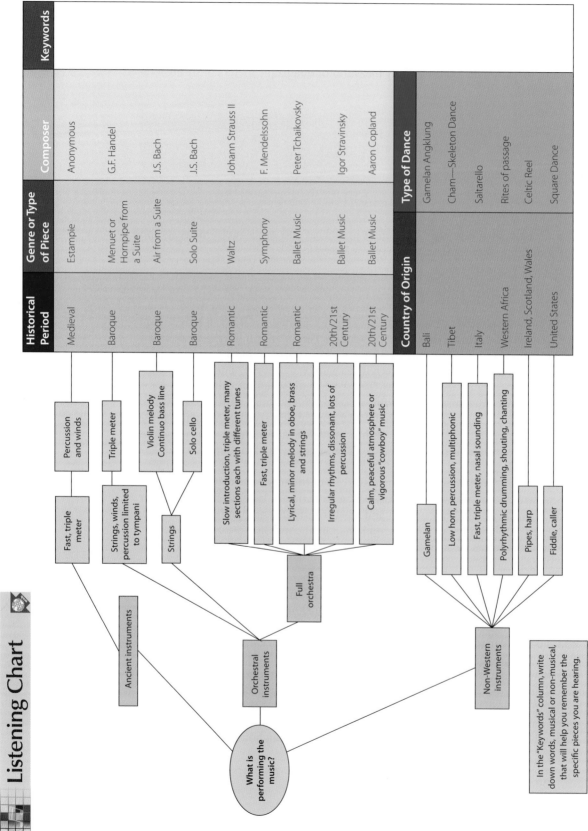

Historical Period	Genre or Type of Piece	Composer	Keywords
Medieval	Estampie	Anonymous	
Baroque	Menuet or Hornpipe from a Suite	G.F. Handel	
Baroque	Air from a Suite	J.S. Bach	
Baroque	Solo Suite	J.S. Bach	
Romantic	Waltz	Johann Strauss II	
Romantic	Symphony	F. Mendelssohn	
Romantic	Ballet Music	Peter Tchaikovsky	
20th/21st Century	Ballet Music	Igor Stravinsky	
20th/21st Century	Ballet Music	Aaron Copland	

Country of Origin	Type of Dance
Bali	Gamelan Angklung
Tibet	Cham—Skeleton Dance
Italy	Saltarello
Western Africa	Rites of passage
Ireland, Scotland, Wales	Celtic Reel
United States	Square Dance

What is performing the music?

Orchestral instruments
- Ancient instruments
  - Fast, triple meter — Percussion and winds
  - Strings, winds, percussion limited to tympani — Triple meter
- Strings
  - Violin melody / Continuo bass line
  - Solo cello
- Full orchestra
  - Slow introduction, triple meter, many sections each with different tunes
  - Fast, triple meter
  - Lyrical, minor melody in oboe, brass and strings
  - Irregular rhythms, dissonant, lots of percussion
  - Calm, peaceful atmosphere or vigorous "cowboy" music

Non-Western instruments
- Gamelan
- Low horn, percussion, multiphonic
- Fast, triple meter, nasal sounding
- Polyrhythmic drumming, shouting, chanting
- Pipes, harp
- Fiddle, caller

In the "Keywords" column, write down words, musical or non-musical, that will help you remember the specific pieces you are hearing.

SUMMARY

The history of dance is as long and as varied as the history of any other art form but perhaps more difficult to trace. Art leaves paintings and sculptures behind as evidence of style, concept, and evolution. Poetry and writing leave the written word. Music has a written language of its own, even though the earliest examples may be difficult to understand and interpret accurately. But dance has nothing to leave behind. There are no physical items such as musical instruments left behind from which we can infer what the movements were like; only images captured by ancient artists on walls and in books. Though there is now a dance equivalent of a written musical language it is not very old. Most dances have been passed from generation to generation through imitation, where one demonstrates how a dance is done, and others remember it as well as they can. What survives today, in a fairly accurate state, of much early and folk dance is the music that accompanied it.

Some dances have been associated with the common people, such as the Estampie and folk dances, while others have been aligned with the rich, such as courtly dance suites. Dance music of the common people tended to rely on a lot of repetition. We see that in the Estampie, the dance music of West Africa, in Celtic reels, and the American square dance. The courtly dance suites of the Baroque period often used a more sophisticated, A-B-A form, such as can be found in the minuet, bourées, and the hornpipe. During the Romantic period the waltz became one of the dances shared by most people in society. It was during this time that dance evolved into the more refined form known as ballet, practiced on the highest level by trained professionals, much like the art of music. But, no matter what the societal station of the dance or the place where it had been performed, or how complex or how simple, there has always been music with the dance. And that music covers the entire spectrum, from the simplest accompaniments to the most esoteric progressive music of the Western world.

SUGGESTED FURTHER LISTENING

Music for the Royal Fireworks—George Frideric Handel

Emperor Waltz—Johann Strauss II

Pizzicato Polka—Johann Strauss II

Polonaise in A-flat major—Frederic Chopin

Hungarian Dance #5—Johannes Brahms

The Nutcracker Suite—Peter Ilych Tchaikovsky

Prince Igor: Polovetsian Dances—Alexander Borodin

La Gioconda: Dance of the Hours—Amilcare Ponchielli

The Firebird—Igor Stravinsky

Pulcinella—Igor Stravinsky

It Don't Mean a Thing if it Ain't Got That Swing—Duke Ellington

Oblivion—Astor Piazzolla

QUESTION ASSIGNMENT

Instructions: Log in to the textbook web site and click on the ASSIGNMENTS tab. In the Chapter Question Assignment area read the instructions and answer the question(s) or provide the asked for information. Be sure to click the SUBMIT THIS FORM button after you complete the Assignment.

Name three types of dances, commonly found as individual movements within dance suites, which are usually composed in an overall A-B-A form.

1. _____

2. _____

3. _____

LISTENING EXERCISES

Instructions: Log in to the textbook web site and click on the ASSIGNMENTS tab. In the Listening Exercises area click on the links to the musical examples for each question and answer the questions. Be sure to click the SUBMIT button after you answer all of the questions.

Listen to each of the musical examples below from the Chapter 4 Playlist while noting the appropriate descriptive prompts on the Listening Chart for Chapter 4 and determine the best answer to each question.

1. "Menuet" from *Water Music Suite in D major* by George Frideric Handel—This dance, for orchestral instruments is in triple meter and begins with the French horns playing the first statement of the melody. Choose the timing below that represents when the strings, winds, and percussion instruments first enter.

   a. 26 seconds
   b. 45 seconds
   c. 60 seconds

2. *On the Beautiful Blue Danube* by Johann Strauss II—This waltz for full orchestra, in triple meter, begins with a slow introduction. The main melody of the piece occurs at approximately the 1:30 second mark. This is followed by many sections each with different tunes. Choose the timing below that represents when the main melody returns later in the piece.

   a. 3:10 seconds
   b. 5:30 seconds
   c. 8:40 seconds

3. "Lake in the Moonlight" from *Swan Lake* by Peter Ilyich Tchaikovsky—This full orchestra piece makes use of a lyrical minor key melody that is constructed in two parts. The entire melody is initially played by the oboe. The first half of the melody starts from the beginning and goes until the 30 second mark. The second half of the melody begins there and lasts until approximately the 1:02 second mark. At that point the brass instruments take over playing the first part of the melody. Choose the timing when the strings take over playing the second half of the melody.

   a. 1:20 seconds
   b. 1:32 seconds
   c. 2:10 seconds

Chapter 5

Songs

FOCUS POINTS

Western Art Song Tradition
Troubadour Songs
Lute Songs
Art Songs
Orchestral Songs
Song Cycles

Folk Song
Love Songs
Work Songs
Songs of War

Popular Song
Tin Pan Alley
Blues Songs
Jazz Songs
Rock and Roll
Urban Folk
R&B
Blues Rock
Metal
Country
Pop
Alternative
Hip-Hop/Rap

Some of the first sounds we hear in life are songs sung by our mothers. Our exposure to songs starts in infancy with lullabies and nursery rhymes and continues through school with patriotic songs, folk songs, and the popular songs of our time. We sing songs when we play children's games. Songs are an integral part of our growing experience, they help us remember facts and information. Learning the alphabet is easier when sung to the tune of *Twinkle, Twinkle Little Star* rather than trying to remember the sequence of letters without the aid of that simple melody. Songs form a bond between us, they tell our stories.

Beyond being a child's learning tool, songs have played a significant role in the development of culture and the recording of history. Before the written language there was the sung language, our connection to pre-history. The earliest fragments of written songs are more than two thousand years old, but the visual evidence of singing goes back even further, to statues and images more than a thousand years older. Throughout most of history the majority of people in the world did not know how to read or

Nocturne by Ben Shahn (1898–1969). Art © Estate of Ben Shahn/Licensed by VAGA, New York, NY. Image copyright © Scala/Art Resource, NY write. Information about culture, history, wars, and great events were often put into song form to facilitate remembering them. The cultural history of much of the world has been passed along through song. Today's popular songs are more likely to be love songs than historical epics but they still bind us one to another, connecting us in ways words or music alone cannot.

There is also something very personal about a song, a single voice communicating with anyone willing to listen. Songs express the most closely held thoughts and feelings we harbor within us. Through songs we can look into the minds and hearts of those who came before us as they reveal who they were and how they viewed the world. And by sharing their songs we connect with those from the past who, we often find, really weren't so different from ourselves. If the history of song teaches us anything it is that people have not changed that much over the centuries, and they share the same basic values across the expanse of the planet.

FOLK SONGS, ART SONGS, AND POPULAR SONGS

Songs can generally be classified as belonging to one of three categories; folk songs, art songs, or popular songs. For the purpose of our discussion, these categories will exclude songs (arias) such as you would find in an opera or a large-scale sacred vocal work since those types of songs have been discussed earlier.

Folk music icon Pete Seeger plays the banjo and sings at the Woody Guthrie Tribute Concert at Severance Hall in Cleveland. © Neal Preston/Corbis

A folk song is a traditional song of the people of a country or culture. Often a folk song exists without any original written version to document its origins. Folk songs usually consist of just the words and a melody. A written out accompaniment is not part of a folk song. Also, the composers of many folk songs are unknown, the songs having originated far back in a culture's history. Most folk songs are passed along from generation to generation through the oral tradition. One person sings the song and others pass it on as best they can remember it. This is a fairly unreliable method by which to pass along music. Subtle changes in the words and/or the music are common when music is passed along through the oral tradition. Folk songs are usually in a simple strophic form, a form in which repeated sections of music are played with changing text for each repetition. This form makes them especially easy to remember and pass along in this manner. Folk songs may also include a chorus—a section of a song with both a repeating melodic line as well as text.

For the purposes of our discussion an art song can be any composed song, from the Medieval period to the present, intended for concert or formal presentation. This would include the courtly songs of the Medieval through Baroque eras in addition to the traditional designation of these songs as coming from the Classical period to the present. Art songs exist in a fairly reliable written form. Sometimes the words are original, written by the composer himself, or they may be a pre-existing poem that has been set to music. Art songs usually have an accompaniment provided by an instrument such as the guitar, the lute (the forerunner of the guitar), or the piano. Art songs are often in strophic form, but they may also incorporate a chorus in addition to the verse. A more loosely structured format may also be used in an art song where there is no repeating verse or chorus. This type of through composed form allows the music to be presented in a way that may better illuminate the words as the story of the song unfolds.

The term "popular song" is a fairly recent invention dating from the late nineteenth century. That may seem like a long time ago to be considered recent, but in comparison to the history of both folk and art songs popular songs can be considered a relatively new kind of song. The emergence of a separate and distinct type of song in the late nineteenth century can be traced to the widespread ownership of pianos among the middle class in both Europe and the United States. An entire industry devoted to the printing of sheet music, written to be played and sung in the home by amateurs, developed at this time. This burgeoning industry helped popular songs become a centerpiece of social activity and enjoyment. The widespread availability of radios in the early twentieth century further accelerated the distribution of songs in a way that had heretofore been unimaginable, increasing the demand for printed music. The format for many early popular songs was basically strophic, sometimes with a chorus, with a fairly simple accompaniment. A variation on strophic form that achieved widespread popularity was the "aaba" form where the "a" sections were verses of repeating music with changing text and the "b" section consisted of different words set to a different melodic line. Contemporary popular songs usually consist of verses and choruses with an additional section called the bridge. The bridge is a short section of a song that is different melodically from either the verse or chorus and provides some variety to the repetitive nature of the verse and chorus structure. The extraordinary demand for popular music fueled the rise of an entire musical industry that reflected the diversity of American culture in the twentieth century. Jazz, rock and roll, R&B, country, and hip-hop are all outgrowths of this demand for popular songs.

REPRESENTATIVE FOLK SONGS

English Folk Songs

The traditional English folk song, *Greensleeves,* is constructed of both verses and a chorus. It is a lament over lost love. Its composition is sometimes attributed to King Henry VIII of England from the sixteenth century. This condensed version begins with a verse of text followed by the chorus. The second "verse" is simply hummed by the performer after which another statement of the chorus brings the song to a close. As you listen to this example can you tell what differences there are between the verses and the chorus?

Greensleeves—
Traditional English Folk Song (poss. Henry VIII of England, 1500s)

Verse
Alas, my love, you do me wrong,
To treat me so discourteously.
And I have loved you so long,
Delighting in your company.

Chorus

Greensleeves was all my joy
Greensleeves was my delight,
Greensleeves was my heart of gold,
And who but my lady Greensleeves.

Verse (hummed)

Chorus

The previous example was sung to a simple chordal accompaniment using a guitar and a bass. The accompaniment consisted of chords that were either strummed or arpeggiated. Arpeggiated means the notes of the chord were played one at a time rather than simultaneously. These are traditional acoustic instruments commonly used to accompany folk songs.

The following example is a British sea chantey, a type of work song historically sung by sailors to accompany their labor. This song was probably sung without any accompaniment while at sea, but in this version a recorder and guitar provide a spare introduction and accompaniment. *Blow the Man Down* has a rhythm that fit the motion of the labor involved, hauling lines on a ship. That is a typical characteristic of work songs. We also hear a type of singing common in much folk music, responsorial singing (also known as call and response). In this type of singing one voice, the leader, sings a line or two and that is answered by a group of voices with a musical response. This kind of performance practice is found all over the world in both the folk and religious music of many peoples. Both traditional Roman Catholic Church music and many contemporary African-American churches employ responsorial singing.

Blow the Man Down—
Traditional English Sea Chantey

What characteristics do the previous examples share? What are some differences between them? How are they different from songs that you know today? What are the similarities to songs today?

AFRICAN FOLK SONGS

One of the challenges we encounter when listening to folk music from other parts of the world is that it is often sung in languages that we don't understand. Do you think that vocal music written for other languages has inherently different characteristics from English language songs? What do you think those differences might be?

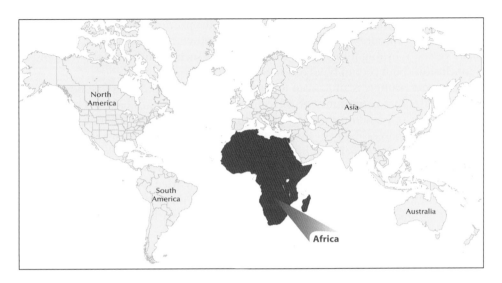

We will listen to two examples of African folk song, one in the language of the Shona people of southern Africa and one in English. The first song is *Gumbukumbu,* a tale of a young child walking with his mother from one village to another over a difficult hill. The mother encourages her son to be strong in order to complete the climb while cautioning that if he should fail his weakness will be reflected in his own children. This is a song that teaches the virtues of determination and being strong in the face of difficulties.

The song exhibits much repetition, like a song in a typical verse format. We hear several voices in this performance, one that seems to be more prominent, and the others which sing as a group in the background. Whenever the more prominent voice, the leader, sings the others respond to it. This is another example of responsorial singing as mentioned above. In many African-American churches in America the minister and the lead singers from the choir engage in a kind of musical conversation with the congregation and the rest of the choir. Exclamatory phrases by one of the leaders are followed by responses, both verbal and musical, from the remainder of the choir and the congregation.

An African mbira. Corel

Another performance characteristic of this song is the use of the mbira as an accompanying instrument. The mbira is sometimes called a "thumb piano." The instrument consists of a hollow box (it can be a wooden box or an empty dried out gourd of some kind) with metal strips of varying lengths attached to it. The number of metal strips that can fit on an mbira is somewhat limited due to its size, so the melodic use of the instrument is usually confined to providing a repetitive melodic motif rather than any extensive melodic or harmonic material. The metal strips are flipped by the thumbs to produce the changing pitches. There is a percussive aspect to the instrument as well. Seeds, dried beans, small rocks, or any small, hard objects may be placed inside the box creating a percussive effect when it is shaken.

 Gumbukumbu—
Traditional African Folk Song

Gumbukumbe, my mother's child, we are climbing a hill and we must keep fit and strong to go on climbing. If you don't take it seriously, you will never make it, or you may, but your children will not make it as you did.

The words of this song are not as extensive as the previous examples, just a couple of sentences. This allows the song to be learned much more easily than songs with many verses. Why might this be the case with songs such as this? Does this lead you to a conclusion about certain types of songs?

The next example is an African folk song sung in English. It was first heard in the United States in a community of African-American people, called the Gullah, who have lived on an island off the coast of South Carolina for many generations. The remoteness and inaccessibility of this island led to the development of a distinct dialect among the Gullah consisting of bits of African languages as well as English, in a curiously unique blend. Members of the Gullah community trace the origins of this song, *Kumbaya,* to their ancestral home in Africa. A clear written link has not been documented but that just reinforces the "folk" attributes of this song. The oral tradition by which it has been passed along through time is the primary link with the cultural origins of the song, not the written record.

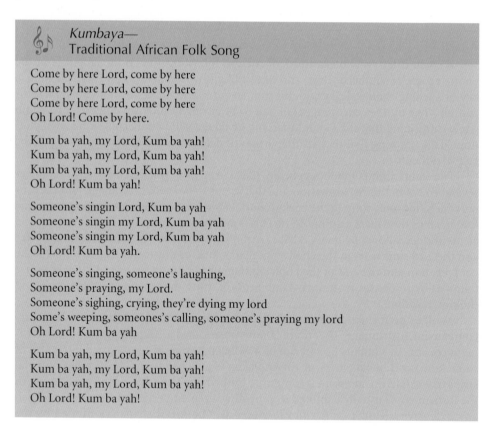

Kumbaya—
Traditional African Folk Song

Come by here Lord, come by here
Come by here Lord, come by here
Come by here Lord, come by here
Oh Lord! Come by here.

Kum ba yah, my Lord, Kum ba yah!
Kum ba yah, my Lord, Kum ba yah!
Kum ba yah, my Lord, Kum ba yah!
Oh Lord! Kum ba yah!

Someone's singin Lord, Kum ba yah
Someone's singin my Lord, Kum ba yah
Someone's singin my Lord, Kum ba yah
Oh Lord! Kum ba yah.

Someone's singing, someone's laughing,
Someone's praying, my Lord.
Someone's sighing, crying, they're dying my lord
Some's weeping, someones's calling, someone's praying my lord
Oh Lord! Kum ba yah

Kum ba yah, my Lord, Kum ba yah!
Kum ba yah, my Lord, Kum ba yah!
Kum ba yah, my Lord, Kum ba yah!
Oh Lord! Kum ba yah!

The accompaniment in this recording is entirely vocal. Harmony is provided by the group of accompanying voices in a responsorial style while a bass line is provided by a solo singer imitating the sound of an acoustic bass.

What Makes Music—Voices

Male Voices

The human voice is the most basic instrument. It is generally divided into four main types according to register (relative highness or lowness) and gender (male or female).

There are two commonly recognized male voices.

Tenor—The higher-pitched male voice.

Bass—The lower-pitched male voice.

There are a number of other types of male voices that are either extreme versions or gradations of the tenor and bass. The baritone has a range between the tenor and the bass. Another, more rare and quite remarkable, male voice is the basso profundo. This is a bass voice with an exceptional richness as well as the ability to reach notes lower than the normal range of a bass voice. At the other extreme is the counter tenor. This is an extremely high-pitched male voice, sometimes sung falsetto, a tone quality that is lighter and not as full-bodied as normal singing. A type of voice that was common during the Baroque period, but fell out of favor soon afterwards, was the castrato. A castrato was a male singer who had been castrated prior to puberty before the voice had changed from a high-pitched boy's voice to a lower-pitched man's voice. This was a very popular voice in the 17th and 18th centuries. The boy soprano is the voice of a young boy who has not reached puberty. This voice possesses a very pure tone and usually does not employ the use of vibrato.

Wayne Hu, Levi Hernandez, Steve Aiken, Eric Barry, and Matt Curran in a scene from Opera Memphis' 2012 production of *La Boheme* by Giacomo Puccini.
Photo courtesy of Opera Memphis, Sean Davis photographer.

The mature male voices (of today), in order from highest to lowest:

Counter Tenor
Tenor
Baritone
Bass
Basso Profundo

AMERICAN FOLK SONGS

Once in America, both English and African peoples developed folk music that reflected their separate heritages and living conditions. The descendants of Europeans sang songs they brought with them from Europe but also created new songs dealing with the westward settlement of the North American continent, love songs and songs inspired by the Revolutionary and Civil Wars. Songs of African descendants often reflected the difficulties inherent in being an enslaved population and the yearning for freedom that was their strongest desire. This was often reflected in songs that expressed a strong belief in the benevolence of a loving God who would ultimately deliver them from their oppression but also in words of striking sadness and pain.

Folk Song Inspired by War

The Cruel War is a song from the American Revolution which has resurfaced during subsequent conflicts, especially during the Vietnam War. It expresses the pain of separation felt by those who remain at home when young men go off to fight. The typical verse structure is augmented by a

The Wounded Drummer Boy by Eastman Johnson (1824–1906).
Copyright © Scala/Art Resource, NY

repeating phrase at the end of each verse. This is not quite a fully separate chorus, but serves essentially the same function.

The Cruel War—
Traditional Folk Song

The cruel war is raging, Johnny has to fight
I want to be with him from morning 'til night.
I want to be with him, it grieves my heart so,
Won't you let me go with you?
No, my love, no.

I'll go to your Captain, get down upon my knees,
Ten thousand gold guineas I give for your release.
Ten thousand gold guineas, it grieves my heart so,
Won't you let me go with you?
No, my love, no.

Tomorrow is Sunday, Monday is the day
That your Captain calls for you, you must obey.
Your Captain calls for you, it grieves my heart so,
Won't you let me go with you?
No, my love, no.

Johnny, oh Johnny, I think you are unkind,
I love you far better than all humankind.
I love you far better than tongue can e're express.
Won't you let me go with you?
Yes, my love, yes.

I'll pull back my hair, men's clothing I'll put on.
I'll pass for your comrade as we march along.
I'll pass for your comrade, and none will ever guess.
Won't you let me go with you?
Yes, my love, yes.

Folk Song Born of Slavery

All the Pretty Little Horses may be familiar to many readers but probably not with the complete, original lyrics. Many people today have heard this song as a lullaby when they were children. When sung as a lullaby only the first verse is sung. But the second verse contains some emotionally powerful lyrics not suitable for a calming lullaby. The song is a musical snapshot of a painful era in our country's history. A slave mother who worked in the slave owner's house would often have to leave her newborn child in the fields with others while she tended to the master's home. This song captures the pain she must have felt hearing her baby crying out to her from the primitive conditions of the field.

All the Pretty Little Horses—
Traditional Folk Song

Hush-a-bye don't you cry
Go to sleep, little baby.
When you wake you shall have
All the pretty little horses.
Blacks and bays, dapples and grays
All the pretty little horses.

Way down yonder in the meadow
Lies a poor little lambie.
Bees and the butterflies picking on its eyes
Poor little thing is crying mammy.
Blacks and bays, dapples and grays
All the pretty little horses.
When you wake you shall have
All the pretty little horses.

The **spiritual** is a kind of folk song of the African-American people of the southern United States that is often based on a biblical story. Spirituals emphasize a strong belief in God's goodness and his eventual deliverance of the enslaved people from the bonds of slavery. To hear an example of the spiritual listen again to *Brother Mosely Crossed (Smote) the Water* from Chapter 2.

Folk Song to Accompany Work

Folk songs were often associated with the trade or labor of common people. These **work songs** were sung by laborers in the course of performing their work or as a testimonial to the kind of work they did, and constitute a significant portion of the folk songs in existence.

The story of John Henry has as many variations as there are versions of the song. This "steel driving man" was the epitome of strength, a symbol of the slaves' hope of overcoming their bondage. It recounts the efforts of a black man who could beat the white man's steam-driven machine, even if it cost him his life. This song is an excellent example of the transformations that a song can go through over the years when it is passed down through the oral tradition. Several versions of the song are included in your playlist. Listen to the first few verses of each version. Note how not only the words change from one version to another but how the melody itself is quite different. What does this tell you about the authenticity of folk songs? Do you think the versions we know today are the way they sounded years ago?

John Henry—
Traditional American Work Song

What can we learn from these folk songs about songs in general? What are some common characteristics of the songs we have heard?

Folk songs are the musical lifeblood of a people. Love, work, freedom, faith, these are the recurring themes of folk songs shared by people the world over. Whether they come from England, Africa, America, or any number of other cultures, these songs share similar concepts of structure and performance. All are based to some degree on verses of text, sometimes with choruses. Is that a concept that spread from one culture to another around the world, or is it something so basic to the singing of songs that it has emerged independently wherever people have gathered in song?

A Unique Type of Folk Song

Bulgarian Folk Song

Bulgarian folk song came to the attention of most of the world in the 1990s after the release of a set of recordings called *Le Mystère des Voix Bulgares (The Mysterious Voices of Bulgaria)*. The music presented on these recordings was for the most part traditional Bulgarian folk songs performed not by untrained villagers from the countryside, but by highly specialized singers in sophisticated arrangements for women's choir. Folk singing has been a long-established tradition in Bulgaria and is an important part of everyday life. All aspects of Bulgarian life, the good as well as the difficult, are represented by songs, and children in school are taught the culture's folk songs from a very young age.

The folk songs of Bulgaria differ significantly from those of other cultures in that they employ musical concepts that are difficult to perform, such as singing dissonant intervals. In most folk music, the harmony is very basic and almost exclusively consonant; that is, the combinations of pitches sound pleasant together. These pleasant, consonant intervals are referred to as thirds (notes that are three notes of a scale apart) and fifths (notes that are five notes of a scale apart). But, in Bulgarian folk music, we often hear dissonant harmonies consisting of intervals of seconds and sevenths (two and seven notes of a scale apart, respectively), the most grating combinations of pitches, and the most difficult for singers to perform. Adding to the difficulty of executing these types of harmonies is the fact that they are often performed by massed voices in choirs, especially women's choirs. Each of the singers in these ensembles must be of the highest caliber in order for the music to achieve the desired result.

And that result is truly exceptional. As you listen to the following example take note of how the music alternates between consonant and dissonant, how the rhythm is very flexible, without a constant pulse, and how the quality of the voices is exceptionally piercing. The effect is at once hypnotic, chilling, and beautiful. This song was written early in the twentieth century when Bulgaria was fighting for its independence from the Ottoman Empire.

Pilentze Pee (Little Bird)—
Traditional Bulgarian Folk Song. Translated by Milena Albrecht.

Little bird singing and saying,
here are the powerful firearms,
here are the sharp swords.
Big field,
behind the field
in a green forest
on a big tall tree,
little bird is singing and saying,
whoever has a vigorous horse
to ride it,
whoever has a beautiful girl
to love her.
There are rebellious years coming
until the end of our souls.

ART SONGS IN THE WESTERN HISTORICAL PERIODS

During the Medieval (500–1450) period there were a large number of songs written by members of the nobility exalting both a pure, chivalrous love for women and a heavenly devotion to the church through participation in the Crusades. France was a particularly active center for the writing of these songs. The poet/musician/noblemen from the southern part of France who wrote these songs were called troubadours, while those from the north were called trouvéres. These terms can be interpreted as meaning "inventors." The songs they wrote have notated melodies but the rhythm is often unclear. There may be some kind of accompaniment indicated or not, leaving the performance of their songs open to widely varying interpretation. By their nature "troubadour songs" (a convenient term applicable to songs of this type) were best suited for performance inside private residences or in small outdoor venues.

A Troubadour before a Royal Couple. From *Las Cantigas de Santa Maria* by Alfonso el Sabio. Thirteenth century. Copyright © Bridgeman-Giraudon/Art Resource, NY

The Renaissance (1450–1600) witnessed the emergence of a widely popular kind of song called the lute song. Especially prominent in England and Italy, the lute song consisted of a vocal part accompanied by a lute, the forerunner of the modern guitar. The accompaniments for these songs were either written out by the composer or indicated simply by the designation of an appropriate harmony, leaving the exact performance interpretation up to the performer. Just as in the songs from the Medieval period there is some room for individual interpretation of the accompaniment.

During the Baroque (1600–1750) period the majority of songs were written for inclusion within larger genres such as operas, oratorios, or cantatas. While independent songs were indeed written during this period, notably by the English composers Henry Purcell and John Blow, they have not maintained a place of prominence in the repertory of singers today. The principal contribution to song writing from this time period was an emphasis on the emotional content of the text.

The Classical (1750–1825) period, especially the years toward the end of the era, was the time when the independent art song was established as a major vocal genre. The Austrian composer Franz Schubert (1797–1828) was the most prominent composer in this genre. His art songs, fully composed for both voice and piano, elevated the piano from simply an accompanying instrument to a full partner in the dramatic narrative of each song. That was the concept Romantic period composers inherited and accepted as the model for the genre.

Composers of the Romantic (1825–1900) period continued to employ the style Schubert developed for the art song but incorporated an ever more adventurous harmonic palette typical of music of the late nineteenth century. Austria and Germany became the countries where the majority of art songs were composed during this time, and it became common to use the German word for art songs, lieder, when discussing these works. An innovation of this time pertaining to lieder was the composition of these songs with orchestral accompaniment instead of piano by composers such as Gustav Mahler. This took the art song out of the relatively intimate performance venues it had always resided in and into the concert hall for larger audiences.

During the twentieth century the art song was eclipsed as a significant genre by the popular song. However, some notable contributions to the genre were made by American composers Aaron Copland (1900–1990), and Ned Rorem (b. 1923).

A Medieval Troubadour Song

Conon de Bethune (ca. 1150–1220) was a twelfth-century French nobleman whose song, *Ahi! Amours* (*Alas Love*), is an excellent example of a Medieval troubadour song. It gives us a clear picture of the mindset of someone in Bethune's position from that time in history touching on the topics of courtly love and duty to the church through participation in the Crusades. The Crusades were a series of church-sponsored military campaigns that began in 1096 and continued for almost two hundred years (though several minor crusades were mounted well into the seventeenth century). These massive undertakings were bound for the Middle East for the purpose of re-establishing Christian control over the Holy Land.

In *Ahi! Amours* the singer expresses his pain at leaving the woman he loves while recounting his obligation to do God's bidding. As a healthy, rich man he must travel to the Holy Land to take back Jerusalem from the "Turks." The song describes those who must go on the Crusades and those who are exempt. In addition, it adds a rebuke to those who stay behind and "sin with cowards and wicked men . . ." The song paints a vivid picture of the world in which Bethune lived. The performance included in your playlist makes use of two rebecs, early forerunners of the violin family, a lute and a tabor, a small percussion instrument. The song is basically strophic with short instrumental interludes that connect the verses as well as serving as a short introduction. Is this performance an authentic recreation of the way Bethune intended it? Perhaps not, but it certainly *could* have been performed in this manner.

Ahi! Amours (Alas Love)—
Conon de Bethune, ca. 1150–1220

Ahi! Amours, con dure departie me convendra faire pour la meillour ki onques fust amee ne servie! Deus me ramaint a li par sa doucour las! Qu'ai j edit? Ja ne m'en part je mie; ains va mes cors servir nostre seignour, Mes cuers remaint del tout en sa baillie.	Alas! Love, what a hard parting I shall have to make from the best lady ever to be loved and served! May God in his goodness bring me back to her as surely as it is true that I leave her with great pain; Alas! What have I said? I am not leaving her; even if my body goes to serve our Lord, my heart remains entirely at her service.

Tuit li clergie et li home d'eage,	The clergy and old men
ki en aumosne et en bien fait manront,	who will be diligent in doing good works
partiront tuit a cest pelerinage,	will also take part in this pilgrimage;
et la dames qui chastement vivront.	And so will the ladies who will live chastely
at loiaute font a cues qui I vont,	If they keep faith with those
et s'eles font par mal conseil folage,	who are going overseas.
a lasches genz et mauvais le feront,	If they sin they will sin with cowards
car tuit li bon iront en cest voyage.	For all good men will be on this journey.
Deus est assis en son saint iretage:	God is besieged in His holy inheritance.
ore I parra con cil le secorront,	This is the hour when we shall show how those
cui il jeta de la prison ombrage,	whom He saved from the cross
quant il fu mors en la crois que Turc ont.	which the Turks have taken will help Him.
sachiez, cil sont trop honi qui n'iront,	Those who do not leave will be dishonored
s'il n'ont poverte ou vieillece ou malage:	unless they are held back by poverty, old age or sickness;
et cil qui sain joene et riche sont	those who are healthy, young and rich
ne pueent pas demorer sans hontage.	Cannot remain here without shame.
Las! Je m'en vois plorant des ieus du front	Alas! I go weeping bitterly to that place
la u Deus veut amender mon corage,	where God wants to purify my heart;
et sachiez bien qu'a le meillour du mont	I know that on this journey I will think of the best person
penserai plus que ne faz a voyage.	That is on this earth, more than I can say.

A Renaissance Lute Song

The **lute song** of the Renaissance was a courtly song prominent among English composers such as John Dowland, Phillip Rosseter, and Thomas Campion. During this time it was expected that educated people at court should be able to both sing and play an instrument. The lute song was the perfect vehicle for exhibiting one's ability in music. The following song describes the virtues of a simple country girl, Amaryllis, as contrasted with the vain needs of the sophisticated ladies at court. It is a short song composed of verses and a chorus. It is easy to imagine it being sung by a gentleman at court with a limited vocal range and an adequate ability on the lute.

A lute player—the lute was the most popular instrument during the Renaissance. Corel

 I Care Not for These Ladies—
Thomas Campion, 1567–1620

I care not for these ladies
That must be wooed and prayed
Give me sweet Amaryllis
The wanton country maid,
Nature Art disdaineth,
Her beauty is her own:

Chorus
And when we court and kiss
She cries 'Forsooth, let go!'
But when we come where comfort is
She never will say no.

(continued)

If I love Amaryllis
She brings me fruit and flowers
But if we love these ladies
We must bring golden showers
Give them gold that sell love
Give me the nut-brown lass

Chorus

These ladies must have pillows
And beds by strangers wrought
Give me a bower of willows
Of moss and leaves unbought,
And fresh Amaryllis
On milk and honey fed,

Chorus

A Classical/Romantic Art Song

Franz Schubert (1797–1828) was a prolific Austrian composer of art songs of the late Classical and early Romantic periods who composed over 600 works in this genre. The subjects of Schubert's lieder cover the gamut of human emotion and experience, from common love songs to supernatural tales and silly ditties. One of Schubert's contributions in elevating the art song from a short, relatively minor musical genre to one of larger significance was the development of the song cycle, a collection of songs that shared a common theme. Schubert's song cycle, *Winterreise* (*A Winter's Journey*), is a poignant and moving collection of songs dealing with lost love and despair. Almost all of Schubert's lieder are for voice with piano, but the piano is much more of an equal partner in these works rather than just a vehicle for harmonic accompaniment. The piano often plays an introduction that sets a definite mood before the first word is sung and provides vivid musical motives representing ideas or images described in the songs. Most of the songs are in strophic form, but some are through composed, unfolding as the story does. The following example is through composed and presents imagery that is dark and sinister, typical of many Romantic period composers' obsession with things of that sort. The words are by Schubert's contemporary, Johann Wolfgang von Goethe, and the story plays on the fears that all children have of the "Boogeyman." Even as adults this story has the ability to put a knot in our stomachs through the emotional and dramatic presentation of the musical and poetic material. And that was the essence of the Romantic period, emotion and drama. Most music of that time was intended to make the listener "feel" something, even if that something was unsettling.

Schubert at the Piano by Gustav Klimt (1862–1918).
Copyright © Erich Lessing/Art Resource, NY

Biographical Spotlight

Franz Schubert.
© 2013, Nicku, Shutterstock, Inc.

Franz Schubert

Franz Peter Schubert was born on January 31, 1797, in what is now Vienna, Austria, and died there on November 19, 1828. His short life was marked by long stretches of relative poverty ameliorated by the kindness of a supportive group of friends and admirers. He often resided in the homes of these friends for extended periods of time in order to save on expenses. He lived during the waning years of the Classical period and was instrumental in the move toward the style that would come to mark the Romantic era.

Schubert received some early musical training from his father, a schoolmaster, and his older brother. He attended a school for aspiring singers, the Stadtkonvikt, where his abilities were better able to flourish with the result being his scholarship-financed education as a member of the Imperial Court Chapel Choir. Schubert's teachers included the most influential composer at the court, Antonio Salieri. He learned the violin, and became the leader of the school's orchestra, sang in the choir, and became an adept conductor. Just when all seemed on track for a brilliant musical career the 15-year-old Schubert's changing voice forced his departure from the school. He soon enrolled in a teacher's college and upon graduation obtained a position at his father's school. He never stopped composing while half-heartedly pursuing a teaching career, and as soon as his music began to gain some measure of success he abandoned teaching to compose exclusively.

Schubert's life was devoted to composing music above all else. He tried to support himself in the manner of other composers of his day who did not have a court appointment, by giving music lessons to pupils, staging concerts, and publishing his music, but he was not successful in any of these endeavors, and did not pursue them for any length of time. He relied on the benevolence of his friends and family who always came to his aid, providing temporary homes and financial support. As his music became increasingly well known he was better able to financially fend for himself. He gained a devoted following among the wealthy in Vienna, and musical gatherings centered around his presence and his music, dubbed "Schubertiads," became the high point of upper class socializing.

Schubert was a prolific composer in most of the major genres of his time. His 600+ lieder were only the most exceptional among hundreds of compositions that he produced in an endless stream one after the other. He wrote over a hundred works for the piano and for piano four-hands (piano duets), dozens of sacred works including six complete masses, nine complete symphonies, and numerous chamber works. While his nearly twenty dramatic works for the stage never found an accepting audience, it was the human element inherent in his lieder that was to become the hallmark of the Romantic period.

The last four years of Schubert's life were marked by an ongoing battle with his failing health while still writing some of his most celebrated music. It is believed he died from syphilis and the effects of mercury poisoning, which was a common treatment at the time. His legacy as a composer continued to grow after his death, and today he is regarded as one of the greatest of the Austrian composers.

Biographical Spotlight Exercise

Instructions: Log in to the textbook web site and click on the **Assignments** tab. Click on **Chapter 5** and scroll to the **Biographical Spotlight area**. Answer the question based on the information in the biography above.

Which type of music of Schubert's never found an accepting audience?

1. Dramatic works for the stage
2. Art songs
3. Chamber works

Erlkönig (The Erlking)—*
Franz Schubert

Erlkönig

Wer reitet so spaet durch Nacht und Wind?
Es ist der Vater mit seinem Kind;
Er hat den Knaben wohl in dem Arm,
Er fasst ihm sicher, er haelt ihm warm.

"Mein Sohn, was birgst du so bang dein Gesicht?" -
Siehst, Vater, du den Erlkoenig nicht?
Den Erlenkoenig mit Kron' und Schweif? -
"Mein Sohn, es ist ein Nebelstreif."

(The Erl-King Speaks)
"Du liebes Kind, komm, geh mit mir!
Gar Schoene Spiele, spiel' ich mit dir;
Manch' bunte Blumen sind an dem Strand,
Meine Mutter hat manch guelden Gewand."

Mein Vater, mein Vater, und hoerest du nicht,
Was Erlenkoenig mir leise verspricht? -
"Sei ruhig, bleibe ruhig, mein Kind;
In duerren Blaettern saeuselt der Wind."

(Erl-King)
"Willst feiner Knabe, du mit mir gehn?
Meiner toechter sollen dich warten schoen;
Meiner toechter fuehren den naechtlichen Reihn,
Und wiegen und tanzen und singen dich ein."

Mein Vater, mein Vater, und siehst du nicht dort
Erlkoenigs Toechter am duestern Ort? -
"Mein Sohn, mein Sohn, ich seh' es genau:
Es scheinen die alten Weiden so grau."

Erl-King
"Ich liebe dich, mich reizt deine schoene Gestalt;
Und bist du nicht willig, so brauch' ich Gewalt."
Mein Vater, mein Vater, jetzt fasst er mich an!
Erlkoenig hat mir ein Leids getan! -

Dem Vater grauset's, er reitet geschwind,
Er haelt in Armen das aechzende Kind,
Erreicht den Hof mit mueh' und Noth;
In seinen Armen da Kind war todt.

Johann Wolfgang von Goethe (1749–1832)

The Erl King

O who rides by night thro' the woodland so wild?
It is the fond father embracing his child;
And close the boy nestles within his loved arm,
To hold himself fast, and to keep himself warm.

"My boy, upon what dost thou fearfully gaze?"
"O father, see yonder! see yonder!" he says;
"O, 'tis the Erl-King with his crown and his shroud."
"No, my son, it is but a dark wreath of the cloud."

(The Erl-King Speaks)
"O come and go with me, thou loveliest child;
By many a gay sport shall thy time be beguiled;
My mother keeps for thee many a fair toy,
And many a fine flower shall she pluck for my boy."

"O father, my father, and did you not hear
The Erl-King whisper so low in my ear?"
"Be still, my heart's darling—my child, be at ease;
It was but the wild blast as it sung thro' the trees."

(Erl-King)
"O wilt thou go with me, thou loveliest boy?
My daughter shall tend thee with care and with joy;
She shall bear thee so lightly thro' wet and thro' wild,
And press thee, and kiss thee, and sing to my child."

"O father, my father, and saw you not plain
The Erl-King's pale daughter glide past thro' the rain?"
"Oh yes, my loved treasure, I knew it full soon;
It was the grey willow that danced to the moon."

Erl-King
"O come and go with me, no longer delay,
Or else, silly child, I will drag thee away."
"O father! O father! now, now, keep your hold,
The Erl-King has seized me—his grasp is so cold!"

Sore trembled the father; he spurr'd thro' the wild,
Clasping close to his bosom his shuddering child;
He reaches his dwelling in doubt and in dread,
But, clasp'd to his bosom, the infant was dead.

Translated by Sir Walter Scott.

---

*The English text provided here is a freely interpreted translation typical of the time period. For a more modern translation please see the Appendix.

What do you think the repeating piano notes of the introduction represent? What sort of challenges does the singer have to confront in performing this piece? What do you think of the ending? What literary or musical devices did the composer use to paint this musical picture for the listener? Was he successful in your opinion? Why or why not?

Did you enjoy this piece? It's definitely not a "pleasant" piece of music. You probably can't remember a tune from it either. Do those things make it un-enjoyable? Think about how this piece differs from all of the songs listened to previously. Is this song fundamentally different or only marginally so? List the qualities that this song shares with the other songs and the qualities that differentiate it. Which kind of song do you like better? Why?

Art Songs with Orchestral Accompaniment

The Romantic period was a time of extremes in music. Composers frequently attempted to do new things or try old things in new ways. The art song had traditionally been written for a solo voice with a minimal instrumental accompaniment, a piano, a lute, etc. But the Romantic period mindset had composers thinking big. **Gustav Mahler** (1860–1911), a late Romantic Austrian composer, wrote numerous songs for voice with orchestral accompaniment. Often these compositions were groups of songs dealing with a common theme, an orchestral song cycle. *Das Lied Von Der Erde* (*The Song of the Earth*) *Lieder eines fahrenden Gesellen* (*Songs of a Wayfarer*), *Das Knaben Wunderhorn* (*The Young Boy's Magic Horn*) and *Kindertotenlieder* (*Songs on the Death of Children*) are song cycles Mahler composed with orchestral accompaniment.

The Romantic period composer's preoccupation with mortality is evident in much of Mahler's work, *Songs on the Death of Children,* being perhaps the most difficult subject matter ever confronted. The *Song of the Earth* is representative of the orchestral song cycles of Mahler. It is scored (written) for both tenor and alto soloists and a large orchestra. It is a personal statement of resignation in the face of the difficulties of life. Mahler wrote *Das Lied* in 1908 soon after the tragic death of his four-year-old daughter as well as other personal setbacks. The fifth song of the six-song cycle, "The Drunkard in Spring," conveys the despair the narrator feels in the face of life's hardships by hiding in the stupor of drunkenness. Many Romantic period artists held a similarly bleak outlook on life and turned to various drugs as a palliative for their woes.

"The Drunkard in Spring" from *Das Lied Von Der Erde*— Gustav Mahler

Wenn nur ein Traum das Leben ist,	If life is only a dream,
Warum denn Müh und Plag?	why then toil and trouble?
Ich trinke, bis ich nicht mehr kann,	I drink until I can no longer,
Den ganzen, lieben Tag!	all the lovely day!
Und wenn ich nicht mehr trinken kann,	And if I cannot drink,
Weil Kehl und Seele voll,	because my throat and soul are full,
So tauml' ich bis zu meiner Tür	I stagger to my door
Und schlafe wundervoll!	and sleep wonderfully!
Was hör ich beim Erwachen? Horch!	What do I hear when I awake?
Ein Vogel singt im Baum.	Listen! A bird singing in the tree.
Ich frag ihn, ob schon Frühling sei,	I ask him whether it is already spring—
Mir ist als wie im Traum.	To me, it's like a dream.
Der Vogel zwitschert: "Ja! Der Lenz	The bird twitters, "Yes! Spring
Ist da, sei kommen über Nacht!"	is there, it came over night!"
Aus tiefstem Schauen lausch ich auf,	From the depths of concentration I listen,
Der Vogel singt und lacht!	the bird sings and laughs!

(continued)

Ich fülle mir den Becher neu	I fill my cup again
Und leer ihn bis zum Grund	and empty it to the bottom
Und singe, bis der Mond erglänzt	and sing, until the moon shines
Am schwarzen Firmament!	in the black firmament!
Und wenn ich nicht mehr singen kann,	And when I can sing no more,
So schlaf ich wieder ein,	I fall asleep again,
Was geht mich denn der Frühling an!?	for what do I care about spring?
Laßt mich betrunken sein!	Let me be drunk!

How did the art song change from the Medieval period through the Romantic? What characteristics, if any, were constant throughout that time? What characteristics were unique to different historical periods?

THE EMERGENCE OF POPULAR SONG

The nineteenth century was a pivotal time in the history of western music. It was during that era that the seeds of change were sowed that lead to the emergence of popular music as the predominant music of the twentieth century. The increasing popularity of a less complex, more immediately appealing, style of music was fueled by song writers eager to provide sheet music for home performances by amateurs. The presence of a piano in the home was a status symbol of the time, and informal gatherings to sing songs were a common social activity. Until the mid-nineteenth century the musical world in America was a secondary afterthought to the longstanding musical traditions of Europe. The absence of cultural allegiances to certain musical styles allowed music in America to evolve in a way not aligned with the aristocratic ties of Europe. The American people were more accepting of music less sophisticated than their European counterparts. Consequently, the emergence of popular music was primarily an American phenomenon.

Stephen Foster

A portrait of American song composer Stephen Collins Foster, attributed to Thomas Hicks (1823–1890). Copyright © National Portrait Gallery, Smithsonian Institution/ Art Resource, NY

Stephen Foster (1826–1864) was an American songwriter whose best known songs include *Oh! Susanna, Old Folks at Home, Jeanie with the Light Brown Hair, Camptown Races* and *Beautiful Dreamer*. While offense is often taken today at some of the lyrics used by Foster when referring to African-Americans of his time, he was, in reality, at the forefront of changing attitudes about African-Americans. His portrayal of African-Americans as having the same feelings, desires, and ideals as whites was novel and provocative, especially when those songs were often written for Minstrel Shows. His reference to an African-American slave woman in the song, *Nelly Was a Lady*, as a "lady" presented her as an equal to anyone. Foster's songs often conjured up sentimental feelings of home, love, and the land, especially the South. While it may be easy to assume from his songs that Foster was a Southerner he was in fact born in Pittsburgh and spent most of his life there and in New York, where he died in 1864.

A simple melody and accompaniment are the hallmarks of American popular song of the nineteenth century. A common form used in many popular songs of the time was "aaba" over the course of 32 bars (measures) of music applied to each verse, as in the example on page 137.

PERSPECTIVE—WORDS IN SONG

Songs are most often described as words set to music, implying that the words exist first and stir some musical inspiration in a composer with the result of the association being a song. That has indeed been the predominant process by which songs have come into existence throughout history. In the case where the same person writes both the text and the music, most often the words have come first and the music created to appropriately illuminate the words.

There are, however, exceptions to this common practice. In the case of songwriting teams, such as in the writing of musicals and contemporary popular song, the process may be truly collaborative. Both the words and the music emerge from this symbiotic relationship more or less concurrently. Also, a traditional existent melody may be given a new text specifically created to fit that tune. This practice is fairly common in the creation of National Anthems, our own being a prime example. (See Chapter 7 for details.)

Most composers of art songs have relied on the poetry of others as the textual basis of their songs. Franz Schubert (1797–1828) relied on the poetry of his German contemporaries such as Wilhelm Müller (1794–1827), Ludwig Rellstab (1799–1860), Heinrich Heine (1797–1856), and Johann Wolfgang Goethe (1749–1832) for many of his lieder. American composer Aaron Copland's (1900–1990) setting of the poetry of Emily Dickinson (1830–1886) is noteworthy for the way the music captures the unique nuances of Dickinson's verse. Benjamin Britten (1913–1976) set fellow Englishman William Blake's (1757–1827) *Songs and Proverbs* in song form. Blake's *Songs of Innocence and Experience* have been set to music by musicians as widely divergent as contemporary classical composer, William Bolcom (b. 1938), and the Mexican progressive rock band, Anda al Sinaia.

The relationship between words and music however is sometimes an uneasy one. For example, perhaps the most renowned composer of art songs of the past fifty years, American composer Ned Rorem, in an interview in 1998 said, ". . . a song is a bastard. It is uniting two art forms that didn't ask to be forced together." Rorem went on to describe how there is more than one way to set a given text to music. For one commissioned work he set each of eight different poems to music twice. Each of the two settings was purposely quite different from the other, giving the same words different meanings.

A relatively new poetic/musical form of expression is the setting of poetry to a musical background without assigning a melodic line to the text. This type of poetry reading to music has grown in acceptance over the last fifty years and has produced a musical experience of significant contemporary relevance. The poetry of the "beat generation" of the 1950s and 1960s was often read in coffeehouses with a minimal, sometimes improvised, musical accompaniment. The poems were often statements of personal reflections or societal observations. Over the past several decades that format has evolved into one of somewhat more structure with the words being carefully placed within a composed musical framework. In this structure the words become an integral part of the musical experience without being musical. That is, the words have no imposed melodic component thrust upon them, remaining pure poetry within a musical context. The jazz-inspired work of poet Robert Creeley (1926–2005) in collaboration with composer/bassist Steve Swallow (b. 1940) is significant in this genre. Poet Sekou Sundiata's work exploring the experience and customs of black culture has a funkier, Afro-Cuban, musical genesis.

Perhaps the wedding of words to music and the unique characteristics of each was best summed up by Bob Dylan in the liner notes to his 1963 album, *The Freewheelin' Bob Dylan*. As part of his description of the creative process he said, "Anything I can sing . . . I call a song. Anything I can't sing I call a poem."

Songs

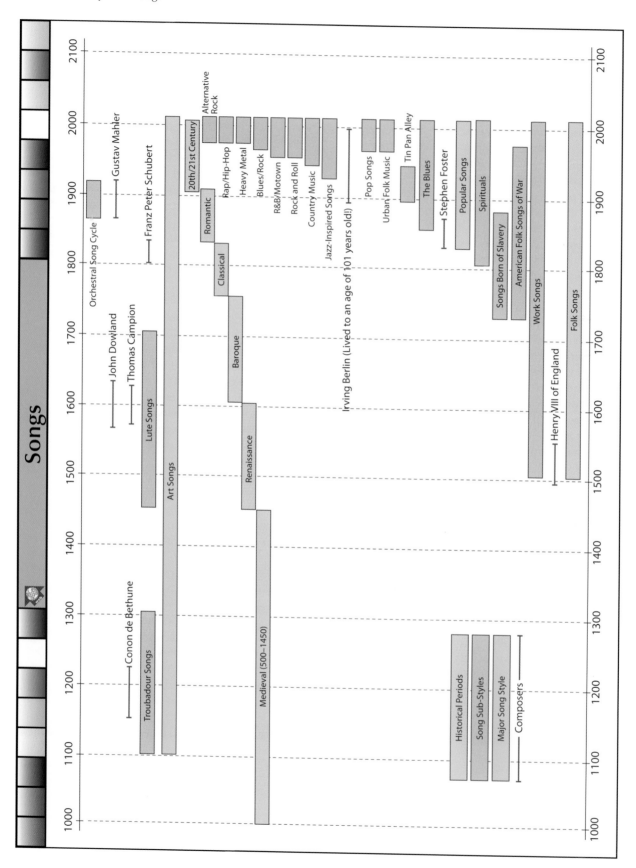

Troubadour Songs

Conon de Bethune

John Dowland

Thomas Campion

Lute Songs

Franz Peter Schubert

Gustav Mahler

Orchestral Song Cycle

Art Songs

Medieval (500–1450)

Renaissance

Baroque

Classical

Romantic

20th/21st Century

Alternative Rock

Rap/Hip-Hop

Heavy Metal

Blues/Rock

R&B/Motown

Rock and Roll

Country Music

Jazz-Inspired Songs

Irving Berlin (Lived to an age of 101 years old!)

Pop Songs

Urban Folk Music

Tin Pan Alley

The Blues

Stephen Foster

Popular Songs

Spirituals

Songs Born of Slavery

American Folk Songs of War

Work Songs

Henry VIII of England

Folk Songs

Historical Periods

Song Sub-Styles

Major Song Style

Composers

> ♪ *Jeanie with the Light Brown Hair—*
> Stephen Foster
>
> | | |
> |---|---|
> | I dream of Jeanie with the light brown hair, | *a*–8 bars |
> | Borne, like a vapor, on the summer air; | |
> | I see her tripping where the bright streams play, | *a*–8 bars |
> | Happy as the daisies that dance on her way. | |
> | Many were the wild notes her merry voice would pour, | *b*–8 bars |
> | Many were the blithe birds that warbled them o'er: | |
> | Oh! I dream of Jeanie with the light brown hair, | *a*–8 bars |
> | Floating, like a vapor, on the soft summer air. | |

THE BLUES

The nineteenth century was the formative period for the style of music called the **blues**. Primarily a vocal genre, the blues grew out of the African-American slave culture of the southern United States. The lyrics often focused on the difficulties inherent in the challenging life experiences of the slave underclass. Broken homes, broken love, and broken lives became the stories of the blues. In this regard the blues can be viewed as an authentic folk music style, having grown out of the life experiences of a culture. But it is for what the blues led to in regard to popular music of the twentieth century that sets it apart from traditional folk music. The blues became the bedrock of rock and roll. Two qualities of the blues stand out as important for their incorporation into popular music of the twentieth century, a repeating **chord progression** that was the framework of each verse, called the **twelve-bar blues**, and instrumental **improvisation**.

Twelve-Bar Blues Chord Progression

A brief discussion of the twelve-bar blues format for blues songs is important because it became the basic structure for so much popular music of the twentieth century. The form of a blues song is based on a repeating harmonic pattern, a chord progression. This recognizable sequence of chords underlies the melody, and the same chord progression is repeated for the changing words of each verse. In order to understand the sequence of chords in the twelve-bar blues chord progression we need to understand how chords are named.

Empress of the Blues by Romare Bearden (1914–1988). Art © Romare Bearden Foundation/Licensed by VAGA, New York, NY. Image copyright © Smithsonian American Art Museum, Washington, DC/Art Resource, NY

Chord Names

A chord that is built upon the first note of a scale is called the I chord. The chords built upon subsequent notes of the scale are called by the corresponding Roman numerals as well. For example, if a chord is built on the fourth note of a scale it is called the IV chord. The fifth note of the scale, the V chord. Most blues songs use these three chords in a specific sequence. The I chord is played first for four bars (measures), each of which has four beats. For example, if you feel the rhythmic beats of a blues song in groups of four, and count four of those groupings (bars) of beats, all of that music will have the same harmony, the I chord. At that point the chord changes to the IV chord for two bars, bars 5 and 6. The chord then changes back to the I chord for two bars, the V chord for one bar, the IV chord for one bar, and then back to the I chord for two bars for a total of twelve bars. That is a basic twelve-bar blues chord progression.

The diagram below shows a typical twelve-bar blues format. The top line represents the twelve bars with the first beat of each measure in bold face. The second line is simply a representation of each beat within each bar. The third line shows the chord that is played during each bar. The chords in parentheses are alternate possibilities.

1234	**2**234	**3**234	**4**234	**5**234	**6**234	**7**234	**8**234	**9**234	**10**234	**11**234	**12**234
/ / / /	/ / / /	/ / / /	/ / / /	/ / / /	/ / / /	/ / / /	/ / / /	/ / / /	/ / / /	/ / / /	/ / / /
I	(IV)	(I)		IV		I		V	IV	I	I(V)

Early pioneers in the blues were singers like Bessie Smith, Alberta Hunter, and Memphis Minnie. Robert Johnson, guitarist and singer from Mississippi, is generally acknowledged as the person who standardized the twelve-bar blues as the basic framework for blues songs. Johnson, according to legend, sold his soul to the Devil at the crossroads of Highways 61 and 49 in Clarksdale, Mississippi, in order to be the greatest blues guitarist ever.

Early blues songs might be accompanied by just a guitar, especially songs that came from the delta region of Mississippi. Later songs from urban areas often used a piano as accompaniment. Modern blues songs have typical rhythm sections of piano/guitars, bass and drums, sometimes adding horns as well. The guitar is the favored solo instrument for the blues. The example we will hear is a modern version of the blues that uses the repeating twelve-bar blues format Robert Johnson helped create. The playing of the first twelve bars of the song features the guitar improvisation that is such a large part of blues music. The vocal verses use guitar improvisations as punctuation marks to the lyrics. A second twelve-bar improvisation is inserted between the verses.

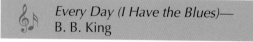

Every Day (I Have the Blues)—
B. B. King

TIN PAN ALLEY

The term Tin Pan Alley refers to both a place and the business of songwriting that was centered there from the 1890s to the 1930s. The place was actually a street in New York City, W. 28th St, where many of the music publishing businesses that constituted Tin Pan Alley were located. These publishers hired composers and lyricists to produce songs on demand. Some of these songs were intended for specific performers looking for a hit song. Others were for the general public to purchase as sheet music for voice and piano. A song's success was measured by how many copies of the sheet music were sold rather than by how many recordings since the recording industry was still in its infancy at that time. Some of the more familiar Tin Pan Alley composers include Irving Berlin (*Easter Parade, White Christmas, Blue Skies, Puttin' on the Ritz*), George M. Cohan (*I'm a Yankee Doodle Dandy, Give My Regards to Broadway*), and George Gershwin (*I Got Rhythm, Swanee*) etc.

Tin Pan Alley songs covered a wide range of styles from older, Stephen Foster type songs to increasingly popular new musical styles like ragtime and jazz. As the "jazzy" sound, with its syncopated rhythms, became ever more prominent in popular music, Tin Pan Alley composers incorporated that sound into their songs.

 Puttin' on the Ritz—
Irving Berlin

JAZZ SONGS

Jazz is a style of music dating from the early twentieth century in America that incorporated style characteristics from both ragtime and the blues. Syncopated rhythms of ragtime and blue notes, repeating chord progressions, and improvisation from the blues melded into this new style that erupted across America and the world. Initially jazz was performed predominantly by African-American musicians for African-American audiences, but the appeal soon spread across all strata of American society. In jazz songs, as in most of the song types we have discussed, verses and choruses alternate. But an added characteristic of jazz songs are improvised sections of scat singing, a vocal equivalent of instrumental improvisation during which the singer vocalizes nonsense syllables over the chords of the verses and/or chorus of the song.

 Blue Skies—
Irving Berlin

Jazz songs also explored topics more controversial in nature. Since jazz songs were performed primarily by and for African-Americans, they sometimes became the eloquent voice of a people still haunted by the intolerance that followed the abolition of slavery. The song, *Strange Fruit*, became a classic embodiment of this spirit. Written by Abel Meeropol under the pseudonym Lewis Allan, its haunting lyrics and imagery became a rallying point for the movement to put an end to the lynching of African-Americans in the South.

 Strange Fruit—
Lewis Allan (Abel Meeropol)

Southern trees bear strange fruit,
Blood on the leaves and blood at the root,
Black bodies swinging in the southern breeze,
Strange fruit hanging from the poplar trees.

(continued)

Pastoral scene of the gallant south,
The bulging eyes and the twisted mouth,
Scent of magnolias, sweet and fresh,
Then the sudden smell of burning flesh.

Here is fruit for the crows to pluck,
For the rain to gather, for the wind to suck,
For the sun to rot, for the trees to drop,
Here is a strange and bitter crop.

ROCK AND ROLL

Chuck Berry (1965) doing his famous "duck walk." Courtesy of Photofest, NY

The 1950s were the decade that gave birth to rock and roll. Many of the first rock and roll songs were based on the twelve-bar blues format with a faster tempo than traditional blues songs. One of the distinguishing characteristics of rock and roll was the presence of a backbeat. A backbeat is a rhythmic quality in which a strong hit on a drum is placed on the second and fourth beats of a four-beat measure instead of the first and third beats. Historically, the first beat of a measure, in a four-beat bar, had been the most strongly emphasized beat, with the third beat, being the next strongest. Jazz and the blues first used the backbeat as a rhythmic quality, but rock and roll made the backbeat, along with fast tempos and loud volume, part of the signature sound of that style also.

Rock and roll was unique in the history of music in that it was geared primarily toward an adolescent audience. The relative affluence of American teenagers after World War II created the first generation that, as a whole, did not need to work in order to help support their families. Prior to that time teenagers either worked in factories, in family businesses, or on the farm. Idle time and spare cash were not a part of growing up. But the natural restlessness of youth combined with the relative financial freedom of the time created a market that had never existed before. Rock and roll was born to serve that market.

Early innovators of the rock and roll style were African-American artists like Chuck Berry and Little Richard, who based most of their songs on the blues format. But it was the white artists of the time like Bill Haley and the Comets and Jerry Lee Lewis who were more commercially successful. It is ironic that today both Chuck Berry and Little Richard are more widely heard and more commercially successful than they were in the days when they helped create rock and roll. Most rock and roll songs used a basic rhythm section of piano/guitars, bass, and drums with the vocal line being the most prominently featured melodic component. The melody was usually not very complex, didn't span a wide range of notes, and lent itself to a very strong vocal quality, often bordering on shouting. Verses of instrumental improvisation were common. Amplified instruments and a highly charged, energetic performance were required of live rock and roll.

 Good Golly Miss Molly—
Little Richard

Roll Over Beethoven—
Chuck Berry

 Rock Around the Clock—
Bill Haley and the Comets

What characteristics do these three early rock and roll songs share? Compare melody, harmony, rhythm, form, timbre, and texture. How do these characteristics compare with earlier types of songs we have discussed?

The Impact of Rock and Roll

Rock and roll was the catalyst for a number of other popular song styles of the second half of the twentieth century. It wasn't that the musical characteristics of rock and roll were necessarily incorporated into all of these other styles but the pervasiveness of rock allowed a number of sub-genres of rock to develop and find sustainable markets. The overwhelming popularity of rock and roll permanently eclipsed both classical music and jazz, and that created an entirely new industry: the music industry. In the early twentieth century the goal of the publishing houses was to sell sheet music. Radio and movies helped put music before the public, familiarizing them with songs they might want to purchase. Later, the availability of recordings for in-home enjoyment further added to the distribution of songs. The advent of television in the 1950s became the most powerful method yet to bring music into the home in an intimate way never before available. Both the music and the "performer" were now there to help sell the music. Seeing and hearing both the performer and the music were much more effective at selling the music than just hearing it on the radio. But the point was not to sell sheet music anymore but to sell recordings. The recording industry became the most powerful force in popular music and led to the development of the new styles of the 1960s until today. The recording industry nurtured artists of varying musical styles in an effort to cultivate enough of a following for each style to be commercially viable.

Rock and Roll Icons

In the history of popular music there have been a few artists who have had an extraordinary effect on all who came after them. **Elvis Aaron Presley** (1935–1977) was born in Tupelo, Mississippi, but is always thought of as the most important of the rock and roll artists from Memphis, Tennessee. Presley's voice was unusually versatile for a rock and roll singer. He could sound like a hillbilly country boy or a soulful crooner. Combined with the frenetic energy he brought to his performances, Elvis Presley was unlike any other singer of the 1950s.

Presley recorded *That's All Right Mama* in 1954 at Sun Studios, producer Sam Phillips' legendary recording venue in Memphis. He saw reasonable success at Sun but switched to the larger RCA Records in 1955 and there developed a more refined sound that found wider acceptance. The year 1956 was a breakout year in many respects for Presley. He recorded his first big hit, *Blue Suede Shoes*, had his first national television appearance on The Ed Sullivan Show, a popular variety program of the time, starred in the first of many movies, *Love Me Tender*, and mounted his first Las Vegas show, all in 1956.

(continued)

More than any single stylistic quality, what Presley brought to rock and roll music was a level of acceptance and visibility in the general public's mind heretofore unknown. Yes, there had been big name musical/movie stars before, like Frank Sinatra for example, but Presley's presence on the public stage brought rock and roll into the public consciousness at a level never before seen, and from which it has never really disappeared.

In England another musical juggernaut was forming in the early 1960s. **The Beatles**, John Lennon, George Harrison, Paul McCartney, and Ringo Starr, were gaining a large share of the British rock and roll audience while Elvis Presley was "The King" of rock and roll in the United States. What later came to be called "The British Invasion" of the United States began when The Beatles appeared on The Ed Sullivan Show in 1964, as Elvis had eight years earlier. This performance added to the media hysteria that had built up in anticipation of their arrival in America. Their number 1 hit song, *I Want to Hold Your Hand*, was the first of many for the group and in retrospect seems incredibly innocuous by present-day standards, especially since The Beatles were often portrayed at the time as purveyors of cultural destruction. But with their carefully combed "long hair," suits and ties, and innocent lyrics, it is difficult to find validation for the resistance they instilled in adults of the time.

Musically, The Beatles started out as a fairly common sounding pop group, rhythm and lead guitars, bass and drums with vocals. Most of their early songs were simple love songs, *I Want to Hold Your Hand, She Loves You*, etc. Along the way, however, they branched out into styles and explored subject matter that stretched the definition of rock and roll and pop music. In the "Sgt. Pepper's Lonely Hearts Club Band" album (1967) they delved into psychedelic lyrics (*Lucy in the Sky with Diamonds*), Indian influences and orchestrated arrangements (*Within You, Without You*), and songs with socially conscientious subjects (*A Day in the Life*). The White Album (1968), which followed the Sgt. Pepper's album, continued in this vein of experimentation and stylistic trailblazing. Considering that they were together for a total of only ten years, from 1960–1970, The Beatles were an amazingly versatile and adventurous group, stretching the definition of rock and roll while challenging the accepted norms of popular music.

The British invasion continued with **The Rolling Stones**, a group that probably had a more lasting influence on the sound of rock and roll than either Elvis or The Beatles. Led by singer Mick Jagger and guitarist Keith Richards, The Rolling Stones cultivated more of a "bad boy" image than The Beatles and remained more firmly rooted in a more hard-edged, sexually-charged, brand of rock and roll. Early hits like *(I Can't Get No) Satisfaction* (1965), *Mother's Little Helper* (1966), and *Jumpin' Jack Flash* (1968) fixed in the public's mind their association with sex, drugs, and blues-based rock and roll respectively.

Blue Suede Shoes—
Elvis Presley

(I Can't Get No) Satisfaction—
The Rolling Stones

OTHER POPULAR STYLES

Urban Folk

The rebellious era of the 1960s and 1970s brought about an increased interest in reviving the simple folk music style of the past as well as promoting songs protesting the United States' involvement in the Vietnam War. This urban folk music, as represented by artists such as Peter, Paul, and Mary, Simon and Garfunkel, Judy Collins, and Bob Dylan, among others, was characterized by acoustic instruments, new presentations of old folk songs, social commentary and a purposefully restrained performance style. Urban folk music's appeal was primarily to a white, middle-class audience.

 The Times They Are a' Changin—
Bob Dylan

R&B/Motown

R&B, short for rhythm and blues, has been a style associated primarily with African-American performers from the 1960s to the present leading to other sub-styles such as hip-hop. The style, as represented by Motown Records, reached the height of its popularity in the 1960s through the 1970s. It featured African-American performers singing songs for African-American audiences. Also known as "**soul music**" and later "**funk**," the smooth sophistication of this music belies its hard-edged rock and roll heritage. The music of early African-American rock and roll artists was often referred to as R&B, as was later music of performers such as James Brown and Rick James, so the term has different connotations depending on the music being discussed. Groups such as The Temptations and The Supremes brought the Motown sound to a wider, integrated, audience through their intricate dance moves, polished harmonies, and non-controversial lyrics. Those groups often featured a lead singer with the rest of the group singing back-up. This often resulted in a kind of call-and-response style of music similar to the responsorial singing found in much non-western music.

Aretha Franklin and James Brown (1988). Courtesy of Photofest, NY

 My Girl—
The Temptations

Blues/Rock

The 1960s and 1970s saw a revitalized interest in the basic blues music of the past, but this time it was coupled with the driving power of rock and roll. This style was known as **blues/rock** and was fostered initially by English bands and artists who revered the purity of the blues style and sought to revive it with the new energy that rock and roll had brought to popular music. One of the foremost artists in this style was/is Eric Clapton, guitarist and singer with groups such as John Mayall's Blues Breakers, The Yardbirds, Cream, and Derek and the Dominoes. Clapton continues to be a popular solo artist today. Blues/rock was a basically straightforward, if somewhat more highly charged, re-creation of the blues. Virtuosic guitar improvisation became one of the hallmarks of this style.

 Crossroads—
Robert Johnson, performed by Cream

I went down to the crossroads, fell down on my knees.
I went down to the crossroads, fell down on my knees.
Asked the lord above for mercy, save me if you please.

(continued)

I went down to the crossroads, tried to flag a ride.
I went down to the crossroads, tried to flag a ride.
Nobody seemed to know me, everybody passed me by.

I'm going down to Rosedale, take my rider by my side.
I'm going down to Rosedale, take my rider by my side.
You can still barrelhouse, baby, on the riverside.

You can run, you can run, tell my friend-boy Willie Brown.
You can run, you can run, tell my friend-boy Willie Brown.
And I'm standing at the crossroads, believe I'm sinking down.

Heavy Metal

A very aggressive style of rock music known as **heavy metal** developed in the early 1970s and continued to gain in popularity into the 1980s. Heavy metal music drew on the high energy and virtuosic improvisation of the blues/rock style and became synonymous in the public's mind with long hair, sex, drug use, satanic connections, and over-the-top live performances. The overt display of symbols and lyrics relating to those subjects put metal music on a crash course with public sentiments concerning the debasement of modern culture through its popular music. Though most of those characteristics had been linked previously to nearly every type of popular music, metal music seemed particularly well suited to attract an abundant amount of controversy. Heavy metal spawned numerous sub-styles, each with its own idiosyncratic characteristics, often linking it with one of the above-named negative connotations. Styles such as hair metal, thrash metal, and death metal did little to dispel notions that this music wasn't somehow connected to these issues. Overly aggressive and grandiose, heavy metal groups such as Judas Priest, Black Sabbath, and Metallica employed extraordinarily virtuosic guitar playing and high drama which often concealed significant social commentary and depth of feeling in the lyrics. Then again, some of the music was also for the sheer exhilaration of the volume and energy in live performance.

 Metal Meltdown—
Judas Priest

Country

Johnny Cash on *VH1 Storytellers* (1998). Courtesy of Photofest, NY

Country music had its roots in the folk music of the southern and western United States and drew on the characteristic styles from those areas to reach its present day form. Folk fiddling of the early settlers and their ancestors from Europe is present in the popularity of the **bluegrass** style of country music today. The folk ballad influence of early Americans is present in the simple verse/chorus format of most country songs. **Western swing** is a type of country music with an easy-going, upbeat sound suitable for dancing and made popular in many Western movies. Much country music is akin to the spirit of the blues with topics such as broken love, hard times, and too much drinking playing prominent roles in the themes of songs. Nashville has historically been the center of country music recording and performance with the recording companies dictating the course of development of the style for much of its history. Country music uses the distinctly recognizable southern accent as a desirable characteristic, which imparts a certain authenticity to this folk-based music. Some important names in the history of country music include Hank Williams, Patsy Cline, Merle Haggard, Waylon Jennings, and Johnny Cash.

 Folsom Prison Blues—
Johnny Cash

Pop Music

A type of music with a somewhat broader appeal than the targeted styles discussed above developed over the past 40 years, crossing generational and racial lines and is commonly referred to as pop music. Without the distinct characteristics of the above-mentioned styles, pop music often appeals to the listener through catchy tunes or "hooks" that are easily recognizable and words that are easy to remember. Pop songs usually consist of verses, choruses, and a bridge, often with an instrumental introduction. Pop music is virtually all vocal music with only the smallest percentage being purely instrumental. High-quality recordings and the backing of large recording studios have been the hallmarks of pop music. The overriding theme of most pop music is love. Michael Jackson, Elton John, Whitney Houston, Celine Dion, and Britney Spears are some successful pop music artists.

 Candle in the Wind—
Elton John, Lyrics by Bernie Taupin

Alternative Rock

Alternative rock had its genesis in the Punk rock music of the 1970s. Seminal groups such as The Ramones, The Sex Pistols and The Clash put forth a primitive, bare-bones version of rock music that was devoid of musical sophistication. Punk rock songs typically used just a few basic chords, avoided self-indulgent improvisational solos, and adopted a philosophy that rejected established social conventions.

The term "Alternative Rock" came into popular usage during the 1980s as a convenient label for the emerging anti-mainstream, indie (independent), and post-Punk rock music dominating college radio stations at that time. R.E.M. (1980–present), Nirvana (1987–1994), Pearl Jam (1990–present), and The Red Hot Chili Peppers (1983–present), were bands that came to be labeled as "Alternative." The musical styles of alternative bands varies greatly but can generically be described as avoiding musical conventions of bands commercially successfully in other identifiable styles such as hip-hop, pop, metal, etc.

Alternative rock bands have not shied away from dealing with difficult subjects, such as suicide in the song *Jeremy* by Pearl Jam. But while the Punk and early alternative bands sought to distance themselves from the traditional measures of commercial success groups such as The Red Hot Chili Peppers have achieved levels of popularity equal to or surpassing many groups in the "commercial" styles.

 Jeremy—
Pearl Jam

Listening Chart

Historical Period	Type of Song	Composer/Artist	Keywords
Medieval	Troubadour Song	Conon de Bethune	
Renaissance	Lute Song	Thomas Campion	
Romantic	Art Song/Lied	Franz Schubert	
19th Century	Popular Song	Stephen Foster	
Romantic	Song Cycle	Gustav Mahler	
20th/21st Century	Blues	B.B. King	
20th/21st Century	Tin Pan Alley	Irving Berlin	
20th/21st Century	Jazz Song	Irving Berlin	
20th/21st Century	Jazz Song	Abel Meeropol	
20th/21st Century	Rock and Roll	Little Richard	
20th/21st Century	Urban Folk	Bob Dylan	
20th/21st Century	R&B/Motown	The Temptations	
20th/21st Century	Blues/Rock	Cream	
20th/21st Century	Heavy Metal	Judas Priest	
20th/21st Century	Country Music	Johnny Cash	
20th/21st Century	Rap/Hip-Hop	Eminem, Run-D.M.C., T.I., Jay-Z, L'il Wayne	
19th Century	American Folk	Traditional	
18th Century	American Folk	Traditional	
18th Century	American Folk	Traditional	
Renaissance	English Folk	Henry VIII ?	
19th Century ?	African Folk	Traditional	
20th/21st Century	African Folk	Traditional	

What is performing the music?

- Voice with ancient instruments
  - French — Verses with interlude
  - English — Verses, lute
- Voice with piano
  - German — Through composed
  - English — Verses with interlude
- Voice with orchestra
  - German — Orchestra and voice
- Voice(s) with a band
  - 12-bar blues, guitar improvisation
  - Big band, improvisation, catchy tune
  - Big band, scat singing
  - Muted trumpet, social commentary
  - 12-bar blues, backbeat, improvisation
  - Acoustic sound, social commentary
  - Four-part harmony
  - Fast, 12-bar blues, improvisation
  - Distortion, fast, virtuosic improvisation
  - "Twangy" guitar, simple steady rhythm
  - Rhythmically spoken lyrics
- Voice(s) with guitar
  - Guitar (banjo, hammer) "John Henry"
  - Verses, "All the Pretty Little Horses"
  - Verses, harmony, "The Cruel War"
- Voices alone
  - Verses and chorus, "Greensleeves"
  - Solo voice with harmony, "Kumbaya"
- Voices with mbira accompaniment
  - Responsorial singing

In the "Keywords" column, write down words, musical or non-musical, that will help you remember the specific pieces you are hearing.

Higher Ground—
The Red Hot Chili Peppers

Rap/Hip-Hop

Rap music is a style of rhythm-based urban music dating from the 1970s. The term hip-hop was initially coined to describe not only a certain style of music but other aspects of urban culture as well, such as graffiti art and break dancing. The term rap refers specifically to the music of hip-hop culture. Originally performed by DJs (disc jockeys) playing records in clubs, raps were rhythmically spoken rhymes over percussive accompaniment taken from commercial recordings. Rap lyrics often dealt with the harsh realities of life on the street in the ghetto. The lyrics have often been controversial in the way they deal with violence, women, and drugs. The violence that has been a significant part of hip-hop culture, and the entire sub-style of gangsta rap has alienated many from this type of music. One of the earliest hip-hop groups was Run-D.M.C. Band members Joseph Simmons, Darryl McDaniels, and Jason Mizell were instrumental in bringing hip-hop into the mainstream of American popular music. The influence of hip-hop culture, including rap music, can be found throughout society today with musical influences appearing in other styles of music and the baggy clothing and excessive jewelry of rap artists becoming staples of fashion for both black and white youths. Ironically, one of the most commercially successful rap artists has been a white rapper called Eminem, the stage name of Marshal Mathers. Having made a success of himself from very humble beginnings, Eminem seeks to instill a sense of pride and confidence in the listener who may be from similar circumstances.

Hard Times—
Run-D.M.C.

Lose Yourself—
Eminem

Hip-hop music reached its most widespread level of notoriety through the style called Gangsta rap. News stories about rappers involved in shootings coupled with misogynistic lyrics denigrating women, common in many songs, prompted public discussions about the appropriateness of rap music in the 1990s. The shootings of artists like Tupac Shakur and Notorious B.I.G., both murdered in hip-hop industry-related incidents, slowed the up to then growing acceptance of the style. Hip-hop music has since moved beyond the Gangsta rap style to one that emphasizes a somewhat more positive outlook. Many of the most popular hip-hop artists of recent times, such as T.I., L'il Wayne and Jay-Z among others, promote self-reliance and hard work in their lyrics as the path to success. T.I., the stage name of Clifford Joseph Harris, Jr., has himself served time in prison. He has even been the star of a popular television program, *T.I.'s Road to Redemption*. In that program the artist reached out to young men whose lives were filled with violence and self-defeating habits. He used his own life as an example of how you can alter your behavior and be successful. Most recently T.I. has starred in another television program, *T.I. and Tiny: The Family*, which follows the artist after his release from prison putting his family and professional lives back together.

♪♪ *Swagga Like Us*—
T.I., Jay-Z, L'il Wayne

SUMMARY

We have heard songs from long ago, the near past, and the present. We have heard songs from our own country and far away lands. We have heard songs that have existed only in the minds and voices of those who sang them for hundreds of years before being written down. What conclusions can we draw about songs in general from this brief survey? What is the importance of experiencing songs?

"All (folk songs) are based to some degree on verses of text. . . ." That statement from early in the chapter seems to be a universal truth. It is indeed the rare song that does not have verses. The answer to whether this concept arose independently in diverse cultures throughout the world or spread from one to another has probably been lost forever in the mists of pre-history. But the question really shouldn't be how this basic concept arose in all the corners of the world but rather once it did why did it remain the single most common aspect of song regardless of the historical era or the place in which it appeared?

The author does not pretend to know the answer to this question but would like to hazard a reasonable guess. Before the understanding of the written word was common, the stories of people were often told through song. Remembering an entire story/song in exacting detail is a difficult task. But breaking it up into small, easily remembered verses helps in organizing our thoughts. Also, in the telling/singing of a long story/song a verse forgotten by one person might be remembered by another, keeping the story intact. The concept of the verse may have arisen as a practical tool for remembering an entire story. This is just this author's guess. Can you think of another possible reason for the universality of the verse as the basis of song?

"Through songs we can look into the minds and hearts of those who came before us as they reveal who they were and how they viewed the world." That sentence taken from the opening of this chapter takes on an added dimension of importance when we think that the image we have of earlier times, molded by the songs from those times, will be reflected back on us by future generations through our songs. What do our songs today reveal about us? What kind of people will those a thousand years hence think we were? It's an interesting question. Songs reflect who we are as a people and as individuals, what we do, the things we value. What *do* our songs reveal about us?

SUGGESTED FURTHER LISTENING

Once, Twice, Thrice, I Julia Tried—Henry Purcell

Come Again—John Dowland, performed by Sting

She Never Told Her Love—Franz Joseph Haydn

Die Forelle—Franz Schubert

Four Last Songs—Richard Strauss

Mack the Knife—Kurt Weill and Bertoldt Brecht, performed by Bobby Darin

The Cat Came Back—Aaron Copland

To a Young Girl—Ned Rorem

She Loves You, Yeah, Yeah, Yeah—The Beatles

Papa Was a Rolling Stone—The Temptations

All Shook Up—Elvis Presley

Bohemian Rhapsody—Queen

Walk this Way—Run-D.M.C. with Aerosmith

The Little Black Boy from *Songs of Innocence and of Experience*—William Bolcom

The Shepherd from *Songs of Innocence and of Experience*—Anda Al Sinaia

Mandela—Sekou Sundiata

QUESTION ASSIGNMENT

Instructions: Log in to the textbook web site and click on the ASSIGNMENTS tab. In the Chapter Question Assignment area read the instructions and answer the question(s) or provide the asked for information. Be sure to click the SUBMIT THIS FORM button after you complete the Assignment.

Name the following:

1. The country whose folk music contains a great deal of dissonant harmony.

2. The Austrian composer who wrote over 600 art songs.

3. The Roman numeral representing the chord that occurs during the fifth bar (measure) of a twelve-bar blues chord progression.

LISTENING EXERCISES

Instructions: Log in to the textbook web site and click on the ASSIGNMENTS tab. In the Listening Exercises area click on the links to the musical examples for each question and answer the questions. Be sure to click the SUBMIT button after you answer all of the questions.

Listen to each of the musical examples below from the Chapter 5 Playlist while noting the appropriate descriptive prompt on the Listening Chart for Chapter 5 and determine the best answer to each question.

1. *Ahi! Amours (Alas Love)* by Conon de Bethune—This Medieval period Troubadour song for voice with ancient instruments is sung in the composer's native language of French. You can tell the instruments are not modern instruments by the nasal quality of their sound. The song is constructed of verses with an interlude between each verse. The music that serves as the interlude is also used an introduction to the song. Choose the timing below that represents when the first interlude is played.

    a. 50 seconds
    b. 1:40 seconds
    c. 2:10 seconds

2. *Erlkönig* by Franz Schubert—This German song, for voice with piano, begins with a short introduction played by the piano alone. In this through-composed song the more commonly used verses are not apparent. The story unfolds as each character speaks. Choose the timing below that represents when the character of the Erlkönig first speaks.

    a. 27 seconds
    b. 1:02 seconds
    c. 1:36 seconds

3. *Every Day (I Have the Blues)* B. B. King—This song for voice with a band, is in a twelve-bar blues format. It begins with a playing of the twelve-bar blues chord progression with a guitar improvisation as an introduction. Choose the timing below that represents when the third playing of the twelve-bar blues chord progression begins. Count the instrumental introduction as the first playing of the chord progression.

    a. 25 seconds
    b. 55 seconds
    c. 1:45 seconds

Music for Mourning

FOCUS POINTS

Vocal Music of Mourning
Requiem Masses
Songs
Orchestral Song Cycles
Spirituals
Dogon Funeral Music
Native American Funeral Music

Instrumental Music of Mourning
Threnody
Funeral March
Dirge
New Orleans Jazz Funeral

The importance of music in accompanying the rituals, ceremonies, and events of life cannot be overemphasized. In most cultures, birthdays, weddings, coming of age ceremonies, as well as the rituals surrounding the passing of life, include music. In mourning the loss of people within a society we acknowledge the importance of the individual, their contribution to the culture, their part, whether great or small, in the life of the community. The grief felt by mourners on the occasion of an individual's death can be eased through the shared experience of music. Music can ennoble the memory of the deceased, provide a time of contemplation for the mourners, celebrate the completion of a life well lived. Music of mourning can be sad and poignant or triumphant and celebratory.

Ludwig van Beethoven's funeral procession in 1827. Copyright © Erich Lessing/Art Resource, NY

An illuminated page from *The Book of Hours*—the main prayer book used in medieval Europe—indicating appropriate prayers and rituals for a Requiem Mass.
Copyright © Erich Lessing/Art Resource, NY

Music deemed appropriate for mourning may be as simple as a song expressing a very personal reflection on the loss. It could also be a large-scale work for symphony orchestra and choir proclaiming eternal salvation while providing reassurance to the living. It might be a purely instrumental composition on either a small or grand scale evoking a mood of sadness, grief or horror. It might also be a raucous jazz tune played by a group of musicians marching through the streets of New Orleans.

THE REQUIEM MASS

In Chapter 2 we discussed the genre of the Mass. The musical mass was based on specific Latin texts from the Roman Catholic Church that had been in use since Medieval times. The group of texts that was typically set to music was called the "ordinary" of the Mass. Those "ordinary" texts were present in the celebration of the ritual of the mass regardless of the time during the ecclesiastical year when a particular mass was celebrated. In the Catholic Church different times of the year represent "feasts" celebrating diverse aspects of the church's beliefs.

The **requiem** is a specific type of mass, one celebrated in memory of someone who has died. Most requiems, especially the older ones dating from the eighteenth century and earlier, make use of some of the texts from the ordinary of the mass such as the Kyrie, Sanctus, and Agnus Dei in addition to texts specific to the Requiem Mass. Texts appropriate for specific masses are called the "**proper**" of the mass. Some common texts specific to requiem masses include:

> **Requiem Aeternam (Introit)**—Eternal rest grant unto them, Oh Lord . . .
>
> **Lacrimosa**—That day is one of weeping . . .
>
> **Dies Irae**—The day of wrath . . .
>
> **Domine Jesu (Offertorium)**—Oh Lord Jesus Christ, King of Glory . . .
>
> **Pie Jesu**—Merciful Lord Jesus . . .
>
> **Lux Aeternam**—Eternal light shine upon them . . .
>
> **Libera Me**—Deliver me, Oh Lord, from eternal death on that awful day . . .
>
> **In Paradisum**—May the angels lead you into paradise . . .

Not all requiems contain all of the above texts. Some requiems contain none of them at all. The texts above are from the Roman Catholic Church and many Protestant denominations do not include those texts in their liturgy. In general, requiems have more variety in their content than masses. Requiems may be written in honor of individuals who have died, in memory of those killed in wars, or sometimes by composers confronting a sense of their own mortality as they advance in age.

Gregorian chants concerning the dead can be traced back to the Medieval period, but it was during the Renaissance that the Requiem Mass became a common, multi-movement genre. That format has remained essentially unchanged to this day with contemporary composers continuing to write requiems. Some requiem masses of note have been composed by **Wolfgang Amadeus Mozart** (left unfinished at his death and completed by one of his students), **Hector Berlioz, Giuseppe Verdi, Gabriel Fauré,**

Biographical Spotlight

© 2013, Stocksnapper, Shutterstock, Inc.

Giuseppe Verdi

Giuseppe Verdi, known mostly for his writing of Italian operas in a thoroughly Romantic style, was born on October 10, 1813, and died on January 27, 1901. At the time of his birth Italy was not yet the unified country it is today, as unification would not happen until 1861. The town in which Verdi was born, Le Roncole, was actually under French administration at the time, so this most Italian of composers began life as a French citizen.

He studied at various locations into his twenties, eventually moving back to the city of Busseto close to the place of his birth. Wherever he lived Verdi cultivated the favor of admirers who facilitated his first performances, including that of Countess Clara Maffei. The Countess was one of the financial backers of the *Risorgimento* movement to unify the fractured Italian peninsula into a single country. She was renowned for hosting gatherings of artists and political figures supportive of the *Risorgimento* in her Milan home, which included the young Verdi. The relationships Verdi formed among this group would influence him for the rest of his life. In 1836, back in Busseto, Verdi became first the teacher, and then the husband, of Margherita Barrezzi, the daughter of one of his benefactors. Tragedy compounded tragedy as each of their two children died within the next three years followed by Margherita's death at the age of 26 a year later.

The tragic events of his first marriage occurred while Verdi was writing his first opera, *Oberto*, which premiered to moderate success in 1839. He was engaged to write three more operas, but it wasn't until *Nabucco* premiered in 1842 that he truly captured the attention of the music world. Verdi later said that the words, "... *may the Lord inspire you a harmony of voices, which may instill virtue to suffering,*" sung by the chorus of Hebrew slaves in the famous chorus "*Va, Pensiero*" (*Fly, thought . . .*) in that opera, gave him the strength to continue to write. During the production of *Nabucco*, Verdi met the soprano Giuseppina Strepponi with whom he began a long relationship and eventually married in 1859.

What followed *Nabucco* were twenty-six additional operas including some of the greatest ever written. Among those are *Rigoletto, Il Trovatore (The Troubadour), La Traviata (The Fallen Woman)*, and *Aida*, up until 1893 when his last opera, *Falstaff* was premiered. Two non-operatic works of Verdi's have also found a permanent place in today's concert halls: the *Requiem Mass* and *Quatro Pezzi Sacri (Four Sacred Pieces)*, the latter completed in 1897 and premiered the following year.

Verdi's involvement with the *Risorgimento* movement has perhaps been exaggerated but there is no doubt he was committed to the idea of a unified Italy and was willing to serve the newly formed country in any way he could. His name, literally, became synonymous with the unification movement through the widespread use of the political slogan "*Viva Verdi*" where "*Verdi*" was an acronym for "**V**ittorio **E**manuele **R**e **D'I**talia" (Victor Emmanual King of Italy). Verdi served terms in both the Chamber of Deputies and in the Italian Senate.

Verdi's second wife, Guiseppina Strepponi, died in 1897 after sharing more than half a century with the revered composer. After her death Verdi ceased composing. He died in 1901 and was buried next to her on the grounds of the *Casa di Riposo per Musicisti*, a rest home for aging opera singers and musicians that Verdi had built in 1896.

Biographical Spotlight Exercise

Instructions: Log in to the textbook web site and click on the **Assignments** tab. Click on **Chapter 6** and scroll to the **Biographical Spotlight area**. Answer the question based on the information in the biography above.

Which of Verdi's operas was the first to truly capture the music world's attention?

1. *Rigoletto*
2. *Nabucco*
3. *Falstaff*

Maurice Duruflé, Johannes Brahms, Benjamin Britten, and, more recently, John Rutter and Andrew Lloyd Webber.

Requiems may be experienced either in church settings or in concert halls. The largest requiems, such as those written by Verdi and Berlioz, call for instrumental forces beyond what most churches can accommodate and therefore are heard most frequently in concert halls. In addition to the large numbers of instruments required to perform these pieces, another consideration is the excessive reverberation often found in large churches. That reverberation can be an unwanted characteristic considering the very high volume and complexity of some of the sections within these requiems. Other requiems, with less extensive instrumentation, are often performed in churches. The requiem by Fauré, with its restrained use of brass and percussion instruments, is a good example of this kind of work.

The Dies Irae

One of the most frequently used texts in requiem masses is the Dies Irae (Day of Wrath) text, which depicts The Last Judgment, when all souls will be held accountable for their sins. The setting of these words is usually an opportunity for composers to unleash their most electrifying and creative musical ideas. Use your own imagination to conjure up images, both visual and musical, for these words:

> The day of wrath, that day will
> dissolve the world in ashes,
> as David and the Sibyl (oracles) prophesied.
>
> How great will be the terror,
> when the Judge comes
> who will smash everything completely!
>
> The trumpet, scattering a marvelous sound
> through the tombs of every land,
> will gather all before the throne.

These words evoke the end of the world with trumpets calling all before God for The Last Judgment. Apocalyptic images are easy to conjure up to words such as these. What images do you see in your mind's eye when you read this? What sort of sounds would *you* use if you were writing the music?

Two memorable settings of the Dies Irae text were written by Wolfgang Amadeus Mozart (1756–1791) and Giuseppe Verdi (1813–1901). Both composers painted vivid musical pictures in their settings of the Dies Irae, employing the musical styles of their respective Classical and Romantic eras. It is an interesting parallel that both composers were especially renowned for their operatic writing. Perhaps this accounts for the inherent dramatic quality of both settings.

The *Requiem Mass in D minor* by Wolfgang Amadeus Mozart was the last work written by the composer before he died in 1791. It was left unfinished with the remainder completed by two other composers, Joseph von Eybler and Franz Xaver Süssmayr, a student of Mozart's. The majority of the reconstructed portions of the *Requiem* were contributed by Süssmayr. Some of those sections were based on incomplete sketches left by Mozart and some portions were completely new material. Süssmayr's additions ranged from filling out incomplete orchestrations of movements to writing entire sections in Mozart's style. The only movement believed to have been composed entirely by Mozart is the opening "Requiem aeternam."

Mozart's *Requiem* was written on a commission from a Count von Walsegg-Stuppach under slightly mysterious conditions. It is believed the Count may have wanted to claim authorship of the work for himself, but the evidence is conjectural at best. The commission was arranged through an intermediary, and whether Mozart ever met the Count is unclear. It was not unusual for composers during the Classical period to occasionally affix their name to a composition not their own, but it was usually done with the full knowledge, and compensation, of the composer.

The following excerpt from Mozart's *Requiem* is from the second movement entitled "Sequence." A sequence was a type of poetic Medieval chant of the Roman Catholic Church. The sequence used in requiem masses was written by Thomas of Celano, ca. 1200, and begins with the "Dies Irae" text. In this example the full power of the Classical period orchestra is combined with choral writing that alternates between homophonic and imitative statements of the text. Toward the end of Mozart's life, he increasingly incorporated imitative compositional techniques reminiscent of the preceding Baroque period.

What are some of the techniques used by the composer to amplify the dramatic nature of the text?

 Sequence (Dies Irae excerpt) from *Requiem Mass in D minor*— Wolfgang Amadeus Mozart

Sequentia	**Sequence**
Dies irae, dies illa	Day of wrath, that day
Solvet saeclum in favilla,	Will dissolve the earth in ashes
Teste David cum Sibylla.	As David and the Sibyl (oracles) bear witness.
Quantus tremor est futurus	What dread there will be
Quando judex est venturus	When the Judge shall come
Cuncta stricte discussurus.	To judge all things strictly.

Giuseppe Verdi wrote *Messa da Requiem* in memory of Alessandro Manzoni, an Italian author and poet. The work is sometimes referred to as the *Manzoni Requiem*. Verdi was an extraordinarily successful opera composer and a prominent figure in Italian politics. He was an advocate for a unified Italy, which at the time was a collection of autonomous nation/states.

Verdi's operas include such perennial favorites among opera goers as *Rigoletto*, *Il Trovatore (The Troubadour)*, *La Traviata (The Lost One)*, *Othello*, and *Aida*. An early opera, *Nabucco*, told the story of the Hebrews exiled from their homeland, which many construed as Verdi's slightly veiled reference to the Italians' political plight at the time. Verdi's *Requiem* was written for four vocal soloists, chorus, and orchestra, which might otherwise constitute the performing needs of an opera. It's not surprising that Verdi's *Requiem* is operatic in style, full of drama and powerful emotion.

The *Messa da Requiem* is in seven movements. As you can see below, this work contains some texts from the ordinary of the mass (Kyrie, Sanctus, Agnus Dei) as well as texts specific to the requiem.

Funeral procession for Giuseppe Verdi in Milan, 1901. Copyright © Bildarchiv Preussischer Kulturbesitz/Art Resource, NY

    I. Requiem and Kyrie
   II. Sequence (Dies irae)
  III. Offertorio
  IV. Sanctus
   V. Agnus Dei

VI. Lux aeterna
VII. Libera me

The first excerpt is the opening of the second movement, "Sequence," which begins with the Dies Irae text in a wild setting for the full orchestra and chorus. Hammer blows on the tympani and bass drums alternate with punctuating chords in the orchestra announcing the day of final judgment. Verdi overwhelms the listener with both the orchestra and choir at the top of their volume and intensity levels.

Sequence (Dies Irae excerpt) from *Messa da Requiem*— Giuseppe Verdi

Sequence	**Sequence**
Dies irae, dies illa,	Day of wrath, that day
solvet saeclum in favilla,	Will dissolve the earth in ashes
teste David cum Sibylla.	As David and the Sibyl bear witness.
Quantus tremor est futurus,	How great will be the terror,
quando judex est venturus,	When the Judge shall come
cuncta stricte discussurus	To judge all things strictly.

The opening passage diminishes into quiet fear at the coming of the Judge. At this point a distant trumpet is heard several times, each time gaining in volume as if coming closer. This section of the Sequence begins with the words "Tuba mirum spargens sonum" (The Trumpet, scattering a marvelous sound). A full brass fanfare then erupts, followed closely by the full orchestra and chorus calling forth to judgment the souls of the living and the dead. Verdi achieves a level of drama rare even for him in this section of the Sequence. Off-stage brass positioned in the balcony, the hallways, and the backstage areas surrounding the stage imitate the call of "The Trumpet." Their relentless calling forth to judgment reaches a full crescendo when the off-stage brass instruments are joined by the on-stage orchestra and voices. The audience is overwhelmed by a wave of sound that washes over them from all sides. This opening section of the Sequence ends with the solo bass voice solemnly intoning the word "Mors" (Death) several times.

II. Sequence	**II. Sequence**
Chorus	*Chorus*
Tuba mirum spargens sonum,	The trumpet, scattering a marvelous sound
per sepulcra regionem,	through the tombs of all lands,
coget omnes ante thronum.	will drive mankind before the throne.
Bass	*Bass*
Mors stupebit et natura,	Death and Nature shall be astonished,
cum resurget creatura,	when all Creation rises again
judicanti responsura.	to answer to the Judge.

The dramatic opening returns twice more to unify this extended movement, perhaps the most memorable setting of this text in any requiem. Verdi's personal memorial to a friend has become one of the most frequently performed requiems of all time, and in so doing has attained the status of a universal statement of mourning.

Have you ever experienced music like this at a time of mourning? Do you think it is appropriate? Does it fit the occasion, or is it out of touch with your view of how to remember someone who has died? It is interesting to note that this piece is often programmed as part of a concert series without regard to whether anyone in particular will be memorialized by its performance. Does this mean it is just another concert piece? Or is it that the work has transcended the mourning of any individual and is a statement about death for all humanity?

What Makes Music—Musical Instruments

The Brass Family

Instruments of the orchestra are grouped into four families according to certain characteristics. All members of this family are made out of brass and produce their sounds by buzzing the lips inside a cup-shaped mouthpiece.

Trumpet—This is the smallest and therefore highest-pitched instrument in the brass family. There is a smaller version of the trumpet called the Piccolo Trumpet, an extremely high-pitched trumpet common in music from the 17th and early 18th centuries.

French Horn—The French horn is a mellow sounding adaptation of the hunting horn. It can also sound quite forceful.

Trombone—This instrument is larger and lower pitched than the trumpet and French horn and does not use valves to change notes like the other brass instruments. Instead it uses a movable slide to change the length of the tubing and thereby the pitch.

Tuba—The tuba is the largest and lowest-pitched brass instrument.

The standard performing ensemble for these instruments is the Brass Quintet, consisting of two trumpets, one French horn, one trombone, and one tuba. This is a very homogenous sounding group, like the string quartet, where all members produce their sound in the same way.

View the video of English composer Benjamin Britten's *Young Person's Guide to the Orchestra* performed by the YouTube Symphony Orchestra on the chapter video playlist.

The brass family of instruments is featured from :56–1:16, and each of the brass instruments is featured individually beginning at the 9:34 mark.

The Memphis Brass Quintet: Dan Phillips, French horn; John Mueller, trombone; Kevin Sanders, tuba; Kyle Milsap, trumpet; and Ben Lewis, piccolo trumpet. Photo courtesy of Dr. Randall Rushing

A Requiem without the Dies Irae

Gabriel Fauré (1845–1924) was a Romantic period French composer whose *Requiem in D minor* stands in stark contrast to the requiems of Mozart and Verdi. The movements of Fauré's requiem are the following:

    I. Introit et Kyrie
   II. Offertoire
 III. Sanctus
  IV. Pie Jesus
   V. Agnus Dei and Lux Aeterna
  VI. Libera Me
 VII. In Paradisum

French composer
Gabriel Fauré (1845–
1924). Copyright © Reunion
des Musees Nationaux/
Art Resource, NY

Note the absence of the Sequence, from which both the Dies Irae and Tuba mirum texts come. In Fauré's requiem there is no mention of a "Day of Wrath" or the possibility of eternal damnation. The inclusion of the "In Paradisum" text, with its comforting words of eternal repose in heaven, offers reassurance to the living that the departed are truly at rest. Fauré's religious skepticism put him at odds with the approach taken by many composers who painted vivid musical pictures of The Last Judgment in their requiems.

Fauré began composing the *Requiem* soon after the death of his father, and by the time he completed it his mother had also died. The work is very much an expression of his personal loss but also an affirmation of his own beliefs concerning death. Fauré viewed death not as something to be feared but rather as a "happy deliverance."

The composition of Fauré's requiem began in 1888 as a smallish piece for his own church in Paris. Initially it was just four movements with strings (minus violins), harp, tympani, and organ accompanying the choir and soprano soloist. Several years later he added two more movements plus bassoons, trumpets, horns, violins and a baritone soloist. Finally, in 1900, a large version with full woodwinds and brass was published. Performances today often employ the intermediate edition, opting for the full complement of movements but with a reduced orchestration. This version fits the peaceful, reserved mood of the piece very well.

🎼 In Paradisum from *Requiem in D minor—*
Gabriel Fauré

In Paradisum
In paradisum deducant te angeli,
in tuo adventu
suscipiant te martyres,
et perducant te
in civitatem sanctam Jerusalem.
Chorus angelorum te suscipiat,
et cum Lazaro quondam paupere
aeternam habeas requiem.

In Paradise
May the angels lead you into paradise,
may the martyrs receive you
in your coming,
and may they guide you
into the holy city, Jerusalem.
May the chorus of angels receive you
and with Lazarus once poor
may you have eternal rest.

The requiem, with its performing forces of vocal soloists, chorus, and orchestra, is the largest musical genre dedicated to the observance of the passing of life. As such, it holds a special place in the experience of music for many people. When a requiem is performed as a memorial the setting is already fraught with emotion. An intense composition such as Verdi's or Mozart's can amplify the depth of the emotional experience beyond what one would normally feel during a musical performance. The Fauré work might serve to ease the grief felt at such a time and offer a sense of peace and acceptance otherwise difficult to achieve. Requiems serve as our farewell to the dead and our affirmation to the living.

SONGS OF MOURNING

Most songs are about the living. It is the rare song that mourns the loss of life. But sometimes a grand statement such as that made by a Requiem Mass isn't the most appropriate vehicle to express the emotions that accompany the loss of life. The Requiem Mass reflects certain societal beliefs and does so with traditional texts that might not fit the unique outlook of an individual composer. When dealing with death sometimes a lone voice singing can best communicate the emotions felt at such a difficult time.

The contemporary singer/guitarist, Eric Clapton, wrote a moving musical memorial after the accidental death of his young son. The song, *Tears in Heaven,* struck a sympathetic chord with the public, unusual for such a tragically personal song. Clapton performed the song in all of his concerts for years afterward as his own way of dealing with his loss. It is a simple song in strophic form with acoustic instruments accompanying the voice. The text is quite personal and written in the first person, very different from the approach of using the ancient Latin texts of the requiem.

Tears in Heaven—
Eric Clapton

Another approach to using song to express the grief and sadness surrounding death is song with orchestral accompaniment. In the previous chapter we discussed this type of song in regard to the orchestral song cycle, a group of songs based on the same subject matter. *Kindertotenlieder* (*Songs on the Death of Children*) is just such a song cycle. Written by the late Romantic period composer Gustav Mahler (1860–1911), these musical settings of such tragic poetry explore different aspects of a parent's loss of a child. The poems on which the songs are based were written by Friedrich Rückert, a German poet, after two of his own children died within two and a half weeks of each other. Rückert, devastated by the loss, wrote over 400 poems on the subject. Mahler chose five to set to music. They reveal the thoughts perhaps only someone so close to the deceased could have: personal, small in scope, yet overwhelmingly tragic. Each poem is a vignette from a life shattered.

"Nun will die Sonn . . ." Movement I from *Kindertotenlieder*—
Gustav Mahler (Now the sun will rise . . .)

Movement 1
Nun will die Sonn' so hell aufgehn,
Als sei kein Unglück die Nacht geschehn!
Das Unglück geschah nur mir allein!
Die Sonne, sie scheinet allgemein!

Du mußt nicht die Nacht in dir verschränken,
Mußt sie ins ew'ge Licht versenken!
Ein Lämplein verlosch in meinem Zelt!
Heil sei dem Freudenlicht der Welt!

Movement 1
Now the sun will rise as brightly
as if no misfortune had occurred in the night.
The misfortune has fallen on me alone.
The sun—it shines for everyone.

You must not keep the night inside you;
You must immerse it in eternal light.
A little light has been extinguished in my household;
Light of joy in the world, be welcome.

Instrumental Music of Mourning

Purely instrumental music cannot truly be "about" something. At least not in the same way words can express thoughts, emotions, and ideas. But instrumental music can by its "mood" imply emotions or intensify feelings we already have when played in the appropriate context. For example, at a football game where emotions run high as the fans root for their respective teams, the playing of fight songs, school alma maters, and stirring music of all kinds can further heighten the excitement of the crowd. Likewise, in a scary scene from a movie, tense, eerie music can literally move you to the edge of your seat in anticipation of what will happen next. Heard in other settings, those

PERSPECTIVE—*ON THE TRANSMIGRATION OF SOULS*

by John Adams

The horrific attacks on the United States on September 11th, 2001 were the catalyst for the creation of innumerable songs, poems, works of art, and memorials of every kind. The need to memorialize the dead and reassure the living was widespread and necessary in order to put the events of that day into a form, if not understandable, that could at least be dealt with psychologically. One of the most powerful works to emerge from that cauldron of anger and sorrow was a musical composition called *On the Transmigration of Souls* by the American composer John Adams.

The work was first performed by the New York Philharmonic under the direction of conductor Lorin Maazel on September 19th, 2002 for the one year anniversary of the attacks. The word "transmigration" means to move from one place, or state of being, to another. The composer's intention for this composition was that the word apply not only to those who died in the attacks but to those still living. In an interview posted on his Web site Adams states ". . . I mean it to imply the movement of the soul from one state to another. And I don't just mean the transition from living to dead, but also the change that takes place within the souls of those that stay behind, of those who suffer pain and loss and then themselves come away from that experience transformed."

In describing his intentions for the listener in the same interview Adams said, "My desire in writing this piece is to achieve in musical terms the same sort of feeling one gets upon entering one of those old, majestic cathedrals in France or Italy. . . . You feel you are in the presence of many souls . . . and you sense their collective energy . . ." The work is written for orchestra, chorus, children's chorus, and a pre-recorded soundtrack. The soundtrack contains sounds of the city, recitations of the names of the victims and quotations from notes left by relatives and friends of the missing at the site of the attacks. Adams weaves the soundtrack seamlessly into his atmospheric writing and the simple, often poignant words bring a very personal level of experience to this composition mourning the loss of so many lives.

On the Transmigration of Souls begins and ends with the sounds of the city. In between, the orchestra elicits both peaceful and anxious moods while providing an appropriate setting for the choral sections. While the spoken words are clear enough to understand while listening to the recorded performance of this piece, the text sung by the choruses is better appreciated with the printed text visible. The full text is posted on the following Web site: www.earbox.com/W-soulstext.html

The following outline may be helpful while listening to this work.

00:00	City sounds
00:39	"Missing . . . missing . . . missing . . ."
00:59	Choir with minimal accompaniment
01:13	Names
03:00	Recitations recede and orchestra comes to the forefront
03:50	Trumpet melody
04:08	Choir melody (quotations) overlaps trumpet
05:30	Texture thins out, orchestra recedes

Changing textures: Chorus, orchestra, recitations

09:54	Quiet rhythmic percussion
11:10	Crescendo, full orchestral sound
11:48	Orchestra quiet, recitations
12:29	Choir enters—A series of poignant personal reminiscences
15:45	Music becomes more animated, builds to 18:02
18:02	Choir re-enters with frantic orchestral accompaniment
19:58	Peaceful atmosphere restored
20:30	Recitation of names interspersed with quotations
24:20	City sounds

pieces of music might very well suggest to a listener similar emotions. Such is the imaginative power of music. But the effect is magnified when the music is experienced in a place or during an event evocative of the music's inherent mood. Composers have long been aware of music's ability to paint "pictures" in the listener's mind. They have often given descriptive names to pieces to stir the imagination or enhance the emotional context in which the music is experienced. Music that represents something extra-musical, like a scene in nature, a story line, or an idea such as love, sadness or fear, is called "program music." We refer to this kind of music as "programmatic."

The Funeral March

One type of program music that is appropriate for this chapter's topic is called a "funeral march." Obviously by using that descriptive name the composer wants you to think along certain lines when listening to the music. A funeral march is usually a slow piece of music with a steady, plodding beat in a minor key that evokes feelings of sadness and grief. It can either be a stand alone, complete piece of music or a single movement from a multi-movement work.

Perhaps the most famous funeral march is the third movement from the *Piano Sonata #2 in B-flat minor* by the Polish composer, Frederic Chopin (1810–1849). Chopin was a Romantic period composer who wrote almost exclusively for the piano. Composers during the Romantic period often specialized in certain types of music for which they had an affinity. A sonata is a type of instrumental piece, usually in three or four movements, either for a solo piano or for another instrument with a significant piano accompaniment.

 3rd Movement "Funeral March" from *Piano Sonata #2 in B-flat minor*— Frederic Chopin

As soon as you heard the first few notes of this funeral march you probably said something to the effect of, "Oh, I've heard that music before." You probably heard it in a cartoon or a movie when something sad happened. It has become *the* cliché for sad music. But the familiar opening theme is only a part of this music, not the entire composition. Can you describe the different sections of this piece? How many sections are there? What is the overall structure of this movement? Within each large section are there changes of mood and character? Why would a composer do that?

Another famous funeral march is the second movement of the *Symphony #3 in E-flat major,* subtitled The Eroica (Heroic) Symphony, by Ludwig van Beethoven (1770–1827). Beethoven initially intended to name this work the "*Bonaparte Symphony*" in honor of Napoleon Bonaparte. Beethoven felt that Napoleon represented a new, positive political force for Europe. But after Napoleon crowned himself Emperor the dedication was changed to read, "Composed to celebrate the memory of a great man." Listen to the "Marcia Funebre" (Funeral March) movement from this symphony and compare it to the Chopin.

Frederic Chopin Playing the Piano in Prince Radziwille's Salon by Henryk Siemiradzki. © Fine Art Photographic Library/ Corbis

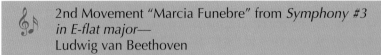

2nd Movement "Marcia Funebre" from *Symphony #3 in E-flat major*—
Ludwig van Beethoven

What similarities can you hear in these two funeral marches? What differences can you perceive? These pieces were not intended to be performed at someone's funeral but rather during a concert where each of these movements was a part of a larger composition. Does that seem appropriate to you or weird?

Threnody

The next example of instrumental music for mourning is quite different in every respect from the Chopin and Beethoven pieces. In this music there is no melody to recognize, no rhythm to feel, no traditional harmony to suggest sadness. The title of the piece is *Threnody to the Victims of Hiroshima,* by the twentieth-century Polish composer, Krzysztof Penderecki (b. 1933). The term "threnody" means "song of lamentation" or "song of mourning" from the Greek word "threnoidia."

Penderecki's "*Threnody*" was written in 1959 and premiered in 1960. It was written for a string orchestra of 52 players consisting of violins, violas, cellos, and basses. On first hearing, it might be difficult for the listener to recognize these traditional instruments since they are required to be played in unusual ways. Striking the instruments, scraping the strings, using the wood of the bow instead of the horsehair, snapping the strings percussively against the fingerboard are all techniques employed in this piece. Not only are the performing techniques unusual but the compositional techniques are extreme as well. Traditional concepts of melody, harmony, and rhythm are non-existent in this composition. They are replaced by closely spaced clusters of notes, tone clusters, instead of traditional harmonies. Approximate rhythmic notations are used that leave the exact timing and manner of the performance to be partly determined by the conductor and the individual players. The result is music of extraordinary dissonance that relates in a way that perhaps no other musical language could the horror of the event that it portrays.

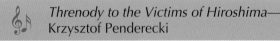

Threnody to the Victims of Hiroshima—
Krzysztof Penderecki

What are your impressions of this piece? Does it stir images in your mind's eye? It certainly isn't traditional music as we know it, but it is musical in its treatment of sound as a tool for communicating. As a memorial to those killed by the atomic bomb at Hiroshima, perhaps it is fitting that an event heretofore never experienced is portrayed by a type of music heretofore never heard.

The *Adagio for Strings*

The *Adagio for Strings* by the twentieth-century American composer Samuel Barber (1910–1981) is a work that has morphed from a single movement within a multi-movement concert piece into a stand-alone work synonymous with "music of mourning." The "*Adagio*" was originally the second movement of a string quartet that Barber had written in 1936 and was not intended as a memorial composition. At the request of Arturo Toscanini, the highly influential conductor of the NBC Symphony

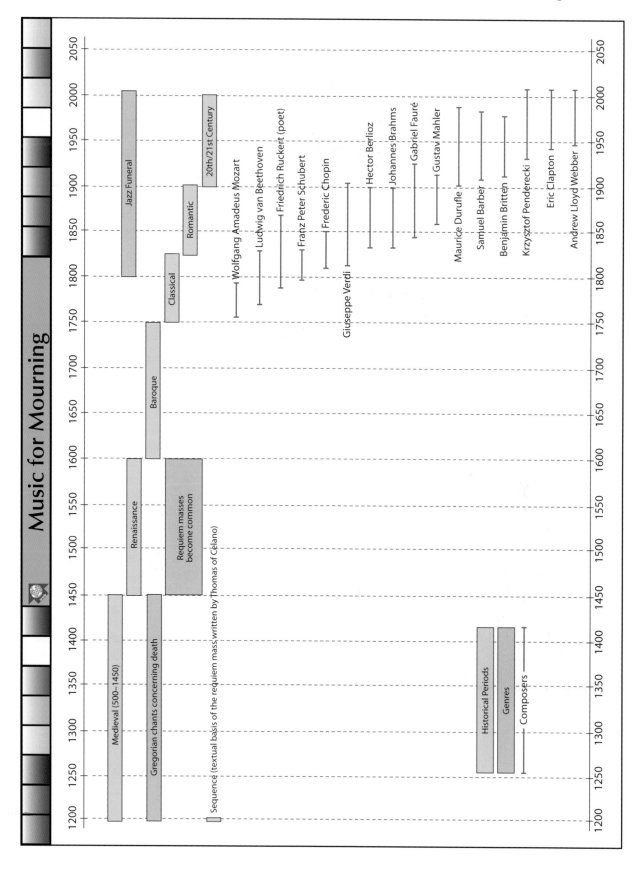

Orchestra, Barber reworked the movement for a full string orchestra. The revised version employed multiple players on each part along with double basses, which were not included in the original scoring. This created a richly textured work of unusual intensity.

The elegiac quality of the *Adagio* lends itself naturally to the observance of the passing of life. It gained widespread acceptance as music of mourning after it was played at the funeral of President Franklin Delano Roosevelt in 1945. The work subsequently was used during the funeral services of other important and notable people such as President John F. Kennedy and Princess Grace of Monaco. The *Adagio for Strings* has also been heard in a number of movies, including *A Clockwork Orange, Elephant Man,* and *Lorenzo's Oil,* adding to its widespread exposure outside of the concert hall. Perhaps most significantly, the piece added poignancy to horrific scenes of war in the movie *Platoon.* While this composition may not have been written specifically for mourning, it may capture better than any other piece the sadness, intensity, and final acceptance of the loss of life.

The work is based on a flowing, lyrical melody that builds inexorably to an intensely climactic sustained chord. After a brief pause, the initial calmness returns and the piece concludes in the placid embrace of peaceful repose.

 Adagio for Strings—
Samuel Barber

Dogon Funeral Music

Dogon funeral mask. © 2013, Henk Paul, Shutterstock, Inc.

The **Dogon** people of Mali, in West Africa, observe the passing of life with a number of rituals involving music, dance, and elaborate costumes. The collective name for all of the funeral rituals of the Dogon is "**Dama.**" Dogon funeral rituals commence immediately after a death has occurred and continue at various times for months afterwards and then yearly as communal remembrances of all who have died during the previous year. In many African cultures funeral rituals are extremely important as it is believed that rituals that are incomplete, or not performed properly, allow the spirits of the dead to remain in this world bringing misfortune on their families. Only upon completion of properly executed funeral rites are the spirits of the dead allowed to pass into the afterlife.

A characteristic of significance with regard to the funeral rituals of the Dogon are the masks that are unique to each village. The purpose of the masks varies, with some representing creation, the earth, animals, people the deceased knew in life, neighboring enemies, and others intended to assist in guiding the deceased to the afterlife.

The music that accompanies the dancing and displaying of the masks consists mostly of drumming and chanting but can also include animal calls and melodic singing performed as a counterpoint to the chanting. The chanting speaks of the deceased's life and depicts the journey to the afterlife. The subject of the chanting changes as different masked groups enter the ritual.

Dogon Funeral Music

The New Orleans Jazz Funeral

In most cultures a funeral is a time for quiet reflection on the memory of the deceased. Outward displays of joy and frivolity are generally looked down upon as being inappropriate to the occasion. An exception to that approach to funerals is the **New Orleans Jazz Funeral**. During these ceremonies the deceased is accompanied to the grave by a slow moving, marching brass band playing melancholy **dirges**. A dirge is any slow, sad music for a funeral. But after interment the band returns to town playing exuberant, celebratory music. This tradition is an adaptation of customs brought to America by slaves from Africa where funeral rituals were more often celebrations of a life, rather than a mourning of a death.

New Orleans jazz band, Olympia, playing in a funeral procession. © Philip Gould/Corbis

Just a Closer Walk with Thee—
Jazz Funeral Dirge

 When the Saints Go Marching In—
Traditional

Native American Funeral Music

The music of Native American cultures is as varied as the many geographical regions from which it comes. While it is impossible to summarize in so short a space as this the distinct characteristics associated with so many tribal styles it is safe to say that much Native American funeral music makes extensive use of percussion instruments in a rhythmically repetitive manner. Drums and rattles play a prominent role along with many varieties of vocal chanting and melodic singing in which extensive repetition is also found. Much Native American music has historically been tied to the rituals of life, passing on historical information, and celebrating the natural world. Music in Native American culture is often performed in conjunction with dance, especially as a storytelling device.

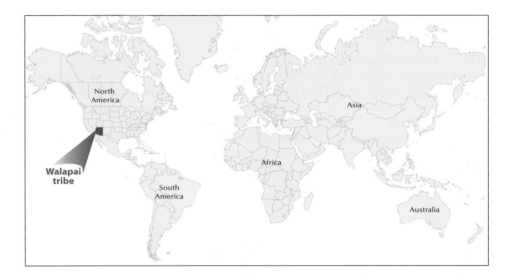

In the following two examples the repetitive nature of music from diverse Native American peoples can be heard. The first example, *Funeral Song,* from the Walapai people of Arizona, and the second example, the *Warrior Death Song,* of the Assiniboine tribe from the northern Great Plains of the United States and Canada, each exhibit different repetitive qualities.

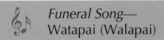 *Funeral Song—*
Watapai (Walapai)

Listening Chart

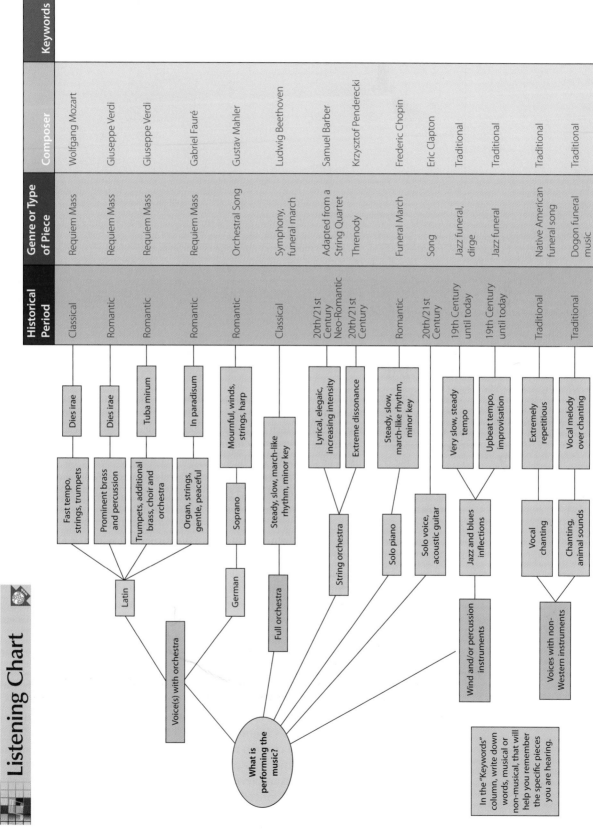

Historical Period	Genre or Type of Piece	Composer	Keywords
Classical	Requiem Mass	Wolfgang Mozart	
Romantic	Requiem Mass	Giuseppe Verdi	
Romantic	Requiem Mass	Giuseppe Verdi	
Romantic	Requiem Mass	Gabriel Fauré	
Romantic	Orchestral Song	Gustav Mahler	
Classical	Symphony, funeral march	Ludwig Beethoven	
20th/21st Century Neo-Romantic	Adapted from a String Quartet	Samuel Barber	
20th/21st Century	Threnody	Krzysztof Penderecki	
Romantic	Funeral March	Frederic Chopin	
20th/21st Century	Song	Eric Clapton	
19th Century until today	Jazz funeral, dirge	Traditional	
19th Century until today	Jazz funeral	Traditional	
Traditional	Native American funeral song	Traditional	
Traditional	Dogon funeral music	Traditional	

Flowchart nodes:

What is performing the music?

Voice(s) with orchestra → Latin → Fast tempo, strings, trumpets → Dies irae
Latin → Prominent brass and percussion → Dies irae
Latin → Trumpets, additional brass, choir and orchestra → Tuba mirum
Latin → Organ, strings, gentle, peaceful → In paradisum
German → Soprano → Mournful, winds, strings, harp
Full orchestra → Steady, slow, march-like rhythm, minor key
String orchestra → Lyrical, elegaic, increasing intensity / Extreme dissonance
Solo piano → Steady, slow, march-like rhythm, minor key
Solo voice, acoustic guitar
Jazz and blues inflections → Very slow, steady tempo / Upbeat tempo, improvisation
Wind and/or percussion instruments
Vocal chanting → Extremely repetitious
Chanting, animal sounds → Vocal melody over chanting
Voices with non-Western instruments

In the "Keywords" column, write down words, musical or non-musical, that will help you remember the specific pieces you are hearing.

Warrior Death Song (for Sitting Bull)—
Assinboine (Assiniboine)

SUMMARY

This chapter began with a look at the Requiem mass, an "institutional" means of acknowledging the passing of life from the perspective of the Catholic Church. Established religions all have rituals, often accompanied by music, which serve as a communal way of dealing with the end of life. Certain texts in the liturgy of the Catholic Church have been used as the basis of the Requiem mass since Medieval times. One text in particular, the Dies Irae (The Day of Wrath), has played an especially important role in Requiem masses, referring as it does to the day of The Last Judgment when all souls will be called to account for their lives. While some of the most memorable Requiem masses have contained remarkable settings of the Dies Irae text, Mozart's and Verdi's for example, some Requiem masses have dispensed with the Dies Irae altogether, such as Faure's.

Requiem masses may be the grandest musical settings dealing with death, but simple songs account for a large portion of the music dedicated to easing the pain at the end of life. Instead of representing a particular religion's point of view about dying it allows for a more intimate expression of loss, one that may be easier for an individual to connect with on a personal level. Songs of mourning may be accompanied by a single instrument, such as the guitar or the piano, a small ensemble of instruments, or a full orchestra.

Instrumental music of mourning takes many forms, from solo instrumental pieces to full orchestral works. The funeral march is a type of piece that can be a freestanding work in its own right or, as is more common, a single movement in a multi-movement composition. Chopin's *Piano Sonata #3 in B-flat minor* and Beethoven's *Symphony #3 in E-flat major* each contain movements called *"funeral marches."* Instrumental music of mourning is sometimes conceived of as such, Penderecki's *Threnody for the Victims of Hiroshima,* for example, or it can sometimes find its place in that category by virtue of the emotional connection it makes with people. Barber's *Adagio for Strings* would be an example of that type of piece.

Music of mourning within any given culture can take on unique characteristics reflecting differing views on the passing of life. The Dogon people of Mali in western Africa hold funeral rituals for days on end, sometimes being completed months after a death has occurred, incorporating music, dance, and elaborate costumes. The music can contain chanting, imitative animal calls, and melodic singing. In the cultural heritage of the people of New Orleans, the passing of life is accompanied by slow, sad music, "dirges," while the body is being carried to the cemetery which then changes to upbeat, celebratory, music after the body has been interred. In this way expressions of sadness at the passing of life are acknowledged while also celebrating a life well lived. In the music of many Native American peoples, chanting and repetitive percussion sounds are common characteristics. The repetitive nature of Native American music is sometimes related to the desire to achieve perfection for the pleasure of God. Native American music of mourning almost always accompanies ritual dancing.

SUGGESTED FURTHER LISTENING

Day is Done (Taps)—Daniel Butterfield

Go Rest High on that Mountain—Vince Gill

Psalm 23—Kathy Troccoli

Masonic Funeral Music—Wolfgang Amadeus Mozart

Ave Maria—Franz Schubert

"In Paradisum" from *Requiem in D minor*—Gabriel Fauré

"Siegfried's Death and Funeral Music" from *Götterdämmerung* (*Twilight of the Gods*)—Richard Wagner

"Aasa's Death" from *Peer Gynt*—Edvard Grieg

Pavane Pour Une Infante Defunt (*Pave for a Dead Infant*)—Maurice Ravel

"Nimrod" from *Enigma Variations*—Edward Elgar

"Adagietto," 4th movement from *Symphony #5*—Gustav Mahler

QUESTION ASSIGNMENT

Instructions: Log in to the textbook web site and click on the ASSIGNMENTS tab. In the Chapter Question Assignment area read the instructions and answer the question(s) or provide the asked for information. Be sure to click the SUBMIT THIS FORM button after you complete the Assignment.

Name the type of funeral music characterized by slow, sad music being played before interment followed by upbeat, celebratory music afterward? Where did this type of funeral music have its origins?

Funeral Music: _____

Place of Origin: _____

LISTENING EXERCISES

Instructions: Log in to the textbook web site and click on the ASSIGNMENTS tab. In the Listening Exercises area click on the links to the musical examples for each question and answer the questions. Be sure to click the SUBMIT button after you answer all of the questions.

Listen to each of the musical examples below from the Chapter 6 Playlist while noting the appropriate descriptive prompt on the Listening Chart for Chapter 6 and determine the best answer to each question.

1. "Tuba mirum" (The Trumpet Shall Sound) from *Messa da Requiem* by Giuseppe Verdi—This piece for voices with orchestra is sung in Latin, the traditional language of the Catholic Church. Trumpets, placed strategically around the auditorium or church where it is performed, call back and forth at ever increasing volume. They are joined by additional brass instruments until the choir and orchestra provide the culminating climactic forces. Choose the timing when the choir makes its first entrance.

    a. 60 seconds
    b. 1:40 seconds
    c. 2:10 seconds

2. *Adagio for Strings* by Samuel Barber—This piece, for string orchestra, begins calmly and repeats its lyrical, elegiac melody with increasing intensity. Choose the approximate timing that represents the most intense moment of the piece.

    a. 1:25 seconds
    b. 4:30 seconds
    c. 5:20 seconds

3. *Dogon Funeral Music*—This example, for voices with non-Western instruments, makes use of chanting, animal sounds, and a vocal melody over the chanting. One of the prominent instruments used is a type of flute made out of wood rather than metal. Choose the timing when you first hear the distinctive sound of this unique sounding flute.

    a. 1:20 seconds
    b. 2:45 seconds
    c. 3:45 seconds

Chapter 7

Music for Celebration, Inspiration, and Commemoration

FOCUS POINTS

Music of Celebration
Songs
Wedding Music
Dances

Music of Inspiration
Fanfares
Marches
National Anthems

Music of Commemoration
Concert Overtures
Works with Narration

Music plays a central role in the significant events of our lives. The power of music to affect the listener can add joy to a celebration, create a sense of common purpose at inspirational events, or serve as a communal bond when historic events or personages are commemorated. Birthdays and weddings incorporate music as part of the celebration. Political and sporting events usually begin with some type of musical proclamation such as the National Anthem or a fanfare. Parades commemorating national holidays include bands playing marches and other types of inspirational music. National and religious holidays have stimulated the writing of numerous musical compositions, and graduation ceremonies from college and high school always have music as part of the proceedings. Virtually every important event in our lives has a musical component.

Other art forms do not play as prominent a role in our celebrations as does music. Occasionally poems are written to commemorate events or mark a celebration but the frequency of their inclusion in such events is not as ubiquitous as musical performances. The creation of paintings, statues or stage plays to mark important events is even less common. A musical performance is an inclusive, communal activity when it is part of an event and as such it can intensify the emotions of those in attendance. Just how music affects our experience of important events will be the topic as we examine music of celebration, inspiration and commemoration.

A Kitty Band procession in Scotland. Corel

MUSIC FOR CELEBRATION

Birthday parties almost always include the song *Happy Birthday.* We have come to expect it. New Year's Eve celebrations often culminate in the singing of *Auld Lang Syne* and *The Star Spangled Banner* is the familiar opening proclamation at sporting events across America. Of course these events could take place without these specific musical compositions. But these pieces have become such an integral part of these events that if they were *not* present it would be out of the ordinary. We take it for granted that music will not only accompany but play an essential role in the celebrations of life. Any of the above-mentioned compositions could be replaced by other music appropriate to the occasions. It just so happens that these particular pieces have acquired such a level of acceptance at these specific events that we have come to expect to hear them whenever we gather to celebrate birthdays, weddings, etc.

Where did *Happy Birthday, Auld Lang Syne,* and *The Star Spangled Banner* come from and how did they become incorporated into our cultural traditions? Have they been around forever, like traditional folk songs anonymously passed down from generation to generation, or were they composed recently and interjected into our celebrations purposefully? Since these pieces have attained such a prominent place in our culture it is appropriate that we take a brief look at them to understand how they became such an integral part of our celebrations.

Happy Birthday

The origin of *Happy Birthday* is a roundabout tale that began with two sisters from Kentucky, Mildred and Patti Hill. Sometime around 1893 Mildred wrote the familiar melody that would eventually become *Happy Birthday.* Patti, who was an elementary school teacher, wrote a verse of words that would be appropriate for a school teacher to sing to her students at the beginning of each school day.

> Good morning to you,
> Good morning to you,
> Good morning dear children,
> Good morning to all.

After a few years this simple greeting was turned around by students into:

> Good morning to you,
> Good morning to you,
> Good morning dear teacher,
> Good morning to all.

The student-modified version spread throughout the country and became a common morning salutation from students to teachers.

There is no documented evidence that the now familiar *Happy Birthday* lyrics were actually written by either of the Hill sisters but the song we know today, with the current words, appeared both in print and on the Broadway stage in two musicals, *The Band Wagon* (1931) and Irving Berlin's *As Thousands Cheer* (1933).

Santa's Birthday Party by R. T. Jones (ca. 1940–1950), including characters from *Alice in Wonderland, Alice through the Looking Glass, Snow White, Red Riding Hood, Reluctant Dragon, Aesop's Fables, Mother Goose*, and others. Copyright © Ricco/Maresca Gallery/Art Resource, NY

Jessica Hill, another sister, recognized the ever-increasing popularity of the song and took legal action to have *Happy Birthday* acknowledged as the creation of her sisters. She was awarded the copyright to *Happy Birthday* on behalf of her sisters in 1934. Due to several quirks in the copyright laws the song is still protected under copyright until 2030. That means that a performance of the song in a public place or in media of any kind requires that royalties be paid to the copyright holder.

The singing of *Happy Birthday* has become the centerpiece, along with the birthday cake, at birthday celebrations in America and many other countries around the world. Another, secondary, musical tradition is part of birthday parties in Mexico and South America. The dancing of a waltz by the birthday girl and her father, upon the girl having reached the age of fifteen or sixteen, is the acknowledgment of attaining a degree of maturity for girls throughout that region. There are other examples of musical components of birthday celebrations but none has attained the almost universal status of *Happy Birthday*.

Auld Lang Syne

The early history of the song *Auld Lang Syne* is lost in the mists of the Scottish sixteenth century. This song is traditionally sung in many countries, including the United States, at 12:00 midnight on New Year's Eve. "Old Long Ago," as it is usually interpreted, is a statement of friendship tinged with a touch of nostalgia. Though it is thought that the poet Robert Burns penned at least some of the words of the poem, today's version is probably a synthesis of Burns' words and older phrases. The melody is a traditional Scottish tune. The commonly accepted wording of the song is as follows:

Should auld acquaintance be forgot
And never brought to mind?
Should auld acquaintance be forgot
And days of lang syne?
For auld lang syne, my dear,
For auld lang syne,
We'll take a cup of kindness yet,
For auld lang syne.

 Auld Lang Syne—
Traditional Scottish Folk Song performed by Guy Lombardo's Orchestra

In America, *Auld Lang Syne* signals the end of one year and the beginning of another, but in other countries the song (or just its melody) has been adopted as a graduation song (Japan and the Philippines), a funeral song (Taiwan), and it even served as Korea's national anthem for a period of time.

What is it about these songs that have allowed them to become such fixtures at these celebrations? It is most likely the participatory character of the songs; everybody in attendance sings them. By joining in the singing each person in attendance becomes an active part of the celebration, not just an observer. It is part of the ritual of the occasion to sing these songs and rituals are indispensable to our celebrations, both sacred and secular. Virtually all religious rituals include the congregation in the active participation of the spiritual observances of the church. It shouldn't be surprising that our secular celebrations have adopted a similar approach to the inclusion of music.

Musical performance celebrating the marriage of the Dauphin of France by Giovanni Pannini (1691–1765). Copyright © Reunion des Musees Nationaux/Art Resource, NY

The *Wedding March* from *A Midsummer Night's Dream*

A piece of instrumental music that is often included in wedding celebrations is the *Wedding March* from the incidental music to the play *A Midsummer Night's Dream*. This music was written by the nineteenth-century German composer **Felix Mendelssohn** (1809–1847), based on the Shakespeare play of the same name. As mentioned in Chapter 3, "Incidental music is music that is composed to accompany a stage production such as a play." Mendelssohn's music from *A Midsummer Night's Dream* is some of the most frequently played incidental music of all time, performed in concert independently from the staging of the play. The "Wedding March" is written in a form we call **rondo** form. It consists of a **theme** played during the opening part of the piece, the "A" section, which is repeated a number of times, with contrasting sections of music interspersed between repetitions of the "A" theme. The following is a visual representation of this type of formal structure:

A—B—A—C—A—D—A

The "A"s represent the main melodic idea, the main theme, and the other letters represent sections based on different melodies. Rondo form pieces can have fewer or greater numbers of sections than this diagram represents. Listen to the excerpt and diagram the format for this specific piece.

 Wedding March from *A Midsummer Night's Dream*—
Felix Mendelssohn

An instrumental composition such as Mendelssohn's *Wedding March* usually accompanies the parts of a celebration during which some activity takes place. In this case it is played when the bride and groom exit the venue after the ceremony is completed. Another frequently used instrumental composition is the "Bridal March" from the opera *Lohengrin* by the German operatic composer Richard Wagner, better known as *Here Comes the Bride*. That music is played when the bride enters the ceremonial venue and walks down the aisle before the ceremony has taken place.

Jewish Wedding Music

In Jewish wedding ceremonies songs play a significant role, with the service interspersed with both contemporary and folk songs. Dancing at a Jewish wedding reception usually includes a type of folk music circle dance called a Hora, with the traditional *Hava Nagila* (*Come Let Us Be Glad*) being the most frequently included dance music.

 Hava Nagila (Come Let Us Be Glad)—
Traditional Jewish Folk Dance

A style of traditional Jewish music known as Klezmer is also often heard at weddings and other types of Jewish celebrations. Klezmer music has a unique sound that is produced by the combination of certain melodic and harmonic characteristics and the types of instruments that are used. Klezmer music developed among traveling musicians who played at celebrations of all kinds in Jewish communities throughout Eastern Europe. Virtuosic improvisation and vocal inflections by the instruments are characteristic of this music. Modern Klezmer ensembles include instruments such as the violin, clarinet, trumpet, flute, cello, bass, and drums.

Wedding Dance—
Traditional Jewish Klezmer Music

Instrumental music serves to set the mood or accompany dancing at celebrations. It often provides a framework, being performed at both the beginning and end of an event, within which the celebration is experienced. In this way the celebration rituals we experience are defined by the music that accompanies them.

Mexican Hat Dance

The Jarabe Tapatío, or **Mexican Hat Dance**, is a piece of music and a dance that have come to be regarded as the national dance of Mexico. The music is a compilation of traditional Mexican folk tunes fashioned into a unified composition in the late nineteenth century by Mexican composer **Jesús Rubio**. The music is most frequently performed by a **mariachi band**, a combination of trumpets, violins, and several sizes and varieties of guitars, including a very large one that serves the function of a bass. Mariachi music originated in the Mexican state of Jalisco as did the Hat Dance. The word "tapatío" in the name refers to Jalisco as the place of origin.

While not tied to any particular celebration, the Mexican Hat Dance may be heard, and seen, at any public celebration in Mexico throughout the year. The most widely known Mexican celebratory event is Cinco de Mayo, Fifth of May, which has come to be known around the world as a celebration of Mexican traditions and ethnicity. It is at events like this, as well as at smaller celebrations like weddings, that the Mexican Hat Dance is often performed. The name, Mexican Hat Dance, is a reference to the part of this courtship dance where the man throws the large wide-brimmed hat that he is wearing, a sombrero, to the ground for the woman to pick up, thus sealing their union in love.

Jarabe Tapatío—
Jesús Rubio

MUSIC OF INSPIRATION

Music has long been used to inspire people, especially in matters of political and national regard. Fanfares have announced the arrival of important personages from ancient kings and queens to modern presidents, bestowing a sense of power and importance on the people who represent our countries. National anthems are musical representations of countries, often invoking some historical or cultural point of reference important in the history of a particular nation. Marches have historically accompanied soldiers into battle, instilling a sense of camaraderie and common purpose through the uniformity of their movements to the music. Music inspires and exhilarates when heard in the shared experience of a common purpose.

Fanfares

A **fanfare** is a short composition for brass and percussion instruments used to announce the arrival of an important person or to mark the beginning of a ceremonial occasion. Notated fanfares date from as early as the Medieval period, and pictorial representations indicate that brass and percussion instruments accompanied soldiers into battle during the Roman empire. Fanfares today are used in circumstances similar to those throughout history. When the President of the United States enters a room, a fanfare called *Hail to the Chief* is played. In the past a similar piece might have announced the arrival of a king.

Armed Forces parade. Corel

Hail to the Chief—
Ceremonial Fanfare

Large ceremonial events are often begun with the playing of a fanfare. In modern times one of the most widely experienced fanfares is the music that marks the beginning and ending of the Olympic Games. Not only is this music used at the opening and closing ceremonies, but it is also heard throughout the games at medal ceremonies, when television coverage begins or ends, and after commercial breaks. This repeated playing gives the music an extraordinary amount of public exposure. When the Olympic Games are in session the fanfare that signifies the games is heard by more people in the world than any other piece of music. Fanfares for the Olympic Games have become a part of the cultural fabric of the entire world.

Bugler's Dream, a fanfare written by Leo Arnaud, had represented the Olympic Games from 1930 until 1984 when a new fanfare was **commissioned** by the Olympic Committee. They chose American composer **John Williams** (b. 1932), already famous for his movie music, to write a new *Olympic Fanfare* for the 1984 games in Los Angeles. It is a fairly extended composition as fanfares go, but it is the familiar brass flourish with which the piece opens that immediately identifies it. Listen first to the opening flourish and then the entire composition.

Olympic Fanfare (opening flourish)—
John Williams

This music probably sounds familiar to you even if the Olympic Games are not in session at this moment.

 Olympic Fanfare (entire composition)—
John Williams

Aaron Copland acknowledges the accolades of the audience at an all-Copland program celebrating his 85th birthday. The New York Philharmonic, under Zubin Mehta, performed *Fanfare for the Common Man*, and other works by the composer. © Bettmann/Corbis

Fanfares usually accompany ceremonial occasions, but one that has acquired a permanent place in the concert repertory of symphony orchestras and concert bands is the *Fanfare for the Common Man* written by American composer Aaron Copland (1900–1990). In 1942 Copland was commissioned by the Cincinnati Symphony Orchestra and its conductor, Eugene Goosens, to write a fanfare honoring those currently serving in World War II. The resulting composition has the signature imprint of Copland's "American" sounding music. Honoring the "everyman" that represented America, Copland penned a work both representative of the country and inspiring to it at the same time. Copland liked the piece so much he incorporated it into the final movement of his *Symphony #3*.

 Fanfare for the Common Man—
Aaron Copland

What makes a "good" fanfare? All of the above examples share certain qualities, but they also have significant differences. What are they? Does this music do what it is supposed to do, inspire you? How does it attempt to do that?

National Anthems

A **national anthem** is a composition adopted as the "official" song used to represent a country. The majority of national anthems invoke nationalistic pride with references to the inherent courage and strength of the people, victories in battles fought, events of historical importance, and the blessings of the land in which they live. The words to *The Star Spangled Banner*, the national anthem of the United States, were written by Francis Scott Key, a prominent Baltimore lawyer. Key was inspired to pen his memorable verses upon seeing the tattered flag of the United States still flying over Baltimore's Fort McHenry after a 25-hour bombardment by the British in 1814. The words were first published in newspapers as a four-verse poem entitled, *The Star Spangled Banner,* with Key's suggestion that they be sung to the melody of a popular English drinking song, *To Anacreon in Heaven,* by John Stafford Smith. The poem, set to the Smith melody, was soon in print and became a common fixture at most patriotic occasions. *The Star Spangled Banner* became the national anthem by vote of Congress in 1931. As is the custom for most songs, including national anthems, *The Star Spangled Banner* is composed of several verses of text sung to the same melody each time. As was discussed in Chapter 5, this type of format is called **strophic form**.

What Makes Music—Musical Instruments

The Percussion Family

Instruments of the orchestra are grouped into four families according to certain characteristics. The percussion family includes any instrument that is hit or struck to make a sound.

These instruments are usually divided into two types, pitched and non-pitched. Some of the pitched percussion instruments include: Marimba, Xylophone, Bells, and Tympani (tunable kettle drums). Some of the non-pitched percussion instruments include drums, cymbals, gongs, ratchet, and triangle.

There is no standard performing ensemble for percussion instruments. Any grouping of percussion instruments is called a Percussion Ensemble and may consist of any and all instruments.

View the video of English composer Benjamin Britten's *Young Person's Guide to the Orchestra* performed by the YouTube Symphony Orchestra on the chapter video playlist.

The percussion family of instruments is featured from 1:34–1:50 and some of the percussion instruments are featured individually beginning at the 12:08 mark.

The University of Memphis Percussion Ensemble, Frank Shaffer (center), Director
Photo courtesy of The University of Memphis, Dr. Randall Rushing, photographer

National anthems became commonplace in the nineteenth century during an era when nationalistic fervor was high throughout Europe and the establishment of many clearly defined national boundaries was in the formative stages. The term used to describe works of music, art, and literature that are inspired by such nationalistic feelings is called nationalism. Nationalism can be expressed in music by various means such as writing operas or ballets based on folk tales, historical events, or important people of a country. It can also take the form of ethnic dances, music describing places in one's homeland, or in the writing of national anthems.

Fourth of July parade. Corel

National anthems are heard today at patriotic celebrations, sporting events, school assemblies, and at the beginning and end of the broadcast day of some television stations. The version of *The Star Spangled Bannner* heard on your playlist features the first and last verses of the song.

The Star Spangled Banner (verses 1 and 4)—
words by Francis Scott Key, music by John Stafford Smith

Oh, say can you see by the dawn's early light
What so proudly we hailed at the twilight's last gleaming?
Whose broad stripes and bright stars thru the perilous fight,
O'er the ramparts we watched were so gallantly streaming?
And the rocket's red glare, the bombs bursting in air,
Gave proof through the night that our flag was still there.
Oh, say does that star-spangled banner yet wave
O'er the land of the free and the home of the brave?

Oh! thus be it ever, when freemen shall stand
Between their loved home and the war's desolation!
Blest with victory and peace, may the heav'n rescued land
Praise the Power that hath made and preserved us a nation.
Then conquer we must, when our cause it is just,
And this be our motto: "In God is our trust."
And the star-spangled banner in triumph shall wave
O'er the land of the free and the home of the brave!

Marches

A **march** is a musical composition usually written for a military band in duple meter and performed at a tempo approximating two beats per second. Marches have long been used in the armed forces to accompany marching formations of soldiers but have become a part of popular culture owing to their inclusion in parades, at sporting events, and as regular features on band and orchestra concerts. The preeminent American composer of marches was **John Philip Sousa** (1854–1932). Sousa's marches were written for a military-type band consisting of brass and wind instruments with percussion.

The formal structure of Sousa marches follows a fairly consistent pattern: a short introduction; several **stanzas** of music (each with a different melody); a **trio** section characterized by a contrasting style of melody; and a **breakstrain**, a vigorous interjection between statements of the trio. The second playing of the trio usually introduces an instrumental **obbligato** countermelody. An obbligato is a virtuosic accompanying line of music, usually played by a single instrument. A countermelody is simply a second melody heard in conjunction with the main melody. The final playing of the trio, called the **grandioso**, is usually loud and may introduce another countermelody heretofore not heard. Sousa is credited with standardizing the march form, which can be outlined as follows using his most famous march *The Stars and Stripes Forever* as a model:

Canadian Royal Marching Band. Corel

Introduction (short)—4 bars
1st strain—16 bars—repeated
2nd strain—16 bars—repeated
Trio—calm, smooth—32 bars
Breakstrain—loud trombones—24 bars
Trio (with piccolo obbligato)—32 bars
Breakstrain—loud trombones—24 bars
Trio (Grandioso)—with a chorus singing a verse of Sousa's original text—32 bars

The Stars and Stripes Forever is, by Act of Congress, the official march of the United States of America and the march Sousa included on virtually all of the programs he conducted after it was written. He wrote the march on Christmas Day 1896 while on a boat heading back to America from Europe. Sousa wrote lyrics that could be sung throughout the piece, but it is rare for text other than the verses below to be included in modern performances.

 The Stars and Stripes Forever—
John Philip Sousa

Hurrah for the flag of the free!
May it wave as our standard forever,
The gem of the land and the sea,
The banner of the right.
Let despots remember the day
When our fathers with mighty endeavor
Proclaimed as they marched to the fray
That by their might and by their right
It waves forever.

Music inspires us through textural references to common cultural and national beliefs and shared ideals. We are moved by its rhythmic energy and the intensity of the instrumentation employed. These qualities, inherent in inspirational music, have remained relatively unchanged throughout history.

MUSIC OF COMMEMORATION

A significant amount of music has been written in observance of major historical events or as commemorative pieces dedicated to the lives of great persons. These kinds of compositions often are initially performed at celebrations conducted in observance of the anniversary of the event or the birth/death of the honored person. Subsequently these pieces either diminish in frequency of performance on such anniversaries or gain new life as concert pieces performed on orchestra, band, or choral concerts separate from the occasions they were first intended to honor. The majority of commemorative pieces date from the late eighteenth century onward. The political unrest fostered by both the French and American Revolutions and the burgeoning sense of nationalism across Europe at that time contributed to the composition of much music in this vein. The general acceptance of programmatic music during this time also helped commemorative pieces become established as an integral part of the musical landscape.

The Concert Overture

The concert overture is a popular genre for commemorative musical compositions with the *1812 Overture* by Peter Ilyich Tchaikovsky and the *Festive Overture* by Dmitri Shostakovich (1906–1975) being two of the most popular. Shostakovich was, like Tchaikovsky, a Russian composer but unlike his fellow countryman, whose composing was dictated by his own muse and the tastes of his audience, Shostakovich was caught up in the political intrigues subsequent to the Russian Revolution of 1917. He even became a member of the Communist Party later in life. This made it necessary for Shostakovich to frequently tailor his composing to the political realities of the moment. The result is a larger than might be expected number of compositions from a major composer commemorating historical and political events. The exact nature of Shostakovich's relation to his political superiors is still a subject of some considerable debate.

The *Festive Overture* was commissioned by the Bolshoi Theatre in 1954 for the 37th anniversary celebration of the Russian Revolution. Shostakovich reportedly wrote the piece in two days. It opens with a fanfare in the brass that serves as an introduction to the very fast main body of the work, played first by the clarinet and then the violins. Short, punctuating melodic ideas follow in the brass and then the second, more lyrical, theme enters in the lower strings. Alternating statements of all of the previous melodic material come next along with some thematic material heard for the first time. The introductory fanfare returns just before the end of the piece, providing an overall A-B-A framework for the composition. But the piece does not end there. After the second playing of the fanfare material a short coda brings back the second, lyrical, melody in a double time version to conclude the piece. Double time is a term used to describe a musical idea that is played at twice the speed it was first heard.

Festive Overture—
Dmitri Shostakovich

La rue Montorgeuil, Paris, during the celebrations of June 30, 1878 by Claude Monet (1840–1926). Copyright © Erich Lessing/ Art Resource, NY

The *1812 Overture*

One of the most frequently performed commemorative compositions is the *Overture Solennelle*, more commonly known as the *1812 Overture*, by the nineteenth-century Russian composer Peter Ilyich Tchaikovsky (1840–1893). The piece was written in commemoration of the retreat from Russia of Napoleon's army in 1812, and was premiered in August of 1882 for the Moscow Art and Industrial Exhibition. The piece was originally to be performed a year earlier at the dedication of the Cathedral of Christ the Saviour in Moscow, but that outdoor performance, intended to incorporate real cannon fire and pealing church bells, was cancelled. A disappointed Tchaikovsky had to settle for a traditional indoor concert performance a year later. The composition is both programmatic and nationalistic in that it tries to represent a battle between opposing armies (programmatic) while stirring Russian patriotic feelings in recalling the Russian victory over the French (nationalism). Both the Russian and French national anthems are used in the piece along with a Russian church hymn and Russian folk song-like melodies. It is interesting to note that the anthems used by Tchaikovsky were the anthems in use when the piece was written in 1882 which were different than the anthems in use at the time of the battle in 1812. Also of note is the fact that there really was no decisive battle for Moscow in 1812. The French had occupied the city for some time and decided to retreat when most of the city burned and their resources had been nearly depleted. The retreating army left with only a fraction of its men surviving.

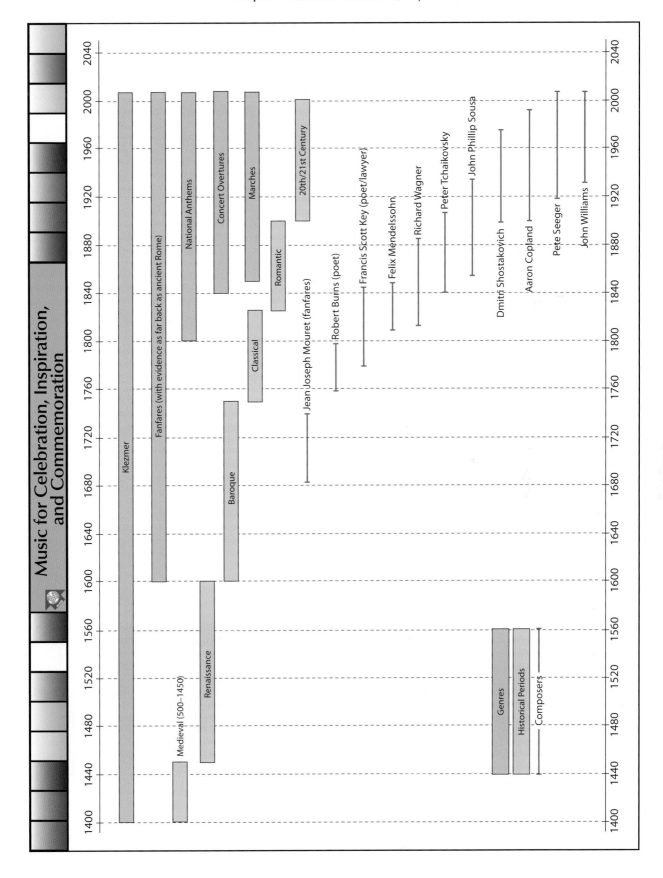

Music for Celebration, Inspiration, and Commemoration

Klezmer

Fanfares (with evidence as far back as ancient Rome)

National Anthems

Concert Overtures

Marches

20th/21st Century

Romantic

Classical

Baroque

Renaissance

Medieval (500–1450)

Jean Joseph Mouret (fanfares)

Robert Burns (poet)

Francis Scott Key (poet/lawyer)

Felix Mendelssohn

Richard Wagner

Peter Tchaikovsky

John Phillip Sousa

Dmitri Shostakovich

Aaron Copland

Pete Seeger

John Williams

Genres

Historical Periods

Composers

PERSPECTIVE—MONUMENTS AND MEMORIALS

Statues, paintings, buildings, monuments, prose, and poetry, in addition to music, are all media through which people or events of the past are remembered and honored. Through these commemorative efforts one can be inspired by bravery exhibited in battle, contributions of individuals or entire peoples to society, sacrifices made on behalf of others, or any honorable or heroic act. When celebrated through music, prose, or poetry, entire stories can be retold, histories recounted, multi-faceted people and events illuminated and explored. Or, they may simply examine one aspect of a person or event. The ways in which music honors individuals or events of the past has been the focus of this chapter. But when a painting, statue, or building is created it is a static object that must convey the essence of a once-living person or a complicated event.

Abu Simbel—Egypt.
Corel

The Great Sphinx
at Giza—Egypt. Corel

Some of the earliest monuments erected to commemorate the lives of people of importance were the Great Pyramids at Giza and the stone carvings at Abu Simbel, both located in Egypt. The pyramids are believed to have been constructed during the period called the *Fourth Dynasty*, approximately 2700–2550 BC. Abu Simbel is a monument consisting of four statues of pharaoh Rameses II constructed in approximately 1300 BC. The pyramids are tombs for the pharaohs who had them built and Abu Simbel was built to honor both the life of Rameses II and his victory in a battle at the city of Kadesh. These monuments are meant to impress and intimidate by their sheer size and majesty, not necessarily to inform or educate the observer. Another Egyptian monument, The Great Sphinx at Giza, is a large stone statue with the face of a man and a lion's body. Why it was built is not known. It also is believed to date from the *Fourth Dynasty*.

Commemorative statues from Ancient Greece date from approximately 500 BC. Prior to that statuary was often symbolic in its representation of people without any attempt on the part of the sculptor to accurately portray the features of specific individuals. Some of the first examples of lifelike statuary are seen in the depiction of Harmodius and Aristogeiton. These Greek warriors overthrew the then ruling family which lead the way to the establishment of democracy in Greece. The statue known as *Winged Victory of Samothrace*, though incomplete, is also an important example of commemorative statuary from ancient Greece dating from ca. 200 BC. These examples are visual commemorations of noteworthy political and military turning points.

Prior to the nineteenth century most commemorative statues and buildings were created as celebrations of military victories. Memorials to those who died were far less common. One of the most poignant memorials to those who gave their lives for others is the *Lion Monument*, also known as *The Dying Lion of Lucerne*. Sculpted out of a rock wall in Lucerne, Switzerland in 1819 by Bertel Thorvaldsen, the sculpture depicts a mortally wounded lion among the shattered representations of the French regime. The monument commemorates the Swiss Guards who lost their lives in the French

The Dying Lion of Lucerne—Lucerne,
Switzerland. Corel

PERSPECTIVE—MONUMENTS AND MEMORIALS

Jefferson Memorial—Washington, D.C.
Corel

Marine War Memorial
—Washington, D.C. Corel

Washington Monument
—Washington, D.C. Corel

Revolution. The inspiring *Marine Corps War Memorial* near Washington, D.C., which shows American troops raising the U.S. flag over Iwo Jima during the Second World War, was created as a memorial to all marines who have lost their lives in battle.

A building erected as a memorial must at once inspire and educate. Its architectural design must simultaneously capture the attention and invite the observer in. Washington, D.C. was conceived as a city of monuments and memorials. Initially those buildings were primarily commemorations of presidents of the United States. The Washington Monument and Lincoln and Jefferson memorials are the most well-known examples of that kind of commemorative structure. A broadening concept of whom and what could be memorialized and celebrated has lead to the inclusion of buildings as var-

ied as the Holocaust Museum, a memorial to the Jewish people killed by the Nazis in World War II, the National Museum of the American Indian, and the Martin Luther King, Jr. National Monument.

One statue that has come to symbolize an entire nation is *Liberty Enlightening the World*, better known as the *Statue of Liberty*, in New York. The statue was a gift from the people of France to the people of the United States in 1886. The *Statue of Liberty* has become a universal symbol celebrating the ideal of freedom. The inscription on the pedestal of Emma Lazarus' poem, *The New Colossus*, includes the famous line, "Give me your tired, your poor, your huddled masses yearning to be free . . ."

Liberty Enlightening the World—The Statue of Liberty. Corel

Lincoln Memorial—Washington, D.C.
Corel

Biographical Spotlight

Peter Ilyich Tchaikovsky

© 2013, Oleg Golovnev,
Shutterstock, Inc.

Peter Ilyich Tchaikovsky was born on May 7, 1840, and died on November 6, 1893. He was a Russian composer who flourished at a time when a distinctly Russian style of music was being advocated by many in his homeland. Schooled in a more European, that is, Germanic, approach to composition, he showed that a recognizably Russian style of music could be achieved without withdrawing completely from the tradition represented by Bach, Mozart, and Beethoven.

Tchaikovsky was born into a middle-class family and was given music lessons beginning at the age of five. He was a talented if not exceptionally gifted student, easily learning all aspects of music but showing little of the creative genius that would mark his later years. At the age of ten his parents enrolled him in a distant boarding school specializing in the training of civil servants. Tchaikovsky's mother, Alexandra, contracted cholera and died when he was fourteen years old, leaving him devastated. He was sent back to school where he sought refuge in music, attending numerous performances and resuming his study of the art for which he would become known. He successfully concluded his studies with an appointment at the Ministry of Justice at the age of nineteen but this extended period of separation from his family, and especially the death of his mother, troubled Tchaikovsky for the rest of his life.

While working at the Ministry of Justice Tchaikovsky enrolled in the new St. Petersburg Conservatory of music and engaged seriously in the study of composition. After a year he became convinced that his future lay in music and resigned his post at the Ministry. After graduation he was offered a professorship at the Moscow Conservatory where he fashioned a living teaching, composing, and engaging in musical criticism.

Tchaikovsky's reputation as a composer grew slowly but steadily. He battled episodes of great depression followed by periods of relative equanimity. His career ran parallel with those of the Russian "Five": Mikhail Glinka, Nicolai Rimsky-Korsakov, Alexander Borodin, Cesar Cui, and Modest Mussorgsky, whose aim in composing was to establish a firmly "Russian" school of music, and their harsh criticism of his music caused Tchaikovsky great distress. He eventually fostered a cordial relationship, first with Balakirev and then with the others, which greatly relieved the stress on Tchaikovsky and allowed him to concentrate on composing as he saw fit rather than pleasing others.

Tchaikovsky married a former student, Antonina Miliukova, briefly in 1877, but the marriage was destined for failure. It is conjectured that Tchaikovsky may have married in an attempt to hide his homosexuality and spare his family the difficulties that such a revelation would have caused. Whatever the reason, it forced Tchaikovsky to come to terms with his sexuality and he never again sought a romantic relationship with a woman. Tchaikovsky did, however, establish a most intense and interesting relationship with a woman named Nadezhda von Meck, a wealthy widow with whom he maintained a thirteen-year relationship solely through letters. In von Meck, Tchaikovsky found someone who shared almost every aspect of his artistic and emotional self. The relationship resulted in von Meck's financial support of Tchaikovsky, allowing him to resign his professorship and devote himself solely to composing. Their letters reveal a relationship based on a shared love of music that allowed each to express themselves fully even if they sometimes differed on particulars. They agreed at the outset that they were never to meet and as far as can be determined, they never did. In 1890, when von Meck's financial situation deteriorated and she could no longer afford to pay for Tchaikovsky's support, the relationship ended rather abruptly. By that time he was in great demand as a composer and conductor, a celebrated and honored son of Mother Russia, and was not in need of her financial support. But the emotional grounding she had given him for thirteen years was gone and it left him despondent. He spent the last three years of his life travelling extensively, conducting concerts, receiving awards and adulation in Russia, Europe, and the United States.

Tchaikovsky's compositions encompass most of the musical genres of his time. His symphonies, especially the last three, are staples of the modern orchestral repertory. Lesser known to today's audiences are his operas but the overwhelming popularity of his concert overtures *Romeo and Juliet* and the *1812 Overture*, the *Violin* and *Piano Concertos*, and his ballet scores to *Swan Lake*, *Sleeping Beauty*, and *The Nutcracker*, make him one of the best known and most beloved of the Romantic period composers.

Biographical Spotlight Exercise

Instructions: Log in to the textbook web site and click on the **Assignments** tab. Click on **Chapter 7** and scroll to the **Biographical Spotlight area**. Answer the question based on the information in the biography above.

Which of the following is a true statement?

1. Tchaikovsky never composed music for the ballet.
2. Tchaikovsky maintained a thirteen-year relationship with a woman named Nadezhda von Meck solely through letter writing.
3. Tchaikovsky never left his home country of Russia.

Russian nationalism was a powerful force when Tchaikovsky was alive, and he considered himself a fairly nationalistic composer. However, he is not usually grouped with the other Russian nationalists, Nicolai Rimsky-Korsakov, Alexander Borodin, Cesar Cui, Modest Mussorgsky and Mili Balakirev, known collectively as The Five (or alternatively, The Russian Five or The Mighty Five), since his music retained a strong European influence. The Five contended that the primary purpose of their music should be to advance Russian nationalistic fervor. But Tchaikovsky's compositions such as the *1812 Overture*, with its overt appeal to Russian sensibilities, certainly confirm his own estimation of his nationalistic intentions.

The *1812 Overture* is approximately 17:00 in length. It is constructed in several distinct sections. As you listen to it make note of the beginnings and endings of sections and try to describe how Tchaikovsky goes from one section to another. Does one section come to a complete stop before the next one begins? Or are the sections connected by transitions that serve to seamlessly go from one to the other? Is there anything that connects what happens at the beginning of the piece to what happens at the end?

The opening of the *1812 Overture* is a setting of a Russian Orthodox hymn, "God, Preserve Thy People," sometimes played by a cello and viola choir or sung by a vocal chorus.

Section I:
Mighty Lord, preserve us from jeopardy.
Take Thee now our faith and loud crying in penitence.
Grant victory over our treacherous and cruel enemies
And to our land bring peace.
Almighty Lord hear our lowly prayer,
And by Thy shining holy light.
Grant us, O Lord, peace again.
Almighty Lord hear our prayer
and save our people
Forever, forever!

2:19—Section II:
This is an unsettled section that builds in intensity with alternating presentations of the theme in an ominous mood. This section diminishes in volume when the sound of the French national anthem, "**La Marseillaise**," is heard representing the advancing threat to Russia by the French army.

5:04—Section III:
Forebodings of a battle with a faster tempo, a few crashing cymbals, marshal trumpet calls and rapid notes in the strings depicting a generally unsettled mood.

7:17—Section IV:
This section features Russian folk song-like melodies in a setting that invokes feelings of calm strength and resolve.

9:46—Section V:
The previous section **segues** into this battle scene in which the French have the upper hand with "La Marseillaise" prominently featured. Previously heard Russian themes are brought back once more before the finale.

12:40—Section VI: Finale
The finale begins with the French anthem heard again amidst rapid notes throughout the orchestra. A crescendo brings forth the first explosions of the triumphant Russian cannons Tchaikovsky calls for in the score. A long descending melodic line in the full orchestra heralds the entrance of the chorus once again singing the hymn, "God, Preserve Thy People," heard at the beginning of the piece but in a much more forceful setting. The "Marseillaise" interrupts this expression of Russian nationalism but is soon relegated to an accompanying role by the chorus singing the Russian national anthem, "**God Save the Tsar**."

God save the noble Tsar!
Long may he live, in pow'r,
In happiness,
In peace to reign!

The piece ends in a triumphant wash of sound. The orchestra, military band, cannons, and tolling church bells signal the Russian people's rejoicing at the retreat of Napoleon's army from Russian soil.

1812 Overture—
Peter Ilyich Tchaikovsky

This piece has become one of the most frequently played "patriotic" pieces of music in the United States, even though it is a Russian commemorative composition with the French national anthem prominently featured. The *1812 Overture* has not always been associated with American patriotic celebrations. In 1974 the *1812 Overture* was featured on a Fourth of July outdoor concert by the Boston Pops Orchestra conducted by Arthur Fiedler. This televised broadcast was complete with military band, church bells, and real canon fire. Prior to that performance the work was only occasionally programmed by American orchestras. The concert was broadcast on television stations across the country, and the connection of this piece to an American commemorative celebration was cemented. Once the work was divorced from its Russian patriotic connotations in the minds of Americans, it became an adopted patriotic work of the United States, played at Fourth of July celebrations across the country.

Lincoln Portrait

A composition written as a commemorative piece in honor of a person of historical significance is the *Lincoln Portrait* by twentieth-century American composer **Aaron Copland**. The *Lincoln Portrait,* scored for full orchestra and narrator, was written in 1942 during World War II as part of Copland's desire to contribute to the war effort. The piece was premiered by the Cincinnati Symphony in May and repeated on the Fourth of July in Washington, D.C., in front of the Lincoln Memorial with the great American poet Carl Sandburg narrating. The inspiring words of Lincoln fit the American psyche at the time, so soon after the Japanese attack on Pearl Harbor the previous December 7th. Copland's music struck a resonant chord in the hearts of Americans with its intentionally "American" sound and subject matter. The narration quotes from Lincoln's Annual Message to Congress from 1862, the Lincoln-Douglass debates of 1858, and the Gettysburg Address from 1863. The *Lincoln Portrait* has become one of Copland's most frequently performed compositions.

The statue of Abraham Lincoln in the Lincoln Memorial in Washington, D.C. © 2010, JupiterImages Corporation

   The piece opens with a solemn introduction. A solo clarinet then plays a traditional folk song melody, "Springfield Mountain," in tribute to Springfield, Illinois, where Lincoln spent his formative years. A fast section follows, during which Copland presents a variation of *Camptown Races* by Stephen Foster. Quoting these two American songs contributes to the uniquely "American" sound of Copland's music. Both themes are treated extensively in a fairly long **development section**. The narrator then begins the narration accompanied by the musical themes previously heard.

 Lincoln Portrait—
Aaron Copland

Narration from Aaron Copland's *Lincoln Portrait*

7:50—"Fellow citizens, we cannot escape history."

That is what he said. That is what Abraham Lincoln said.

"Fellow citizens, we cannot escape history. We of this congress and this administration will be remembered in spite of ourselves. No personal significance or insignificance can spare one or another of us. The fiery trial through which we pass will light us down in honor or dishonor to the latest generation. We, even we here, hold the power and bear the responsibility." [Annual Message to Congress, December 1, 1862]

He was born in Kentucky, raised in Indiana, and lived in Illinois. And this is what he said. This is what Abe Lincoln said.

He said: "The dogmas of the quiet past are inadequate to the stormy present. The occasion is piled high with difficulty and we must rise with the occasion. As our case is new, so we must think anew and act anew. We must disenthrall ourselves and then we will [shall] save our country." [Annual Message to Congress, December 1, 1862]

(continued)

10:30—When standing erect he was six feet four inches tall, and this is what he said.

He said: "It is the eternal struggle between two principles, right and wrong, throughout the world. It is the same spirit that says 'you toil and work and earn bread, and I'll eat it.' No matter in what shape it comes, whether from the mouth of a king who seeks to bestride the people of his own nation, and live by the fruit of their labor, or from one race of men as an apology for enslaving another race, it is the same tyrannical principle." [Lincoln-Douglas debates, 15 October 1858]

12:00—Lincoln was a quiet man. Abe Lincoln was a quiet and a melancholy man. But when he spoke of democracy, this is what he said.

He said: "As I would not be a slave, so I would not be a master. This expresses my idea of democracy. Whatever differs from this, to the extent of the difference, is no democracy."

13:25—Abraham Lincoln, sixteenth president of these United States, is everlasting in the memory of his countrymen. For on the battleground at Gettysburg, this is what he said:

He said: "That from these honored dead we take increased devotion to that cause for which they gave the last full measure of devotion. That we here highly resolve that these dead shall not have died in vain. That this nation under God shall have a new birth of freedom and that government of the people, by the people, and for the people shall not perish from the earth." [Gettysburg Address]

Commemorative music reminds us of who we are and what we have been through as a people. It reinforces our shared cultural and national histories. It strengthens the connections that bind people one to another.

A SONG OF CELEBRATION, INSPIRATION, AND COMMEMORATION

We Shall Overcome is a song illustrative of all three types of music we have discussed in this chapter. The song has been associated with labor struggles and the Civil Rights movement in the United States since the 1940s. It is often sung on the anniversary of important dates in the struggle for equality. *We Shall Overcome* is sung by those seeking to strengthen the bond between themselves and others in pursuit of the redress of social wrongs. "We Shall Overcome" has become a fixture in performances on the national holiday commemorating the life of Dr. Martin Luther King, Jr.

After the attacks on the United States on September 11, 2001, *We Shall Overcome* also became associated with the tragic events of that day. Soon after the attacks, Bruce Springsteen's version of the song appeared as the musical background to a compilation of video images from that day that was broadcast repeatedly by NBC News. Springsteen's rendition of the song had already been recorded in 1998 for a tribute album in honor of Pete Seeger. The images and the music created an indelible impression on the collective American psyche.

The origins of the song are somewhat murky, but it is fair to say that the commonly sung version is an amalgam of several gospel songs with additional lyrics added by American folk singer Pete Seeger (b. 1919). The legal rights to *We Shall Overcome* are held by Seeger and fellow folk singers Guy Carawan and Frank Hamilton.

Listening Chart

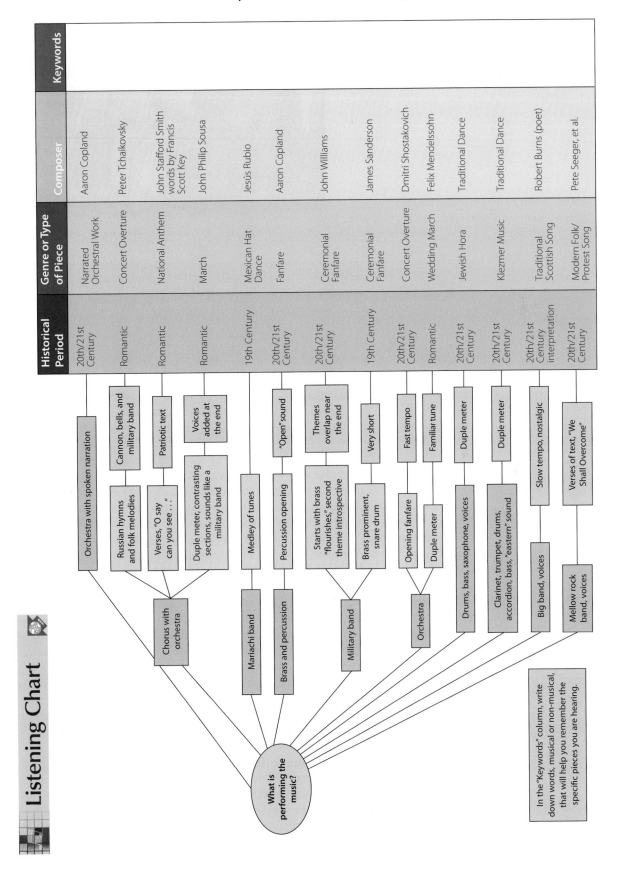

Historical Period	Genre or Type of Piece	Composer	Keywords
20th/21st Century	Narrated Orchestral Work	Aaron Copland	
Romantic	Concert Overture	Peter Tchaikovsky	
Romantic	National Anthem	John Stafford Smith words by Francis Scott Key	
Romantic	March	John Philip Sousa	
19th Century	Mexican Hat Dance	Jesús Rubio	
20th/21st Century	Fanfare	Aaron Copland	
20th/21st Century	Ceremonial Fanfare	John Williams	
19th Century	Ceremonial Fanfare	James Sanderson	
20th/21st Century	Concert Overture	Dmitri Shostakovich	
Romantic	Wedding March	Felix Mendelssohn	
20th/21st Century	Jewish Hora	Traditional Dance	
20th/21st Century	Klezmer Music	Traditional Dance	
20th/21st Century interpretation	Traditional Scottish Song	Robert Burns (poet)	
20th/21st Century	Modern Folk/Protest Song	Pete Seeger, et al.	

What is performing the music?

- Orchestra with spoken narration
- Cannon, bells, and military band — Russian hymns and folk melodies
- Patriotic text — Verses, "O say can you see . . ."
- Voices added at the end — Duple meter, contrasting sections, sounds like a military band — Chorus with orchestra
- Medley of tunes — Mariachi band
- "Open" sound — Percussion opening — Brass and percussion
- Themes overlap near the end — Starts with brass "flourishes," second theme introspective — Military band
- Very short — Brass prominent, snare drum
- Fast tempo — Opening fanfare — Orchestra
- Familiar tune — Duple meter
- Duple meter — Drums, bass, saxophone, voices
- Duple meter — Clarinet, trumpet, drums, accordion, bass, "eastern" sound
- Slow tempo, nostalgic — Big band, voices
- Verses of text, "We Shall Overcome" — Mellow rock band, voices

In the "Keywords" column, write down words, musical or non-musical, that will help you remember the specific pieces you are hearing.

The Selma-to-Montgomery freedom marchers, including Dr. Martin Luther King, Jr. (r) and Rev. Ralph Abernathy (2nd from left). King was to lead the marchers the last four miles to the state capitol.
© Bettmann/Corbis

 We Shall Overcome—
Pete Seeger, Guy Carawan, and Frank Hamilton

SUMMARY

Chapter 7 has dealt with music that we encounter in the everyday events of our lives. Some of this music, such as that which accompanies birthday and wedding celebrations, helps us observe the major turning points that are common to people the world over. While some of this music is tied directly to the culture from which it originated, Jewish wedding music and the *Mexican Hat Dance* for instance, some music has transcended the culture from which it came to become accepted by people from other cultures, such as has been the case with the song *Happy Birthday*.

Where the above music accompanies the personal celebratory events of our lives, there is also music that attends the shared events that shape our national or cultural identities. This music inspires us to strengthen our sense of community within the national or international framework. Fanfares that are played at large-scale events such as the Olympics or inaugural celebrations, marches that instill a sense of military discipline and respect, and national anthems that serve as a focal point for people of a shared national heritage are all types of music that inspire us in some way.

Commemorative music serves to remind us of who we are, where we came from, and what we aspire to be as communities, nations, and as peoples. Many commemorative pieces, such as Copland's *Lincoln Portrait*, remain indelibly linked to the event or person in whose honor they were written. But some commemorative music has gone beyond being tied to an individual event or person and taken on a larger role as a standard part of the concert repertory, Tchaikovsky's *1812 Overture* comes to mind in that regard. Shostakovich's *Festive Overture*, while having been written as a commemorative piece for the Russian Revolution, is performed just as, if not more, frequently here in the United States.

Music of celebration, inspiration, and commemoration is an important part of the cultural fabric of society. It is the tie that binds together the different facets and rituals that attend the milestone events of our lives, our national and cultural histories, and our communal memories. By an unstated agreement we allow these pieces of music to represent a shared view of the most significant events in our individual lives and in the histories of our cultural and national communities.

SUGGESTED FURTHER LISTENING

"Rondeau" from *First Suite in D major*—Jean Joseph Mouret

"La Rejouissance" from *Music for the Royal Fireworks*—George Frideric Handel

Ma Vlast—Bedrich Smetana (Six pieces commemorating the composer's homeland)

Here Comes the Bride—Richard Wagner (Melody is from the "Bridal Chorus" heard at the beginning of Act III of the opera *Lohengrin*)

Festive Overture—Dmitri Shostakovich

America (My Country 'Tis of Thee)—Melody based on the English national Anthem, *God Save the Queen*, words by Samuel Francis Smith

America the Beautiful—Melody by Samuel Ward, words by Katherine Lee Bates

Silent Night—Franz Gruber

We Gather Together—Traditional Thanksgiving Song

Bless This House—Traditional Thanksgiving Song

The Pines of Rome—Ottorino Respighi

The Great Gate of Kiev from *Pictures at an Exhibition*—Modest Mussorgsky

How Great Thou Art—Carl Boberg

Blessed Assurance—Fanny Crosby

A Mighty Fortress Is Our God—Martin Luther

QUESTION ASSIGNMENT

Instructions: Log in to the textbook web site and click on the ASSIGNMENTS tab. In the Chapter Question Assignment area read the instructions and answer the question(s) or provide the asked for information. Be sure to click the SUBMIT THIS FORM button after you complete the Assignment.

Which type of musical composition (genre) discussed in Chapter 7 has notated examples going as far back as the Medieval period and can trace its origins through pictorial representations back to the Roman empire? Name a modern (Twentieth-Century) example of this type of music.

Genre: _____

Modern Example: _____

LISTENING EXERCISES

Instructions: Log in to the textbook web site and click on the ASSIGNMENTS tab. In the Listening Exercises area click on the links to the musical examples for each question and answer the questions. Be sure to click the SUBMIT button after you answer all of the questions.

Listen to each of the musical examples below from the Chapter 7 Playlist while noting the appropriate descriptive prompt on the Listening Chart for Chapter 7 and determine the best answer to each question.

1. *Olympic Fanfare* (full version) by John Williams—This piece for military band, but just as often heard played by a symphony orchestra, starts with brass "flourishes" playing the main theme. Several additional themes are added throughout the piece, and these themes overlap near the end of the piece. Choose the timing when the first statement of the second theme, introspective in nature, occurs.

   a. 34 seconds
   b. 1:02 seconds
   c. 2:21 seconds

2. *The Stars and Stripes Forever* by John Philip Sousa—This piece, performed by a chorus with orchestra, sounds like a military band. It is a march in duple meter; that is, the meter is in repeated groupings of two beats. In this performance there are voices added at the end. Choose the timing when the voices enter.

   a. 20 seconds
   b. 1:59 seconds
   c. 2:51 seconds

3. *1812 Overture* by Peter Ilyich Tchaikovsky—This concert overture, for voices with orchestra, makes use of traditional Russian hymns, and folk melodies. One of the prominent features of this piece is its use of cannon, bells, and a military band. The chorus opens the piece singing one of the hymns, *God Preserve Thy People.* The chorus returns near the end to sing the Russian national anthem, *God Save the Czar.* Choose the timing at which that occurs.

   a. 12:40 seconds
   b. 13:18 seconds
   c. 14:17 seconds

Chapter 8

Music for the Concert Hall

FOCUS POINTS

Baroque	*Classical*	*Romantic*	*Twentieth/ Twenty-First Centuries*
Concerto	Sonata	Ballade	Piano Pieces
Concerto Grosso	Symphony	Tone Poem	Ballet
Fugue	String Quartet	Concerto	Concerto
Dance Suite	Concerto	Symphony	Symphony
Imitative Polyphony	Thematic Development	Nationalism	Expressionism
	Formal Structure	Program Music	Serialism
		Impressionism	Neo-Classicism
			Avant-garde
			Minimalism
			Crossover

DEVELOPMENT OF THE CONCERT TRADITION

Attending a **concert** is something we take for granted today. It is just one of any number of ways we can enjoy music. Paying an admission fee to listen to musicians ply their trade did not become commonplace until the latter part of the Baroque (1600–1750) period. The types of performances available to the general public were more likely to be productions of single large, vocal compositions, such as an **opera** or an **oratorio**, rather than an instrumental concert. Prior to that time most people experienced music primarily as part of an event or activity such as a religious observance or during public festivities and seasonal celebrations. Hearing music in a concert hall was reserved for the wealthy, aristocratic ruling class who could afford to hire composers and musicians to write and perform music in their homes and for their courts. Those concerts were often performed in extravagantly decorated private concert halls on the estates of the **patrons** who financed the performances. The public concerts that did take place were often done in makeshift concert halls such as converted rooms in public buildings or churches.

A modern concert hall. © 2010 JupiterImages Corporation

As public concerts became more frequent toward the end of the Baroque period, public concert halls began to appear in the larger cities across Europe. The ability of musicians to draw income from concerts staged in these venues became an increasingly important outlet for both musical creativity and financial support, which heretofore had been restricted almost solely to the churches or the courts. Throughout the ensuing Classical period performances in public concert halls became more frequent, and by the Romantic period most musicians earned their livings without any church or court affiliation. The advent of publishing houses through which compositions could be sold and broadly distributed increased the awareness of a composer's music beyond geographical restrictions, further increasing the performance and income opportunities for a composer.

Concerts during the late eighteenth and throughout the nineteenth centuries were very long events that could last anywhere from 2–4 hours. They frequently featured the compositions of a single composer who might even have been the financial backer of the performance. Compositions included on a program were often new works being heard for the first time presented by the person who wrote them. The types of instrumental genres that became fixtures of orchestral programs included symphonies, concertos, overtures, and tone poems. Throughout the nineteenth century concerts became more frequent and attended by an ever-widening spectrum of the population. The establishment of philharmonic and choral societies to promote and sustain symphony orchestras and choral organizations further accelerated the ever-increasing number of public concerts and fueled the growing support of public concerts by the middle class. Concerts featuring orchestral music, sometimes with a choral component, became increasingly common. Choral groups retained a prominent place in church music and appeared regularly as an important part of orchestral presentations so the increase in the number of orchestral concerts was not mirrored by a similar increase in purely choral programs.

In the twentieth century the length of concert performances was shortened, and a fairly standard format gradually evolved for orchestral programs. A concert would typically begin with a short piece, such as an overture from an opera or a concert overture, which would be followed by a concerto featuring a renowned soloist. An intermission would precede the longest and final piece on the concert such as a symphony, an extended tone poem, or a large-scale choral composition with orchestral accompaniment. Programs might be constructed along a "theme" such as "*Beethoven: Early, Middle, and Late,*" using pieces that represented the different times in Beethoven's composing life. More often though the practice of choosing pieces that represented an array of historical eras and styles in order to provide a little something for everyone was the way most programs were constructed. That way of presenting compositions in concert has remained the basic format of orchestral programming up to the present day. The performance format of other ensembles is not nearly as entrenched as orchestral concerts. Choral and band concerts exhibit much more variety in their presentations. Chamber music concerts usually feature one type of small ensemble, such as a string quartet, and draw from the repertoire for that instrumentation, which often does not have as much variety as the genres for orchestra. Consequently, a program featuring a string quartet (the ensemble) may very well consist of two or three string quartets (the genre).

Music from the Medieval and Renaissance periods usually appears on concerts devoted to early music. Since the orchestra as a standard performing ensemble began to take shape during the Baroque period, music from earlier eras does not often find its way onto an orchestral program. Choral music from the Medieval and Renaissance is more likely to appear on choral concerts, and instrumental music from those periods is sometimes heard on chamber music concerts and in recital. A recital is a small-

▬▬ Musical Experiences before the Twentieth Century ▬▬

It is important to understand that the only way a person living before the twentieth century could hear music was in a live performance. There were no recordings, no radio, no videos, movies, or television. Furthermore, the repeated hearing of any piece of music could only be achieved through its appearance on multiple programs, and that was not very likely to happen within the same city because audiences tended to go to concerts to hear new works by their favorite composers. Large undertakings like operas were the exception. Operas would normally have a number of performances scheduled from the outset due to the extraordinary costs involved in mounting such expensive productions. The repeated performances offered the opportunity to recoup more revenue in order to offset production costs. So while the norm today is to hear pieces of music over and over again, affording us a degree of intimate familiarity with individual compositions unheard of in the past, the norm before the twentieth century was to hear a piece of music one time. Imagine a world where a piece of music came into your life and disappeared again after one performance. If that were the case today, would music play as significant a role in your life as it does?

scale concert presented by an individual or a small group of performers in an intimate setting.

MUSIC FOR THE CONCERT HALL—HISTORICAL PERIODS, COMMON GENRES, AND COMPOSERS

BAROQUE PERIOD, 1600–1750

Style and Characteristics

During the Baroque period music was composed either for a court or a church. Court music was mostly instrumental and church music mostly vocal and two distinct styles developed along those lines. Instrumental music of the Baroque retained a high degree of imitative polyphony from the previous historical era, the Renaissance, while church vocal music became more homophonic in order to make the words more easily understood. A group of Italian intellectuals known as the Florentine Camerata espoused this type of vocal writing, and their influence was such that clarity of the presentation of the text became paramount in vocal music. Both instrumental and vocal music of the Baroque was highly embellished with frequent use of ornaments, the addition of "extra" notes to the written melodic line. Some of the common ornaments included: the trill, the rapid alternation between the written note and the note above it; the turn, a series of pitches that encircled the written note; and the appoggiatura, a stressed note that was not part of the harmony which resolved to a consonant pitch within the chord. Performers were expected to add ornaments in a stylish way that added to the written line but not to the extent that it overwhelmed it. Consequently, Baroque music can have a wide degree of variation between any two performances, even by the same performer. The addition of ornaments was up to the performer with only an occasional indication in the music by the composer as to when ornaments might be added. There was also a unique ideal in the approach to dynamic levels in the

Three Musicians of the Medici Court by Antonio Domenico Gabbiani (1652–1726). Copyright © Erich Lessing/Art Resource, NY

Baroque period called terraced dynamics. That is where there are no gradations between loud and soft, no crescendos or decrescendos, just sudden shifts from a loud dynamic level to a soft one. The harpsichord, the forerunner of the piano, mirrored this ideal. The harpsichord could not produce a gradual increase or decrease in the volume level but could make sudden changes from loud to soft (or soft to loud) by engaging or dampening additional sets of strings within the instrument.

Musical Elements

During the Baroque period the musical elements of melody, harmony, rhythm, form, timbre, and texture took on many characteristics that are similar to the concepts that govern these musical components today. Melodies tended to be presented in high-pitched instruments and were often fairly long and lyrical. The harmonic language of the time employed a generally fast harmonic rhythm. That means that the harmony changed frequently, often from one beat to another. The Baroque period was the historical era when the harmonic language we use today was firmly established and composers explored harmonic progressions, series of chords, extensively. Most pieces were either in a clear major or minor tonality but sometimes pieces in minor keys ended on major chords. The term tonality often refers to the key of the piece. This means that the music is centered around a specific pitch. Tempo in the Baroque period was generally steady throughout a movement. See below for a discussion of forms common to the period.

Baroque Instruments

The bowed stringed instruments in use today, the violin family, replaced the viol family of stringed instruments during the Baroque period. Wind instruments were generally not as refined or precise in terms of tone production and exactness of pitch as modern instruments. Recorders were commonly used instead of flutes. The other woodwinds of the time, the oboe and bassoon, had a more nasal tone quality than today's counterparts, and the clarinet had yet to be invented. The Baroque trumpet had no valves with which to change pitches. In order to facilitate the playing of melodies, trumpet parts were written in the highest register of the instrument where the slightest changes in the position of the lips within the mouthpiece made possible the playing of virtuosic melodic lines. The French horn also had no valves and was similarly challenged in the execution of melodic lines. The harpsichord and the organ were the most prominent keyboard instruments of the time. The mechanism that produced the sound on the harpsichord plucked the strings inside the instrument rather than striking them as in a modern piano. That produced a timbre with a distinctly metallic quality unique to that instrument. Instrumental music frequently had a polyphonic texture, whereas vocal music tended to be primarily homophonic with imitative polyphony reserved for large choral movements.

BAROQUE PERIOD

Some Prominent Composers	Genres
Arcangelo Corelli, 1653–1713	Concerto, Concerto Grosso, Trio Sonata
Antonio Vivaldi, 1678–1741	Concerto, Concerto Grosso, Opera
Johann Sebastian Bach, 1685–1750	Concerto, Concerto Grosso, Suite, Passion, Cantata, Fugue, Toccata
George Frideric Handel, 1685–1759	Concerto, Concerto Grosso, Suite, Oratorio, Opera

The Baroque Orchestra

The violin family of instruments, the violin, viola, cello, and bass, became the foundation of the orchestra during the Baroque period. Orchestras during that time were small by today's standards with strings distributed in the following numbers:

4–6 1st violins
4–6 2nd violins
2–4 violas
2–4 cellos
1–2 basses

There was no standard woodwind component to the orchestra at this time, but flutes, or their predecessor the recorder, were used frequently, as were oboes and bassoons. The most prominent brass instrument was the trumpet with French horns used occasionally. Tympani, the large kettle drums, were the most commonly used percussion instruments.

The Basso Continuo

Underlying all of the music of the Baroque period was an instrumental ideal called the basso continuo. This was a combination of a harpsichord, the predecessor of the piano, and a low-pitched instrument such as a cello, bass, or bassoon, that provided a harmonic foundation and a rhythmic engine for the ensemble. The continuo part was written in a kind of shorthand called figured bass that was based on the notes in the bass line. While the low-pitched instruments played the actual written notes, the harpsichord player would create a full harmonic accompaniment based on a series of numbers that were written above the bass notes. The numbers indicated certain pitches that would fit the harmony over any given bass note and the harpsichord player would improvise a harmonic accompaniment appropriate to the tempo and mood of the piece. It is in many ways similar to the modern day lead sheet in contemporary music that indicates the harmony but not how to play it.

Baroque Instrumental Genres

Orchestral dance suites, discussed in Chapter 4, concertos, and concerto grossos (concerti grossi) were popular genres for the orchestra of the Baroque period. A concerto is a three-movement orchestral work that features one solo instrument.

A concerto grosso is similar but it features a small group of soloists instead of just one. Antonio Vivaldi (1678–1741), an Italian composer known for his writing of concertos for stringed instruments, especially the violin, is credited with formalizing the three-movement format of the concerto. Below is the format for a typical concerto or concerto grosso of the Baroque period.

> 1st Movement—Allegro (fast), Ritornello Form
>
> 2nd Movement—Adagio (slow), A-B-A or Theme and Variations Form
>
> 3rd Movement—Allegro (fast), Ritornello Form

Ritornello form was used especially for concerto grossos because the structure of the form allowed for the easy featuring of the small group of soloists. The term ritornello literally refers to the returning chorus in a song. Ritornello form was essentially a modified version of A-B-A. For example, the diagram:

$$A\text{-}B\text{-}A\text{-}C\text{-}A\text{-}D\text{-}A\text{-}E\text{-}A$$

might be an accurate depiction of a movement in ritornello form. The "A" section, would be played by the entire orchestra, often including the soloists, and they would play the main theme of the movement. On subsequent returns of the "A" section, the theme, or just a fragment of it, might be played. This "A" section is called the "tutti," the Italian word for "all," indicating that everyone plays during this section. It is also sometimes referred to as the "ripieno." The other sections, based on different melodic material, would be played by the soloists along with the basso continuo. These sections are called the "concertino." Thus the form allowed the soloists a relatively softer accompaniment when they were featured and one in which they could present ever changing musical ideas. The orchestra provided the repeating theme that gave the movement a sense of continuity and the basso continuo held it all together. Antonio Vivaldi frequently used ritornello form in the fast movements of his concerti, and this practice became the standard for the period.

Concerto Grosso

The first movement of a concerto or concerto grosso would typically be in ritornello form with the solo instruments being featured both individually and as a group. The German composer Johann Sebastian Bach (1685–1750), wrote a set of six concerti grossi that he sent to the Margrave of Brandenburg in 1721 in hopes that the Margrave would offer him a position at court. While Bach's appeal for a court appointment was not successful, the pieces, collectively known as the *Brandenburg Concertos*, have become the most popular examples of the concerto grosso genre. Each work is for a different group of solo instruments. The second "concerto" uses violin, oboe, recorder, and trumpet soloists along with a string orchestra and basso continuo. The first movement of this work is in ritornello form with each of the soloists being featured separately at first and then in various combinations.

 Brandenburg Concerto #2, 1st movement—
Johann Sebastian Bach

Concerto

The second movements of concertos from the Baroque period were usually fairly short movements with a minimal accompaniment in the orchestra, sometimes reduced to just the basso continuo. The following example from the *Lute Concerto in D major* by Antonio Vivaldi uses sustained strings in the accompaniment along with the continuo. One of the primary performance attributes of the Baroque period was the ability of the performer to improvise by adding ornamentation to the basic melodic line, especially during repeated sections. The lute was the forerunner of the modern guitar.

Italian composer Antonio Vivaldi. Copyright © Scala/Art Resource, NY

 Lute Concerto in D major, 2nd movement— Antonio Vivaldi

The Fugue

Another Baroque genre closely tied to a specific structure was the fugue. A fugue was a keyboard genre, primarily written for the organ, in which a main theme, the subject, was presented numerous times at different pitch levels with sections of different music, called episodes, interspersed throughout. Fugues were often linked with a preceding improvisatory work such as a toccata, prelude, or fantasia. Johann Sebastian Bach was the greatest composer of these keyboard genres.

Johann Sebastian Bach was especially noted for his organ playing ability. During his lifetime Bach was much more renowned for that than for his composing. He was a master of writing in the polyphonic style even while the tastes of the public were shifting toward the more homophonic style of the coming Classical period. In that regard Bach was considered an "old fashioned" composer during his lifetime. Several of his sons were more popular with the public than he was. His mastery of the compositional technique of imitative polyphony made him particularly well suited to compose fugues for the organ.

What Makes Music—Musical Instruments

Keyboards

Another major type of instrument is the entire keyboard family. Instruments that use a keyboard include the Piano, Harpsichord, Organ, and Synthesizer.

Piano—The piano is a string instrument that is played in a percussive manner by employing a series of hammers inside the body of the instrument that hit the strings to produce sound. The piano usually has 88 keys. There are also three foot pedals to soften, sustain, and selectively sustain, notes. The piano

A Grand Piano. © 2013, marijaf, Shutterstock, Inc.

keyboard is touch-sensitive in that the harder you depress the keys the louder the notes will sound. This is how it got the name pianoforte, literally, the soft/loud.

Harpsichord—This instrument was a forerunner of the piano. The sound is produced by a series of plectrums plucking the strings inside the instrument. Unlike the piano, the volume of the sound does not increase according to how hard you depress the keys on the keyboard. In order to increase the dynamics

A Flemish Harpichord. © 2013, Linda Bucklin, Shutterstock, Inc.

(continued)

you must call into use another set of strings inside the instrument by means of a lever or some other device located on the side of the instrument.

Organ—This instrument uses air forced through pipes of varying lengths and thicknesses to produce different pitches. It can either be mechanically or electronically operated and often has more than one keyboard that the player can set to have different tonal qualities. The organ also has a set of keys that are operated by the feet of the player that play the lowest pitched notes.

Synthesizer—A synthesizer is an electronic instrument that often uses a keyboard similar to a piano, which produces sound based on digitally stored and manipulated files. These sounds can either be recreated sounds of acoustic instruments or new sounds created by digitally manipulating the stored files.

Pipe organ incorporated into the design of a concert hall. © 2013, Pavel L. Photo and Video, Shutterstock, Inc.

The *"Little" Fugue in G minor* is so called in order to distinguish it from the *"Great" Fugue in G minor,* another, longer work in the same form. Once you understand the format for a fugue, it unfolds in a predictable manner and the enjoyment of it comes from being able to follow the theme as it is presented at different pitch levels and in conjunction with other, subordinate, melodic lines. A fugue begins with the main theme, called the subject, being played in its entirety without any accompanying music. After the first statement of the subject it is presented again at another pitch level, either lower or higher, with an accompanying melodic line. A secondary melody of this nature is often called a countermelody. This sequence of presentations of the theme, called the exposition, continues until a short period of music is heard during which the subject is not played. When there is a section of music without the subject being played, that section is called an episode. Statements of the subject with accompanying countermelodies are interspersed with episodes until the piece ends. In the following example, listen for how many times the subject is presented.

 Little Organ Fugue in G minor—
Johann Sebastian Bach

Now listen to the same piece again, but instead of counting entrances of the theme listen to what else is going on while the subject is being played and also listen for episodes. What function do you think episodes serve in a fugue?

 Little Organ Fugue in G minor—
Johann Sebastian Bach

Now listen one last time to an orchestrated version of the same piece. Are there any differences in the presentation of the subject in this version? Which version do you prefer? Why?

♪ *Little Fugue in G minor* (orchestrated)—
Johann Sebastian Bach

Does the fugue sound like a logical composition to you? After hearing this one several times do you think you could predict what might happen in a different fugue? Try listening to the fugal section from the *Toccata and Fugue in D minor* by Bach to see if you can.

Biographical Spotlight

Johann Sebastian Bach.
© 2013, Nicku, Shutterstock, Inc.

Johann Sebastian Bach

Johann Sebastian Bach was born on March 23, 1685, in Eisenach, Germany, and died on July 28, 1750, in Leipzig. He was the eighth child in a family already well-known for their musical accomplishments and he left a legacy that profoundly affected music to this day. He was orphaned at the age of 9 after which he lived for a period with an older brother, Johann Christoph Bach, the organist at a prominent church in the town of Ohrdruf. Johann Sebastian set off on his own in 1700 when his brother could no longer afford to support him. He moved to Lüneburg where orphans such as he could attend school in return for singing in the choir at St. Michael's Church. During the time spent with his brother and the two years he spent in Lüneburg, Bach became exceptionally adept at the organ, the playing of which he would be renowned for the rest of his life.

From 1703 to 1706 Bach held violinist and other positions in Weimar and Arnstadt, from where we have evidence of his first compositions, before moving to Mühlhausen in 1707. There he married a second cousin, Maria Barbara Bach, and started to seriously explore his compositional abilities. After only a year Bach returned to Wiemar but to a much improved position as organist and orchestra member at the court of Duke Wilhelm Ernst, at twice the salary of his previous position. The Bach family increased by three with the births of Catharina Dorothea in 1708, Wilhelm Friedemann in 1710, and Carl Phillip Emmanuel in 1714. Twins born in 1713 did not survive. As his family grew Bach sought better paying positions but remained in Wiemar as the Duke continued to raise his salary and appointed him Concertmaster (the leader) of the court orchestra. Bach eventually got caught between the competing interests of his employer the Duke and his successor, Ernst August, and was even imprisoned for a short time before being relieved of his position. The time spent in Wiemar, 1708–1717, was one of exceptional creativity for Bach. He wrote numerous cantatas during that time and much of his best organ music came from that period.

In December of 1717 Bach accepted a new position in Köthen where he would spend the next five years. Bach's new employer, Prince Leopold von Anhalt-Köthen, took Bach and his entire musical entourage with him on extravagant trips and it was during one of those excursions that Maria Barbara Bach took ill and died. Bach was left with four children to care for as another son, Johann Gottfried Bernhard, had been born in 1715. In 1721 Bach married Anna Magdalena Wilcken, a soprano with whom he had worked for several years. Over the course of their marriage Anna Magdalena would bear 13 children but only 6 would survive to adulthood. The male children, Gottfried Heinrich (who eventually developed serious mental impairments), Johann Christoph Friedrich, and Johann Christian, were all trained in music and became accomplished musicians, while the female children, Elisabeth Juliane Friederica, Johanna Carolina, and Regina Susanna, led lives outside of the musical spotlight. Prince Anholt-Köthen's initially excessive spending on musical pursuits eventually declined, and as the musical atmosphere in Köthen dwindled along with it Bach sought positions in Berlin, Hamburg, and Leipzig, eventually accepting the position of Cantor (the head musician in a church) at St. Thomas' Church and School in Leipzig. Bach would remain in Leipzig from 1723 until his death in 1750.

(continued)

The years spent in Leipzig saw Bach working harder than ever, frequently composing a new cantata each week for the church services, rehearsing the choirs five days a week, providing choirs for four different Leipzig churches each Sunday, teaching Latin to the boys at the school, composing and overseeing the musical performances at funerals and weddings, all for less money than he had made in Köthen. Adding to his heavy professional responsibilities Bach and Anna Magdalena endured the deaths of several of their children at very young ages. So while he was at the high point of his professional life in terms of composing new works Bach was also dealing with challenges that would have crushed the spirit of someone without the inner strength he possessed. Bach's Lutheran faith was the obvious source of this strength of character. He frequently added the additional letters, "S.D.G," signifying "Soli Deo Gloria"—"to the only God be glory," to his signature on many of his compositions, especially the sacred cantatas.

The extraordinary workload and the increasingly difficult relationship between himself and his employer during the first six years in Leipzig resulted in Bach seeking other musical outlets for both creative and financial satisfaction. This led him to seek and be granted the directorship of the *Collegium Musicum*, a musical organization that gave public concerts at Zimmerman's Coffee House in Leipzig, in 1729. He held this influential position for the next ten years while continuing his duties to a lesser degree at St. Thomas.

During the last decade of Bach's life he travelled regularly to Berlin where his son Carl Phillip Emmanuel was a prominent musician. He also maintained an ongoing relationship with the court in Dresden as his duties in Leipzig diminished. His long-established reputation as a virtuoso organist was now being matched by his acknowledged mastery as a composer, at least within Germany. He died in 1750 after complications from eye surgery for advanced cataracts. After his death his reputation grew as others promoted his music. The Bach Gesellschaft (Bach Society) was formed by his successor at St. Thomas' Church and others for the purpose of publishing his music and thereby bringing his music to the attention of a wider audience. In 1829 the prominent German composer Felix Mendelssohn's performance of Bach's *St. Matthew Passion* continued elevating Bach's reputation among the highest levels of the musical world. Major composers, including Mozart and Beethoven, adopted aspects of his contrapuntal style after studying his works. To this day all students of music study the works and style of Bach, as he is the acknowledged master of the harmonic underpinnings of Western art music.

Biographical Spotlight Exercise

Instructions: Log in to the textbook web site and click on the **Assignments** tab. Click on **Chapter 8** and scroll to the **Biographical Spotlight area**. Answer the question based on the information in the biography above.

Which of the following is a true statement?

1. Bach only worked for churches throughout his lifetime.
2. Several of Bach's sons were important composers in their own right.
3. Bach's music is not studied much by musicians today.

The Trio Sonata and the Sonata

The **trio sonata** was a genre written for two high-pitched melodic instruments, such as the violin, and a basso continuo. The name of this genre implies that it is performed by three players. That is misleading since the basso continuo is composed of at least two players, a keyboardist, and a low-pitched instrumentalist such as a cellist or bassoonist. Consequently four players are required to perform a trio sonata. But the basso continuo was considered such a unified instrumental ideal that the combination of players needed to execute it was considered one item; thus, the term trio was used in the name. The trio sonata was a four-movement genre with a slow-fast, slow-fast organization of movements. The 1st and 2nd and the 3rd and 4th movements were often linked and played without pause. A close relation of this genre was the **sonata**, a composition usually written for a single instrumentalist with basso continuo. That genre required three players to perform it. The sonata had a similar organization of movements, slow-fast, slow-fast.

The following example of a trio sonata movement is by Arcangelo Corelli (1653–1713), the Italian composer whose contributions to the trio sonata genre established it in the form we know today. The two violins sometimes imitate each other and at other times play in harmony with each other. We can also hear in this example a sectional structure to the movement based on the ritornello form of the time. Corelli, a violinist, was also instrumental in establishing the performance technique of the violin.

Sonata, Opus 1 #3, Presto—
Arcangelo Corelli

Italian Terms

It has been the tradition in Western art music to use Italian words when referring to certain aspects of music both in the printed musical score and in the programs provided to the audience. The expression dynamic level, or simply, **dynamics**, refers to the loudness of the music and the term **tempo** refers to the speed of the music. Both of these descriptors are quite subjective and open to individual interpretation by conductors and performers. The **metronome**, a device used for assessing the speed of a piece of music based on the number of beats per minute, was invented in the early nineteenth century. Since then composers have often used both a metronome indication and a tempo term to convey their idea of how fast or slow a piece of music should be performed. Below are some of the commonly used Italian terms for dynamics, along with the abbreviations that are used when they appear in a printed score, and tempos, as they are used as generic names of individual movements in multi-movement compositions.

Dynamics	*Tempos*
pianissimo—very soft *(pp)*	largo—very slowly
piano—soft *(p)*	adagio—slowly
mezzo piano—half soft *(mp)*	andante—moderately slow
mezzo forte—half loud *(mf)*	moderato—moderately
forte—loud *(f)*	allegretto—moderately fast
fortissimo—very loud *(ff)*	allegro—fast
crescendo—gradually louder	vivace—fast and lively
decrescendo—gradually softer	presto—very fast

CLASSICAL PERIOD, 1750–1825

Style and Characteristics

The music of the Classical period is often described as elegant, logical, and balanced. While simplistic in its characterization of this period, the words do help in understanding why the music sounds the way it does, why it is constructed the way it is, and how it was experienced by the audience of the time. The early part of the Classical period in Europe was dominated by the ruling aristocracy who lived in elegant palaces and whose lavish lifestyle necessitated the need for ever-present music for entertaining guests. The wealthy women of the period wore large, elegant dresses, and the men wore powdered wigs defining a sense of style that was at once both refined and artifi-

PERSPECTIVE—BAROQUE TO THE TWENTY-FIRST CENTURY (Part 1)

No work of art exists in a vacuum. It is a product of the time and place from which it comes. Paintings, sculptures and musical compositions are often created for the edification of a patron and as such appeal to a specific aesthetic or cultural perspective. Works of art from the Medieval era were predominantly religious in nature since the church was the primary sponsor of their creation. The Renaissance saw the emergence of more secular music and art when the wealthy courts of the time manifested an increase in power and influence. The socio/economic, political and religious environment has always been instrumental to the type of music written throughout history. A brief overview of these areas from the Baroque period to the twenty-first century may be helpful in placing the music from this chapter in perspective.

Baroque, 1600–1750

Louis XIV, dubbed the "Sun King," ruled France from 1643 until 1715. The extravagantly opulent tone of his court is often seen to have been at odds with the progressive nature of his rule. During his reign he oversaw a restructuring of the administrative, financial and military composition of the country. During this time the Germanic lands, known then as the Holy Roman Empire, and Italy were not the unified countries we know today but rather collections of autonomous areas governed by often competing monarchs. In England Oliver Cromwell rose to power bringing to an end the unchecked supremacy of the monarchy there and expanding English influence abroad.

The King James Version of the Bible was published in England in 1611 which G.F. Handel was to later use for the text of *Messiah*. England saw the rise of several new Christian sects including the Puritans, the Quakers and the Baptists. The Thirty Years War, a conflict between Protestants and Catholics, was fought from 1618–1648. Many European countries were involved in this conflict with the Holy Roman Empire (Germany) being the geographic region most affected by the war. The influence of the Catholic Church was still strong, especially in Italy. The astronomer Galileo Galilei was subjected to condemnation by the church for his scientific writings which were at odds with church teachings. The economies of European countries began a long transition from feudalism to capitalism.

Classical, 1750–1825

The emergence of rationalist philosophical tenets during this time, often called the Enlightenment, is at odds with the resurgence in religious fervor called The Great Awakening. While writers such as Jean-Jacques Rousseau, Immanuel Kant and Voltaire (François-Marie Arouet) espoused philosophies emphasizing human capacity to achieve a good and just world, renewed emphasis on an individual's personal relationship with God was being instilled by Christian preachers in both Europe and America.

This era saw the reinstatement of the monarchy in England with the reigns of Kings George II–IV. Their disagreements over taxation and other issues with the American colonies resulted in the American Revolution in 1776. In France the French Revolution began with the storming of the Bastille, the Parisian jail that was a symbol of the French aristocracy's injustices, in 1789. The French briefly experimented with a constitutional monarchy but in 1792 abolished the monarchy completely, establishing a republican form of government. Napoleon Bonaparte, a French general, staged a coup and established a new form of government with himself as its head. In 1804 Napoleon further consolidated his power and crowned himself Emperor. Napoleon engaged in an extensive series of military campaigns intended to bring all of Europe under his control. His victory over the Austro-Russian army in 1805 led to the dissolution of the Holy Roman Empire. Napoleon's army was finally defeated in 1813 and he was forced into exile. The extensive disruption caused by the Napoleonic Wars led to the convening of the Congress of Vienna, a conference of representatives of the leading European powers, in 1814–1815. This meeting was held for the purpose of redrawing the boundaries of many European countries. One of the most important changes made was to merge the numerous components of the Holy Roman Empire into the German Confederation.

cial. Estates of the wealthy aristocrats included large, intricately designed gardens. The need to impose a sense of order on the natural world is but one example of the emphasis on formal structure during this time. This emphasis on form, within which thematic development takes place, is the predominant characteristic of the music of the Classical period. The latter part of the Classical period was influenced greatly by the growing political unrest that reached its peak in the French and American Revolutions. The tension between the wealthy aristocracy and the emerging middle class is apparent in the increased emphasis on music of a more dramatic nature that became increasingly common toward the end of the period. That more emotionally charged music found its most potent voice in the music of Ludwig van Beethoven. Most of the instrumental music of the Classical period is absolute music. It doesn't try to tell a story, paint a musical picture of a scene in nature, or represent anything other than the musical concepts that manifest themselves through the notes. It exists simply as an art form revealed through musical expression. When listening to instrumental music from the Classical period, our listening should be directed toward how the musical elements are manipulated.

Concert Hall at Esterhazy Castle where many of Haydn's symphonies were first performed.
Copyright © Erich Lessing/Art Resource, NY

Musical Elements

The musical elements of melody, harmony, rhythm, form, timbre, and texture are treated with a general sense of restraint in the Classical period. Melodies tend to be created in two parts of equal length, the first part ascending, and the second part descending. This is sometimes referred to as a "question and answer" melodic style since it reflects the tendency of our voices to rise in pitch when we ask a question and fall when we answer one.

The harmonic language of the time employs a generally slow harmonic rhythm in most of the music. That simply means the harmonies do not change as frequently as they did in pieces from the Baroque period. Most compositions evoke a clear major or minor tonality. Rhythm in the Classical period exhibits a steady beat once the tempo is established in a movement. It can change, but once it changes it usually stays that way for a while. Form in the Classical period is discussed below. The stringed instruments in use during the Classical period were mostly the same as during the Baroque period, but the wind instruments underwent a degree of refinement which allowed a stronger, clearer timbre consistent across most instruments. The harpsichord of the Baroque was gradually replaced by the pianoforte, and finally the piano, which had a mellower timbre and a wider range of dynamics. The prominent polyphonic texture of instrumental music in the Baroque period gave way to a more homophonic approach during the Classical period.

CLASSICAL PERIOD

Some Prominent Composers	Genres
Franz Joseph Haydn, 1732–1809	Symphony, Concerto, String Quartet, Sonata, Opera, Oratorio
Wolfgang Amadeus Mozart, 1756–1791	Symphony, Concerto, String Quartet, Sonata, Opera
Ludwig van Beethoven, 1770–1827	Symphony, Concerto, String Quartet, Sonata
Franz Schubert, 1797–1828	Art Songs (Lieder), Symphony, String Quartet

Single-Movement Forms of the Classical Period

We have seen previously how composers organize music by balancing repetition and contrast in a piece. In the Classical period several forms were used with great consistency by all composers in the writing of individual movements of multi-movement compositions. Most instrumental genres of this time consisted of three, four, or more movements, each of which was composed in a specific form.

The most frequently used single-movement forms of the Classical period were A-B-A form (also known as ternary form or three-part form), rondo form, theme and variations, and sonata form. The simplest of these forms, A-B-A form, uses repeating sections of music at the beginning and end of the movement, the "A" sections, with a contrasting section, the "B" section, in the middle. This ternary form had been in use throughout the Baroque period before Classical period composers adopted it as the standard form for the third movement of four-movement orchestral compositions called symphonies. Rondo form is another extension of A-B-A form, similar to ritornello form of the Baroque period discussed above. In rondo form contrasting sections of music are interspersed between repetitions of the "A" section. Whenever the "A" section returns it usually presents a complete statement of the theme, unlike ritornello form of the Baroque period where fragments of the "A" theme were common. A typical movement in rondo form can be represented by the following diagram.

A-B-A-C-A-B-A

Theme and variations form is just what the name implies, a melodic theme followed by a series of variations on that theme. Variations can be created through altering any element of the music, the melody, the rhythm, the harmony, etc. Theme and variations movements are fun to listen to when you can perceive the original theme's characteristics throughout the variations. The last of the common single-movement forms, sonata form, requires an extended explanation.

Sonata Form

Sonata form takes the characteristics that define the forms discussed above, A-B-A, rondo, and theme and variations, and combines them in a single form. Both A-B-A and rondo form rely exclusively on repetition and contrast to generate interest and unity within a movement. Theme and variations form relies on the concept of varying, or developing, a melodic theme in order to keep the music interesting while endeavoring not to stray too far from the original. Otherwise, the connection between a variation and the theme that inspired it would be broken. A movement in sonata form employs both of these concepts. A sonata form movement is similar to a conversation or an argument where two contrasting themes, one strong, the other more lyrical, are presented initially in different tonal centers or keys, creating a sense of conflict between the themes. These melodic ideas are then developed throughout the movement by changing different aspects of the melody, such as altering the rhythm, playing only parts of the tune, or taking a melody that was originally in a major key and playing it in a minor key. The conflict inherent in the two themes would eventually be resolved when both themes reappear near the end of the movement in their original form and in the same key. This process by which a melodic idea is transformed in numerous ways is called thematic development and was a hallmark of the Classical period.

Sonata form was universally adopted by Classical period composers as the vehicle best suited to frame the thematic development they all sought to emphasize in their works. The Classical period was also known as the Age of Reason and the Age of Enlightenment. Both of these historical descriptors imply that the center of concern during this time was the mind and its ability to understand the world in which it resided. It was generally believed that the universe was an understandable place if only one had enough knowledge about it. To this end, composers attempted to create understandable works in which the audience members could perceive both the structure of the composition and the workings of the composer's mind in manipulating the musical elements. If the listener understood how the music was structured it could be followed with greater ease and the intricacies of the composer's treatment of thematic development perceived.

Sections in a Sonata Form Movement

Sonata form relies on a basic roadmap the listener can follow that can be modified in numerous ways by individual composers or from composition to composition. Sonata form movements are based on three primary sections, exposition, development, and recapitulation. However, most composers add shorter sections into the mix, which allows for a degree of individuality and variety.

Introduction: As the name implies, this is a section sometimes used to begin a movement. It is often in a contrasting tempo to the main body of the movement with a melody that may not be heard again after the introduction ends.

Exposition: This is the first part of the movement where the two contrasting themes are presented, "exposed," to the listener. The first theme, which is usually fairly strong and forceful, is played in the tonic key. That is the tonal center based on the first note of the scale of the key the movement is in.

Transition: This is a section of music that is used to smoothly go from one theme to the other in the exposition or from the development to the recapitulation.

The second theme is then presented in another key, usually the **dominant** (the tonal center based on the fifth note of the scale). The exposition section usually ends on a very strong sounding chord followed by a momentary silence, and the entire exposition is almost always played twice.

Closing: This is a section that brings an appropriate sounding end to a section of music such as the end of the exposition.

Development: This part of the movement is where the composer employs the most thematic development in manipulating the themes. The composer also moves the music through different tonal centers (keys) during this section. The development section is usually the shortest of the three sections of a sonata form movement. The development usually employs a transition section to segue directly into the last major section of the movement.

Transition: This is a section of music that is used to smoothly go from one theme to the other in the exposition or from the development to the recapitulation.

Recapitulation: This last major section of a sonata form movement brings back the two themes as they were heard in the exposition, but this time both themes are played in the tonic key. The feeling of having completed some kind of musical journey at the end of a movement in sonata form is in no small part due to having explored distant tonal centers during the movement and having finally returned to the "home" key.

Coda: A section of music that brings the entire movement to a final sounding conclusion.

Tonal Centers in Sonata Form

Understanding the concept of tonal centers, or keys, in sonata form is important in this respect, the tonic key of a piece of music is where the music "feels" most at rest to us. All other keys imply a feeling of movement away from the tonic or "home" key. The more the music moves into unrelated keys the more we want it to come back "home" to the tonic key. Over the course of the history of Western art music, this reaction, even if it is an unconscious reaction for most of us, has been fostered through the evolution of our use of harmony. It is one of the defining characteristics of Western art music.

CLASSICAL INSTRUMENTAL GENRES

The Symphony

The **symphony** is an orchestral genre that was developed during the Classical period in large part by the Austrian composer **Franz Joseph Haydn** (1732–1809), among others. Haydn is sometimes referred to as the "Father of the Symphony" due to his establishment of the four-movement format that became commonly accepted. The symphony evolved from the Italian opera sinfonia of the Baroque period, a three-movement instrumental composition that served as a prelude to operatic performances. Each movement of a symphony has certain characteristics, such as tempo and formal

The Classical Orchestra

During the Classical period the orchestra came to be fairly standardized in terms of instrumentation. A typical configuration for an orchestra during the Classical period might consist of strings in numbers of 6–8 1st violins, 6–8 2nd violins, 4–6 violas, 4–6 cellos, and 2–4 basses. Woodwinds might consist of 2 flutes, 2 oboes, 2 bassoons, and toward the end of the period, 2 clarinets or bassett horns (early versions of the clarinet) might be included. Brass instruments would be represented by 2 French horns and 2 trumpets. Trombones and tubas were not typically used during this time except for certain effects in operas or military pieces. Tympani, kettle drums, were often used in Classical period symphonies with occasional appearances by cymbals, triangle, and smaller drums.

structure, which allows the listener to predict, to a limited degree, the musical events and how they unfold in most symphonies.

Franz Joseph Haydn was the court composer to the Esterhazy family of Hungary for nearly thirty years. Haydn, along with the musicians he hired, lived on the Esterhazy estate just outside of Vienna, Austria. Throughout his tenure Haydn was given great latitude in experimenting with different manifestations of the genres of the time. Haydn's addition to the symphony of a dance-based movement, the minuet, added an element of elegant familiarity that was enjoyable to the aristocratic audience for which it was intended. The creative freedom that Haydn enjoyed allowed him to try out different combinations and orders of movements until both the symphony and the string quartet genres emerged in the form outlined below.

Franz Joseph Haydn (1732–1809). On the music stand is the score of *Symphony #94*, the "Surprise Symphony." Copyright © Erich Lessing/Art Resource, NY

1st Movement—Allegro (fast), Sonata Form

2nd Movement—Adagio (slow), Sonata or Theme and Variations Form

3rd Movement—Moderato (moderate tempo), Triple Meter, A-B-A Form
This movement was usually based on a dance such as the minuet.

4th Movement—Allegro (fast), Sonata or Rondo Form or a combination of the two.

In the following example from the famous *Symphony #5 in C minor* by Ludwig van Beethoven (1770–1827), listen for two things: the use of the four note motive upon which the movement is based and the different sonata form sections in the music. A motive is a very short, readily identifiable melodic or rhythmic idea. Beethoven's use of the four-note motive is very clever. He not only uses it as a "melodic" motive but as a "rhythmic" motive as well. Throughout the movement, and the entire symphony, three short notes followed by a longer note can be heard, continually reminding the listener about the musical idea upon which the entire symphony is based. In listening for the sonata form sections, it's not essential to be able to identify every minor section that Beethoven employs but try to hear the following:

The presentation of the main theme (motive) at the beginning (you really can't miss that)

The second, more lyrical theme (accompanied in the bass instruments by the rhythmic motive associated with the main theme)

The end of the exposition

The repeat of the above items

The beginning of the development section (it starts with the main theme again)

The return of the main theme at the beginning of the recapitulation

There will be several other twists and turns along the way, that is what makes the music interesting, but don't worry about trying to figure out what they all are. If you can hear the music being presented in sections, with some sections being repeats of familiar material and others providing a degree of variety, then you have heard what is structurally important in this music. One of the rewards of music based on the concept of thematic development is that upon subsequent hearings the details of the composer's compositional ideas reveal themselves on an evermore intricate level, providing an endless source of enjoyment.

 Symphony #5 in C minor, 1st movement—
Ludwig van Beethoven

Beethoven was a composer who bridged the Classical and Romantic periods. His dates place him in the Classical period, as does the basis of his compositional method, thematic development. But the emotional content of his music puts him more in tune with the Romantic period. The time in which Beethoven lived, 1770–1827, was a transitional period during which composers can be classified either way. A composer similar to Beethoven in both the time during which he lived and the emotional content of his music was Franz Schubert (1797–1828). The Romantic nature of Schubert's music can be seen especially in his art songs as discussed in Chapter 5. The Classical disposition of Schubert is more apparent in his instrumental music, particularly in his symphonies and string quartets.

The String Quartet

The *String Quartet in D minor* by Schubert is an excellent example of his Classical period grounding in the forms of that time. The string quartet is a genre that shares the same format as the symphony. The difference is that the ensemble that performs it is a string quartet instead of an orchestra. The string quartet (the performing group) consists of two violins, one viola, and one cello and is what we call a chamber music ensemble. Chamber music is any music for a small group of instruments where all of the instruments play a unique part. That is different from a large ensemble like the symphony orchestra which is composed of sections of instruments in which many players share the same part. For example, the bass section of an orchestra can have anywhere from two to ten bass players all playing the same music.

The *String Quartet in D minor* was written in 1824 and the second movement, marked *Andante con moto* (moderately with motion), is a theme and variations movement based on an art song named "Death and the Maiden" that Schubert had written seven years earlier. The somber theme is treated to a series of five variations followed by a closing coda. The theme and variations form was a favorite of composers of the Classical period for the second movement of multi-movement instrumental works.

 String Quartet in D minor, 2nd movement *(Andante con moto)*—
Franz Schubert

Composition

Musical compositions can be listened to on a number of levels. You can simply listen to the melodies and enjoy the piece as a series of melodic "hooks," to use a term borrowed from pop music referring to the tune that catches your attention. Or you can listen to it as a series of episodes in which moods and melodies change, leading you from beginning to end in a logical manner. You can also listen to a piece of music on a deeper, more sophisticated level. One in which you hear melodies in relation to each other, where harmonic centers shift coherently, where the whole is greater than just the sum of its parts.

In the accompanying image titled, *Composition*, the photographer/artist, Chip Pankey, has created a multi-level visual experience; much like a composer creates when writing a musical composition. There are vertical and horizontal elements, similar to each other but different in their orientation. There are what seem to be animated variations on those two elements in the curved pieces that are obviously related to, and derived from, the static vertical and horizontal elements. The entire work is defined by the outer edge and imbued with the overarching blue hue. How similar is this to a musical composition in which the vertical and horizontal lines could be considered primary and secondary themes, the curved pieces variations on these themes, and the blue tint an overall instrumental timbre? But beyond those considerations there is a complete composition that is more attractive and interesting than the individual elements; a work that has motion, structure, repetition, and contrast; a work that is more than the sum of its parts.

The Concerto

The **concerto** was a genre that had been popular in the Baroque period and carried over to the Classical period without significant structural change. It remained a three-movement form but utilized the single movement forms that were common for the Classical period. The other change in the Classical period concerto was the addition of a **cadenza** in one or more movements. A cadenza is an improvisatory sounding section of music for the soloist to play without the orchestra accompanying. It usually appears toward the end of a movement, giving the soloist the opportunity to display the full measure of their virtuosic ability.

1st Movement—Allegro (fast), Sonata Form

2nd Movement—Adagio (slow), Sonata, A-B-A or Theme and Variations Form

3rd Movement—Allegro, Rondo Form or Sonata/Rondo (a combination of the two)

 Concerto for Trumpet and Orchestra, 1st movement—
Franz Joseph Haydn

The Sonata

The **sonata** was a three-movement instrumental genre that shared the same movement format as the concerto. The difference, as was the case with the symphony and the string quartet, was in the performing forces. Sonatas were written either for one instrument along with a complementary piano part or for a solo piano. Many composers wrote piano sonatas for themselves to perform since most composers were accomplished pianists. One of the most highly regarded pianist/composers of the Classical era was Ludwig van Beethoven. His piano sonatas often reveal a depth of pathos that is often not apparent in his orchestral works. Beethoven is known for the power and strength that is conveyed through his music, but the slow movements of his piano sonatas reveal the quieter, more reflective Beethoven often hard to perceive in his larger compositions. Beethoven's personal life was tragic and difficult. His younger years were spent overcoming the abuses of an alcoholic father and while still in his twenties he faced fear and despair upon discovering that he was going deaf. The voice of the very human side of Beethoven is the one we hear in the second movements of his piano sonatas.

As you listen to the following example from a piano sonata by Beethoven, try to experience it on several different levels. First, listen for the melody and the accompanying harmony and allow yourself to "feel" whatever mood the music is in at any given moment. Secondly, listen for how Beethoven manipulates the theme throughout the movement. Can you identify changes to the theme? Does the theme actually change or is interest generated by some other means? Thirdly, can you identify an overall structure to the movement? Is the form of this movement unusual as far as the slow movements of instrumental pieces go? Does understanding the structure of this movement allow you to enjoy it more or does it get in the way of your listening to the music?

 Piano Sonata, Opus 13, 2nd movement— Ludwig van Beethoven

A solo piano composition such as this would most likely be heard in a **recital** hall rather than in a large concert hall. How might that more intimate setting affect your experience of the music?

ROMANTIC PERIOD, 1825–1900

Style and Characteristics

The Romantic period was the antithesis of the Classical. Where the Classical period emphasized form, the Romantic period stressed freedom of expression. Where the Classical period valued restraint and elegance, the Romantic aesthetic sought exaggeration and an overload of new and unique musical experiences. Romantic composers prized an approach to composition in which each composer found his own musical voice, his own niche, which differentiated him from other composers. Consequently, the number of prominent composers in the Romantic period far exceeds the relatively few composers of stature from the Classical period. Think of it this way, if everyone agreed on what characteristics made a great symphony (as they basically did in the Classical period), and everyone tried to write a great symphony, the best ones would be fairly apparent so there would be relatively few to discuss. But if no one could agree on what made a symphony great (as they didn't in the Romantic period), then everyone would approach the writing of symphonies in different ways, resulting in a greater number of symphonies of interest and many more composers known for writing symphonies. Also, since composers no longer worked as employees of royal courts during

Hector Berlioz conducting one of his symphonies. Satirical print depicting listeners fleeing the noise. Copyright © Erich Lessing/Art Resource, NY

the Romantic period they no longer had to conform to the dictates and tastes of such a narrow segment of the population. Composers in the Romantic era survived based on the attractiveness of their work to the general public which accepted a much wider variety of styles and approaches than the aristocratic ruling class.

Musical Elements

The elements of music are treated in a more liberal manner during the Romantic period. Melodies can be short and easily recognizable **motives** without any kind of structure or they might be long, drawn-out statements in several sections. The harmonic language of this time is stretched to the limits with composers adding more pitches to familiar harmonies, creating a less "functional" type of harmony. In the past harmony functioned as a means to help move the music through tonal centers, giving a piece a sense of movement through space as well as time, eventually returning to the "home" key which signified the end of the composition. Instead, Romantic composers more frequently used harmony as a coloring device to further enhance an already expanded palette of timbres resulting from ever-more exotic instruments and combinations of instruments being used in their works. Rhythm in the Romantic period is very flexible with tempos pushing forward and pulling backward being common instead of the exception. The term **rubato** is used in conjunction with solo piano music to imply that the rhythmic feel should exhibit a constant ebb and flow and not remain static. Form plays a role in Romantic music, but it is not the rigid framework it was in the Classical period. Composers expand or alter forms to suit their fancy and it is the rare composer that sticks to the Classical period forms without some personal modification. No overall texture is predominant in the Romantic period. Homophonic and polyphonic writing can be heard in most composers' works. The expanded instrumentation available to composers results in much experimentation in new and unique instrumental combinations leading to a wider variety of timbres than ever heard before.

ROMANTIC PERIOD

Some Prominent Composers

Gioacchino Rossini, 1792–1868
Franz Schubert, 1797–1828
Hector Berlioz, 1803–1869
Felix Mendelssohn, 1809–1847
Frederic Chopin, 1810–1847
Robert Schumann, 1810–1856
Franz Liszt, 1811–1886
Giuseppe Verdi, 1813–1901
Richard Wagner, 1813–1883
Johannes Brahms, 1833–1897

Modest Mussorgsky, 1839–1881
Peter Ilyich Tchaikovsky, 1840–1893

Genres

Opera
Art Songs (Lieder), Symphony, String Quartet
Symphony, Opera, Overture, Requiem
Symphony, Incidental Music, Concert Overtures
Solo Piano Music, Concerto
Symphony, Concerto, Chamber Music, Solo Piano Music
Solo Piano Music, Concerto, Tone Poem
Opera, Requiem, Sacred Choral Music
Opera
Symphony, Concerto, String Quartet, Sonata, Requiem,
  Solo Piano Music
Opera, Tone Poem
Symphony, Concerto, Ballet, Opera, Concert Overture

Antonin Dvorak, 1841–1904   Symphony, Concerto, Ethnic (Slavonic) Dances
Nicolai Rimsky-Korsakov, 1844–1908 Symphony, Concert Overture

Post-Romantic Period Composers

Gabriel Fauré, 1845–1924   Requiem, Chamber Music
Giacomo Puccini, 1858–1924   Opera
Gustav Mahler, 1860–1911   Symphony, Orchestral Lieder
Claude Debussy, 1862–1918   Tone Poem, Ballet, Chamber Music
Richard Strauss, 1864–1949   Tone Poem, Opera
Maurice Ravel, 1875–1937   Tone Poem, Opera, Ballet, Chamber Music

The Romantic Orchestra

The Romantic period orchestra is generally larger than the Classical period orchestra with increased numbers of stringed instruments and a wider representation of woodwind, brass, and percussion instruments. Clarinets are common by this time in addition to larger and smaller variations of other woodwind instruments. The English horn, a larger version of the oboe, is used frequently; as are the contrabassoon, the larger version of the bassoon; piccolo, the smaller version of the flute; and sometimes the bass clarinet, the largest and lowest version of the clarinet. Trombones are frequently seen in groups of three along with a single tuba, and the French horn section now has four players as the standard. In the percussion section any and all percussion instruments become commonplace.

The Romantic Piano

In the Romantic period improvements in the construction of the piano allowed composers to write with a wider range of expression for an instrument that could play higher, lower, louder, and softer than in the Classical period. Some composers chose the piano to be their primary vehicle of musical expression, such as **Frederic Chopin** (1810–1847) of Poland and, to a lesser degree, **Franz Liszt** (1811–1886) of Hungary. New genres were developed for the piano, which became a popular status symbol among the burgeoning middle class. Many short genres such as the etude, prelude, mazurka, and ballade were popularized by Frederic Chopin as the performing standards of the amateur pianist rose significantly.

Yvonne and C. Lerolle at the Piano by Auguste Renoir. Corel

In the following example by Chopin the episodic nature of the music makes it easy for the listener to imagine a story taking place, with one scene following another. This composition was called a **ballade** by Chopin. The term was derived from the poetic form of the ballad, a storytelling poem in several stanzas. As you listen to this example, jot down your ideas of what the musical scenes represent to you. Does creating a picture in your mind of "what is going on" in the music make it more enjoyable? Today almost all instrumental music is heard in conjunction with visual images, movies, television, etc., so it is very natural for us to want to impose visual imagery on purely instrumental music. It is what we in the twenty-first century have been conditioned through our experience to believe instrumental music is for.

Ballade in G minor—
Frederic Chopin

What kind of story did you "hear" in this music? What characteristics in this music lend it to this kind of visualization? Is it surprising to you that all four of the Ballades by Chopin have been choreographed by ballet companies?

Romantic Period Instrumental Genres

Most of the instrumental genres of the Classical period remain popular in the Romantic period. The symphony, string quartet, concerto, and sonata are stalwarts of the concert repertoire but almost always with some modifications. Composers no longer feel compelled to strictly follow the formats of the previous era, so symphonies may have five movements instead of four, concertos may be written with each movement segueing into the next, and the forms or tempos of individual movements may bear no relation to the Classical models on which they were based.

Two new genres acquire a significant place in the orchestral repertoire of the Romantic period. The tone poem, or symphonic poem, becomes a staple of many composers' output. A tone poem is an extended single-movement orchestral genre that is programmatic. The concert overture, a single-movement orchestral genre that may or may not be programmatic also becomes popular during this time. A concert overture is usually written in some variation of sonata form and is reminiscent of an opera overture.

PROGRAM MUSIC, NATIONALISM, AND IMPRESSIONISM

In contrast to the Classical period, when most instrumental compositions were absolute music, the majority of instrumental works from the Romantic period are programmatic. They tell a story, paint a musical picture of a scene in nature, or represent some other extra-musical concept. Program music is the opposite of the absolute music of the Classical period and is the single most commonly shared characteristic among Romantic period compositions.

Program Music

German composer Richard Strauss (1864–1949). Image courtesy of Erich Lessing/Art Resource, NY

A good example of the tone poem genre is the 1895 work *Til Eulenspiegel's Merry Pranks,* written by the German composer Richard Strauss (1864–1949). This tale of a fourteenth-century German prankster named Til Eulenspiegel, is a series of scenes from the life of this impish rascal told through the picturesque writing of Strauss. The story of "Til" is one of those mythic legends probably based on a true-to-life character whose exploits have grown in the retelling over the centuries. According to the legend, Til Eulenspiegel was renowned for poking fun at authority figures and engaging in mischievous deeds. The name Eulenspiegel translates as "Owl's Mirror" and refers to an old saying that, "One sees one's own faults no more clearly than an owl sees its own ugliness in a looking glass." Strauss did not provide a detailed program outlining the specific events represented in the music, saying rather, "Were I to put into words the thoughts which its several incidents suggest to me, they would not suffice for the listener and might even give offense. Let me therefore leave it to my hearers to crack the nut the rogue has presented them." However, the brief outline below may be helpful in listening to this music for the first time.

00:00	"Once upon a time . . ." violins and clarinets
:17	1st Til theme in horn and other instruments
1:10	2nd Til theme in clarinet
	Being chased through the market place, upsetting baskets of goods, causing a ruckus
2:43	Dressing up like a monk and preaching blasphemy—basses, flutes, violins
3:12	Reaction of crowd—general upheaval—full orchestra
4:55	Solo violin—Love theme
6:05	"Sexy" theme in violins
6:23	1st Til theme in background—Always mischievous, even in love
7:23	Imitating the learned scholars—bassoons
8:23	Laughing at the authorities—2nd Til theme
8:52	Thumbing his nose—trill, full orchestra
10:18	1st Til theme returns
10:36	2nd Til theme returns
	Victorious, roguish march-like section
	Music gets more animated
13:14	Caught by the authorities—Drum roll
	Being brought to the gallows
13:30	Impish 2nd theme intercedes several times
14:28	Hanged—Two low chords
	Spirit rises—woodwinds
15:06	"Once upon a time"—violins
16:13	Having the last laugh!

 Til Eulenspiegel's Lustige Streiche (Til Eulenspiegel's Merry Pranks)—Richard Strauss

After hearing the music with the above suggested "program," listen to it again without referring to any outline and jot down your own images of what the music might be portraying. The composer purposefully did not want to give the listener a detailed program but only wanted to suggest certain scenes. Try writing out your own program now that you know the general images the composer intended to represent. Do you "see" similar images in your mind's eye?

Nationalism

The nineteenth century was an era of great political unrest across Europe. It has been common in times of such political uncertainty for artists to represent their national heritage through their writing, painting, and music. This nationalism in music can be exhibited through the writing of operas and ballets based on historical themes or important people from a particular country. It may also be manifested by incorporating ethnic and national dances into musical compositions as well as writing sets of dances

Onion-shaped domes on Russian Orthodox cathedrals are emblematic of the Russian people and their culture. Corel

unique to a composer's country. Sometimes composers write music evocative of geographic places of interest from their homeland.

The tone poem, *A Night on Bald Mountain*, by the Russian composer Modest Mussorgsky (1839–1881), is an excellent example of a piece that is programmatic and nationalistic. Mussorgsky was one of "The Five" Russian nationalist composers who sought to create a unique Russian style of composition in contrast to the predominant German style. Those composers, Mili Balakirev, Cesar Cui, Alexander Borodin, and Nicolai Rimsky-Korsakov, along with Mussorgsky, purposely chose subject matter and created melodies that would elicit a nationalistic fervor in the listener, an assumed Russian listener. What they could not anticipate was that their efforts would find an eager audience far beyond the bounds of their national borders, an audience intrigued with the exotic melodies and timbres of their Russian homeland.

This piece is based on Russian author Nicolai Gogol's (1809–1852) version of the ancient Russian legend of *St. John's Night on the Bald Mountain*. This legend of a macabre celebration on the night of June 23rd, St. John's Night, lends itself to some of the most vivid programmatic writing of the Romantic period. The music depicts the orgiastic revelry and demonic dances of the underworld led by the god of darkness, Chernobog. Mussorgsky's original composition went through several revisions of his own before Rimsky-Korsakov completed the version usually played today after the composer's death. This version ends with the chiming of church bells at dawn dispersing the dark revelry of the Witches Sabbath.

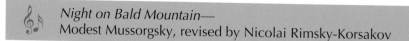

Night on Bald Mountain—
Modest Mussorgsky, revised by Nicolai Rimsky-Korsakov

This piece may sound familiar to you as it was included in an animated movie called "Fantasia" produced by the Disney studios in 1940. In that movie a number of orchestral compositions were presented with animated scenes and stories created by the animation artists.

Impressionism

A distinct style of late Romantic music called impressionism developed in France toward the end of the nineteenth century and carried over into the early twentieth century. The term "impressionism" was first coined by an art critic upon seeing the painting, *Impression, Sunrise*, by the French painter Claude Monet. Impressionism in art, as represented by the works of painters like Claude Monet and Pierre-August Renoir, favored an emphasis on subtleties of light and color rather than on clarity of line and polished representations of objects that had been favored by the Academic Art of the French Academies. Impressionistic music reflected analogous qualities through an emphasis on subtle and new expressions of timbre (tone color) and harmony rather than on extensive development of melodic themes or emphasizing formal structure in musical compositions.

The late nineteenth century was a time when the interaction between artists from diverse disciplines was at the highest point since the Renaissance. Musicians, writers, dancers, and painters often lived in the same communities, frequented the same cafes, and generally created self-contained artistic communities within the great cities of Europe. In 1876, Stéphane Mallarmé, a French writer and poet, wrote a poem entitled *The Afternoon of a Faun* depicting a mythological, half man/half animal creature, a faun, in a summer afternoon's encounter with enchanting wood nymphs. The faun's carnal desires are aroused by the presence of the nymphs, and his memory of them

The Parliament of London by French Impressionist painter Claude Monet (1840–1926). Monet frequently painted the same image at various times of the day to capture the essence of different lightings. Corel

haunts him after they have left. Claude Debussy (1862–1918) used this poem as the basis for his **tone poem** of the same name.

The Afternoon of a Faun premiered in 1894 and was an immediate audience favorite. It was later used in 1912 as the music for a radically different kind of ballet choreographed by the revolutionary Russian dancer Vaclav Nijinsky for Serge Diaghilev's Ballet Russes in Paris.

> *L'Après-midi d'un faun (The Afternoon of a Faun)—* Claude Debussy

Describe how this music is different from the other music you have heard from this chapter. Think about the elements of music, melody, harmony, rhythm, form, texture, and timbre and compare them to how other composers treated those elements. What differences in the treatment of those elements make this music unique?

THE ROMANTIC SYMPHONY

The symphony in the Romantic period was based on the format established by Franz Joseph Haydn in the Classical era but exhibited more flexibility in terms of number and sequence of movements and in the wider range of expressive devices commonly found in music of the nineteenth century. Some Romantic period composers wrote symphonies with three or five movements. Cesar Franck's *Symphony in D minor* has only three movements while Hector Berlioz's *Symphonie Fantastique* contains five. In some instances composers might even end a symphony with a slow movement instead of a loud and fast one, Tchaikovsky's *Symphony #6* is an example of this. While the following work sticks to the traditional Classical period ordering of movements it is a distinctly Romantic work at heart.

THE NEW WORLD SYMPHONY

Antonin Dvořák (1841–1904) wrote the *Symphony #9 in E minor*, subtitled *From the New World*, in 1893 during an extended visit to the United States. Today it is commonly known as *The New World Symphony*. Dvořák, a Czech composer originally from Prague, spent the years from 1892–1895 in the U.S. as the Director of the National Conservatory of Music in New York City. During this time he developed an intense interest in the music of both the African-American and Native American peoples. The primary theme of the second movement of the *Symphony #9* sounded so much like a traditional African-American spiritual that words were put to it by William Arms Fisher, a student of Dvořák's, and it is now known as the spiritual *Goin' Home*. Dvořák stated that he did not use any pre-existing melodies in this symphony but that it contained melodic material inspired by the music of the Native Americans.

The second movement excerpt on your playlist begins with the sustained chords of the brass section followed by the *Goin' Home* theme played by the English Horn, the larger counterpart of the oboe. After listening to this excerpt it is interesting to listen to the "spiritual" version of this melody to hear how Dvořák perfectly captured the nature of the African-American spiritual style in this symphonic genre.

The fourth movement of the *Symphony #9* begins with a folk-like theme in the brass instruments that could be one of the "Indian" sounding themes Dvořák was referring to. Several vigorous secondary themes come and go in the first two minutes until the tempo slows dramatically and a more lyrical theme is introduced. Throughout this movement, and in fact this entire symphony, melodies are always prominent and follow one after the other. It is not usually necessary to try to follow the development of themes in symphonic music of the Romantic era, as you might with music from the Classical period. An understanding that primary themes will come back several times throughout a movement interspersed with other melodies is usually sufficient to fully enjoy the music.

Symphony #9, 2nd movement, Largo—excerpt
Antonin Dvořák

Goin' Home—
Melody composed by Antonin Dvořák,
words by William Arms Fisher

Symphony #9, 4th movement, Allegro con fuoco (Fast with fire)—
Antonin Dvořák

TWENTIETH/TWENTY-FIRST CENTURY 1900–PRESENT

Style and Characteristics

There is no one overriding style or set of characteristics that has defined the concert music of the twentieth and twenty-first centuries. Instead there have been several significant styles that were adopted by composers that have found varying degrees of acceptance with concert audiences. The end of the Romantic period, as exemplified by composers like the impressionist Claude Debussy and the German operatic composer Richard Wagner, found composers questioning the basic tenets of musical composition that composers had accepted for 900 years. Central to the evolution of Western

PERSPECTIVE—BAROQUE TO THE TWENTY-FIRST CENTURY (Part 2)

Romantic, 1825–1900

The nineteenth century was the time during which England, in the guise of the British Empire, rose to become the pre-eminent world power. The reign of Queen Victoria, 1839–1901, is often referred to as the Victorian era. Political stability on the continent was established only briefly after the Congress of Vienna (1814–1815) with rising nationalist movements in the German Confederation and the Kingdom of Sardinia (Italy) and many small-scale revolutionary movements taking root. While a widespread conflict was avoided for several decades, issues concerning who held sovereign authority over the Holy Land led to the Crimean War from 1854–1856. This conflict pitted Russia against an alliance of France, England, Sardinia (Italy), and the Ottoman Empire. By the end of the century, both Germany and Italy emerged as unified nations.

The move away from feudal, agrarian economies continued at an accelerated pace as the Industrial Revolution fueled an ever-increasing urban population. The old order of nobility, clergy, and peasantry gave way to a new stratification of society. The clergy no longer held the sway they once had and the new middle class was itself divided into tradesmen, business owners, and the lowest classes who worked for them. It was this lowest rung of the economic ladder that was attracted to the Socialist and Communist ideals that were gaining in popularity. The upper strata of the middle class became the catalyst for an extraordinary expansion of public artistic presentations. The Anglican Church of England sent missionaries around the world through the extensive network of lands constituting the British Empire.

Twentieth/Twenty-First Century 1900–The Present

Unified Germany's dominating influence throughout Europe led to World War I from 1914–1918. Russia's heavy losses in that war led to the forsmation of the Soviet Union and the adoption of a communist form of government. New countries were delineated at the end of the war in the Treaty of Versailles including Austria, Poland, Finland, Czechoslovakia, and Yugoslavia among others. The world-wide economic depression that began in 1929 alienated many people in the lower classes. Their fears allowed opportunistic individuals such as Adolf Hitler in Germany and Benito Mussolini in Italy to rise to power as the heads of fascist states bent on world domination. World War II began in Europe in 1939 with the German invasion of Poland and expanded to the Pacific when Japan attacked the American Naval Base at Pearl Harbor, Hawaii, in 1941. It ended in 1945 when the Allied Forces (principally the United States, England, France, and the Soviet Union) defeated the Axis Powers (Germany, Italy, Japan) by invading Germany and dropping the newly-invented atomic bombs on the Japanese cities of Hiroshima and Nagasaki.

After World War II, the world's center of influence shifted from Europe to the United States and the Soviet Union, with China playing an ever-increasing role both politically and economically. The Cold War, the period from the late 1940s to the late 1980s, pitted the Western nations led by the United States against the Eastern Bloc of the Soviet Union, China, and the Eastern European countries, in a protracted ideological, economic, and political struggle. Conflicts such as the Korean and Vietnam Wars were in essence proxy wars between these two competing forces. The Cold War ended with the dissolution of the Soviet Union in 1991. The United States, as the only remaining superpower, increasingly became the target of the anger and frustrations of people around the world, whether justified or not. Terrorist attacks by Islamic extremists created an atmosphere heretofore unknown, where nations are threatened not by other nations but by supra-national elements that are difficult if not impossible to confront directly. Religious fundamentalism, exerting its influence through the political structure of nations, changed the character of international relations, especially in regard to the Middle East.

Composition, 1955 by Sonia Delaunay (1885–1979). © Pracusa 2013018

art music had been the concept that a musical composition was based on a tonal center, a pitch upon which a scale and resultant harmonies were derived. The term that came to define that concept was the word "key." Compositions were often named with the key of the piece being a prominent part of the name, such as *Symphony #5 in C minor* by Beethoven. Perhaps the most significant aspect of twentieth/twenty-first-century music was the realization by composers that a tonal center was not essential to a musical composition.

A New Musical Language—Re-Evaluating Common Practices

Composers in the latter part of the nineteenth century and in the early years of the twentieth century began questioning all of the assumptions about music that composers had accepted for centuries. It was the general tenor of the times. In all areas of intellectual endeavor, the ideas that had been central to every discipline were being re-evaluated. In biology the theories of how living things came to be in their present form had been questioned by Charles Darwin and Alfred Russel Wallace. In physics the concept of quantum mechanics explained how particles behaved on the sub-atomic level, while Albert Einstein's General and Special Theories of Relativity revealed nothing less than a completely new view of the entire universe. Based as it was on the idea that space and time were inextricably connected in a new concept called space-time, Einstein's unique insight set the long-accepted Newtonian views of the universe on their heads. Pablo Picasso and other artists created entirely new ways to visually represent the world. Picasso's "cubist" style of the early twentieth century allowed three-dimensional objects to be represented in their entirety on a two-dimensional surface. He did this by deconstructing the subjects he painted and presented all of their parts on the two-dimensional plane of a canvas, even if their shape no longer resembled the object as one would see it in the "real" world. All of these ideas represented radically new ways of explaining the world in which we live. Composers sought nothing less for their art, a completely new musical language.

TWENTIETH/TWENTY-FIRST CENTURIES

Some Prominent Composers	Genres
Richard Strauss, 1864–1949	Tone Poem, Opera
Arnold Schoenberg, 1874–1951	Chamber Symphony, Concerto, Chamber Music
Maurice Ravel, 1875–1937	Ballet, Opera, Chamber Music
Béla Bartok, 1881–1945	Concerto, Chamber Music, Orchestral Works
Igor Stravinsky, 1882–1971	Ballet, Symphony, Chamber Music
Anton Webern, 1883–1945	Chamber Music, Orchestral Works
William Grant Still, 1895–1978	Symphony, Chamber Music, Movies
George Gershwin, 1898–1937	Tone Poem, Rhapsody, Opera, Concerto
Aaron Copland, 1900–1990	Ballet, Symphony, Chamber Music
Dmitri Shostakovich, 1906–1975	Symphony, Opera, Chamber Music
Alan Hovhannes, 1911–2000	Symphony, Chamber Music
John Cage, 1912–1992	Chamber Music
Pierre Boulez, b. 1925	Chamber Music, Orchestral Works
Terry Riley, b. 1935	Chamber Music, Orchestral Works
Philip Glass, b. 1937	Symphony, Concerto, Opera, Chamber Music
Ellen Taaffe Zwilich, b. 1939	Symphony, Concerto, Chamber Music, Orchestral works

Serialism

The most significantly different concept to arise from this attempt to reinvent the musical language of the time was the adoption of atonality as the basis of musical composition. Atonality means that there is no recognizable tonal center in a piece, no home key around which everything else revolves. Since scales and harmonies had always been based on the tonal center of a piece, new concepts regarding melody and harmony were necessary if atonal music were to be realized. The resultant melodic and harmonic traits of atonal music were dissonant, harsh, and unpredictable. Composers found that writing in this style was difficult because there were no patterns or conventions, such as scales and chord progressions, on which to base their music. So they created some. In order not to emphasize any one pitch, which would have resulted in an implied tonal center, composers ordered pitches in random sounding rows or series that they then manipulated as if they were traditional scales, creating melodies and harmonies based on those tone rows. This type of music was alternately known as serialism, being based on a "series" of pitches, or twelve-tone music, since it was based on the twelve pitches that were put in a tone row. The Austrian composer Arnold Schoenberg (1874–1951) is acknowledged as the composer who brought atonal music to the forefront of the musical world. He subsequently created the serial techniques by which atonal musical materials could be organized, which were the basis of twelve-tone music. Other composers, most notably, Anton Webern (1883–1945) and Pierre Boulez (b. 1925), built on Schoenberg's ideas with even more radical extensions of serial technique.

Expressionism

Most twelve-tone music was extremely dissonant and consequently unsettling in its effect on the listener. This type of music fit well with a general artistic trend prominent

The Scream, 1893, by Edvard Munch (1863–1944). Copyright © 2006 The Munch Museum/The Munch-Ellingsen Group/Artist Rights Society (ARS), NY. Image courtesy of Scala/Art Resource, NY

in Germany during the late nineteenth and early twentieth centuries called **expressionism**, which sought to explore the dark side of human experience and the unconscious mind. These ideas were in vogue at the time due in no small part to the influential ideas of the Austrian psychoanalyst, Sigmund Freud. Artists of all types created works of an unsettling nature, the most famous example being the painting *The Scream,* 1893, by the Norwegian painter Edvard Munch. This painting, depicting the unexplained anguish of an androgynous "everyman," whose pain is ignored by the seemingly unmoved couple in the background, has become synonymous with expressionism.

As you listen to the following two movements from a solo piano work by Schoenberg, look at the painting by Munch. Does the music reflect what you are seeing in the painting? What sort of emotional reaction do you have to this music? Is it enjoyable? Do you think the composer intended for it to be enjoyable? Or is there another reason for this music?

 Five Piano Pieces, two movements—
Arnold Schoenberg
Langsam (Slowly)
Sehr rasch (Very quickly)

As was mentioned above in regard to the piano sonata by Beethoven, a solo piano composition such as this would most likely be heard in a **recital** hall, or some other smaller venue, rather than in a large concert hall. What makes a certain type of performance more appropriate for one venue or another; the size of the performing ensemble, the emotional content of the music, the time period during which the music was written?

Primitivism

Many composers in the early years of the twentieth century incorporated dissonance into their music as a common harmonic quality. Some added irregular rhythmic patterns, unpredictable meter changes, and short motivic melodies along with a primal quality that earned it the stylistic name **primitivism**. This type of music made extensive use of percussion instruments and strong, irregular rhythms that conjured up images of primitive societies in Europeans' minds. The Russian composer, **Igor Stravinsky** (1882–1971), wrote the definitive work in this style, the revolutionary ballet *Le Sacre du Printemps* (*The Rite of Spring*), discussed earlier in the chapter on Music for Dancing. With its enormous orchestra, relentlessly driving rhythms, and **unresolved dissonances**, *The Rite of Spring* was the epitome of the primitivistic style.

 The Rite of Spring, excerpt "Adoration of the Earth"—
Igor Stravinsky

Neoclassicism

Europe was devastated after World War I, 1914–1918, with many orchestras disbanded and concert halls and opera houses in ruins. Taking into account the financial difficulties in mounting performances of large works, many composers took to writing smaller-scale works, chamber music, rather than compositions for large orchestras. The emotional angst so thoroughly explored by expressionism before the war found little favor among audiences on the war-torn continent. A less emotional style was desired and the result was neoclassicism, music that was smaller in scope, more restrained in its emotional demands, and reminiscent of earlier eras. During this period between the two World Wars, composers looked to the Renaissance, Baroque, and Classical periods and adapted genres and styles from those eras for modern sensibilities. While a composer might write a symphony, based on the Classical period model, it would incorporate twentieth-century characteristics such as mildly dissonant harmonies and irregular rhythms. Igor Stravinsky, one of the most influential composers of the time, was again a leader, this time in the development of the neoclassical style.

Pulcinella

Shortly after the end of World War I, the Russian impresario Serge Diaghilev asked Igor Stravinsky to re-interpret several musical pieces written by the eighteenth-century Italian composer Giovanni Battista Pergolesi. This re-orchestration of Pergolesi's work was to be the basis of a new ballet for the Ballet Russes. Diaghilev and Stravinsky had previously collaborated on several ballet projects, including *The Rite of Spring*, but this commission would energize the neoclassical direction in which music was heading at the time. The story was based on the traditional characters of the "Commedia dell'arte," the Italian theatrical style prominent from the fourteenth through the eighteenth centuries. The Commedia dell'arte was known for its improvisational acting style in which the story, scenes, acts, and conclusion were worked out beforehand, but the specific words of the actors were improvised while the action unfolded. Over time, recurring characters developed who were represented in these productions through costumes and masks. Pulcinella was one of these characters, a rough sort of hunchbacked clown.

Basing the ballet on eighteenth-century theatrical traditions as well as eighteenth-century music firmly places this composition in the realm of the neoclassical. Stravinsky orchestrated the melodies with a sense of great restraint, retaining the clarity and elegant style of the original while imbuing the music with rhythmic quirks and dashes of harmonic flavor, clearly marking it as a twentieth-century creation.

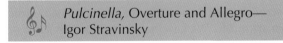

Pulcinella, Overture and Allegro—
Igor Stravinsky

What Baroque or Classical period characteristics can you hear in this music? What twentieth-century characteristics are apparent?

Avant-garde: Experiments in Modern Music

From the 1930s until the end of the century, many composers looked for ever-more unique ways to compose and perform music. The advent of electronic means with which to both record and recreate sounds led to composers like Edgard Varése (1883–1965) creating compositions of recorded sounds manipulated in studios and presented "in concert" by playing a recording of the final version in a concert hall. This "musique concrete," or concrete music, never found much of an audience outside of a small circle of composers and within schools of music but stands as an interesting early attempt to use a new tool with which to create music, much as the computer has been used in recent decades. American composer John Cage (1912–1992) experimented with incorporating chance happenings into his compositions. His infamous composition *4' 33"* consists of a silent piano whose lid over the keyboard is opened for the first movement, closed for the second, and opened again for the third. The "composition" is made up of the chance sounds that happen to occur during the length of the piece. This extreme example of aleatoric music, music that incorporates chance happenings, belies a serious idea that Cage had. He believed that our definition of music shouldn't just be notes played on instruments in concert halls but should include all of the sounds in nature and the world that we tune out every day. Other composers, such as Pierre Boulez (b. 1925), pushed the serial ideas of Schoenberg to the limit, serializing all aspects of the music. This total serialism created music that was intellectually challenging in the extreme.

A prominent avant-garde American composer, Henry Cowell (1897–1965), experimented with novel approaches to tonality and rhythm and advocated unusual performance techniques on traditional instruments. His composition *The Banshee*, written in 1925, for solo piano makes use of some of these techniques including playing directly on the strings inside the piano. By striking the strings and sliding the nails of the fingers lengthwise on the strings, he created tone clusters of numerous adjacent pitches and an eerie "wailing" sound otherwise unobtainable through traditional performance techniques. In traditional Scottish and Irish folklore, the mythological banshee either heralded a forthcoming death or lamented a recent one.

The Banshee—
Henry Cowell

Traditionalism

Throughout the twentieth century, while many composers experimented with novel concepts and unique approaches to musical composition, there was an unbroken line of composers who wrote in a more or less straightforward extension of the tonal music of the Romantic period. These composers did not completely eschew the innovations of the twentieth century but rather incorporated them in a discriminating fashion, creating more audience friendly music. Rather than adopt the new concepts that often intimidated audiences, these composers extended the tradition of tonality-based music and evolutionary changes in Western art music. We have heard the music of some of the most prominent composers in this vein already, Leonard Bernstein (*West Side Story*), Aaron Copland (*Rodeo* and *the Fanfare for the Common Man*), Samuel Barber (*Adagio for Strings*), and Richard Strauss (*Til Eulenspiegel's Merry Pranks*). George Gershwin (1898–1937), who blended traditional classical genres with the emerging jazz style of the time, created one of the most vibrant and popular musical styles of the twentieth century. William Grant Still (1895–1978) was the first prominent African-American composer who infused his work with African-American influences. Still broke through racial barriers both as a composer and conductor and became a successful composer and arranger for both radio broadcasts and Hollywood movies. Another composer whose works are very tonal but who explored exotic concepts from non-Western styles of music in his works was Alan Hovhannes (1911–2000).

A recent extension of the tonal line of traditional music can be found in the minimalism of contemporary composers like Terry Riley (b. 1935) and Philip Glass (b. 1937). Minimalism is characterized by having a traditional tonal center and much repetition with layering of melodic or motivic elements. Terry Riley's composition, *In C,* is often considered the seminal composition in this style. Other composers in the late twentieth and early twenty-first century have made extensive use of "quotations" of themes from earlier composers' works. This gives their compositions a dual character, acknowledging the early influences that are the basis of our current music while exploring the possibilities inherent in modern compositional techniques. Ellen Taaffe Zwilich (b. 1939), sometimes referred to as a neoromantic composer, is a prominent American composer in this vein. The early twentieth-century practices of blending traditional compositions with popular styles has also been a prevalent theme in late twentieth and early twenty-first century compositions. Folk, rock, blues, and jazz influences can be seen in the work of a number of contemporary composers, including the American composer Conni Ellisor.

TWENTIETH/TWENTY-FIRST CENTURY TONALITY-BASED COMPOSITIONS

Rhapsody in Blue

George Gershwin wrote the *Rhapsody in Blue* in 1924 for Paul Whiteman's jazz band/orchestra, and it intrigued both reviewers and audience alike due to its treatment of jazz and classical styles as equals in one composition. Whiteman was an influential figure in New York's musical circles, and his presentation of "An Experiment in Modern Music" concert included the *Rhapsody in Blue*. The term rhapsody is used to describe a free-form musical composition of an effusive nature. The work is for solo piano and "orchestra." The original Whiteman band had only 18 instrumentalists, and the version commonly heard today is for solo piano and full symphony orchestra. The jazzy sounds that give the work its unique appeal had not been incorporated into large-scale classically based compositions prior to this. Gershwin was sufficiently encouraged by the response to the Rhapsody that the blending of the two styles became the hallmark of his compositional style. Other composers such as Leonard Bernstein and Duke Ellington have followed Gershwin's lead in writing music that blends the classical and jazz styles.

George Gershwin (1898–1937) at work. Behind him, posters of his productions. Copyright © Jewish Chronicle Archive/HIP/Art Resource, NY

Rhapsody in Blue—
George Gershwin

Can you identify the "jazzy" sounds in this piece? How are they different from "classical" sounds? What elements of music can be considered jazzy?

Afro-American Symphony

William Grant Still was the first African-American composer of significance, and his work reached far beyond the concert hall through his work in radio and in Hollywood. Still grew up in Little Rock, Arkansas, and after dabbling with the more dissonant compositional styles receiving much attention early in the twentieth century, found his unique musical voice in the African-American-influenced compositions exemplified by the *Afro-American Symphony* written in 1931. The third movement of this symphony, Animato (Animated), uses bluesy, folk music-like tunes reminiscent of spirituals, a banjo, and vibrant rhythms.

Afro-American Symphony, 3rd movement "Animato"—
William Grant Still

Symphony #2, Mysterious Mountain

Alan Hovhannes (1911–2000) was an American of Armenian heritage. Hovhannes's music did not fit any of the prevailing twentieth-century styles, including the Romantic era extensions of Strauss, et al., but found a wider degree of acceptance after the premiere of his *Symphony #2, Mysterious Mountain* in 1955. The work presented a fresh alternative to both the serial composers and the Romantic traditionalists. Hovhannes's writing is very tonal but not in the line of Bach, Beethoven, and Brahms. It is usually based on a mode (scale) other than the major/minor tonalities of traditional Western art music. Often the modal basis of his compositions can be found in music of non-Western cultures. This gives his music an exotic, intriguing sound. The following example from the *Symphony #2, Mysterious Mountain,* is a double fugue, two separate themes treated fugally (imitative polyphony). This combination of exotic, modal writing within a traditional compositional technique such as the fugue makes Hovhannes's music difficult to categorize but eminently listenable.

 Symphony #2, Mysterious Mountain, double fugue excerpt—
Alan Hovhannes

In C

Tonal music in the twentieth/twenty-first centuries has found its most readily accepted outlet in the style developed in the 1960s called **minimalism**. Minimalist music emphasizes repetition, tone color, and rhythmic patterns. Some of the innovators in this style of music were **La Monte Young, Terry Riley, Steve Reich**, and **Philip Glass**. Minimalist music is relatively simple sounding and has gained wide acceptance among composers and the public alike because of its adaptability to almost all musical genres. There have been operas, chamber music works, as well as large orchestral compositions written in this style. Early minimalist works tended to be extreme in their exploration of the minimalist concepts. The example below by Terry Riley, *In C,* is perhaps the most extreme minimalist composition of all time. The work consists of the repeated playing of high-register octave "Cs" on the piano while eleven instruments take turns playing short melodic motives, fifty-three in all, in overlapping rhythms and textures. After all eleven instruments have played one of the motives, they move on to the next one. This creates a subtle, ever-changing mass of sound that shifts the textural shape of the music much as clouds in the sky morph from one "shape" into another, slowly, almost unnoticeably. The effect is mesmerizing, hypnotizing, and, to some people, very annoying. While a composition such as *In C* may not be everyone's idea of great music, the idea behind it is very powerful. Compositions have now been written in all genres based on minimalist concepts.

 In C—
Terry Riley

How does this music affect you? Do you like it? Dislike it? Does it make you relax? Does it make you want to pull your hair out? Listening to *In C* is a challenge in some ways. We expect music to *do* something. Have a beginning, go through some changes, and then come to a final sounding conclusion. We want to hear a balance of repetition and variety. Too much of one or the other and we shut down our ears and brains. We often cease to process what we hear when it doesn't meet our expectations. Minimalist music challenges the very expectations we bring when listening to music. In order to have an enjoyable and rewarding experience with minimalist music, we must change our expectations of what music is and does. The best way to experience any unfamiliar style of music is to approach it with an open mind. There is no question that this music is tonal, we hear the tonal center almost continually throughout the piece. There is no dissonance that requires resolving so there really isn't anything unpleasant, in the traditional harmonic sense, to make it difficult to listen to. What is difficult is what the music does, or doesn't do, to satisfy our expectations of what music should be.

Terry Riley and other minimalist composers have been influenced significantly by their knowledge of music from non-Western cultures, especially Indonesian gamelan music, western African drumming, and the music of India. Indian music can seem to go on for an extremely long time without much "happening." Is it simply a cultural expectation that can be learned and thereby make the music enjoyable? Possibly, but the time and effort necessary may be more than most people are willing to invest to find out. *In C* may be a bit taxing for a first exposure to minimalist music. Try listening to other minimalist works, such as the 4th movement from Philip Glass's *Symphony #3*, for example, to hear how the minimalist approach might be more appealing. Philip Glass has been the most successful minimalist composer, writing film scores, operas, and minimalist compositions in virtually all genres.

> 🎼 *Symphony #3,* 4th movement—
> Philip Glass

Is this music more agreeable to you? Does it sound more like what you expect music to sound like? Does it sound like it is doing something, going somewhere?

CROSSOVER MUSIC

The term "crossover music" commonly refers to one style of popular music that has gained popularity among an audience of another style. It can also mean what composers such as George Gershwin and William Grant Still did earlier in the twentieth century, that is, unite other styles of music, like folk and popular styles, with traditional composition. American composer Conni Ellisor (b. 1957) has combined folk idioms with traditional classical methods in several works to create a style that is easily accessible to the listener while exploring new possibilities within the classical parameters of composition. In her 1996 work *Blackberry Winter,* Ellisor uses one of the simplest folk instruments, the mountain dulcimer, as a featured solo instrument with chamber orchestra. In this work she creates a nostalgic yet vibrant atmosphere, bridging the worlds of traditional folk music and twentieth/twenty-first century composition. The challenge of creating new musical styles through a merging of pre-existing approaches is summed up by Ellisor in the following statement:

American composer
Conni Ellisor.

"... much of the momentum of classical composition is related to modulations [i.e., changing from one key or tonality to another to create a sense of musical journey], and I never realized how true this was until I began working within the limitation of the dulcimer's anchored tonality. My solution was to create orchestral interludes that moved into new tonalities and allowed the dulcimer soloist time to retune the instrument for the next melodic statement. In writing this piece, I wanted to be respectful of the rich heritage of both the dulcimer and the classical chamber orchestra, but I felt a certain liberty in combining these traditions."

In the following example the distinctive sound of the mountain dulcimer opens the movement with a vigorous rhythmic pattern and melodic motive. The dulcimer is then joined by the orchestra, and the movement moves through several mood and tonality changes before ending in a final climactic rush of energy. As the composer's comments above indicate, this work pays homage to classical traditions through the movement through different tonal centers giving the work a sense of direction. The mountain dulcimer's presence provides the timbre of the folk music tradition while the simple melodic structure and rhythmic vitality idiomatic to the instrument reinforce the folk heritage the piece summons to the listener's mind.

 Blackberry Winter, 3rd movement—
Conni Ellisor

The term "crossover music" can also be thought of as rock, jazz, R&B, etc., styles that make use of traditional classical music ideas and techniques. Early rock groups such as The Moody Blues (1960s), Deep Purple (1960s), and the Electric Light Orchestra (1970s) used orchestral arrangements and synthesized sounds to create music that bridged the pop and classical worlds. More recently rock artists like Yngwie Malmsteen and Trey Anastasio have created works for electric guitar and orchestra modeled on the concerto and suite genres of the classical music tradition. Anastasio's *Time Turns Elastic,* written in a collaborative effort with Don Hart and premiered in 2008, explores the lyrical character of the electric guitar similar to how a composer might write for a bowed string instrument such as the violin. Malmsteen's *Concerto Suite for Electric Guitar and Orchestra,* another collaborative work, written with David Rosenthal, highlights the composer's legendary lightning-fast guitar technique in a piece that is reminiscent of the virtuosic showpieces of the nineteenth century, with a decidedly modern twist.

 "Vivace" from *Concerto Suite for Electric Guitar and Orchestra*
Yngwie Malmsteen with David Rosenthal

Listening Chart

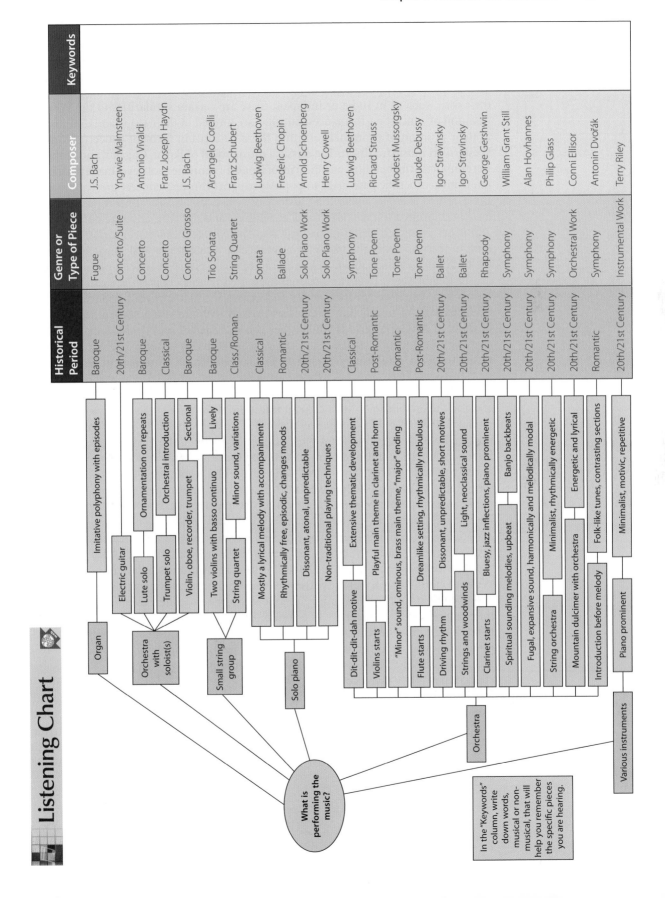

Historical Period	Genre or Type of Piece	Composer	Keywords
Baroque	Fugue	J.S. Bach	
20th/21st Century	Concerto/Suite	Yngwie Malmsteen	
Baroque	Concerto	Antonio Vivaldi	
Classical	Concerto	Franz Joseph Haydn	
Baroque	Concerto Grosso	J.S. Bach	
Baroque	Trio Sonata	Arcangelo Corelli	
Class./Roman.	String Quartet	Franz Schubert	
Classical	Sonata	Ludwig Beethoven	
Romantic	Ballade	Frederic Chopin	
20th/21st Century	Solo Piano Work	Arnold Schoenberg	
20th/21st Century	Solo Piano Work	Henry Cowell	
Classical	Symphony	Ludwig Beethoven	
Post-Romantic	Tone Poem	Richard Strauss	
Romantic	Tone Poem	Modest Mussorgsky	
Post-Romantic	Tone Poem	Claude Debussy	
20th/21st Century	Ballet	Igor Stravinsky	
20th/21st Century	Ballet	Igor Stravinsky	
20th/21st Century	Rhapsody	George Gershwin	
20th/21st Century	Symphony	William Grant Still	
20th/21st Century	Symphony	Alan Hovhannes	
20th/21st Century	Symphony	Philip Glass	
20th/21st Century	Orchestral Work	Conni Ellisor	
Romantic	Symphony	Antonin Dvořák	
20th/21st Century	Instrumental Work	Terry Riley	

In the "Keywords" column, write down words, musical or non-musical, that will help you remember the specific pieces you are hearing.

What is performing the music?

SUMMARY

There are few if any classical musical traditions in the world that encompass the breadth and depth of the music of Western culture intended for concert hall performance. In non-Western cultures that have a significant classical music heritage of their own, such as in India or in Japan, there are certain similarities to the Western tradition of concert performances, but they are limited in their scope and diminishing in their position of prominence within those cultures in favor of concerts from the Western art music tradition. The classical music styles of Japan, Gagaku, and Nohgaku were important in the courts and theatres of Japan for centuries but never made the transition from aristocratic patronage to popular support through concert presentations. In India, which also has a very long history of "classical" music, concert presentations have been limited to recitals of small ensembles, and the type of music on those programs has remained fairly unchanged over the course of many centuries. In fact, in both of these societies the rise in prominence of Western classical music has rivalled the traditional classical music presentations of each culture in concert performances.

In looking back over the material presented in this chapter, one can see an extraordinary variety of musical styles and genres. Each historical period had certain characteristics or trends that composers worked within. Genres sometimes went out of favor in different periods while other genres retained their popularity across the centuries. The musical basis of the changes seen from one historical period to another is the evolution of the harmonic system that is the bedrock of tonality in Western music. The societal basis for the changes across the historical eras is centered on who was paying for the music to be composed and the intended audience. Before the Baroque era, and the establishment of a concert tradition, most musical activity was supported by the church. The Baroque period supported an approximately even division of patronage between the courts and the churches of Europe. The Classical period saw an increase in music supported by the courts and the aristocracy and a corresponding increase in music geared toward that sensibility. The Romantic period composer, no longer able or willing to depend on such aristocratic patronage, wrote for the general public in a purposefully attractive style in order to garner the support of a paying public. The early twentieth-century search for a new musical language and the subsequent adoption by many composers of an intentionally dissonant style turned many classical music patrons toward the emerging popular styles of jazz, Tin Pan Alley songs, and the Broadway musical, leaving classical music in an increasingly tenuous position. Without church or aristocratic patronage and a public increasingly unwilling to pay to attend concerts of dissonant music, composers turned to a new avenue of support for their composing, the university. A position on a university faculty allowed a composer to receive a comfortable income while pursuing the compositional style of their choice, often without regard for whether it was commercially viable or not. Through this means did the dissonant compositional style remain in vogue for most of the twentieth century. While many composers adopted the dissonant styles, others maintained a fairly traditional, tonal, musical outlook throughout the twentieth and into the twenty-first century. In the later years of the era the general consensus was reached that dissonant music did not provide what listeners wanted. The overall approach in the last twenty years or so has been one of tempering the more dissonant qualities with more easily accessible characteristics, principally through a return to tonality-based composition.

SUGGESTED FURTHER LISTENING

Adagio in G minor—Tomaso Giovanni Albinoni

Jesu, Joy of Man's Desiring—Johann Sebastian Bach

Symphony # 41 in C major, 4th movement—Wolfgang Amadeus Mozart

Ave Verum Corpus—Wolfgang Amadeus Mozart

Concerto for Trumpet and Orchestra in E-flat major, 3rd movement—
Franz Joseph Haydn

The Creation—Franz Joseph Haydn

Symphony #7 in A major, 1st movement—Ludwig van Beethoven

Symphony #9 in D minor, 4th movement—Ludwig van Beethoven

Scenes from Childhood—Robert Schumann

Les Preludes—Franz Liszt

Variations on a Theme by Franz Joseph Haydn—Johannes Brahms

Overture to *Ruslan and Ludmilla*—Mikhail Glinka

Prelude to *Tristan und Isolde*—Richard Wagner

The Planets—Gustav Holst

"Four Sea Interludes" from Peter Grimes—Benjamin Britten

Ionisation—Edgard Varése

La Mer—Claude Debussy

Concerto for Orchestra, 2nd movement—Bela Bartok

Les Bandar-Log—Arnold Koechlin

A Survivor from Warsaw—Arnold Schoenberg

Final Alice—David del Tredici

Symphony #3—Henryk Górecki

QUESTION ASSIGNMENT

Instructions: Log in to the textbook web site and click on the ASSIGNMENTS tab. In the Chapter Question Assignment area read the instructions and answer the question(s) or provide the asked for information. Be sure to click the SUBMIT THIS FORM button after you complete the Assignment.

Name three characteristics and two common instrumental genres of music from each of the historical periods from the Baroque period through the Twentieth/Twenty-First Centuries.

Baroque Period
Characteristics:
1. _____
2. _____
3. _____

Baroque Genres:
1. _____
2. _____

Classical Period
Characteristics:
1. _____
2. _____
3. _____

Classical Genres:
1. _____
2. _____

Romantic Period
Characteristics:
1. _____
2. _____
3. _____

Romantic Genres:
1. _____
2. _____

20th/21st Century
Characteristics:
1. _____
2. _____
3. _____

20th/21st Century
Genres:
1. _____
2. _____

LISTENING EXERCISES

Instructions: Log in to the textbook web site and click on the ASSIGNMENTS tab. In the Listening Exercises area click on the links to the musical examples for each question and answer the questions. Be sure to click the SUBMIT button after you answer all of the questions.

Listen to each of the musical examples below from the Chapter 8 Playlist while noting the appropriate descriptive prompt on the Listening Chart for Chapter 8 and determine the best answer to each question.

1. *Concerto for Trumpet and Orchestra* by Franz Joseph Haydn—This piece for trumpet solo accompanied by an orchestra begins with an orchestral introduction; that is, the orchestra plays until the 1:07 second mark before the trumpet makes its first entrance. The soloist and orchestra play, sometimes together, sometimes answering each other throughout the movement until the cadenza occurs. That is the point at which the soloist extemporaneously plays unaccompanied for an extended length of time. Choose the timing at which the cadenza begins.

    a.   2:00 seconds
    b.   3:52 seconds
    c.   5:13 seconds

2. *Ballade No. 1 in G minor* by Frederic Chopin—This piece for solo piano is rhythmically free, meaning that the tempo changes constantly throughout the piece. It is also episodic in that there are many sections, often exhibiting extreme changes of mood. The opening of the piece is quite calm and pensive. Choose the approximate timing when the mood first changes to one of agitated excitement.

    a.   38 seconds
    b.   2:25 seconds
    c.   3:06 seconds

3. *Blackberry Winter* by Conni Ellisor—This piece for mountain dulcimer and orchestra begins with the dulcimer setting an energetic mood that the orchestra picks up and maintains until approximately the 1:38 second mark when the mood relaxes. Choose the approximate timing at which a new, lyrical melody enters played by the violins.

    a.   2:00 seconds
    b.   2:16 seconds
    c.   3:07 seconds

Chapter 9

Music for the Movies

FOCUS POINTS

Early Movies	*1930s, 1940s and 1950s*	*1960s, 1970s and 1980s*	*1990s–Present*
Silent Film	Orchestral Scores	Signature Sounds	Pop Song
Synchronized Sound	Prokofiev	*James Bond*—Barry	Soundtracks
Classical Music	Steiner	*Jaws*—Williams	Operatic Concept
Operatic Concept	Use of Songs	Spaghetti Westerns—	*Star Wars*—
in Use of Motives	Animated Films	Morricone	Williams
	and Shorts	Operatic Concept	*Lord of the*
	Electronics	*Star Wars*—Williams	*Rings*—Shore
	Herrmann		
	Stage Adaptations		
	Operatic Concept (cont)		

During the twentieth century a major new outlet for the experience of music came into being with the advent of "moving pictures," the movies. This theatrical genre allowed for the widespread experience of a dramatic presentation, and its accompanying music, in an endless number of venues through reproduction of the film. The showing of a movie in multiple cities, either simultaneously or over a period of time, allowed more people to view the movie and hear its music in a much shorter time frame than was possible through staged presentations. In the making of a movie the artists necessary to create the film only needed to be brought together once during the filming. The production existed, in essence, forever once it was captured on film. In contrast, each time a staged presentation of a dramatic production was mounted it required the entire cast of characters, support crews, director, musicians, costumes, sets, and time for rehearsals. The distribution of movies was far easier and much more cost effective than remounting productions of musicals or operas. Movies gave the public a musical experience similar to, but in some ways significantly different from, staged musical presentations.

North by Northwest (1959), directed by Alfred Hitchcock, music by Bernard Herrmann. Shown: Cary Grant and Eva Marie Saint.
Courtesy of Photofest, NY

EARLY YEARS OF MOVIE MUSIC

The movies produced before 1927 were silent films. They contained no dialogue, no sound effects, no music. When shown in theatres the films were often accompanied by a live instrumental performance that embellished the action on the screen. The music was provided by a piano, a small ensemble or, in some cases in the larger cities, by a full orchestra. The music was sometimes specifically written for a particular movie and distributed by the movie studio to theatres showing the film. Or it might be a compilation of pre-existing music picked by the performers in the theatre and excerpted to fit the scenes on the screen. Sometimes it was a combination of the two. Tunes from popular songs were commonly used, as were excerpts from well-known classical compositions. Even if an audience member watching a movie had never been in a concert hall, they would almost certainly have heard music written by Tchaikovsky, Beethoven, or any number of classical composers by simply going to the movies. Whatever type of music might be accompanying the action on the screen it was always played in fairly short segments to match the changing scenes. Unlike the established practices in traditional symphonic writing, the development of melodies and the use of established forms would rarely be a consideration in movie music. This episodic nature of music for the movies would remain a defining characteristic of the genre.

One of the first feature-length (over an hour) movies to include a complete musical score was *Birth of a Nation*, directed by D. W. Griffith and released in 1915. This controversial silent movie was based on the novel *The Clansman* by Thomas Dixon in which the Ku Klux Klan was portrayed as a positive force in reconstituting the United States following the Civil War. The film's treatment of music is noteworthy in that it presaged many of the ways music would be used in movies for years to come. In the film African-American slaves and northern carpetbaggers were represented as threats to national harmony while southern gentility was romanticized. Wistful excerpts from popular songs such as *Dixie* and *Swanee River* were used to conjure up images of peaceful Southern days gone by. Those Stephen Foster songs were still fresh enough in the public's mind to be at once recognizable as sympathetic to the southern side in the war. Tunes such as *America* were used to appeal to a wider national sensibility and excerpts from classical compositions such as the *Peer Gynt Suite* by Edvard Grieg (1843–1907) and the *Poet and Peasant Overture* by Franz von Suppé (1819–1895) contributed to the general atmosphere of different scenes.

The Jazz Singer

A milestone in the use of music in feature-length films came in 1927 with the release of *The Jazz Singer*, starring Al Jolson, the most popular stage entertainer of the time. *The Jazz Singer* included scenes utilizing synchronized sound in an otherwise silent movie. Jolson's performance in the film included some of his most popular songs, which were recorded in perfect time with the movements on the screen. The movie-going public was thrilled by the effect. While there had been other instances of synchronized sound in other movies they were all short subject films. The appearance of a major star such as Jolson and the use of synchronized sound in a full-length feature film distinguished *The Jazz Singer* from previously released short "talkies." *The Jazz Singer* established the use of sound in films as no other movie had before.

The *Jazz Singer* is the story of a Jewish boy, Jakie Rabinowitz, whose father hopes will take his place as the Cantor at their synagogue. But the boy loves the "jazz" music of the time and has a falling out with his father over the direction in which his musical interests will take him. Jake Robin, Jakie's adopted stage name, has his big chance starring in a Broadway musical that is set to open on Yom Kippur, the Day of Atonement, the holiest of the Jewish holidays. His father falls ill and Jake has to decide whether he will sing on the stage or take his father's place at the synagogue.

The bulk of the film makes use of the common musical component of silent movies, an accompanying score of original music mixed with excerpts of pre-existing classical compositions, to reflect the general mood of the scenes. But a further refinement of the technique makes use of a recurring melodic motif, the ancient Jewish prayer Kol Nidre. The melody appears in the score as a unifying element throughout the movie whenever Jolson's character is torn by the conflict he feels between his "jazz" career and his religious obligations to follow in his father's footsteps. The melody takes on added significance as the movie progresses because the Kol Nodre is usually sung by the cantor at the synagogue on Yom Kippur, the day that Jake has to decide whether to advance his career or honor his father and his faith.

The use of unifying melodic motifs had become a signature element in late nineteenth-century opera by composers such as Richard Wagner and Giacomo Puccini and became a common technique in film music as well. Even though the film genre was not very old, the musical component of many early films was quite sophisticated, adapting techniques that had been used in incidental music, opera, and ballet for centuries.

The following two examples from *The Jazz Singer* reflect the conflict Jolson's character must resolve. The first, *Toot, Toot, Tootsie, Goodbye,* is in the popular song style he loves and is sung in a club scene in the movie. The second, *Kol Nidre,* is the ancient Jewish prayer that could bring peace between Jake and his father. It is heard in the background throughout the movie as well as in the culminating scene in the Temple.

 Toot, Toot, Tootsie, Goodbye
Gus Kahn, Ernie Erdman, Dan Russo

 Kol Nidre—
Jewish Prayer

"All vows, obligations, oaths, and anathemas, whether called 'konam,' 'konas,' or by any other name, which we may vow, or swear, or pledge, or whereby we may be bound, from this Day of Atonement until the next (whose happy coming we await), we do repent. May they be deemed absolved, forgiven, annulled, and void, and made of no effect; they shall not bind us nor have power over us. The vows shall not be reckoned vows; the obligations shall not be obligatory; nor the oaths be oaths."

ORCHESTRAL SCORES

During the 1930s a number of movies were produced with large orchestral scores written by European-born and trained composers. Many of those musicians had moved to the United States from countries in which people of their ethnicity were being oppressed. In America they found an outlet for their creativity in the Hollywood studios. The music they wrote, if heard simply as musical compositions, would be categorized as "Romantic" in style, in the vein of the late nineteenth-century composers with whom they had studied in Europe. They tended to use large orchestras the way the Romantic period composers had in creating programmatic compositions. In these scores a wide array of textural

Composer Erich Wolfgang Korngold (ca. 1936). Courtesy of Photofest, NY

and coloristic effects were employed to represent the images on the screen. Erich Wolfgang Korngold (1897–1957) and Max Steiner (1888–1971) were the two most prominent composers during that formative period of movie music. Listen to the music these composers wrote for the main title sequences of two of their movies from this time, Steiner's *King Kong* from 1933 and Korngold's *Sea Hawk* from 1940.

 King Kong, Main Title Sequence—
Max Steiner

 The Sea Hawk, Main Title Sequence—
Erich Wolfgang Korngold

You probably know what *King Kong* was about, and the music certainly stirs up images of danger—the giant ape and the scene of natives dancing in a jungle ritual. Do you perceive anything else that the music might be portraying in these opening two minutes that accompany the on-screen credits? *Sea Hawk* is the tale of a swashbuckling, but good-hearted, pirate. Does the opening music paint a musical picture of the open sea and adventure in your mind? It's also a love story. Does the music reflect that also? How?

The most memorable tune associated with a film score from this time period is Max Steiner's lyrical melody from the classic film *Gone with the Wind,* 1939. That epic love story was set against the backdrop of the Civil War in the south. The presentation of music in *Gone with the Wind* is reminiscent of certain aspects of operatic writing. The first music that is heard is called the "Overture," with that word appearing on the screen as the music is played. A static image of a sky at sunset serves as a backdrop to this opening music just as a closed curtain would accompany an overture in an opera. Halfway through the film there is an intermission, again with the word "Intermission" appearing on the screen over a static image. Before the second half begins an "Entracte" is heard, just as a prelude or introduction to an act of an opera would be played.

During the Main Title Sequence immediately following the overture the main theme is framed by other tunes that also appear in the movie. This opening sequence captures the expansive nature of the story. The orchestra makes a grandiose entrance that is followed by a brief statement of a quaint tune while images of slaves working the fields are shown. The main theme follows, accompanied by scenes of the land, slaves in the fields, and the primary settings of the film, Tara and Twelve Oaks plantations, and Atlanta, Georgia. The original music by Steiner melds into a sentimental arrangement of "Dixie" as the credits end and the movie begins.

 Gone with the Wind, Main Title Sequence—
Max Steiner

How does the music that appears at the very beginning of a movie affect your perception of what is to come? From hearing just the above three examples what can you conclude about the approach composers of movie music take in creating music for an opening sequence in a film? Do you think their approach has any precedent in other types of music?

Alexander Nevsky—
A Milestone in Movie Music

One of the most important movies of the first half of the twentieth century, musically speaking, was a Russian propaganda film entitled *Alexander Nevsky*, completed in 1938. The movie featured music by the prominent Russian composer **Sergei Prokofiev** (1891–1953), who together with the film's director, **Sergei Eisenstein**, created the first movie in which the musical considerations were just as important as the visual. This audio/visual symbiosis was radically different from the approach taken by other film makers of the time and revolutionized the musical component of film making from that time forward.

Alexander Nevsky (1938 Russia), directed by Sergei M. Eisenstein, music by Sergei Prokofiev. Shown: Nikolai Cherkasov as Alexander Nevsky. Courtesy of Photofest, NY

In the silent movies that predated *Alexander Nevsky*, the musical component was usually added later to complement what was already on film. In the first "talkies," the musical element was fairly minimal and frequently reverted to a silent movie-type accompaniment, as in *The Jazz Singer,* rather than incorporate the music in an integral fashion with the drama. Prokofiev, however, was convinced that writing the music for *Alexander Nevsky* while filming was still ongoing would be the best way to create music best suited to the story. Eisenstein agreed and their unique collaboration ensued, one that would change the way directors viewed the musical component of a film and the way composers would write music for the movies. In the creation of *Alexander Nevsky*, Eisenstein and Prokofiev continually consulted with each other as to how they would approach each scene. Sometimes the filming was done first and the music written to fit it and at other times the music was composed while the scenes were still being finalized. In one instance the music was written first and the visual images edited to fit the already recorded music. On a concert tour of the United States the previous year, Prokofiev had visited Hollywood and seen how animators at the Walt Disney studios synchronized their images to the pre-recorded music for cartoons, and he convinced Eisenstein that it was possible to do the same with film images.

Alexander Nevsky is the story of a thirteenth-century Russian hero, Alexander of Novgorod, whose defeat of Swedish invaders in a battle that took place on the Neva River earned him the sobriquet Alexander Nevsky. In 1242 an army of German knights invaded Russia, and Alexander again was called upon to defeat the invading forces. The parallels to contemporary history with the rising Nazi influence in Germany in the 1930s were not lost on the Soviet regime at the time. Eisenstein was requested to create this film by the Soviet government as a means of rallying the Russian people in preparation for a possible war with Germany. A temporary defusing of the tensions delayed the distribution of the film, but when relations between Russia and Germany deteriorated once again the film was put into wide circulation and was hailed as an extraordinary achievement in film making.

One of the most musically, and visually, electrifying scenes in the movie is the climactic "Battle on the Ice," which takes place on the frozen Lake Chudskoye. The music depicts the frozen landscape with an eerie chilliness evoked by the stringed instruments. The strings utilize a playing technique called **ponticello**, where the bow is scraped close to the bridge of the instrument producing a raspy sound. The tension of the impending battle is evoked by an ever-increasing rhythmic pulse underscoring a brass-intoned war call. The invading Teutonic Knights (the Germans) are portrayed as crusaders representing Christianity. The Russian Communist regime of the 1930s actively sought to subvert any religious movements in Russia, so the invaders in the film are purposely associated with Christianity. The invaders' ensuing defeat is equated as a defeat of their religion at the hands of the Russians. During the "Battle on the Ice" scene the Germans sing a Gregorian Chant-like melody that Prokofiev composed to Latin words also created for this composition. A rough translation of that text is:

"As a foreigner, I expected my feet to be shod in cymbals.

May the arms of the cross bearers be triumphant.

May the enemy perish!"

As the armies move closer together across the expanse of the frozen lake, the music grows in intensity. An ominous undercurrent is present in the music. The chorus, sung by the Knights, grows in volume and the orchestral texture becomes more complex as the armies draw closer. During this scene the music occasionally drops in volume in order to allow dialogue to be heard. Finally, the armies engage in a pitched battle on the ice of the frozen lake. At that moment the music unexpectedly stops, overtaken by the shouts of the armies and the clanging of their weapons. After a few moments of just the sounds of the battling armies, the music resumes with a much more upbeat character as the Russian forces take the upper hand.

The progression of the music in this scene both foretells the action in the drama and represents it as it unfolds. The tension of the impending battle is heightened by the increasing tension and foreboding character of the music. The changes in fortune during the battle are reflected in the nature of the music. This dual use of music in film became the norm after *Nevsky*. Directors made ever-more sophisticated use of music once the methods of synchronizing sound to the action and the level of editing techniques allowed them to use it in an intrinsically artistic manner rather than as an add-on consideration. The "Battle on the Ice" scene remains an archetype for future battle scenes in film.

The music that Prokofiev wrote for *Alexander Nevsky* was formulated into a secular cantata by the composer that has become one of the most popular choral works of the twentieth century. The "Battle on the Ice" scene is movement number five in the cantata.

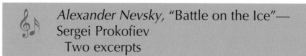

Alexander Nevsky, "Battle on the Ice"—
Sergei Prokofiev
Two excerpts

SONGS IN FILM

After the initial period of developing the techniques necessary to incorporate music into films and the novelty of having sound as a normal component of movies had passed, the presentation of songs in film became an important vehicle for putting songs before the public. In an era before television and the Internet, the movies and radio were the entertainment media shared by most people. The placing of a song in a movie was a calculated risk for the producer because a movie's success could often depend on it. On the other hand, an already popular song might be used in a movie to guarantee a certain level of success of the film or in some cases even have the movie named after the song. Many film musicals were produced from the 1930s onward, films in which both the music and the dancing were interwoven as integral parts of the storyline and songs were also incorporated into otherwise dramatic movies.

In the 1939 movie *The Wizard of Oz*, what was to become one of the most popular songs of the twentieth century, *Somewhere, Over the Rainbow,* music by Harold Arlen with lyrics by E.Y. Harburg, made its screen debut. The 17-year-old Judy Garland sang the song that almost didn't make the final cut of the film. For many people that song summarizes the entire story and makes the film a memorable experience from childhood. The song is typical of many songs from movie musicals of the time in that it actually advanced the story in some way. It was not merely an inserted diversion from the action, as songs from staged musicals of the time often were, but rather a musical element that either moved the story forward, gave an insight into a character or revealed an important complementary view of the situation.

 Somewhere, Over the Rainbow—
music by Harold Arlen, lyrics by E.Y. Harburg

The Wizard of Oz (1939), directed by Victor Fleming. Shown: Ray Bolger, Jack Haley, Judy Garland, Bert Lahr. Courtesy of Photofest, NY

Other notable songs that appeared in movie musicals in the 1940s include *Easter Parade* and *White Christmas* by Irving Berlin, both of which made their debuts in the 1942 film *Holiday Inn.* Each song reached an even higher level of popularity when movies were named after the songs, *Easter Parade* in 1948 and *White Christmas* in 1954. Two other Berlin songs, *Puttin' on the Ritz* and *Blue Skies,* became like-named movies in 1940 and 1946 respectively, capitalizing on their already famous names. George M. Cohan, the popular Tin Pan Alley composer, saw his songs *I'm a Yankee Doodle Dandy* and *Give My Regards to Broadway* turned into movie musicals with the same names as well.

A song that played an especially important role in an otherwise dramatic movie was *As Time Goes By,* written by Herman Hupfield in 1931. That song appeared in the movie *Casablanca* starring Humphrey Bogart and Ingrid Bergman in 1942. The song *As Time Goes By* serves as a painful remembrance for the two lovers, Rick and Ilsa, separated by the war (World War II) but now joined in an episode of political intrigue and personal sacrifice. The song both reminds them of their earlier time together in Paris and the impossibility of ever recapturing their happiness.

 As Time Goes By from *Casablanca—*
Herman Hupfield

AN EVOLVING VIEW OF THE ROLE OF MUSIC IN MOVIES

By the end of the 1940s disparate views on the role of music in movies developed. Some critics and directors thought that the moment you were aware of the music in a movie was the moment the music intruded into the drama and therefore had overstepped its bounds. Others viewed music as a natural complement to the dramatic presentation, much as it had been for centuries in staged dramatic productions. A thoughtful dialogue ensued in which influential figures closely associated with both movies and music discussed their respective points of view.

One of the most popular composers of the time, Aaron Copland, wrote carefully considered opinions on the topic of movie music which were published in *The New York Times* newspaper. In a November 6, 1949, article entitled, *Tip To Moviegoers:*

Take Off Those Ear-Muffs, Copland stated that, "Movie music, . . . is a new form of dramatic music—related to opera, ballet, incidental theatre music—in contradistinction to concert music of the symphonic or chamber music kind. As a new form it opens up unexplored possibilities. . . ." Copland viewed music as a serious contributor to the dramatic product, a kind of adaptation of staged musical genres of the past. Copland went on to outline what he viewed as the ways in which music serves the screen, by:

> *"Creating a more convincing atmosphere of time and place."*
>
> *"Underlining psychological refinements—the unspoken thoughts of a character or the unseen implications of a situation."*
>
> *"Building a sense of continuity."*
>
> *"Serving as a kind of neutral background filler."*
>
> *"Underpinning the theatrical build-up of a scene and then rounding it off with a sense of finality."*

Each of these attributes can be seen in the examples of movie music we have already discussed. The songs associated with the southern United States quoted in *Birth of a Nation* and *Gone with the Wind* certainly set the time and place of those movies. The use of the Jewish prayer, the *Kol Nidre,* in *The Jazz Singer* spoke volumes, without using words, about the main character's psychological state as he wrestled with his decision between fame and family/religion. That melody also built a sense of continuity throughout the film, reminding the viewer that Jakie's decision was looming ever larger in his mind throughout the film. All of the above-mentioned movies also have scenes in which the music is there but plays no pivotal role, serving simply as "background filler." This music sets the mood of a scene just as a physical set provides context within which the action takes place. The "Battle on the Ice" scene from *Alexander Nevsky,* with its inexorable buildup of tension climaxing in the decisive battle may be what Copland had in mind when describing music's role in, "Underpinning the theatrical buildup of a scene . . ." as an attribute of movie music.

Copland's was a uniquely appropriate voice to comment on movie music since he was someone who had been successful in composing both concert music and movie music (*The Red Pony, The Heiress, Our Town, Of Mice and Men*). He was also intimately familiar with writing theatrical music for ballets so his perspective on how movie music differed from traditional music for staged productions demanded a significant degree of respect. Copland's progressive ideas on the legitimacy of film music had a strong influence on the work of other composers of concert and movie music such as Leonard Bernstein and Bernard Herrmann.

In the following excerpt from the 1949 film *The Red Pony* Copland uses music as both source music and background music. Background music sets or reflects the mood of a scene. Source music comes from something that you actually see on the screen such as a band, a radio, or some other thing that you would normally expect to make music. The scene in *The Red Pony* from which this music comes shows a young boy, Tom, feeding chickens on his family's ranch. He is in the middle of a circle of chickens throwing food to them when he imagines the chickens to be circus horses circling around him in a ring under the Big Top. A circus band plays the music that we hear at the beginning of this excerpt, source music. At 32 seconds into the excerpt Tom comes back to reality and the scampering chickens he must chase down. The music we hear at that point reflects the chaos of the scattering chickens, background music. At 1:09 into the excerpt he daydreams of the circus again and we hear the circus music once more, source music.

Chapter 9 Music for the Movies ■ 253

 "Circus Music" from *The Red Pony*—
Aaron Copland

How does this example reflect Copland's ideas on movie music as expressed in the concepts outlined above?

MUSICAL PERFORMANCES AS PIVOTAL SCENES

In both *The Wizard of Oz* and *Casablanca* a song served as a focal point in revealing the emotional state of mind of the principal characters. Some directors have used musical performances on screen as the backdrop for climactic or key scenes in the drama.

A second significant use of music in *Casablanca* occurs during a scene in which Rick's Café Americain, the establishment owned and operated by Humphrey Bogart's character Rick, is filled with both French ex-patriots and German officers. Much of the background drama in *Casablanca* centers around the Germans' control of Casablanca, which is an avenue of escape for those seeking to flee from German-controlled lands, and the individuals who have come to the city seeking to find a way to freedom. German officers in the café are gathered around the piano singing a German patriotic song, *Die Wacht am Rhein (Watch on the Rhine)*, when Ilsa's husband, Victor Laszlo, who is wanted by the Germans for working against them, cannot restrain himself any longer. He walks to the band and orders the musicians to play *La Marseillaise*, the French national anthem. As the band begins to play the patrons in the café take up the song and drown out the Germans, a symbolic representation of what they hope will come to pass politically. This scene from Casablanca and the one discussed above involving *As Time Goes By*, through their use of music, summarize the two intertwined storylines of this film.

 Die Wacht am Rhein/La Marseillaise from *Casablanca*—
See Chapter 9 Video List on Web Site

In Alfred Hitchcock's 1956 remake of his 1934 suspense masterpiece, *The Man Who Knew Too Much*, James Stewart's character follows an assassin to the Royal Albert Hall, perhaps the most famous concert hall in London, in order to prevent him from finding his target during a live performance of a large-scale work entitled *The Storm Cloud Cantata*. The intensity of the drama is matched by the ebb and flow of the drama in the musical performance. A loud cymbal crash, the climactic moment of the musical performance, is the instant when the fatal shot is to be fired.

Bernard Herrmann was the composer of the musical score to *The Man Who Knew Too Much* but the music for that climactic scene was written by another composer, Arthur Benjamin, who had penned the score for Hitchcock's earlier version of the film. When the director, Hitchcock, asked Herrmann to score the remake of the film he told him he was free to write a new composition for the pivotal scene. Herrmann declined, saying *The Storm Cloud Cantata*, written by his predecessor, was perfect and couldn't be improved upon. In that famous scene Bernard Herrmann is the on-screen conductor of the orchestra playing Arthur Benjamin's music.

The Storm Cloud Cantata—See Chapter 9 Video List on Web Site
Arthur Benjamin, from *The Man Who Knew Too Much*

In Steven Spielberg's classic sci-fi film *Close Encounters of the Third Kind* humans and aliens share their first communication through music. Throughout the movie a five-note musical motive serves as a unifying thread, heard by humans whenever the aliens have made their presence known. When the aliens land their spaceship at a facility in the desert an electronic keyboard plays the five-note motive in an attempt to communicate with them. After several statements of the motive, to which the aliens respond with only grunting-type sounds, they eventually complete the last two notes of the motive after the first three are played, implying a level of understanding. From that point on the keyboard player and the aliens extend their communication through a series of complicated musical interactions ending finally in a series of slow, single, low-pitched notes. This scene sums up what the movie has been all about, humans and aliens in a close encounter.

 Wild Signals from *Close Encounters of the Third Kind*—John Williams

STAGED MUSICAL ADAPTATIONS

The popularity of the Broadway musical from the 1940s onward provided a substantial pool of already scripted dramas/comedies from which movie producers could choose material to bring to the movie screen. Virtually all of the successful Broadway musicals found their way onto film in productions that were often more lavish than the original staged presentations. With the ability to change camera angles, edit both the visual and audio components, and otherwise recreate the staged production in almost every way, musicals on film gave an extended second life to many Broadway productions.

The filmed versions of musicals kept them alive in the public's mind even when a live production was not ongoing. This fostered a resurgence of interest in the remounting of live performances of these musicals in schools and community theatres. These shows might have otherwise receded into oblivion, having been out of public view for so long a time. While the filming of musicals did breathe new life into many works, it did allow for one questionable practice that could never have succeeded in the theatre. It became fairly common to dub a trained singer's voice over the visual image of a prominent actress or actor whose singing would not have been of an acceptably high quality. It comes as a surprise to many people to learn that the voices they hear in filmed musicals is sometimes not the voice of the person on the screen. Singer **Marni Nixon** made a career of providing the singing voice for famous faces on the movie screen. Her voice can be heard standing in for such stars as Audrey Hepburn in *My Fair Lady* and for Natalie Wood in *West Side Story*. The dilemma movie producers faced of casting a box office "big name" who couldn't sing while finding a suitable voice to dub over the acting was the hilarious premise of the 1952, made for the screen, musical, *Singin' in the Rain*, starring Gene Kelly and Debbie Reynolds.

Some popular musicals that made the transition from stage to screen included *My Fair Lady, Oklahoma, South Pacific, The Sound of Music, The King and I, West Side Story, Annie Get Your Gun, Fiddler on the Roof,* and *Hello Dolly*. More recently stage hits like *A Chorus Line, Joseph and the Amazing Technicolor Dreamcoat, Evita, Chicago,* and *Phantom of the Opera*, among others, joined the earlier musicals in film adaptations.

Carmen Jones (1954), directed by Otto Preminger, music by Georges Bizet, lyrics by Oscar Hammerstein. Shown: Harry Belafonte as Joe and Dorothy Dandridge as Carmen Jones. Courtesy of Photofest, NY

What Makes Music—The Conductor

The role of the **conductor** has evolved over the centuries. During the Baroque period the conductor was usually the leader of the first violin section who served simply to start the music by waving his violin bow in a manner indicating when everyone should start playing. Today's conductor often serves as the **Music Director** for a large organization, whether it be a professional symphony orchestra, a large choral group, or an academic musical ensemble in a school setting. In addition to standing in front of the group waving their arms during a performance, the Music Director plans all of the programs that the ensemble will perform over the course of a year, chooses guest solo artists, oversees auditions for members wanting to participate in the ensemble, rehearses the ensemble in preparation for performances, and finally, conducts the ensemble in public concerts. The Music Director also serves as the public face of a musical organization, and as such, plays a significant administrative and public relations role, rather than just a musical one.

What a conductor does when they are standing in front of a group waving their arms, in what may sometimes seem like a random manner, is actually a complex mix of important functions. One of the primary things that the conductor does is indicate to the musicians the meter of the music so that everyone in the ensemble knows exactly where they are in the music at all times. This is especially important in music where the meter changes often. There are certain arm-waving patterns that conductors use to indicate the different types of meters, along with each beat within the meter, that the conductor modifies to their own personal style. The conductor also sets the tempo, or

speed, at which the music is played. In addition to indicating the meter and tempo, the conductor also controls the dynamic (volume) level of the music by the relative force of the motions they make while conducting. Catching the attention of individual or sections of musicians as important entrances are about to be made is also a role the conductor plays. The emotional content of the music is reflected in the facial expressions and body language the conductor uses to communicate with the musicians while the music unfolds. These are some of the important aspects of the conductor's role while on the podium during a performance.

Conductor Antoine Marguier conducts the United Nations Orchestra. Martin Good / Shutterstock.com

But, the most important work of a conductor is done before the performance, in rehearsals, where every aspect of the music is examined, discussed, explained, and ultimately understood by all participants so that the performance is a uniform expression of the conductor's vision of how it should sound. In that aspect the conductor is the ultimate authority in a musical ensemble, and the performance is his or her interpretation of each piece of music performed.

One of the more interesting stage adaptations brought to film was the 1954 rendition of *Carmen Jones*, based on a 1943 Broadway production with book and lyrics written by Oscar Hammerstein, the lyricist from the famous Rodgers and Hammerstein song writing team. The stage play was itself based on the immensely popular nineteenth-century French opera, *Carmen*, by **Georges Bizet** (1838–1875). *Carmen Jones* was the Bizet opera reset in the southern United States with an African-American cast. The book was changed to reflect the southern black dialect of the time, but Bizet's music was left largely intact. The role of Carmen was played by Dorothy Dandridge, who was nominated for an Academy Award for her performance, the first black actress to be so honored. This was one of those instances where a professional singer's voice was overdubbed for the songs in the film. The voice that was heard when Dandridge "sang" was of the famed Metropolitan Opera star Marilyn Horne.

The following excerpt from *Carmen Jones* takes place when Carmen, a parachute factory worker, enters the cafeteria where women from the factory and men from the military base mingle during their lunch hour. During this song, sung to the "Habanera" from the opera, she flirts with the target of her next seduction, a soldier named Joe.

"Dat's Love" from *Carmen Jones*—
lyrics by Oscar Hammerstein, music by Georges Bizet

CLASSICAL COMPOSITIONS THAT APPEAR IN MOVIES

Classical music compositions have figured prominently in many film scores. Astute directors in conjunction with composers and music supervisors choose appropriate compositions, or portions of them, as background music for scenes in movies. These pre-existing pieces may constitute only a small part of the musical score for a film with the rest of the music being composed for that specific movie. They might also be part of a pastiche of compositions, somewhat akin to a patchwork quilt, wherein many different compositions, or excerpts from them, are combined to constitute the musical score for a film. The list of classical compositions that have appeared in movies is quite extensive and can be found by following the URL *http://www.allegro-c.de/formate/cmm.htm*. A very brief list of some of the more prominent uses of Classical music in movies follows.

Movie	Composer	Composition
A Clockwork Orange	Ludwig van Beethoven	*Symphony # 9*
Platoon	Samuel Barber	*Adagio for Strings*
2001: A Space Odyssey	Richard Strauss	*Thus Spake Zarathustra,*
	Johann Strauss	*The Blue Danube Waltz*
Dracula	Peter Tchaikovsky	*Swan Lake*

In 1998 minimalist composer Philip Glass was commissioned to add an entirely new musical score written for a string quartet for *Dracula.*

The Shining	Bela Bartok	*Music for Strings Percussion & Celeste*
Somewhere in Time	Sergei Rachmaninoff	*Rhapsody on a Theme of Paganini, Variation #18*
Elvira Madigan	Wolfgang Mozart	*Piano Concerto # 21, Andante*
Shine	Sergei Rachmaninoff	*Piano Concerto #3*
The Last Emperor	Johann Strauss	*The Emperor Waltz*
Apocalypse Now	Richard Wagner	*Ride of the Valkyries*
10	Maurice Ravel	*Bolero*
Die Hard II	Jean Sibelius	*Finlandia*

MUSICAL BIOPICS

Another outlet for music in movies has been the biopic, film biographies about famous musicians and composers. This method of incorporating music on screen allows for filmed concert performances, source music, as well as simply using the music to support the drama. While biopics are intended to be fairly accurate representations of the people they portray, they often include much fictional material in order to better present an engaging story. The movie *Amadeus* is actually a fictional account of Mozart's career based on a play by Peter Shaffer. The play/film made some assumptions about the composer's life that made for better theatre than biography. Some of the better musical biopics are listed below.

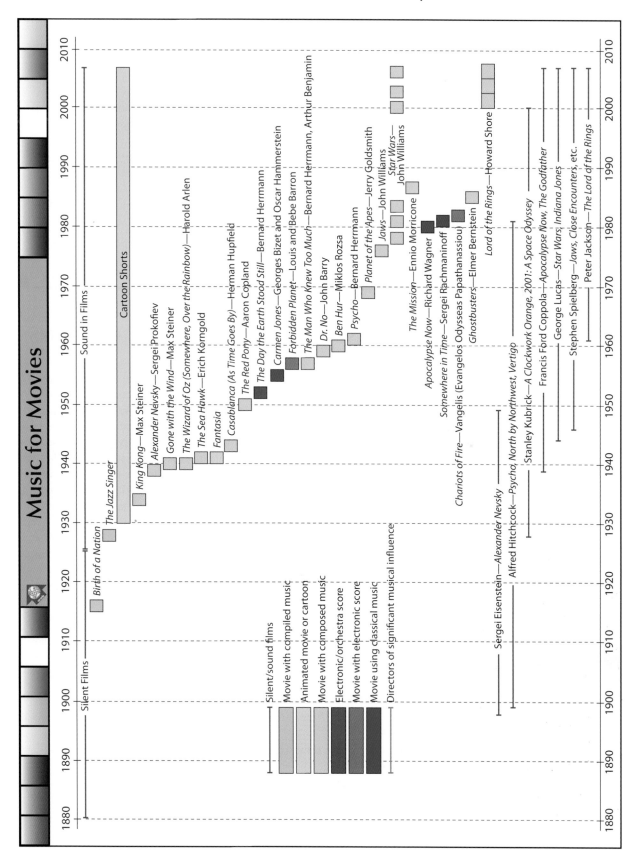

Music for Movies

A timeline spanning 1880 to 2010.

Silent Films / **Sound in Films**

Cartoon Shorts

Birth of a Nation

The Jazz Singer

King Kong—Max Steiner

Alexander Nevsky—Sergei Prokofiev

Gone with the Wind—Max Steiner

The Wizard of Oz (Somewhere, Over the Rainbow)—Harold Arlen

The Sea Hawk—Erich Korngold

Fantasia

Casablanca (As Time Goes By)—Herman Hupfield

The Red Pony—Aaron Copland

The Day the Earth Stood Still—Bernard Herrmann

Carmen Jones—Georges Bizet and Oscar Hammerstein

Forbidden Planet—Louis and Bebe Barron

The Man Who Knew Too Much—Bernard Herrmann, Arthur Benjamin

Dr. No—John Barry

Ben Hur—Miklos Rozsa

Psycho—Bernard Herrmann

Planet of the Apes—Jerry Goldsmith

Jaws—John Williams

Star Wars—John Williams

The Mission—Ennio Morricone

Apocalypse Now—Richard Wagner

Somewhere in Time—Sergei Rachmaninoff

Chariots of Fire—Vangelis (Evangelos Odysseas Papathanassiou)

Ghostbusters—Elmer Bernstein

Lord of the Rings—Howard Shore

Legend:
- Silent/sound films
- Movie with compiled music
- Animated movie or cartoon
- Movie with composed music
- Electronic/orchestra score
- Movie with electronic score
- Movie using classical music
- Directors of significant musical influence

Sergei Eisenstein—Alexander Nevsky

Alfred Hitchcock—Psycho, North by Northwest, Vertigo

Stanley Kubrick—A Clockwork Orange, 2001: A Space Odyssey

Francis Ford Coppola—Apocalypse Now, The Godfather

George Lucas—Star Wars, Indiana Jones

Stephen Spielberg—Jaws, Close Encounters, etc.

Peter Jackson—The Lord of the Rings

Movie	Year	Subject
Song to Remember	1945	Polish pianist and composer Frederick Chopin
Rhapsody in Blue	1945	American composer George Gershwin
Song of Love	1947	German composers Robert and Clara Schumann and Johannes Brahms
The Glenn Miller Story	1954	Big band bandleader Glenn Miller
Benny Goodman Story	1955	Jazz clarinetist Benny Goodman
Gene Krupa Story	1959	Jazz drummer Gene Krupa
Long Without End	1960	Hungarian pianist and composer Franz Liszt
Music Lovers	1970	Russian composer Peter Tchaikovsky
Mahler	1974	German composer Gustav Mahler
Amadeus	1984	Austrian composer Wolfgang Amadeus Mozart
Immortal Beloved	1994	German composer Ludwig van Beethoven
8 Mile	2002	Hip-hop artist Eminem
Ray	2004	R&B star Ray Charles
Walk the Line	2006	Country music star Johnny Cash

MUSIC FOR ANIMATED MOVIES AND CARTOONS

In 1940 the Walt Disney Studios, in collaboration with conductor Leopold Stokowski and the Philadelphia Orchestra, released a unique, full-length animated movie entitled *Fantasia*. The movie sought to explore the visual imagery that could be inspired by classical music compositions. The film consisted of a number of musical compositions serving both as inspiration for, and background music to, animated scenes. Since 1940 the animated sequences in Fantasia have been the first exposure to classical music for many people. Having had those musical compositions linked to visual images on their first hearing has usually meant a lifelong association between the music and the animation. While music is often thought of as a purely "aural" experience, it is a natural tendency for many people to associate music with some kind of visual imagery. This can be done through creating a "picture" in the mind of what the music represents to them or by conjuring up a storyline to go along with the music as it changes character. The Disney animators did no more than what most people already do to a limited degree. Only they possessed an extraordinarily high degree of both creative and animation ability and through those means were able to make their minds' creative musings come to life on the screen.

The musical compositions used in *Fantasia* were the following.

Fantasia (1940), directed by James Algar and Samuel Armstrong. Shown: "Sorcerer's Apprentice" scene. Courtesy of Photofest, NY

Toccata and Fugue in D minor: an orchestrated version of an organ work by Johann Sebastian Bach.

The Nutcracker Suite: a collection of some of the dances from Peter Ilyich Tchaikovsky's ballet *The Nutcracker.*

The Sorcerer's Apprentice: a tone poem by Paul Dukas starring Mickey Mouse.

The Rite of Spring: a reworking of some of the material from Igor Stravinsky's ballet.

The Pastoral Symphony: a condensed version of Ludwig van Beethoven's *Symphony #6.*

Dance of the Hours: ballet sequence from Amilcare Ponchielli's opera *La Gioconda (The Merry One).*

Night on Bald Mountain/Ave Maria: a melding of two compositions, *Night on Bald Mountain* by Modest Mussorgsky and *Ave Maria* by Franz Schubert.

Cartoon Shorts

By the time the full-length *Fantasia* was released, the making of cartoon shorts had become commonplace. These cartoons were often presented in theatres before the featured movie was shown, and they also provided a change of pace between **double features**. Theatres in the early days of movies frequently showed two movies for one admission price. While the Disney Studios put their emphasis on producing movie-length animated features, the **Warner Brothers** company specialized in short animated cartoons that were intended to be additions to the regular movie experience. Warner brothers created two different series of cartoons, "Loony Tunes" and "Merry Melodies." The Warner Brothers Company created such memorable cartoon characters as Bugs Bunny, Daffy Duck, Porky Pig, Tweety Bird, Elmer Fudd, The Road Runner, and Wile E. Coyote.

The music for the Warner Brothers cartoons was a manic mix of short sound effects, classical excerpts, and composed music that exaggerated the impact of the action on the screen. Split-second synchronization of the animation and the music heightened the comic effect. Memorable tunes from classical compositions were incorporated into the Warner Brothers cartoons under the supervision of their musical director, **Carl Stalling** (1892–1972). Many cartoons were also based entirely on adaptations of classical compositions such as Rossini and Wagner operas. Warner Brothers also owned the rights to many of the musical compositions of **Raymond Scott**, a band leader and composer of that era whose music was used in many Warner Brothers cartoons. One Scott composition in particular, *Powerhouse,* was used in 40 different cartoons! The piece is in A-B-A form with the A section being a frantic theme consisting of very fast notes. This section was used in cartoons during chase scenes or other fast-paced sequences. The B section was frequently employed to represent factory scenes or mechanical images of some kind.

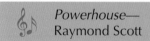

Powerhouse—
Raymond Scott

House Hunting Mice, a 1947 Warner Brothers cartoon, featured Hubie and Bertie, two mischievous mice as they explore a "House of the Future." When they encounter a robot housekeeper the action takes on an increasingly frenetic quality until the overworked robot self-destructs and a small army of replacement robots takes over. *Powerhouse* is first heard at 2:19 into the cartoon when the robot housekeeper suddenly appears from a closet. Subsequent short quotations of *Powerhouse* are heard at approximately 3:40, 4:03, 4:13, 4:38, 5:02, 5:28, and 6:27 into the 7:12 cartoon.

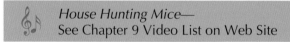

House Hunting Mice—
See Chapter 9 Video List on Web Site

Warner Brothers was also known for the ingenious use of classical music compositions in their cartoon shorts. Two cartoons in particular, *The Rabbit of Seville* from 1950, was based on melodies from Giaocchino Rossini's opera *The Barber of Seville*, and *What's Opera Doc?* from 1957 was a compilation of motives from operas written by Richard Wagner. *Long Haired Hare,* from 1949, parodied both operatic singers and one of the most prominent classical music conductors of the time, Leopold Stokowski.

After the 1950s cartoon shorts were no longer a regular part of the movie going experience. The cartoons that had for so long been an integral part of going to the movies became the much anticipated highlight of many children's Saturday mornings. The cartoons moved from the movie theatre to the television, and the Warner Brothers characters found a permanent home in the living rooms of nearly every young American.

Try taking on the role Disney's animators did in creating *Fantasia.* Listen to the following composition (which was not included in the film) and create a "story" to go along with it. Write down the "scenes" as you see them in your mind while the music progresses and try to come up with a name for your story. It's not as hard as you might think, and it's more fun than you might imagine. Try not to let any pre-existing associations of this music you might have influence your story.

William Tell Overture—
Gioacchino Rossini

How many different scenes did you "see"? Have you heard this music before? Most people have heard this piece before in a cartoon. If you had, did that influence your imagination? Why do you think this music has been used in cartoons?

ELECTRONIC SCORES

Professor Léon Theremin with his invention, one of the first electronic instruments, which has become known simply as a "theremin." © Hulton-Deutsch Collection/Corbis

The 1956 sci-fi film *Forbidden Planet* didn't have any music, in the traditional meaning of the word, but rather employed a completely electronic score of unusual sounds composed by **Louis** and **Bebe Barron** to augment the visuals. Some twentieth-century composers had been experimenting for decades with electronic apparatus such as recording devices, oscillators, and unusual electronic instruments to create previously unheard of sounds. Among these electronic instruments was one invented by a Russian cellist and electronic engineer, Léon Theremin (born Lev Segeivitch Termen), called the **theremin**. Composer **Bernard Herrmann** (1911–1975) incorporated the theremin prominently in his score to the sci-fi movie, *The Day the Earth Stood Still,* 1951. But *Forbidden Planet* was the first full-length film to use electronic music exclusively. The concept was so outlandish that a conflict arose with the American Federation of Musicians, the labor union that represented musicians in Hollywood, and a different word had to be substituted for "music" in the credits to the film. The Barrons were consequently credited with creating the "Electronic Tonalities" rather than the "Electronic Music" and were not compensated as they would have been for composing a musical score.

Forbidden Planet was loosely based on Shakespeare's *The Tempest,* set on another world in the not-too-distant future. The electronic sounds added an otherworldly aspect to the futuristic sets. Compare the main title sequence from this movie with the similar sequences from *Gone with the Wind* or *The Sea Hawk,* heard earlier in this chapter. Does this "music" set the scene for you as well as the more traditional music used in those movies?

PERSPECTIVE 1—MUSIC ON RADIO AND TELEVISION

Almost concurrent with the rise of the movies as a means of disseminating music was the emergence of radio broadcasts. Between 1920 and 1930, radio stations were licensed in all of the states and territories of the United States. As a purely aural medium, radio was well suited for the presentation of music in a variety of guises. Programming soon developed devoted to broadcasting "concerts" of classical and popular music. The Metropolitan Opera in New York began broadcasting productions live to the nation in 1931 and continues to do so today. Gathering around the radio to listen to broadcasts of concerts by popular big bands in the 1930s and 1940s became a common social activity. Popular songs were played on the radio on such programs as *Your Hit Parade*, which broadcasted the top fifteen most popular songs each week from 1935 to 1955. Radio stations frequently hired their own bands and orchestras for the live performance of music heard on their broadcasts. Some of these ensembles, such as the NBC Symphony Orchestra under the direction of Arturo Toscanini, and the CBS Symphony Orchestra, led by Bernard Herrmann, were arguably two of the best orchestras of the time.

Radio programming also included many dramatic presentations such as *The Shadow, The Thin Man,* and *The Crypt.* Serialized presentations of novels and movies on the radio were very popular. These programs used background music to set the mood of the scenes and enhance the drama, much as staged theatrical productions had done for centuries and the movies were doing at the same time in the theatres. Radio comedies used music to punctuate the timing of joke telling and to maintain an upbeat, light mood throughout. Radio programs also pioneered the concept of "theme songs," the readily identifiable musical signatures of specific programs. One of the most recognizable for many years was the theme music for *The Lone Ranger* radio program (and the later television program of the same name). That music, the final portion of Gioacchino Rossini's *William Tell Over-*ture, became commonly known as "The Lone Ranger Theme."

In the 1950s and 1960s, television theme songs became some of the most familiar music in the country. Dramas such as *Dragnet, The Lone Ranger,* and *The Twilight Zone* typically had theme music of the orchestral variety, while comedies such as *Leave it to Beaver, I Love Lucy, The Beverly Hillbillies,* and *The Addams Family* used short, catchy songs for their theme music.

The emerging popular style of rock and roll music was given an unprecedented boost with the advent of the television program *American Bandstand.* Beginning its run as a local show in Philadelphia from 1952–1956, this program featured teenagers dancing to pre-recorded and live performances of the most popular songs of the day. During the "Rate-A-Record" segment of the program, songs were rated by a panel of teens eliciting comments such as, "It had a good beat and I could dance to it, I'll give it a 9." *American Bandstand* became nationally syndicated in 1957 and continued on the air until 1989. *Hootenanny*, a similar type of program featuring folk music, went on the air in the early 1960s as that type of music was gaining in popularity. In the 1970s, *Soul Train*, dedicated to soul and R&B music, began its extraordinary run which continues to today.

MTV, which stands for Music Television, was the first network dedicated to presenting music exclusively. MTV began operation in 1981 and continues today, though with a considerably different format from its original music-only concept. In its early years MTV tended to feature heavy metal and hard rock bands. The success of MTV fostered spin-off and copy cat networks such as VH1 (Video Hits One), geared towards a more adult audience, and CMT (Country Music Television), dedicated to country music. All three networks are now owned by the entertainment conglomerate Viacom.

PERSPECTIVE 2—MUSIC FOR VIDEO GAMES

In the early twentieth century the advent of movies added a new genre to the composers' repertoire for the presentation of music. Movies lent themselves to an adaptation of existing styles of music such as opera, ballet, and incidental music for plays, albeit in a more episodic style. When television appeared later in the century composers again adapted existing styles, primarily incidental music, to this newly available genre. It is fairly rare for an entirely new genre of musical expression to not only come into being, but also to be shared among millions upon millions of people across the world, but that is the case with music for video games. Over the last several decades the growing popularity of video games has spawned a need for musical accompaniments that span the spectrum of musical styles and has served as a catalyst for new styles and compositional approaches. Far from the electronic beeps, sound effects, and minimal music of many early video games such as Pong and Pac Man, the music for video games today is just as likely to be fully symphonic scores supplemented by modern electronic instruments, rock-based songs, or world music-inspired soundtracks. In short, every type of music known prior to the advent of video games has been integrated into game music and prepared for that platform with a new mindset. Composers approach this music in a fresh way, driven by the new reality of a non-linear visual platform, which requires a non-linear concept for the music.

Throughout history music has been conceived in a linear fashion. It has a beginning, goes through various changes during the course of the performance, and then comes to an end. It hasn't mattered whether the music was for the concert hall, opera, ballet, or movies; it has always been thought of in the same way, from beginning to end. Video games, with the ever changing, player-determined, scenarios possibly going in any number of directions, necessitates music that is equally adaptable to this endless branching of scenes and levels of play. Composers have never dealt with such an indeterminate framework within which to compose. It has given composers the opportunity to open themselves to possibilities never before imagined.

Video game composer Clint Bajakian describes what it is like composing for this genre as opposed to writing for a linear genre such as a movie.

"One of the main differences between scoring for film and scoring for games is the respective requirements of music integration. In a game, the music must be edited and scripted to respond musically to the unpredictably timed sequence of events and situations. The closest analogy to this in film would be music editing in a fixed-time linear environment. In a game, music segments and layers must be organized to connect or layer dynamically at run time. The music segments are controlled by code which is designed to track changes in the game's situation and translate those changes on the fly in accordance with the music integrator's vision. What the two media share is the importance of plain old great music composition and production. Once that is achieved however, the two media diverge dramatically. To make a score flow musically and remain appropriate to the game state at all times requires a massive amount of planning, editing, technical work, and a robust audio engine that is capable of sophisticated music manipulation routines designed and implemented by the music integrator."

The variety of video games on the market is reflected in the equally diverse styles of musical composition for them. Epic storylines have larger-than-life sounding soundtracks such as in *Halo*. Atmospheric leitmotifs are evident in the *Myst series*. Interactive musical elements play a central role in *The Legend of Zelda: Ocarina of Time*. In that game the player must learn musical melodies playable by the five buttons on the game controller, mirroring the five holes on the simple musical instrument, the ocarina. Some games and systems even allow gamers to incorporate their own music from their own CDs into the soundtrack for a game.

Music for video games was not taken seriously for a long time, possibly because of the simplistic character of the music in early games, but the music has

PERSPECTIVE 2—MUSIC FOR VIDEO GAMES

gained considerably in respect among musicians as well as the public as the genre has matured, evolved, and become ubiquitous throughout society. Video game music found its ultimate mainstream acceptance in 2011 when *Baba Yetu*, the theme song for *Civiliza-* *tion IV* composed by Christopher Tin, won a Grammy for Best Instrumental Arrangement Accompanying Vocalists. The song, with its world beat-inspired sound, is a Swahili translation of *The Lord's Prayer*.

"Baba Yetu"

Swahili
Baba yetu, Yetu uliye
Mbinguni yetu, Yetu amina!
Baba yetu Yetu uliye
jina lako litukuzwe.

Utupe leo chakula chetu
Tunachohitaji utusamehe
Makosa yetu, hey!
Kama nasi tunavyowasamehe
Waliotukosea usitutie
Katika majaribu, lakini
Utuokoe, na yule, muovu e milele!

Ufalme wako ufike utakalo
Lifanyike duniani kama mbinguni. (Amina)

English
Our Father, who art
in Heaven. Amen!
Our Father,
Hallowed be thy name.

Give us this day our daily bread,
Forgive us
our trespasses
As we forgive those
Who trespass against us
Lead us not into temptation, but
deliver us from evil forever.

Thy kingdom come, Thy will be done,
On Earth as it is in Heaven. (Amen)

 Forbidden Planet, Main Title Sequence—
Louis and Bebe Barron

How would you compare this next excerpt entitled "Battle with Invisible Monster" to the battle music from *Alexander Nevsky?* Any similarities, or is it completely different?

 Forbidden Planet, "Battle with Invisible Monster"—
Louis and Bebe Barron

Other examples of electronically produced music for movie scores can be found in the movies *Chariots of Fire*, 1981, and *Blade Runner*, 1982, with musical scores composed and performed by **Vangelis** (b. 1943). Vangelis is the adopted name of Greek born composer Evangelos Odysseas Papathanassiou. Vangelis' use of **synthesizers**, electronic keyboards that can both imitate traditional instruments and create purely electronic timbres, was the basis of his scores and has become the most common means of producing electronic music since that time. The quality of imitative sounds capable of being produced through synthesizers has increased enormously over the past 30 years since the inception of **sampling**, the process of converting analog sounds produced by acoustical instruments into digital data that can be downloaded into, and reproduced by, electronic instruments such as synthesizers.

The opening credits of *Chariots of Fire* show a group of college runners from a local university training with the British seacoast as a backdrop.

 Chariots of Fire, Main Title Sequence—
Vangelis

Composer **Bernard Herrmann**'s use of the theremin in the score to *The Day the Earth Stood Still* is not an example of an exclusive use of electronic versus traditional music but rather an incorporation of electronic technology within the orchestral texture. The two theremins used in this movie score, both high- and low-pitched ones, are used just like any other instruments in the orchestra and augment the orchestral timbre in a way that adds an otherworldly context to a familiar sound. In the following example you can hear the theremin used in this manner. You may not find it so unusual since after its use in this film it was used not infrequently in many other sci-fi movies, in television programs and even in some pop music from the 1960s and 1970s by artists like The Carpenters and The Beach Boys.

 The Day the Earth Stood Still, "Prelude"—
Bernard Herrmann

Can you hear the wavering sound of the theremins mixed in with the orchestral instruments? The theremin is "played" by the performer moving his hands in the air in proximity to the instrument. The relative closeness of the hands to the box in which the oscillating generator is housed affects both the pitch and the loudness of the notes produced.

THE INFLUENCE OF THE DIRECTOR

While the work of the composer seems obvious in discussing the music for movies, the importance of the director should not be understated. As was apparent in the collaboration of Eisenstein and Prokofiev in *Alexander Nevsky,* the willingness of an open-minded director can raise the level of importance of the music in a film significantly. **Stanley Kubrick** (1928–1999) was such a director. Music always played an important role in his movies and he was open to creative ways of using music as was evident in the 1971 film, *A Clockwork Orange.* That movie included synthesized adaptations of classical pieces by Beethoven, Purcell, and Rossini performed on synthesizers by Walter Carlos. The familiar classical compositions heard in electronically altered versions mirrored the presentation on the screen of a society familiar yet uncomfortably distorted.

Francis Ford Coppola's (b. 1939) use of Richard Wagner's "Ride of the Valkyries" from the opera *Die Walküre* (*The Valkyries*) in his film *Apocalypse Now* was a brilliant modern setting of that work. A "valkyrie" in Norse mythology was a warrior maiden who swept down upon a battlefield to carry off the bravest of the fallen heroes to the home of the Gods, Valhalla. The music in Wagner's opera accompanied a throng of valkyries descending on a battlefield. In Coppola's rendition the music accompanies a swarm of attacking helicopters descending on a battlefield in Vietnam.

"Ride of the Valkyries" from *Die Walküre*—
Richard Wagner

PROMINENT COMPOSERS OF MOVIE MUSIC

Bernard Herrmann, in addition to his groundbreaking use of electronic instruments, was best known for the orchestral scores written for his collaborations with Alfred Hitchcock on some of the renowned director's classic thrillers including *Vertigo,* 1958, *North by Northwest,* 1959, and *Psycho,* 1960. Herrmann also oversaw the sound component of Hitchcock's *The Birds,* 1963, which had no music at all, only bird-like sound effects. Herrmann also wrote the score for Orson Welles' much acclaimed film *Citizen Kane,* 1941. In the 1945 movie *Hangover Square,* the climactic scene required the performance of a piano concerto written by the film's main character. Herrmann composed the original music for this fictional creation. In the following excerpt from *Psycho's* infamous "shower scene" the screeching violins musically represent the stabbing knife and screams of the murder victim.

Shower scene from *Psycho* (1960). Courtesy of Photofest, NY

 "Murder" (Shower Scene from *Psycho*)—
Bernard Herrmann

Miklós Rózsa (1907–1995) provided the music for nearly 100 movies during a long career that began in 1937 and ended with his last film score in 1982. Rózsa is best known for the scores he wrote while the studio composer for MGM Studios from 1949–1961, including *Madame Bovary,* 1949, *Quo Vadis,* 1950, *Lust for Life,* 1956, and for historical epics such as *Ben Hur,* 1959, and *King of Kings,* 1961.

Ennio Morricone (b. 1928) wrote the distinctive scores for many of the most popular "Spaghetti Westerns" directed by Sergio Leone including *For a Fistful of Dollars* (1964), *For a Few Dollars More* (1965), and *The Good, The Bad and The Ugly* (1966), among others. His signature sound in those films was partly due to the use of unusual sounds such as the electric guitar, whistling, and the chanting of a chorus in addition to sound effects such as cracking whips.

One of Morricone's most memorable scores was to the 1986 film *The Mission,* directed by Roland Joffé. In it Morricone blends traditional Western liturgical music with his re-creation of native music of Amazonian tribes. This duality of styles mirrors the competing elements of the story. The young Jesuit priest, Father Gabriel, attempts to contact and convert the Guarani people, a South American tribe previously unfriendly toward Gabriel's predecessors. His first contact with the Guarani takes place when he plays his oboe in the jungle, attracting both their attention and their hostility. This musical excerpt went on to popular success separate from the film in many commercial arrangements.

 The Good, The Bad and The Ugly—Main Theme—
Ennio Morricone

 Gabriel's Oboe from *The Mission*—
Ennio Morricone

Elmer Bernstein (1922–2004) composed many movie scores from 1951–2002, including *The Ten Commandments*, 1956, *The Magnificent Seven*, 1960, *To Kill a Mockingbird*, 1962, *The Great Escape*, 1963, *The Blues Brothers*, 1980, and *Ghostbusters*, 1984.

John Barry (b. 1933) is also a composer with numerous film scores to his credit but is most known for providing the distinctive sound to the James Bond series of movies. The swaggering "James Bond Theme" played by an electric guitar over an orchestral texture with an electric bass firmly sets this music, and the movie it comes from, in the 1960s.

Dr. No, "James Bond Theme"—
John Barry

Jerry Goldsmith (1929–2004) began writing music for television shows in the 1950s and moved to movie scoring in the 1960s. He is best known for writing the music for five of the Star Trek series of films, *Planet of the Apes*, 1968, *The Omen*, 1976, *Alien*, 1979, and *Poltergeist*, 1982.

Howard Shore (b. 1946) has become widely known for the memorable symphonic scores to the *Lord of the Rings* trilogy but has been active writing music for the movies and television since the 1970s. He made extensive use of motives to represent the characters and themes throughout the *Lord of the Rings* trilogy.

John Williams (b. 1932) "*. . . is without a doubt the most popular and widely-heard composer of music for orchestra in the world. . . .*" This quote from John Williams' Web site most likely accurately describes the breadth of this composer's familiarity among moviegoers around the world. He has composed the orchestral scores for many of the most popular movies of all time, including *Jaws*, 1975, *Close Encounters of the Third Kind*, 1977, *Superman*, 1978, *Raiders of the Lost Ark*, 1981, *E.T. The Extra-Terrestrial*, 1982, *Saving Private Ryan*, 1998, *Jurassic Park*, 1993, *Schindler's List*, 1993, all six *Star Wars* movies, 1977, 1980, 1983, 1999, 2002, 2005, the first three *Harry Potter* movies, 2001, 2002, and 2004, and *War of the Worlds*, *Memoirs of a Geisha*, and *Munich*, all in 2005. Williams' collaborations with directors Steven Spielberg, which has lasted over 30 years, and George Lucas have afforded him the opportunity to be a part of some of the greatest cinematic successes of all time. When Williams began scoring movies in the 1970s the tradition of large orchestral movie scores, formalized in the works of Max Steiner and Erich Wolfgang Korngold, had been in decline for some time. Many film directors and producers had turned to using pop music as the basis for their film scores, and Williams is often credited with re-energizing the declining orchestral style. Williams is also known for the theme music he has composed for the Summer Olympic Games in 1984, 1988, and 1996, as well as the Winter Olympic Games in 2002. Williams has also had a successful career as a conductor, having been appointed the Principal Conductor of the Boston Pops Orchestra in 1980 and holding that post until 1993. That position afforded him an unprecedented level of exposure, especially for a composer of film music, through the frequent nationally televised concerts by that ensemble.

Two of the most readily identifiable movie themes ever written are from *Jaws* and *Star Wars*. As you listen to these excerpts try to recall what the experience of seeing those movies was like. Can you ever separate the music from the movies? Should you? Do you think this music would be enjoyable or meaningful if you've never seen the movies?

Sean Connery as James Bond in *Dr. No* (1962). Courtesy of Photofest, NY

Jaws: The Revenge (1987) directed by Joseph Sargent. Even though most of the music for this movie was contributed by Michael Small, the ominous motive created by John Williams for the first *Jaws* movie was used to represent the approaching shark. Courtesy of Photofest, NY

Biographical Spotlight

© 2013, Featureflash, Shutterstock, Inc.

John Williams

John Williams, born February 8, 1932, is an American composer most known for the film scores to movies such as *Jaws, Star Wars, Raiders of the Lost Ark,* and *E.T.: The Extra-Terrestrial.* Williams' father was the drummer for the *Raymond Scott Quintet* (see *Powerhouse* on page 259) a jazz group whose music became well known for its inclusion in many Warner Brothers cartoons. Williams grew up in New York and Los Angeles studying music first at UCLA and then the Julliard School of Music in New York. In between these two formal venues of study, he spent time in the Air Force where he had the opportunity to exercise the practical application of his talents as a conductor and arranger for the Air Force Band.

Williams returned to Los Angeles after completing his studies at Julliard and worked in the Hollywood movie studios playing piano and orchestrating music written by other composers, all the while gaining a reputation as a composer in his own right. He began sharing the music writing duties for low-budget movies such as *The Creature from the Black Lagoon* but soon graduated to being the sole composer for feature films like *The Valley of the Dolls* and *Goodbye Mr. Chips*, both of which received Academy Award nominations for the music. The year 1974 was pivotal in Williams' career, as that was when he began his long association with Stephen Spielberg, with whom he would collaborate repeatedly over the next several decades on films such as *Jaws, Close Encounters of the Third Kind*, *Jurassic Park*, and *Schindler's List*. Williams soon after also become closely associated with the films of George Lucas, starting with *Star Wars*, which employed an operatic approach to using **leitmotifs**, easily recognizable themes linked to individual characters and plot lines. The nineteenth-century German composer Richard Wagner perfected the use of the leitmotif (leading motive) in his four-opera series entitled *Götterdämmerung (Twilight of the Gods)*, connecting characters and the plot throughout all four operas. Williams' use of leitmotifs in the *Star Wars* series of movies resulted in a grand compositional scheme that could be carried from one movie through any number of sequels, just as Wagner had done a century earlier in his operas. Williams used this approach again in the scores to the *Superman, Indiana Jones,* and the first three *Harry Potter* films. In total Williams has written the music for over eighty movies, winning an Academy Award for Best Score five times, a truly extraordinary accomplishment.

Williams has also composed concert and ceremonial music. His most widely known work, outside of the movies, is the Olympic Fanfare (see Chapter 7) that he composed for the 1984 Los Angeles Olympic Games. Beyond that he has composed numerous concertos, a symphony, and other ceremonial music.

Williams has also maintained an extensive conducting career, being named the conductor of the Boston Pops Orchestra in 1980, a post he held until 1993. He has continued to maintain a significant conducting schedule, appearing regularly with the Los Angeles and New York Philharmonic Orchestras.

John Williams' style is similar to the richly Romantic orchestral writing of earlier film composers such as Max Steiner and Erich Korngold. His scores are not mere background filler, but are an integral part of the story-telling process.

Biographical Spotlight Exercise

Instructions: Log in to the textbook web site and click on the **Assignments** tab. Click on **Chapter 9** and scroll to the **Biographical Spotlight area**. Answer the question based on the information in the biography above.

Which of the following is a true statement?

1. Williams has never been associated with the movies of Stephen Spielberg or George Lucas.
2. Williams' music never bears any similarity to the music of Richard Wagner.
3. In addition to composing, Williams has maintained an extensive conducting career.

Listening Chart

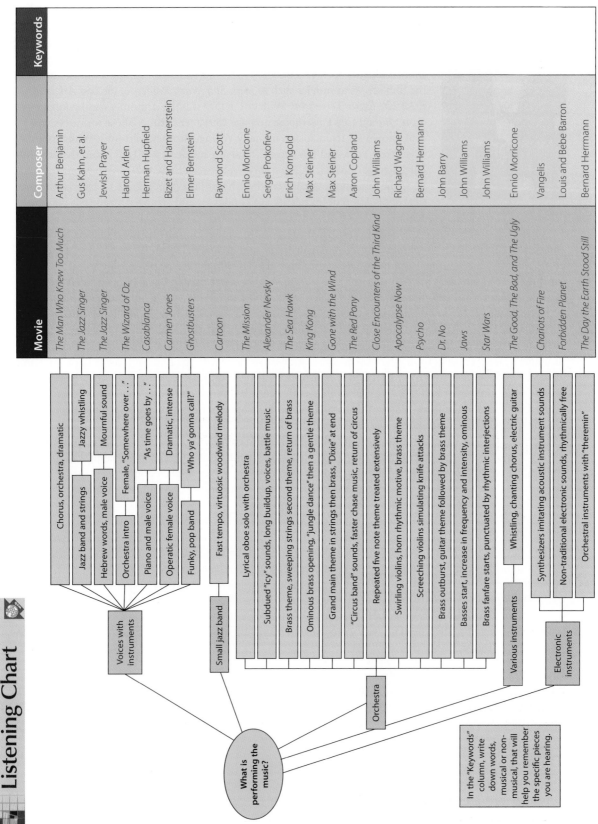

Movie	Composer	Keywords
The Man Who Knew Too Much	Arthur Benjamin	
The Jazz Singer	Gus Kahn, et al.	
The Jazz Singer	Jewish Prayer	
The Wizard of Oz	Harold Arlen	
Casablanca	Herman Hupfield	
Carmen Jones	Bizet and Hammerstein	
Ghostbusters	Elmer Bernstein	
Cartoon	Raymond Scott	
The Mission	Ennio Morricone	
Alexander Nevsky	Sergei Prokofiev	
The Sea Hawk	Erich Korngold	
King Kong	Max Steiner	
Gone with the Wind	Max Steiner	
The Red Pony	Aaron Copland	
Close Encounters of the Third Kind	John Williams	
Apocalypse Now	Richard Wagner	
Psycho	Bernard Herrmann	
Dr. No	John Barry	
Jaws	John Williams	
Star Wars	John Williams	
The Good, The Bad, and The Ugly	Ennio Morricone	
Chariots of Fire	Vangelis	
Forbidden Planet	Louis and Bebe Barron	
The Day the Earth Stood Still	Bernard Herrmann	

What is performing the music?

Voices with instruments
- Chorus, orchestra, dramatic
- Jazz band and strings
- Jazzy whistling
- Hebrew words, male voice
- Mournful sound
- Orchestra intro
- Female, "Somewhere over . . ."
- Piano and male voice
- "As time goes by . . ."
- Operatic female voice
- Dramatic, intense
- Funky, pop band
- "Who ya' gonna call?"

Small jazz band
- Fast tempo, virtuosic woodwind melody

Orchestra
- Lyrical oboe solo with orchestra
- Subdued "icy" sounds, long buildup, voices, battle music
- Brass theme, sweeping strings second theme, return of brass
- Ominous brass opening, "jungle dance" then a gentle theme
- Grand main theme in strings then brass, "Dixie" at end
- "Circus band" sounds, faster chase music, return of circus
- Repeated five note theme treated extensively
- Swirling violins, horn rhythmic motive, brass theme
- Screeching violins simulating knife attacks
- Brass outburst, guitar theme followed by brass theme
- Basses start, increase in frequency and intensity, ominous
- Brass fanfare starts, punctuated by rhythmic interjections

Various instruments
- Whistling, chanting chorus, electric guitar

Electronic instruments
- Synthesizers imitating acoustic instrument sounds
- Non-traditional electronic sounds, rhythmically free
- Orchestral instruments with "theremin"

In the "Keywords" column, write down words, musical or non-musical, that will help you remember the specific pieces you are hearing.

Jaws, "Main Title and First Victim"—
John Williams

 Star Wars, "Main Title Sequence"—
John Williams

SUMMARY

Music for the movies was derived from the long tradition of music that accompanied staged theatrical productions. Those genres included opera, ballet, and incidental music for the theatre. Closer in approach to incidental music than opera or ballet in its episodic nature, movie music nonetheless adopted some of the common characteristics associated with opera and ballet in the use of melodic motives to represent characters and thematic ideas. This approach became an indispensible tool with which to create an emotional or dramatic setting within which the story takes place. The use of the Jewish prayer *Kol Nidre* to represent the backdrop of the main character's Jewish heritage in *The Jazz Singer* is one example of this. The use of melodic ideas to represent aspects of the story was a common characteristic of Richard Wagner's operas in the nineteenth century. In Wagner's operas these melodic ideas were called *leitmotifs,* or leading motives.

Coming into existence during the waning days of the Romantic style of European symphonic music and the simultaneous emergence of the jazz style of American popular music, it is not surprising that most movie music from the first half of the twentieth century falls into either of those two categories or is a combination of the two. Most dramatic films were scored by European composers born into that era, Max Steiner, Erich Korngold, and Sergei Prokofiev for example, and the movies they scored were dominated by the sound of symphonic music applied to the two-dimensional drama on the screen. Movies such as *King Kong, The Sea Hawk, Gone with the Wind,* and *Alexander Nevsky* are examples of this approach. Lighter-themed movies such as musicals were based on the popular sound of jazz and big band music of the 1930s and 1940s. A common element in many movies from the 1940s to the present was the inclusion of songs that in some way served as a focal point in a film. *Somewhere Over the Rainbow* from *The Wizard of Oz* is a memorable example of this. Including a song in an otherwise dramatic movie could also serve as a dramatic vehicle, revealing character traits or advancing the storyline. The song *As Time Goes By* from *Casablanca* does both.

As the genre matured and the resources available to the composer expanded, they used the new electronic tools at their disposal to create a new type of symphonic music as well as incorporate popular music and newly developed electronic techniques into their scores. *The Day the Earth Stood Still, Forbidden Planet,* and *Chariots of Fire* are examples of this. Music can also serve as the underpinning of pivotal scenes in otherwise dramatic films. The extended symphonic/choral piece *The Storm Cloud Cantata* from the movie, *The Man Who Knew Too Much,* and the scene revealing the alien creatures in *Close Encounters of the Third Kind* are the climactic scenes in each of those movies. Music in animated features and cartoon shorts is equally as important as the visual element.

After over a century of writing music for the movies, the styles that are represented and the approaches taken by composers in creating music for this dramatic genre provide a musical experience as varied and interesting as the entire art of music itself.

SUGGESTED FURTHER LISTENING/WATCHING

Fantasia—Animated film by Walt Disney

Fantasia 2000—Animated film by Walt Disney

Jungle Book—Walt Disney

The Benny Goodman Story—The story of the clarinet playing, Swing era band leader.

The Gadfly—Music by Dmitri Shostakovich

Citizen Kane—Music by Bernard Herrmann

Ben-Hur—Music by Miklós Rózsa

High Noon—Music by Dimitri Tiomkin

Schindler's List—Music by John Williams

Hero—Music by Tan Dun

Braveheart—Music by James Horner

Gladiator—Music by Hans Zimmer and Lisa Gerrard

The Lord of the Rings: The Fellowship of the Ring—Music by Howard Shore

QUESTION ASSIGNMENT

Instructions: Log in to the textbook web site and click on the ASSIGNMENTS tab. In the Chapter Question Assignment area read the instructions and answer the question(s) or provide the asked for information. Be sure to click the SUBMIT THIS FORM button after you complete the Assignment.

Which prominent American composer stated that, "Movie music . . . is a new form of dramatic music—related to opera, ballet, incidental theatre music—in contradistinction to concert music of the symphonic or chamber music kind. As a new form it opens up unexplored possibilities . . ."?

Composer: _____

List the five ways in which this composer believed music serves the screen.

1. _____

2. _____

3. _____

4. _____

5. _____

LISTENING EXERCISES

Instructions: Log in to the textbook web site and click on the ASSIGNMENTS tab. In the Listening Exercises area click on the links to the musical examples for each question and answer the questions. Be sure to click the SUBMIT button after you answer all of the questions.

Listen to each of the musical examples below from the Chapter 9 Playlist while noting the appropriate descriptive prompt on the Listening Chart for Chapter 9 and determine the best answer to each question.

1. "Battle on the Ice" from *Alexander Nevsky*, music by Sergei Prokofiev—One of the most musically significant scenes in this historic movie is the "Battle on the Ice." In this orchestra piece the composer sets the mood during the first two minutes using a playing technique for the string instruments called "ponticello" to produce subdued "icy" sounds. The imminent battle is foretold with a long buildup as the music increases in volume and intensity. In addition to the orchestra the composer uses voices to represent the combatants. At what point are the voices first heard?

   a. 2:00 seconds
   b. 2:30 seconds
   c. 3:18 seconds

2. Main Title music from *King Kong*, music by Max Steiner—This orchestra music, played during the opening credits for the movie, represents several main themes of the story. The ominous brass opening sounds allude to the menacing nature of the giant ape. The following "jungle dance" music characterizes the dangerously strange and exotic location where the main characters first encounter the natives and Kong. These are followed by a gentle theme tinged with sadness, unmistakably referring to the female lead character, with whom Kong becomes strangely enamored. Choose the timing when this gentle theme is first heard.

   a. 20 seconds
   b. 57 seconds
   c. 1:19 seconds

3. Main Title from *The Good, the Bad and the Ugly*, music by Ennio Morricone—In the music for a number of "Spaghetti Westerns" composer Ennio Morricone would use various instruments not normally found in a typical orchestra. In this example he uses whistling, an oddly chanting chorus, and an electric guitar. Choose the timing when the electric guitar is first heard.

   a. 26 seconds
   b. 36 seconds
   c. 47 seconds

The Experience of Improvisation

FOCUS POINTS

Improvisation in Classical Music
Ornaments
Cadenzas
Traditional Ensembles
    Playing in a Jazz Style

Jazz Styles
Dixieland
Chicago Style
Big Band/Swing
Bebop
Cool
Fusion

Improvisation in Popular Music
Rock and Rock
Twelve-Bar Blues
Jam Bands

World Music Traditions That Use Improvisation
Indian Raga
Arabic Maqam

IMPROVISATION, A UNIQUELY MUSICAL EXPERIENCE

One of the manifestations of music that is fairly unique among artistic experiences is the practice of musical **improvisation**. To improvise is "to compose on the spur of the moment" according to the Random House Dictionary of the English Language. For many people the idea that music can be created on the spot, seemingly from nothing, is almost unbelievable. To be able to do it confirms their image of musicians as especially gifted in an intangible way. In reality the art of improvising is a carefully crafted aspect of music that reveals as much about the studiousness of improvising musicians as it does about their inspiration. Most improvisation in music takes place within carefully defined parameters that allow for the creative expression of musical ideas in a seemingly effortless stream of consciousness. The musical boundaries that encapsulate improvisation actually allow for the germination of musical ideas rather than restrict it by providing a framework on which the musician builds an improvised solo. This seeming dichotomy, a free improvisation versus specified parameters, gives improvised music a dual nature that many find exhilarating and in many people's minds is the epitome of musical expression.

Workers improvising in the courtyard of a factory, during a strike in 1936. Copyright © Snark/Art Resource, NY

The Improvisatory Framework

What sort of boundaries do improvising musicians work within when they improvise? Often it is a harmonically based consideration that determines the direction and nature of improvisation. It could be as simple as a single chord used as a background harmony over which musicians improvise melodic material, or it can be a chord progression that becomes the backdrop for improvisation. Rhythmic elements also come into play, such as the meter the music is in. The meter provides the time frame within which the melodic improvisation takes place. Sometimes the improvised material is rhythmic instead of melodic. Everyone has heard a drummer take a "drum solo" at one time or another. That is a type of improvisation as well.

The notes that are played during an improvisation often come from the scales upon which a piece is based or that fit a particular concept of harmony. The specific kind of scale that is used as the improvisatory basis for a given harmony varies with the style of music being played, that is what imparts the particular flavor of a certain type of music. For example, an improvised solo in jazz sounds somewhat different from an improvised solo in bluegrass music, which sounds significantly different from an improvisation in an Indian raga. The theoretical bases for the scales used in improvisation are quite complicated and beyond the scope of this text. However, the basic concepts of repetition, contrast, and variation are evident in all styles of improvisation. An overview of some of the different manifestations of improvisation, both in the Western tradition and in music from other cultures, can afford us a better understanding of the depth and breadth of this uniquely musical practice.

Improvisation in Western Art Music

The concept of improvisation has held a place of varying importance in Western music at different times throughout history. During the Medieval period much of the sacred music that was composed was put to paper and preserved fairly well intact. But

A concert by Lionello Spada (1576–1622). Copyright © Reunion des Musees Nationaux/Art Resource, NY

the secular music of the time might only have been sketchily preserved in written form. We saw in Chapter 4, in the case of dance music from the Medieval period, how that music often was written down only as a melodic line. We know from written texts and paintings that many instruments often played dance music, so what did the other musicians play? They probably improvised accompanying music and rhythms that fit the written out melody. From this we can assume that improvisation had to have been a common component of music from that time. It may not have been the kind of improvisation that we are familiar with today, but it was improvisation nonetheless. It is also believed that many musicians of that time did not read music and that pieces were often transferred aurally from one performer to another. We saw in Chapter 5, in our discussion of folk songs, that recreating music in that manner virtually assures a certain amount of improvisational creativity in each performance.

As music was more carefully notated during the Renaissance, the practice of improvisation did not hold as high a place of prominence. But during the Baroque period, the time when our modern concepts of harmony became fairly well formalized, improvisation took on added importance. Musicians were expected to be able to improvise in both instrumental and vocal compositions by adding ornaments to melodic passages. Ornaments were added notes that embellished the printed melodic line, usually during a repeat of a section of the music. Do you recall the *Lute Concerto* by Antonio Vivaldi that we listened to in Chapter 8? The repeated sections of that piece had extensive melodic embellishments, ornaments, which amounted to a type of improvisation. A second hearing of that movement will make that improvised ornamentation apparent.

 Lute Concerto in D major, 2nd movement—
Antonio Vivaldi

Also in the Baroque period, the **basso continuo** represented a type of improvised accompaniment since the keyboard player in the continuo made up the music they played by interpreting symbols and numbers that were written above the bass line. That accompaniment could take any form the player wished. The Baroque period also saw the rise to prominence of the concerto as an instrumental genre. Within the concerto a section came to be included called the **cadenza**, which allowed for an extensive improvisation by the featured performer. The cadenza usually began on the harmony of a single chord held briefly by the orchestra, which then gave way to the unaccompanied, improvised cadenza. The cadenza became an integral part of the concerto throughout the Classical and Romantic periods but eventually lost its true improvisatory character when composers began providing written out cadenzas for the performers that merely mimicked the character of improvised music.

Listen to the following example of a cadenza for the piano that is improvised by the performer. This cadenza is from the first movement of the *Piano Concerto #1 in C major* by Ludwig van Beethoven. It occurs at approximately 12:22 of the movement when the other instruments drop out and the piano embarks on a solo cadenza based on the themes of the movement. The cadenza ends at approximately 14:03 when the pianist plays a scale that naturally leads back to the melody that began the movement. This is a signal to both the orchestra players and the conductor that the soloist is about to end the cadenza.

 Piano Concerto #1 in C major, 1st movement—
Ludwig van Beethoven
Cadenza improvised by Galina Vracheva

The cadenza was designed to show off the virtuosic ability of the performer. What performing techniques does the player employ to display her virtuosity?

Improvisation never became an integral part of Western art music. Its presence has chiefly been represented through Baroque period ornamentation, the basso continuo, and by its continued influence in the improvisatory character of cadenzas and some keyboard genres such as the fantasia, toccata, and the prelude. From the Classical period onward improvisation took a back seat to the carefully notated music that has been the preponderance of Western art music.

Improvisation in the Contemporary "Classical" Context

Some contemporary composers, such as David Balakrishnan, are incorporating improvisatory techniques within composed pieces. Balakrishnan is one of the violinists with the Turtle Island String Quartet, a unique group of instrumentalists who for over twenty years have specialized in adapting jazz improvisation to the traditional classical genre of the string quartet. He writes with intimate knowledge of both classical customs and idiomatic expressions of jazz improvisation. Listen to the Turtle Island String Quartet's rendition of *A Night In Tunisia,* a jazz classic by the trumpeter Dizzy

Turtle Island String Quartet.
Courtesy of Peter Serling

Gillespie (1917–1993). The performance is a combination of carefully crafted composed elements and improvisations by the members of the quartet. As you listen to this performance, try to perceive when they are playing composed music and when they are improvising.

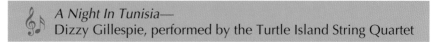

🎼 *A Night In Tunisia—*
Dizzy Gillespie, performed by the Turtle Island String Quartet

Another contemporary composer mixing jazz and classical elements is George Duke (b. 1946), a prolific composer, jazz pianist, and music producer. Duke's extraordinary work for symphony orchestra and jazz ensemble, *Muir Woods Suite,* premiered in 1993 at the Montreaux Jazz Festival and is an ambitious work in the mold of George Gershwin's jazz-influenced compositions from earlier in the twentieth century. Duke goes beyond the fully composed works of Gershwin by incorporating true improvisatory solos for the drums, bass, and piano within the framework of the otherwise composed piece. In the following excerpt from the *Muir Woods Suite,* you can hear sections that are composed but sound improvised, other sections that are true improvisations, and still others that are a combination of the two.

🎼 *Muir Woods Suite, "Phase 5"—*
George Duke

Improvisation in Jazz

The term "jazz" is one of those words that represents something that is difficult to define. As you listened to the previous musical example, the sound of the piece probably struck you as "jazzy." But what does that mean? Just what is jazz? As stated earlier in the text, the term jazz is used to describe a still-evolving style of music that traces its roots to the blues and ragtime music of the late nineteenth and early twentieth centuries. Those styles each contributed certain characteristics to jazz. From ragtime music jazz inherited syncopated rhythms. The blues contributed the use of a repeating chord pattern as the basis of a song, altered "blue notes" in the scale and improvisation over the repeating chord pattern. The term "blue notes" refers to notes of a scale that are lowered in pitch from the traditional scales during the performance of certain styles of music, like the blues and jazz. The lowered notes are often the pitches that would normally be the third, fifth, and seventh notes of a major scale. Jazz is often played by a small ensemble consisting of a rhythm section composed of piano, bass, drums, and sometimes a guitar, augmented by any combination of other instruments such as the saxophone, trumpet, trombone, clarinet, etc. The size and composition of jazz ensembles changed over the course of its history, and the makeup of the ensembles is often part of the determining characteristics of a jazz style.

New Orleans/Dixieland Jazz

The first jazz style of the early twentieth century developed in and around New Orleans and came to be called Dixieland jazz. Dixieland music was usually played by a fairly small group, a rhythm section along with several other instruments. It employed group improvisation that emphasized rhythmic as well as melodic alterations of the tune over a repeating chord pattern. In the following example, played by one of the legends of jazz, Louis Armstrong (1901–1971), you can hear the group improvisation at the beginning when the clarinet and trombone are improvising while the trumpet alternately plays the melody and improvises. After the voice sings two verses of the song, the clarinet takes a turn improvising over the chord changes. The voice, Louis Armstrong's, sings another verse and the trombone takes an improvised solo over the same chords. Finally all three solo instruments improvise simultaneously over the chord changes to bring the song to an end.

When the Saints Go Marching In—
performed by Louis Armstrong

Chicago Style Jazz

The Chicago style of jazz of the 1920s placed more emphasis on solo improvisations. Louis Armstrong, as the leader of his own bands The Hot Five and The Hot Seven, was one of the most prominent figures in this style of jazz. In the *West End Blues* you can hear the instrumentalists take turns improvising along with the unique style of vocal improvisation called scat singing. As the name implies, Chicago jazz developed in the city of Chicago.

West End Blues—
Louis Armstrong and His Hot Five

Biographical Spotlight

© 2013, David Davis, Shutterstock, Inc.

Louis Armstrong

Louis Armstrong was born in New Orleans on August 4, 1901, and died in his own home in Queens, New York on July 6, 1971. He grew up in poverty on the streets of New Orleans. His father, William Armstrong, left the family while Louis was still a baby, and his mother, Mary, left him in the care of family members after turning to prostitution out of financial desperation. He attended the Fisk School for Boys until 1911 but dropped out and spent his time hanging out and getting into trouble on the streets of New Orleans. Armstrong sang on the streets as part of a quartet of young boys while working for a hauling company owned by a family of Jewish immigrants, the Karnofsky family. They took in the young Armstrong to live with them for a year, where he saw for perhaps the first time that the racial discrimination he felt as a poor African-American was not unique to members of his race but was shared by the relatively well-off, Jewish, Karnofsky family as well. In gratitude for their kindness he wore a Star of David throughout his life.

In 1913 he was sent to the Colored Waif's Home, a reform school for African-American boys, after firing a gun into the air during New Year's Eve festivities. He stayed there for a year, which was where he first learned to play the cornet, an instrument similar to the trumpet but with a mellower tone quality, under the tutelage of Peter Davis. Once back on the streets he continued to hone his skills on the cornet before replacing Joe "King" Oliver, another musical mentor and one of the most popular musicians in

(continued)

New Orleans, in the Kid Orly Band, in 1917. A year later Armstrong married Daisy Parker and the couple adopted a young son, Clarence, after his mother, a cousin of Louis', died. Clarence fell off a porch and hit his head, leaving him mentally disabled. Armstrong continued to care for Clarence through his several subsequent marriages and arranged for his continued care after his own death. Clarence outlived his adoptive father, passing away in 1998.

The years from 1919 to 1925 saw a number of changes in Armstrong's location and family life. In 1919 he headed to St. Louis to play in riverboat bands, and in 1921 returned to New Orleans. In 1922 he moved to Chicago at the invitation of Joe Oliver to join his band, the Creole Jazz band. He and Daisy divorced in 1923. In Chicago he met and married his second wife, Lillian Hardin, a band leader herself, in 1924. Lillian would come to exert significant influence over Armstrong's career over the next decade. Armstrong soon moved to New York to play with Fletcher Henderson's Orchestra, the hottest jazz band in New York at the time, and there he made many now-famous recordings. In 1925 he went back to Chicago and recorded with his own bands, "Hot Five" and "Hot Seven." They never did live performances, only recordings, but the performances on those recordings are legendary, preserving forever for everyone to hear the Chicago style that he was so influential in establishing.

The years 1930 to 1935 saw more city-hopping with stints in Los Angeles, Chicago, and in 1932, back to New Orleans. Lillian's influence over Armstrong's career began to wane during this period, and in 1931 he and Lillian separated. He toured Europe for several years, coming back to the U.S. in 1935. Armstrong had played in gangster-owned clubs in Chicago where he became friends with Joe Glaser, a mob-connected associate of Al Capone. Armstrong hired Joe Glaser as his manager to handle the business end of the band and to straighten out his tangled financial and legal affairs. Glaser would remain with Armstrong until his death. Glaser formed an orchestra as Armstrong's own band, the Louis Armstrong Orchestra, composed mostly of musicians from New Orleans and King Oliver's old band, with whom Armstrong was familiar and comfortable. Relieved of managing the business of the band and working with hand-picked musicians, Armstrong spent the next ten years just making music and touring ceaselessly. Armstrong and Lillian divorced in 1938, after which he briefly married a longtime girlfriend named Alpha Smith. Armstrong quickly divorced her, and married Lucille Wilson, with whom he stayed for the rest of his life. During the 1930s Armstrong also became well known for his singing as well as his cornet playing. He appeared in a number of movies and recorded songs that featured his distinctive, gravelly-sounding voice. In 1947 the Louis Armstrong Orchestra was dissolved as their big band style became dated, and Glaser replaced it with the smaller Louis Armstrong All-Stars.

The band travelled to Africa, Asia, Europe, and South America, often on State Department-sponsored goodwill tours, as well as across the United States many times over the next 20 years. They kept up an extraordinarily busy schedule, often playing over 250 concerts per year. In 1963 Armstrong had a No. 1 hit song with *Hello Dolly*, written by Jerry Herman, which was his best-selling recording ever, and which won a Grammy award in 1964 for Best Male Vocal Performance. In 1968 he recorded *What a Wonderful World*, a song written by Bob Thiele and George Davis Weiss, which has become something of a cultural fixture.

Armstrong appeared in 35 movies between 1930 and 1970, and footage of him was even included in one movie posthumously. His presence on the world stage as a jazz musician, pop singer, television, and movie celebrity, made him one of the most recognized people on the planet. His influence on the development of jazz is inestimable. Louis Armstrong, also known as "Satchmo" or "Pops" throughout his life, died a peaceful death in his sleep in 1971 in the house he had shared with his wife Lucille for 38 years.

Biographical Spotlight Exercise

Instructions: Log in to the textbook web site and click on the **Assignments** tab. Click on **Chapter 10** and scroll to the **Biographical Spotlight area.** Answer the question based on the information in the biography above.

Which of the following is a true statement?

1. Armstrong's career was centered solely in Chicago.
2. Armstrong was known only as an instrumentalist.
3. Armstrong had two early mentors, Peter Davis and Joe "King" Oliver.

Big Band or Swing

In the 1940s the big band was the most common ensemble featured in jazz. During this time the prominence of improvisation declined in favor of more highly orchestrated compositions. The larger ensembles of this time, with sections of trumpets, trombones, and saxophones, plus the requisite rhythm sections, required a more fully composed approach to performance than the smaller ensembles of earlier days. These big bands also played in larger venues to accommodate the stronger sound the increased number of instruments produced. In **big band** music improvisation was still executed by individual performers, but it manifested itself in the form of shorter solos within the more highly structured compositions. Often the big band leader was the premier soloist with other members of the band also contributing improvisations as needed. Big band music is also referred to as **swing** music for the easygoing, danceable quality the music often exhibits. In big band music a frequently included short introduction is followed by the main tune, after which the melody may be heard again with interjections by the horn sections. Improvised solos occur during a repeat of the melody or an accompanying horn motif over a chord pattern previously heard. Famous big band leaders of this time include Duke Ellington, Benny Goodman, Tommy and Jimmy Dorsey, Glenn Miller, and Count Basie.

Count Basie and His Orchestra (ca. 1950s). Courtesy of Photofest, NY

 One O'Clock Jump— Count Basie and His Orchestra

 Take the "A" Train— Billy Strayhorn, performed by the Duke Ellington Orchestra

 In the Mood— Glenn Miller Big Band

Bebop Jazz

The late 1940s and early 1950s saw a reaction against the formulaic compositions of the swing era in the jazz style known as **bop** or **bebop**. Some of the major figures associated with this style of jazz were saxophonist **Charlie Parker** (1920–1955), trumpeter **Dizzy Gillespie** (1917–1993), and pianist **Thelonious Monk** (1917–1982). This style of jazz was quite intellectually adventurous. It stretched the musical boundaries of jazz by incorporating more extended and sometimes dissonant harmonies, unpredictable chord progressions, and melodic lines that were often not very lyrical. The basic format for most jazz tunes from this era is a variation on the traditional A-B-A form. The main melody, called the **head**, is played at the beginning. This is followed by an extended section of improvisation, either by one player or each player in the ensemble in turn, which is then followed by a return of the main melody at the end of the piece. In this format the A-B-A form closely resembles sonata form of the Classical period by utilizing a middle section that is based on the material from the main melody. In sonata form that was called the development section. A better description of this type of form in jazz might be A-A'-A, where A' represents the improvisation(s) on the "A" section. In the following piece by Thelonious Monk, many of these qualities are apparent. What differentiates the composed sections from the improvisations?

>
> *Straight No Chaser—*
> Thelonious Monk

What is your reaction to this music? How does it make you feel? What qualities in the music elicit those feelings?

Here is another example of bebop jazz by another of the musicians credited with creating the style, trumpeter Dizzy Gillespie. Earlier you heard a version of his composition, *A Night in Tunisia,* as interpreted by the Turtle Island String Quartet. Compare that to this original version.

> *A Night in Tunisia—*
> Dizzy Gillespie

How does the improvisation in this type of jazz differ from what you have heard in the earlier styles? Can you sing or hum the melodies from either of these pieces?

Cool Jazz

Jazz saxophonist Stan Getz (ca. 1950s). Courtesy of Photofest, NY

Cool jazz of the late 1950s and 1960s was a more restrained, understated variety of bebop jazz. It featured virtuosic improvisations with a calm presentation, as if seemingly effortless to execute. Brushes often replaced drumsticks with more emphasis on the cymbals than before. This style was intended to be performed by small ensembles in small, intimate settings, such as clubs created for the purpose of presenting small jazz ensembles. Major figures in this style of jazz include Miles Davis (1926–1991), Stan Getz (1927–1991), Dave Brubeck (1920–2012), and The Modern Jazz Quartet.

> *Yvette—*
> Stan Getz

Modal Jazz

The next stylistic development in jazz was the adoption of a new system of improvisation based not on a chord progression or a melodic idea but rather on one of the basic elements of a piece called the mode. A mode is a kind of scale. Early in the development of Western music a series of melodic modes were adopted by Catholic Church musicians, upon which the music they composed was based. Two of those modes became the major and minor scales that formed the basis of harmony in Western music. The other modes were relegated to a minor position of prominence in most Western music. Modal jazz based its improvisatory element on exploring the potential of some of these ancient modal concepts. In modal jazz an improvisation would be created around the notes present in a particular mode. This put the emphasis more on creating interesting melodic ideas within the modal pitches rather than playing variations on a melody or that fit into a preset series of chords. Two of the most important musicians in the development of modal jazz were Miles Davis and John Coltrane (1926–1967).

> *So What—*
> Miles Davis

Hearing the differences in improvisatory approaches between modal jazz and earlier varieties may be difficult for most people. The important thing in discussing this approach is that it represents an ongoing evolutionary trend within jazz to constantly move in new directions, to find new ways of allowing the individual voice of the performer to be heard. In essence, that is what jazz has been all about.

Fusion

In 1969 Miles Davis gathered a group of musicians together for a three-day recording session that culminated in the album *Bitches Brew,* a set of extended compositions many consider the beginnings of **fusion jazz**. Fusion is a type of jazz that incorporates aspects of rock music and other styles. The final tracks on *Bitches Brew* were the result of studio engineering that pieced together disparate improvisations from the sessions with composed material. The pieces on the album are quite long with distinct sections much as is found in extended "classical" music compositions. In both the recording techniques and the fusion of jazz, rock, and funk styles, Davis was again at the forefront of the evolutionary changes in jazz.

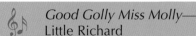

Bitches Brew—
Miles Davis

The last 30 years have seen a number of stylistic niches evolve and develop a certain following. Among these, free jazz, as the name implies a more unrestricted type of jazz, Latin jazz, based extensively on rhythmic qualities of Latin- and African-derived music, and for lack of a better term, traditional jazz, a style that looks to older varieties of jazz for its ideals and inspiration, have been the most prominent jazz styles. While the popularity of jazz has diminished significantly since the 1940s it retains a noteworthy place in the history of music as the first important American contribution to the world's music. It is also the first stylistic movement in Western music to have improvisation as one of its central elements.

Improvisation in Rock Music

Early Rock and Roll

Improvisation has been an integral part of rock and roll music since its early days in the 1950s. Many early rock and roll songs were based on the twelve bar blues chord progression or a close variation of it. Consequently, at least one verse of many songs was devoted to an instrumental improvisation. Listen again to the early rock and roll songs we discussed in Chapter 5 and you will hear examples of this limited improvisation in each of the songs.

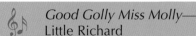

Good Golly Miss Molly—
Little Richard

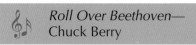

Roll Over Beethoven—
Chuck Berry

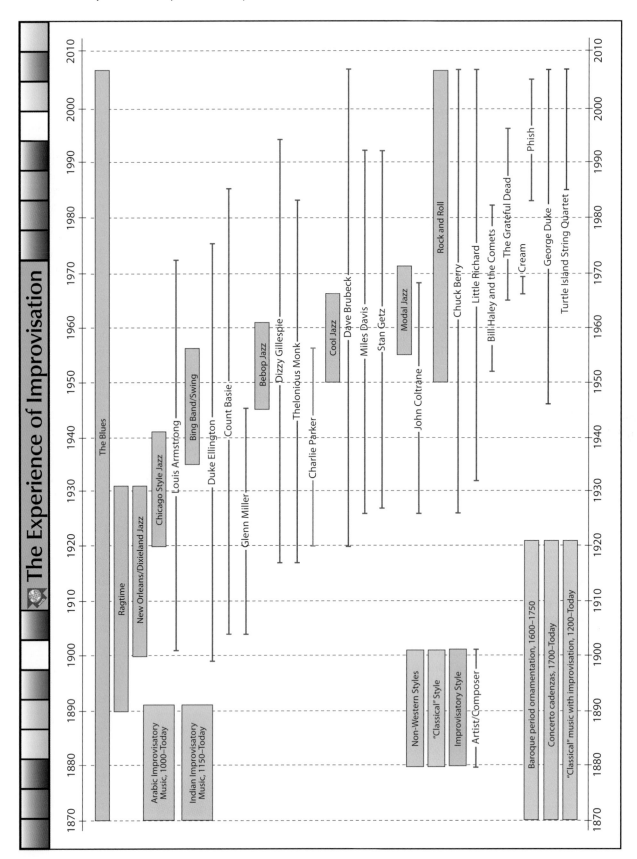

PERSPECTIVE—IMPROVISATION IN THEATRE AND DANCE

The practice of improvisation in music is the culmination of a thorough knowledge of the harmonic, melodic, and rhythmic elements on the part of the performer. It is a performance practice that comes to life when executed in front of an audience. As such, it replaces the accurate reproduction of a composer's ideas with a spontaneous variation on it. In the practice of improvisation the performer takes on the composer's role, if only partially, by modifying the specified elements of a piece and transforming them during the performance. It is that aspect of improvisation in music, the fact that it occurs almost exclusively during a performance, which distinguishes it from how it is used in theatre and dance.

Improvisation in theatre and dance is more often used as a tool to stimulate creative ideas rather than as a performance practice to be aspired to. Some types of dance are more improvisatory in character than others, such as the tango for example. And some types of dance that have historically been purely choreographed have recently begun to incorporate improvisatory elements, such as ballet. When discussing dance it is helpful to make a distinction between social dance and concert dance. Social dancing is the type of dance people generally engage in for pleasure while concert dance is presented for an audience. Improvisation is much more common in social dance than in concert dance.

In concert dance, improvisation is more often a choreographer's device rather than a performer's. Dance, being a physical and visual art form, relies on the choreographer's imagination to "picture" physical shape, line, form, and movement in the performance space. How those elements interact, are balanced, and structured cannot be done on paper, as a composer might try out different ideas on manuscript paper. Through improvised movement the choreographer can see and feel what is physically possible and turn those improvisations into movement that can be repeated by the performers. In this way the choreographer's improvisation can lead to new ideas rather than simply repeat what he or she has seen others do. In ensemble performances, dancers must recreate their movements exactly or else they risk getting in the way of the other dancers. It is rare for a dancer in a concert presentation to improvise anything other than a short solo section of a piece.

A fairly recent development in the world of dance, from the early 1970s, is a style called "Contact Improvisation." As the name implies, Contact Improvisation uses contact between two dancers, or dancers and inanimate objects, as a catalyst for improvised movement. While some contend that this is a major new dance genre, others see it more as an interesting addition to the existing world of concert, as well as social, dance. In the concert setting, Contact Improvisation is usually done without musical accompaniment.

The use of improvisatory dialogue in the theatrical presentations of the Italian Commedia dell'arte, prominent from the fourteenth through the eighteenth centuries, is the foremost example of improvisation in theatrical performance. The basic storyline and characters within the plays were agreed upon beforehand with the dialogue extemporaneously spoken by the actors. The measure of an actor's ability in this genre was the degree to which he could seamlessly play off of the words spoken by his colleagues.

In the modern theatre, improvisation is used mostly as a training activity to sharpen an actor's sense of timing and stage presence. An actor's ability to improvise in reaction to unforeseen circumstances while on stage is an essential performance skill. While some improvisatory theatre is presented in public, it constitutes a very small portion of theatrical performances. Improvisations are sometimes staged by a director or actors to elicit new ideas or bring a fresh perspective to a scene.

Rock Around the Clock—
Bill Haley and the Comets

In all three of these songs at least one verse was an instrumental improvisation based on the repeating chord pattern of the song. This is essentially the same approach to improvisation that the blues and jazz musicians had taken earlier in the century and which continued in contemporaneous jazz.

Improvisational Rock—Cream

As rock music morphed into the many sub-styles of the 1960s and 1970s, certain types of rock kept the improvisational element and some even expanded on it to the point that it became one of the defining characteristics of those styles. Foremost in bringing improvisational rock to the forefront of popular music was the British group Cream. The music of this three-man band, consisting of a guitar, bass, and drums, was an homage to the blues-based foundation of rock and roll. All three of the members of Cream—Eric Clapton, guitarist, Jack Bruce, bassist, and Ginger Baker, drummer—were virtuosic performers in their own right, but together they brought a new level of improvisatory interaction to rock music that hadn't been experienced before. In concert performances Cream's improvisations often went on for twenty minutes or more. The type of improvisation practiced by Cream varied from song to song. Sometimes the improvisation was based on chord progressions, as we heard on the Robert Johnson blues song *Crossroads* in Chapter 5. At other times they would do an extended modal improvisation as in the song *Spoonful,* written by Willie Dixon. Cream was one of a number of blues-based bands, such as John Mayall's Bluesbreakers, the Yardbirds, and the Animals, that came out of England in the 1960s.

In the following performance the majority of the written part of the song, the lyrics and melody, are played and sung at the beginning. The general feel of the song is established during this opening section. At approximately 2:48 into the song the voice drops out and the improvisation begins. There are no changing chords from this point on until the voice returns near the end of the performance, bringing back the melody that began the piece. At approximately 4:02 into the piece the drummer hits the center part of a cymbal which is an audible signal to the rest of the band that a rhythmic change is about to take place. A double time (twice as fast) feel in the tempo occurs soon after at approximately 4:10 when the bass player doubles the speed at which he has been playing his notes. This kind of pre-arranged, onstage communication between players is common in long improvisations. As this performance progresses there are a number of distinct sections, each with its own mood, tempo, and nuance. As you listen to this performance, see if you can hear any other "signals" that might be given between the players. Here's a hint, listen carefully at 13:22 into the piece.

Spoonful—
Willie Dixon, performed by Cream

The Grateful Dead and Phish

Many other bands adopted improvisatory styles to varying degrees, but two bands made it the basis of their performing personae, the Grateful Dead and Phish. Both groups specialized in long, free-form improvisations. Phish's improvisations sometimes took wildly incongruous turns, even incorporating vocal improvisations as well as instrumental. Each group had an extraordinary guitarist who wrote much of the band's music and led the improvisatory explorations, Jerry Garcia for the Grateful Dead and Trey Anastasio for Phish. During live performances Phish used audible and visual signals to indicate upcoming changes in the character of an improvisation. These signals were well rehearsed and contributed to the band's ability to extend improvisations in sometimes unpredictable ways. An unusual approach Phish took in composing the songs for one album was to record extensive improvisations first and then write songs to fit the improvisations, instead of incorporating improvisations into an already composed song.

Phish. Courtesy of Photofest, NY

The Grateful Dead was formed in 1965 and remained intact until the death of Jerry Garcia in 1995. Many of the Grateful Dead's loyal fans, referred to as "Deadheads," followed the band from concert to concert, experiencing not only their "jam band" musical style but also the drug culture that was an ongoing part of the "Deadhead" experience. Phish attracted a somewhat less drug-centered following until the breakup of the Grateful Dead when many Deadheads began following Phish in a manner similar to how they had followed the Dead. Phish was continuously active as a band from 1983 until 2000 when they announced their breakup. Two years later a reunion concert was performed and the band continued to play concerts sporadically until 2004. The following song, *You Enjoy Myself*, performed by Phish, is a complex composition incorporating composed as well as improvisational sections and is representative of the type of extended pieces for which they were known.

You Enjoy Myself—
Trey Anastasio, performed by Phish

Improvisation in Non-Western Music

The practice of improvisation is more common in the music of certain non-western countries than in others. India and the Near Eastern countries of Arabia have a long established tradition of musical improvisation that is similar to improvisation in Western music but with significant differences. The music from northern India, Hindustani music, was influenced by Arabian music after Islamic invaders conquered the northern provinces of India in the late twelfth century. Music from southern India, Carnatic music, shows less Arabian influences and may be considered a more pure variety of classical Indian music.

Rain Dance—Mega Raga, from Golkonda, India, ca. 1765. Copyright © Bildarchiv Preussischer Kulturbesitz/Art Resource, NY

Improvisation in both Arabic and Indian musical styles is based on melodic elements rather than harmonic ones, as is common in Western music. We have seen in the discussion of improvisation in jazz and Western classical music that the improvisation is almost always based on an underlying harmony or chord progression. Modal jazz comes closest to the non-Western concepts of improvisation in that it was based on a mode, a type of scale, and not on the harmonic foundation supporting the melody. That is how non-Western improvisation is often executed as well. A particular piece is based on a certain "scale," even though it may not be called a scale in that musical tradition, and the musicians improvise using pitches based on that scale. In Western improvisation that concept would usually lead to melodic improvisation in which the performers relate their improvised music to the melody that was presented at the beginning of the piece. In much non-Western improvisation there is no attempt to reconcile the improvised melodic ideas with the main melody of a piece. The improvisation is based solely on the scale pitches and not from a melody derived from it.

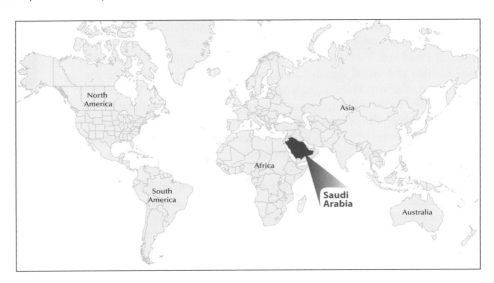

Arabic Improvisatory Music

Music from the Arabian Peninsula and surrounding countries is based on an octave divided into 24 pitches, twice the number in Western music. From those 24 pitches, only 7 are used to create the scales/modes on which individual pieces are based. This is the same number of pitches used in Western music, but the intervals, or spaces, between the pitches differs from that in Western music, giving Arabic music its unique sound. The scale/mode equivalent in Arabic music is called the maqam, or the plural form, maqamat.

An Arabic oud. Corel

The oud is one of the most common Arabic stringed instruments, similar to the lute in size and shape but without frets. Frets are the raised bars on guitar and lute fingerboards that define the pitches. The lack of frets on the oud, along with its nylon or gut strings, contributes to its unique timbre. Other common Arabic instruments include the quanan, similar to an autoharp in shape, which is played with a plectrum while the instrument rests on the knees, and the nay, a type of long flute made of cane. Borrowed from European music is the violin, which, since the middle of the nineteenth century, has become a standard instrument in Arabic music.

In Arabic music there is no emphasis put on polyphonic textures as there is in much Western music, and little if any importance is placed on thematic development in the Western sense. Small groups of pitches are used as melodic building blocks that are based on different notes of the mode that underlies the piece. These groups of pitches are then used to form the basic outlines of improvised melodic lines. The rhythmic pulse of an improvisation can alternate from calm and tenuous to fast and driving.

Oftentimes when listening to non-Western improvisatory music our ears and minds try to impose an order, or form, on the music. This can lead to expectations that certain things will, or should, happen at certain times. That is a Western expectation of what music is or should be and will lead to an unfulfilled musical experience. Rather than listening "for" certain things to happen, a listener should listen "to" what happens during an improvisation. The difference is subtle but important. When listening "for" something we are anticipating the future. When listening "to" something we are experiencing the present. Arabic improvisation occurs in the present, where it is best experienced and enjoyed.

Maqam Kurd—
Traditional Arabic Improvisation

Indian Improvisatory Music

The music from India consists of two distinct types, Hindustani music from the north, and Carnatic music from the south. The Hindustani style is what most people today associate with "Indian" music. All Indian music is derived from ancient **Vedic** religious texts, the **Vedas**, which pre-date the modern Hindu religion. Vedic culture dates from approximately 1500 BC until 500 BC, which makes the music of India one of the oldest continuously experienced types of music in the world.

An Indian sitar.
Corel

One of the commonly used instruments in Indian music is the **sitar**, a plucked stringed instrument with two sets of strings, one melodic and another resonating set that provides an unchanging "harmonic" background sound under the melody. The "frets" under the melodic strings are raised off of the neck of the instrument in a curved shape, which produces a unique, metallic timbre. The **tamboura** is another stringed instrument, usually having three strings, that provides a **drone** harmony in the background to the sitar. A drone harmony is one in which the notes do not change from one chord or harmony to another but instead provide an unchanging background sound to melodies produced by other instruments. A common percussion instrument in Indian music is the **tabla**, similar in appearance to, but larger than, a set of bongos. The tabla player has the ability to alter the pitch and resonance of the tabla by pressing on the heads of the individual drums in various ways.

What Makes Music—Musical Instruments

Plucked Strings

There are a number of stringed instruments that do not use a bow to make their sound. These instruments make their sound by having their strings plucked or strummed either by the fingers themselves or by using a plectrum, a small plastic or metallic item used for that purpose. Some of these instruments include the **guitar**, **banjo**, **mandolin**, **lute**, and **ukulele**. They all have various numbers of strings, can be played by either plucking or strumming the strings, and have frets embedded in the neck to indicate where the fingers should be put down in order to change the pitches. These instruments have a flat bridge, not a curved one like the bowed strings, no sound post inside to help amplify the sounds, and no bass bar to augment the low notes as do the bowed string instruments mentioned previously.

There is one other plucked string instrument that is unlike the ones mentioned above, and that is the **harp**. The harp does not have a fingerboard on which to press the strings. Rather, the strings are stretched tightly in the air, and they are plucked by both hands while a series of foot pedals are depressed or released in order to change the pitches.

© 2013, Ansis Klucis (FotoAka), Shutterstock, Inc.

© 2013, Fedorov Oleksiy, Shutterstock, Inc.

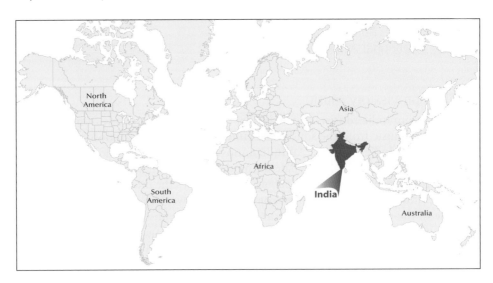

The Raga

While much Indian music is vocal, including much improvisatory Carnatic music from the southern half of the subcontinent, the most commonly heard Indian music in the west is the **raga**. A raga is an improvisatory piece of music based on a series of pitches, similar to but more complex and subtle than a scale, from which melodies are derived. The raga is an intricate system of musical relationships of pitches and references to religious principles derived from the ancient Vedic texts. As such, it dictates the appropriateness of specific ragas for certain types of occasions, times of the day, or seasons of the year.

The performance of a raga can best be explained by the sequence in which certain events take place. The beginning of a raga is usually slow and dreamlike, with the basic "scale" that the piece is based on outlined by the sitar player while the tamboura provides a drone accompaniment. No rhythmic element is present at the beginning. After the basic parameters of the melodic component of the raga are played by the sitar player, the percussion instrument, the tabla, will enter establishing a rhythmic pulse. The rhythmic element of a raga is called the **tala**. From that point on the sitar and tabla players will engage in both melodic and rhythmic improvisation, playing off each other as one or the other changes the tempo or mood of the piece. The sitar player will explore different musical ideas based on the melodic raga while the tabla player explores the rhythmic tala. The synergy between the two players can produce exhilarating passages of unbridled energy or calm reflective moments.

Raga: Tilik Shayam—
Performed by Ravi Shankar

As in the Arabic music heard earlier, Indian improvisation is melodic and not based on any harmonic considerations. The drone "harmony" of the tamboura is more a quality of the timbre of the music than the harmony. Also, as in Arabic music, the expectation of something "happening" in Indian music will also lead to frustration for a Western listener. The full enjoyment of this music comes from allowing the music to unfold as the performers create it without expecting it to "do" something. The minimalist music discussed in Chapter 8 was significantly influenced by this type of non-Western music. What similarities in approach between minimalist music and non-Western improvisation can you perceive?

Listening Chart

Period/Type of Jazz/Rock	Type of Improvisation	Composer/Artist	Keywords
Baroque	Ornamentation	Antonio Vivaldi	
Baroque	Cadenza	Johann Sebastian Bach	
20th/21st Century	Classical/Jazz	Turtle Island String Quartet	
20th/21st Century	Classical/Jazz	George Duke	
New Orleans	Group	Louis Armstrong	
Chicago	Individual	Louis Armstrong	
Swing/Big Band	Harmonic/Melodic	Count Basie Band	
Swing/Big Band	Harmonic/Melodic	Duke Ellington Band	
Swing/Big Band	Harmonic/Melodic	Glenn Miller Band	
Bebop Jazz	Harmonic	Thelonious Monk	
Bebop Jazz	Harmonic	Dizzy Gillespie	
Cool Jazz	Harmonic	Stan Getz	
Modal Jazz	Modal	Miles Davis	
Fusion Jazz	Harmonic/Modal	Miles Davis	
Rock and Roll	12-Bar Harmonic	Little Richard	
Rock and Roll	12-Bar Harmonic	Chuck Berry	
Rock and Roll	12-Bar Harmonic	Bill Haley	
Blues/Rock	Harmonic/Modal	Cream	
Jam Band/Rock	Extended	Phish	
Maqam Kurd	Melodic/Modal	Traditional Arabic	
Raga	Melodic/Modal	Traditional Indian	

Diagram — "What is performing the music?"

Grouping categories:
- Lute solo with string orchestra
- String orchestra with soloists
- String quartet
- Orchestra/jazz soloists
- Jazz/Big band
- Rock band
- Non-Western instruments

Keyword descriptions:
- Ornamentation on repeated sections
- Extended harpsichord cadenza
- Free rhythm at beginning, running bass line
- Piano, bass, drums improvs
- Group improvisation, trumpet featured
- Trumpet intro, scat singing
- Piano tune, solos, brass interjections
- Sax tune, brass interjections, some solos
- Sax tune, brass interjections, some solos
- Piano featured, dissonance
- Bass, percussion, muted trumpet start
- Soft sax, brushes on drums, restrained
- Piano, bass start, trumpet solo
- Low pulses, dissonant chords, trumpet
- 12-bar blues, sax/piano improvisation
- 12-bar blues, guitar improvisation
- 12-bar blues, guitar improvisation
- Long, extended improvisation, bluesy
- Long, extended improvisation, varied
- Oud, rhythmically free, melodic
- Sitar, tabla, microtones, melodic

In the "Keywords" column, write down words, musical or non-musical, that will help you remember the specific pieces you are hearing.

SUMMARY

Why is improvisation such an important component of so many types of music from so many cultures, but not nearly as important in other art forms? Improvisation certainly exits in the theatre and is an important element in theatrical and some dance performances, but it certainly isn't the basic concept underlying those genres as it is in so many varieties of music. From all the styles of jazz, including Dixieland, Chicago style, big band, bebop, cool, and fusion, to the blues, rock and roll, and bluegrass, there would be none of these styles if it weren't for improvisation.

Improvisation has played an important role in Western art music from the beginning. During the Medieval period the melodic line of secular dance pieces would often be the only music written down. The rest of the parts, for however many other instruments might be part of a particular performance, would be improvised. The Baroque period, that formative era when so many of the principles and concepts still governing Western art music were developed, was based in large part on the concept of improvisation. Improvised ornaments added to repeated melodic lines, and the basso continuo practice requiring the keyboard player to improvise their part based on a system of symbols and numbers written above the bass line, both have modern counterparts in the music of today. The improvised cadenzas of the Classical period are perhaps the high point of pure improvisation in Western art music. Twentieth and twenty-first century composers have sought ways to incorporate improvisation and improvisatory-sounding music into traditional classical genres. George Gershwin, the Turtle Island String Quartet, and George Duke are some who have successfully done this.

The evolution of jazz throughout the twentieth and into the twenty-first century has been a condensed version of the evolution of Western art music. From the polyphonic, improvised melodic lines of Dixieland, to the more homophonic, single-line improvisations of Chicago style, to the "Romantic" large-scale big band music of the 1940s, to the reactionary, dissonant, bebop style, the general trends in jazz have mirrored the evolutionary characteristics of one thousand years of Western art music in a mere one hundred years of jazz.

As rock and roll eclipsed jazz as the preeminent American popular music style in the 1950s, improvisation maintained a prominent role in that style as well. As many early rock and roll songs were based on the twelve-bar blues format, improvisation would appear in at least one or two repetitions of that chord progression. From the 1960s onward, some artists; Cream, The Grateful Dead, and Phish for example, emphasized the improvisatory aspect of their music in long, many-faceted, improvisatory excursions that extended the length of many of their songs to twenty or thirty minutes in live performances.

The music of virtually the entire Indian culture and much Arabic music would not exist if there were no improvisation. In the music of those cultures where less emphasis is put on the harmonic element of music, the manipulation of the melodic element through extended improvisation makes that much more prominent and important.

There is something inherently appealing about the creation of music "on the spot," as improvisation is often called. If reaffirms our unique place in nature as imaginative beings capable of creating something that wasn't there before. Perhaps that is what we ultimately seek in our musical experience.

SUGGESTED FURTHER LISTENING

The Thrill Is Gone—B.B. King with Eric Clapton

Spain—John Coltrane

Feel's So Good—Chuck Mangione

Bag's Groove—Milt Jackson and the Modern Jazz Quartet

Giant Steps—John Coltrane

Heliocentric Worlds—Sun Ra

Transformations—James Emery

African American Epic Suite—Yusef Lateef

Traintime—Cream

"Great Improvisations from Goran Bregovic Orchestra"—http://youtube.com/watch?v=g9WNF_2-3gI

QUESTION ASSIGNMENT

Instructions: Log in to the textbook web site and click on the ASSIGNMENTS tab. In the Chapter Question Assignment area read the instructions and answer the question(s) or provide the asked for information. Be sure to click the SUBMIT THIS FORM button after you complete the Assignment.

List the three basic musical concepts evident in all styles of improvisation.

1. _____

2. _____

3. _____

Name the section of music within a concerto during which improvisation occurs.

1. _____

LISTENING EXERCISES

Instructions: Log in to the textbook web site and click on the ASSIGNMENTS tab. In the Listening Exercises area click on the links to the musical examples for each question and answer the questions. Be sure to click the SUBMIT button after you answer all of the questions.

Listen to each of the musical examples below from the Chapter 10 Playlist while noting the appropriate descriptive prompt on the Listening Chart for Chapter 10 and determine the best answer to each question.

1. "Phase 5" from *Muir Woods Suite* by George Duke—This piece for orchestra and jazz soloists has sections that are fully composed, both for the orchestra alone and with the soloists, and sections that are completely improvised, just for the soloists. The solo piano, bass, and drums improvise both as a group and individually. Choose the timing where the piano begins an extended featured solo accompanied by the bass, drums, and the orchestra.

   a.   2:00 seconds
   b.   2:50 seconds
   c.   4:38 seconds

2. *Good Golly Miss Molly* performed by Little Richard—This song, played by a typical 1950s era rock band, is in a twelve-bar blues format. One of the repetitions of the 12 bars features a saxophone and piano improvisation. Choose the timing at which that improvisation begins.

   a.   17 seconds
   b.   1:12 seconds
   c.   1:30 seconds

3. *Raga Tilak Shyam*, traditional Indian raga, performed by Ravi Shankar—This Indian raga, performed by non-Western instruments, including the sitar, the tamboura, and the tabla, features many examples of microtones; that is, the bending of the pitch. Choose the timing when the tabla first enters.

   a.   1:19 seconds
   b.   4:19 seconds
   c.   7:35 seconds

Glossary of Key Terms

A

A cappella   Unaccompanied vocal music.

A-B-A   Type of single-movement form consisting of an opening section of music with certain characteristics, a contrasting section, and then a return to the original music at the end. Also known as three-part form or ternary form.

Absolute music   Music without a "program" that exists for its own sake and does not try to represent any extra-musical idea.

Achi Llama   Tibetan folk dance, performed outside of the monasteries for the purpose of preserving and retelling historical facts, legends, and myths of their culture.

Aesthetic   The perception of beauty and how we react to it.

Age of Enlightenment   Term used to refer to eighteenth-century Europe during which the philosophical outlook was based on knowledge and a rational view of the world.

Age of Reason   Term used to refer to European rational philosophy from approximately 1600–1800, including the Age of Enlightenment.

Air   A lyrical type of dance music, but not a real dance, often incorporated into Renaissance and Baroque dance suites.

Aleatoric music   Music that incorporates some element of chance in either the composition or performance of the music. Advocated by American composer John Cage.

Allemande   French dance in a fast 4/4 time.

Alternative rock   Style of rock music that avoids the musical conventions of other identifiable, commercially successful, styles.

Alto   The lower-register female voice.

Appoggiatura   A melodic "ornament" from the Baroque period that consisted of a stressed note that was not part of the harmony played on the beat that resolved to a consonant pitch within the chord after the beat.

Aria   A lyrical vocal piece, a song, usually for a solo voice with orchestral accompaniment. Common in operas, oratorios, and cantatas.

Arpeggiated   In reference to a chord, it indicates the playing of the individual notes of the chord sequentially rather than simultaneously.

Art song   A song for solo voice with accompaniment intended for concert or formal presentation in which both the solo voice part and the accompaniment are written out by the composer.

Asymmetrical meter   Meter in which the number of grouped pulses changes instead of remaining constant.

Atonal music   Music without a tonal center, or key. Developed in the early twentieth century by Austrian composer Arnold Schoenberg.

Atonality   The absence of a tonal center in music.

B

Backbeat   A rhythmic quality in which the second and fourth beats of a four-beat measure are emphasized. Common in rock and roll.

Background music   Music in a movie that sets or reflects the mood of a scene.

Ballade   A piano genre of the Romantic period developed by Frederic Chopin that is episodic in nature, derived from early poetic forms such as the English ballad and French ballade.

Ballet   A type of dance with a rigorous set of movements and techniques by which to execute those movements. Started as a royal court entertainment danced by amateurs and evolved into full-evening story-telling productions.

Ballets Russes   The ballet company run by Serge Dighilev, noted impresario, in Paris.

Bar   A measure of music. In ballet also a device used in the training of dancers.

Baritone   Male voice that has a range between the tenor and the bass.

Baroque   Historical period of music dating from 1600–1750.

Bass (Double Bass, Contra Bass, Bass Fiddle)   The largest and lowest pitched of the bowed string instruments. The bass is played standing up or sitting on a stool and is often played **pizzicato**; that is, plucked with the fingers rather than stroked with a bow.

Bassadance   A slow-paced French dance from the Renaissance.

Basso continuo   The Baroque period instrumental practice of coupling a low-pitched sustaining instrument such as a cello, bass, or bassoon with a harpsichord, to provide a firm harmonic and rhythmic foundation for the music.

Basso profundo   A bass voice with an exceptional richness as well as the ability to reach notes lower in pitch than the normal range of a bass voice.

295

Bassoon   The largest member of the woodwind family and sounds the lowest. It is a double-reed instrument like the oboe.

Beat   The basic, underlying pulse of the music. Similar to your heartbeat. It can be fast or slow, depending on the mood of the music.

Bebop   A style of jazz from the late 1940s and 1950s that incorporated more extended and sometimes dissonant harmonies, unpredictable chord progressions and melodic lines that were often not very lyrical. Also called "bop."

Big band   Type of popular jazz-influenced music of the late 1930s and 1940s for a large ensemble consisting of a rhythm section plus sections of trumpets, trombones, and saxophones. Also called "swing" music.

Biopic   A movie biography of a famous person.

Blue notes   In the blues and jazz, the lowered pitches of the major scale, usually the 3rd, 5th, and 7th, that give the melodic element of the music its unique "bluesy" or "jazzy" sound.

Bluegrass   Style of country music that features virtuosic fiddle and mandolin playing.

Blues   Style of vocal music developed in the nineteenth century by African-American people in the American south that mostly dealt with the difficulties of life. Based on a repeating series of chords called the twelve-bar blues (see twelve-bar blues).

Blues/rock   Style of rock music from the 1960s and 1970s that was based on the blues format with high volume levels and virtuosic guitar improvisations.

Bop   A style of jazz from the late 1940s and 1950s that incorporated more extended and sometimes dissonant harmonies, unpredictable chord progressions, and melodic lines that were often not very lyrical. Also called "bebop."

Bourrée   A French dance in a moderate 2/2 time.

Boy soprano   The voice of a young boy who has not reached puberty. This voice possesses a very pure tone and usually does not employ the use of vibrato.

Brass quintet   The standard performing ensemble for the brass family of instruments, consisting of two trumpets, one French horn, one trombone, and one tuba. This is a very homogenous sounding group, like the string quartet, where all members produce their sound in the same way.

Breakstrain   A section of a march characterized by a loud, vigorous melody appearing between statements of the trio.

Bridge   Part of a popular song that connects a verse with the chorus and provides contrast to the repetitiveness of the verse/chorus format.

C

Cadenza   The point in a concerto, toward the end of a movement, when the soloist extemporaneously improvises on themes previously presented in the movement. Most cadenzas are in fact written out beforehand and performed in an improvisatory fashion rather than being truly improvised.

Call and response   See "responsorial singing."

Call to Prayer   In the Muslim world the music that is sung five times daily by the "muezzin" telling Muslims it is time to pray. In modern times this has often been replaced by a recording rather than a person singing from a tower called a minaret.

Caller   In an American square dance, the person who calls out which steps are to be danced next.

Camerata   Sixteenth-century group of Italian intellectuals who espoused a monodic style of vocal music in order to allow the meaning of the words to be clearly understood.

Cantata   Sacred vocal genre consisting of multiple movements performed during a church service. Common in the Baroque period as well as today.

Canzon   Renaissance period instrumental genre employing imitative polyphony.

Carnatic   Refers to music from southern India.

Castrato   A male singer who had been castrated prior to puberty before the voice had changed from a high-pitched boy's voice to a lower-pitched man's voice. This was a very popular voice in the 17th and 18th centuries.

Catholic Counter-Reformation   The Catholic Church's effort in the sixteenth century to counter the reform movement lead by Martin Luther. The Council of Trent, held from 1545–1563, defined the theological tenets of the Catholic Church that differentiated it from the reform movement.

Cello (Violoncello)   A bowed string instrument that is considerably larger than both the violin and the viola and is held between the legs while sitting on a chair.

Celtic   The term used to refer to the cultural characteristics of European people who once shared a common sub-group of the Indo-European languages. Most commonly used to refer to the people of Ireland, Scotland, and Wales.

Cham   Sacred dance of Tibetan Buddhism.

Chamber music   Music for a small group of players in which each line of music is performed by only one instrument. Usually intended for performance in a small venue such as the "chambers" of a large estate.

Chicago (style of jazz)   Type of jazz developed in the 1920s that placed more emphasis on solo improvisations than the Dixieland style that preceded it.

Chinese Opera   Traditional musical theatre genre of China combining music, costumes, makeup, scenery, mime, dance, and acrobatics characterized by a generally boisterous presentation of musical materials.

Choral society   A philanthropic group organized for the purpose of promoting and financially supporting a choral organization. Became popular in nineteenth-century Europe.

Chord   The combination of three or more pitches. Chords create harmony.

Chord progression   A logical-sounding series of chords.

Chordal   Used in reference to an accompaniment that is basically chords without additional melodic material.

Choreographer   The person who decides on the dance moves for a staged performance.

Chorus   Either a large choir of mixed voices or a repeating section of text and music.

Christmas carol   A song based on the Christmas story or related ideas.

Clarinet   A high-pitched, single-reed, woodwind instrument. It uses one piece of cane pressed tightly against a piece of plastic or glass through which air is forced to give it its characteristically mellow tone quality.

Classical   Historical period of music. Approximately 1750–1825.

Closing   A section of music found in sonata form movements that brings either the statement of the first theme or the exposition to a final-sounding conclusion.

Coda   A section of music frequently found in sonata form movements that brings the entire movement to a final-sounding conclusion.

Coloratura Soprano   Soprano voice that is extremely high and also quite agile in that it can jump from one note to another with great ease in the very highest register.

Commedia dell'arte   An Italian improvisatory theatre style prominent from the fourteenth through the eighteenth centuries.

Commission(ed)   Payment for a piece of music to be composed at a future date. A work that has been paid for before it has been written is said to have been "commissioned."

Concert   A public performance of music in a formal setting by a group of musicians.

Concert overture   A single-movement orchestral genre of the nineteenth century, usually programmatic and in an extended sonata form, intended as a stand-alone piece on a concert rather than as a prelude (overture) to a stage presentation such as an opera or a ballet.

Concert performance   Performance of music originally intended for a stage production, such as a ballet or opera, without the staging.

Concertino   In a concerto grosso, the small group of soloists with basso continuo.

Concerto   A three-movement instrumental genre from the Baroque period onward for one soloist with orchestral accompaniment with a movement structure of 1-Fast 2-Slow 3-Fast.

Concerto grosso   A three-movement instrumental genre from the Baroque period for a small group of soloists with a movement structure of 1-Fast 2-Slow 3-Fast.

Conductor   The leader of a musical ensemble whose gestures in rehearsals and concerts indicate meter, tempo, dynamic level, and, through facial expressions and body language, the emotional content of the music.

Consonant   Sounds that feel at rest, stable, pleasing.

Cool (jazz)   Style of jazz from the late 1950s and 1960s that was a more restrained, understated variety of bebop jazz. It featured virtuosic improvisations with a calm presentation, as if seemingly effortless to execute.

Copyright   Legal term that accords the creator of a piece of music (or any other intellectual property) the right to control its use, reproduction, and performance.

Countermelody   A secondary melody in a contrapuntal texture.

Counter tenor   An extremely high-pitched male voice, sometimes sung falsetto; a tone quality that is lighter and not as full-bodied as normal singing.

Country (music)   Style of music from the southern and western United States utilizing fairly simple chords and forms with stories predominantly about broken love, hard times, prison, and drinking.

Courante   A French dance in fast 3/4 time.

Crescendo   The gradual increase in the dynamic level (volume).

Crusades   A series of military campaigns undertaken by the Roman Catholic Church from 1096 until approximately 1300 to retake control of the Holy Lands from the "Turks" (Muslims).

Cubism   An early twentieth-century style of art promoted by Pablo Picasso and Georges Brasque in which geometrical shapes of deconstructed figures are rearranged on a canvas to represent three-dimensional objects on a two-dimensional surface.

Cubist   The adjective form of cubism. See cubism.

Cymbals   Non-pitched, metallic percussion instruments played by hitting them together or with wooden sticks.

D

Dama   Collective name for all of the funeral rituals of the Dogon people of Mali in West Africa.

Dance of the Skeleton   A type of religious dance of Tibetan Buddhism invoking the transitory nature of life.

Dancing master   From the Renaissance until the mid-nineteenth-century dancing instructors employed by wealthy patrons to both teach and perform dances.

Decrescendo   The gradual decrease in the dynamic level (volume).

Development   A section in a sonata form movement during which the main themes are manipulated in various ways and several key centers are explored before returning to the main theme in the following section, the recapitulation.

Dies Irae   "Day of Wrath . . .," a traditional Roman Catholic Church text describing The Last Judgment. This text is frequently included in requiem masses.

Dirge   Any slow, sad music appropriate for a funeral.

Dissonant   Harmonies that have a harsh, grating quality.

Dixieland   A type of early jazz that is usually played by a small group consisting of a rhythm section along with several other instruments. This type of jazz employs group improvisations that emphasize rhythmic as well as melodic alterations of the tune over a repeating chord pattern. Also known as New Orleans jazz.

Dogon   West African tribe centered in Mali. Noted for their use of elaborate masks in funeral rituals.

Dominant   In tonal music the harmony based on the fifth note of the scale.

Domine Jesu (Offertorium) "Oh Lord Jesus Christ, King of Glory . . .," a traditional Roman Catholic Church text imploring deliverance from eternal punishment. This text is frequently included in requiem masses.

Double feature The presentation of two movies for the price of one. A common practice in the early days of film.

Dramma Giocoso A "jocular drama." A staged musical work that combines aspects of comic and serious opera. Most notably written by Mozart.

Drone A constant, unchanging pitch or combination of pitches. Common in Indian music.

Drums Non-pitched percussion instruments played with wooden sticks.

Duple meter Meter with two beats, or multiples of two beats, in each measure.

Dynamics Term that refers to the volume level, or loudness, of the music.

E

Eighth notes Notes that each receive 1/2 of one beat. Two eighth notes are equal to one quarter note (which receives one beat).

Episode In a fugue, a section of music during which the subject (main theme) is not heard.

Estampie A Medieval dance usually in a fast triple meter.

Esterhazy A family of nobility and the name of their estate in Eisenstadt, Austria. During the Classical period when Franz Joseph Haydn was the composer for the family, the property belonged to the Hungarian Empire.

Exoticism Romantic period practice of incorporating characteristics of music of other cultures into Western art music.

Exposition The first major section of a sonata form movement during which the main themes are presented (exposed) to the listener in two different keys (tonal centers). The exposition is usually repeated. In a fugue the term refers to any section of the piece when the theme is heard.

Expressionism An early twentieth-century musical style associated with composers such as Schoenberg, Webern, and Berg. The music is dissonant and unsettling and often deals with dark subjects.

F

Fanfare A short composition, usually played by brass, and possibly percussion instruments, to announce the arrival of an important person or to mark the beginning of a ceremonial occasion.

Fantasia A free-form, improvisatory-sounding keyboard genre of the Baroque period frequently paired with a highly-structured form such as the fugue.

Fantasia An animated feature-length film from the Walt Disney Studios released in 1940 that featured fanciful animations set to classical music compositions.

Fiddle A violin, usually with a more flattened bridge in order to facilitate the playing of more than one string at a time.

Flute A high-pitched woodwind instrument made out of silver, gold, or platinum. Its sound is produced by blowing air over an open hole, much like when you make a sound by blowing over the top of a soda bottle.

Folk Art Any traditional art form representative of, and shared by, a certain people or culture.

Folk song A type of song common to the people of a nation, ethnic group, or culture, the origins of which are usually not documented in written form.

Form The structure of a musical composition. In individual movements form usually is based on how the themes (main melodies) are manipulated. In entire compositions it refers to the overall outline of movements or other large sections such as the acts of an opera.

French Horn This member of the brass family is a mellow sounding adaptation of the hunting horn.

Frequency of vibration The rate at which the air is set in motion which causes a pitch to be perceived.

Frets The raised bars on the necks of guitars and lutes that define the pitches.

Fugue Baroque period keyboard genre employing imitative polyphony with contrasting material.

Funeral march A type of composition, often a single movement from a multi-movement work, with a slow, steady, march-like beat and an overall somber countenance.

Funk A style of R&B music emphasizing syncopated rhythms, the presence of horn sections, and an aggressive bass line.

Fusion A type of jazz that incorporates aspects of rock music and other styles.

G

Galliard A fast-paced French dance in triple meter, often paired with the slower pavane.

Gamelan A Balinese and Javanese collection of primarily percussion instruments, gongs, cymbals, drums, played as an ensemble.

Gamelan angklung A smaller version of the gamelan.

Gamelan beleganjur A gamelan of more portable instruments, used primarily while walking during rituals and celebrations.

Gamelan gong A large gamelan.

Gangsta rap Style of rap music preoccupied with violence and the denigration of women.

Genre A type of music, such as a symphony, concerto, etc., or a piece of music in a general style, such as chamber music, opera, etc.

Gigue An English dance in fast 3/4 time.

Gong Non-pitched percussion instrument played by hitting it with a large mallet.

Gospel Music   Worship music of predominantly black churches in the United States characterized by performances by large choirs, often singing in unison, with soloists who improvise over the choral background. Also refers to the music of many southern white Christian churches but the style of performance is quite different from black gospel music in that it is usually performed by a smaller group employing traditional harmonies.

Grandioso   In a march, the final playing of the trio which is usually loud and may introduce another countermelody heretofore not heard.

Gregorian chant   Medieval period, monophonic, vocal music of the Roman Catholic church.

Guitar   A plucked string instrument with frets embedded in the neck to indicate where the fingers should be placed in order to change the pitches.

H

Harmonic rhythm   The relative rate at which harmonies change in a musical composition. In a piece where the harmonies change frequently, it is said to have a fast harmonic rhythm. In a composition where the harmonies stay the same for a relatively long time before changing, it is said to have a slow harmonic rhythm.

Harmony   Element of music that is literally all of the pitches that are not the melody. Harmony adds a richness of sound to the melody and can convey emotional aspects of the music such as feelings of happiness or sadness, tension, or peacefulness, etc.

Harp   A plucked string instrument that does not have a fingerboard on which to press the strings. Rather, the strings are stretched tightly in the air and they are plucked by both hands, while a series of foot pedals are depressed or released in order to change the pitches.

Harpsichord   A forerunner of the piano. The sound is produced by a series of plectrums plucking the strings inside the instrument.

Head   In jazz, the beginning of a piece that contains the main melody.

Heavy metal   A style of rock music emphasizing virtuosic guitar playing, over-the-top live dramatic presentations, and piercing vocal lines.

Hindustani   Refers to music from northern India.

Hip hop   A style of music, dance, and art developed in the inner cities of the United States in the 1970s. The musical component, rap music, is derived from R&B that combines spoken rhyming lyrics with a percussive accompaniment.

Homophonic   Type of texture consisting of a prominent melody with subordinate accompanying material.

Hook   An immediately recognizable melody, rhythm, or sound to catch the listener's attention.

Hora   A traditional Jewish circle dance.

Hornpipe   An English dance in 3/2 time with a characteristic syncopation on the first beat of each measure.

Hymn   Any religious song intended for the express purpose of praising God.

Hymnal   A printed collection of hymns.

I

Idiomatic   Term used to describe music that is especially well suited to the performance characteristics of a particular musical instrument.

Imitative polyphony   Polyphonic texture in which each voice imitates what a previous voice has already stated.

Impresario   The person who runs an opera or ballet company.

Impressionism   Late nineteenth-century musical style associated with the French composer Claude Debussy. The name comes from the painting style of the time in which subtleties of light and color were emphasized over form and line. In music the analogous concepts were emphasis on subtleties of timbre (tone color) and harmony rather than thematic development and form.

Improvisation   The creation of music during a performance.

In Paradisum   "May the angels lead you into paradise . . .," a traditional Roman Catholic Church text regarding the entrance of the soul into heaven. This text is frequently included in requiem masses.

Incidental Music   Music written to accompany a play. Often includes an overture, numerous dances, and interludes.

Interval   Two pitches sounded simultaneously or the distance between two pitches.

Introduction   A section of music that precedes the main body of a movement such as an introduction before the exposition section of a movement in sonata form.

J

Jam Band   A rock group that specializes in improvisatory music.

Jazz   A style of popular American music developed in the twentieth century characterized by syncopated rhythms and improvisation.

Jig   An English dance in a fast triple meter felt in one.

K

Kabuki Theatre   Traditional Japanese theatre combining music, acting, elaborate make-up, and costumes.

Ketjak   A kind of rhythmic chanting from Bali.

Key   The tonal center of a piece, or section of a piece, of music from which the melodies are taken and around which the harmonies are based.

Kh mei   The Tuvan name for throat singing.

Klezmer   A type of Jewish folk music distinguished by specific melodic and harmonic characteristics, virtuosic improvisation, and instrumental vocal inflections.

L

Lacrimosa   "That day is one of weeping . . .," a traditional Roman Catholic Church text describing the weeping that will accompany The Last Judgment. This text is frequently included in requiem masses.

Lead sheet   A type of contemporary sheet music in which the harmony of a song is indicated by the names of the chords and perhaps a diagram of them.

Libera Me   "Deliver me, Oh Lord, from eternal death on that awful day . . .," a traditional Roman Catholic Church text beseeching deliverance from eternal damnation. This text is frequently included in requiem masses.

Libretto   The words of an opera often available for audience members during operatic performances.

Lieder   German word for art songs.

Lute   A plucked string instrument that was a forerunner of the guitar.

Lute song   Renaissance era song for solo voice with lute accompaniment.

Lux Aeternam   "Eternal light shine upon them . . .," a traditional Roman Catholic Church text asking that the perpetual light of salvation shine on the saved through the granting of mercy. This text is frequently included in requiem masses.

Lyricist   Someone who writes lyrics.

Lyrics   The words of a song.

M

Magnificat   Sacred vocal genre based on the Virgin Mary's response to her being told she will bear the Son of God.

Major   Kind of harmony that sounds happy, triumphant, or bright.

Major key   Tonal center with a generally bright or triumphant feel to it.

Maqam   The scale equivalent in Arabic music.

Margrave of Brandenburg   The title of the ruler of the German province of Brandenburg. A margrave was a governor of noble rank.

Mariachi band   A combination of trumpets, violins, and several sizes and varieties of guitars associated with music of Mexico.

Marimba   A pitched percussion instrument made of different-sized wooden blocks played with mallets.

Mass   Musical setting of the texts associated with the Roman Catholic Church's ritual of the mass.

Mbira   Traditional African folk instrument consisting of a hollow box or gourd with metal strips of differing lengths attached that can be flipped by the thumbs to provide accompaniment to songs. Also called a thumb piano.

Measure   A bar of music, the defining unit of the meter of a piece.

Medieval   Historical period of music dating from 500–1450 AD.

Melismatic   Style of singing where many pitches are sung to one syllable of text.

Melody   The element of music that refers to the tune that we can recognize and remember. Consists of pitches with distinct rhythmic characteristics.

Menuet (minuet)   A French dance in a moderate 3/4 time and A-B-A form.

Meter   The organization of beats into regularly recurring groups of beats.

Mexican Hat Dance   A piece of music and the associated dance often regarded as the national dance of Mexico.

Mezzo-soprano   Female voice whose pitch range lies between an alto and a soprano.

Microtones   Pitches in between two "regular" notes. If you think of two adjacent notes on a piano, microtones would be pitches that exist between those pitches. Often heard in non-Western music, blues, jazz, rock, and spirituals.

Minimalism   Late twentieth-century style characterized by having a traditional tonal center and much repetition and layering of melodic or motivic elements. La Monte Young, Terry Riley, Steve Reich, and Philip Glass were innovative composers in this style.

Minor   Kind of harmony that sounds sad, melancholy, or ominous.

Minor key   Tonal center with a generally dark or melancholy feel to it.

Minstrel show   Type of American stage entertainment common in the nineteenth century featuring songs, dances, and comedy routines often with white performers performing in black face.

Minuet (menuet)   A French dance in a moderate 3/4 time and A-B-A form.

Modal jazz   Jazz style that bases improvisations on modes rather than changing harmonic elements.

Mode   One of twelve scales commonly used in music of the Catholic Church during the Medieval and Renaissance periods.

Monodic   Vocal style that employs a single melodic line with unobtrusive accompaniment.

Monophonic   A kind of texture that consists of a single melodic line.

Monophony   A monophonic texture.

Morality play   An early (Medieval–Renaissance) dramatic musical genre depicting the struggle of good versus evil.

Motet   Sacred, polyphonic vocal genre dating from the thirteenth century through the eighteenth century.

Motif   A short, readily identifiable, melodic, or rhythmic idea.

Motive   A short, readily identifiable melodic, or rhythmic idea.

Movement   A part of a large musical composition with a beginning and end but does not constitute the entire composition. Similar to a single act of a multi-act play.

Multiphonics   The singing of two or more pitches simultaneously. Practiced by Tibetan Buddhist monks and Tuvan (Mongolian) shepherds. Also known as throat singing.

Music Director   The conductor of a musical ensemble who has the additional responsibilities of overseeing programming, choosing guest soloists, auditions, and serves in an administrative role as the public face of a musical organization.

Musical   Also called the Broadway Musical, is a theatrical production consisting of music, singing, dancing, and usually contains dialogue.

Music supervisor   The person charged with oversight of all aspects of the musical component of a film. Not necessarily the composer of the music but often a compiler of appropriate music and overseer of how it is incorporated into the film.

Musique concrete   Literally "concrete music," an early attempt at using electronic recording equipment to manipulate sounds from the real world to create compositions that exist only on magnetic tape.

N

National anthem   The official song representing a country.

Nationalism   A general trend in nineteenth-century music in which composers sought to emphasize their national, cultural, and ethnic heritage by incorporating national stories and myths, folk tunes, and dances into their compositions.

Native American funeral music   Music performed during funerals characterized by the extensive use of rattles, drums, vocal chanting, and singing, all in a rhythmically repetitive manner.

Neoromanticism   A twentieth-century style which looked to the Romantic period for stylistic and emotional ideals.

Neoclassicism   A twentieth-century style fostered by Igor Stravinsky and Paul Hindemith which looked to earlier historical eras for formal and textural ideals. Regarded as a reaction against late Romantic era emotionalism.

New Orleans Jazz   A type of early jazz that is usually played by a small group consisting of a rhythm section along with several other instruments. This type of jazz employs group improvisations that emphasize rhythmic as well as melodic alterations of the tune over a repeating chord pattern. Also known as Dixieland jazz.

New Orleans Jazz Funeral   A custom in New Orleans where sad music is played by a marching brass band on the way to the burial of the deceased, but after interment is complete, joyful, celebratory music is played as the band marches back to town.

O

Obbligato   A virtuosic accompanying line of music, usually played by a single instrument.

Oboe   A high-pitched, double-reed, woodwind instrument that produces its sound by having two pieces of cane, that are shaved very thin, tied together, with air forced between them. This produces a sound that is often characterized as somewhat nasal in character.

Off-stage   The term used when instrumentalists perform from a location not on the stage. Frequently used for effect with brass instruments as in the call of the "last trumpet" announcing the "Last Judgment" in requiem masses.

On pointe   Ballet term referring to dancing on the tips of the toes.

Opera   Staged musical genre combining singing, acting, costumes, and scenery with an accompanying orchestra in a pit below, and in front of, the stage.

Opera Buffa   Comic opera. Common during the Baroque and Classical periods.

Opera Seria   Serious opera. Common during the Baroque and Classical periods.

Operetta   A light opera genre popular in nineteenth-century England and Austria.

Oral tradition   The non-written practice of passing songs along from people to people through performance.

Oratorio   Dramatic, sacred genre of the Baroque period consisting of arias, recitatives, and choruses. Usually based on biblical stories and texts. Performed in concert format, that is, not acted out on stage.

Orchestral dance suite   A genre for orchestra consisting of a series of dance movements.

Orchestrated   The term refers to a piece originally written for an instrument such as the organ or piano then subsequently arranged for an orchestra.

Orchestration   The term used to describe the assignment by composers of specific instruments to musical lines in a composition.

Ordinary   Five specific texts from the mass consisting of the Kyrie, Gloria, Sanctus, Credo, and Agnus Dei. These are the texts that appear in all masses.

Organ   A keyboard instrument uses air forced through pipes of varying lengths and thicknesses to produce different pitches. It can either be mechanically or electronically operated and often has more than one keyboard that the player can set to have different tonal qualities. The organ also has a set of keys that are operated by the feet of the player, which play the lowest-pitched notes.

Organum   A two-part sacred vocal work for a pre-existing Gregorian chant and one additional melodic line.

Ornament   Any one of a number of melodic embellishments, common in the Baroque period, that could either be indicated in the music by the composer or added by the performer as a demonstration of virtuosic and/or improvisatory ability.

Oud   Common Arabic stringed instrument, similar to the lute in size and shape but without frets, which along with its nylon or gut strings, contributes to its unique timbre.

Overture   A single-movement orchestral composition that precedes a dramatic presentation such as an opera, musical, ballet, or oratorio.

P

Patron   A financial supporter of artists and artistic productions.

Patronage   The practice of financially supporting a composer either by a wealthy nobleman or a church.

Pavane   A slow, stately French dance often paired with a contrasting Galliard.

Pelog   Type of seven-tone scale common in Balinese music in which only five tones are usually used. The tones don't match the divisions of the octave common in Western music, resulting in an out-of-tune sound to Western ears.

Pentatonic   Literally "five sounds," usually refers to any five-tone scale. Common in much non-Western music and recognizable as the basic sound of much Oriental music.

Percussion Ensemble   Any group of percussion instruments that performs as an ensemble.

Performance practice   The practical application of the knowledge of how a particular style or genre of music should be performed.

Perotin   Medieval period composer noted for the writing of organum.

Philharmonic   A philanthropic group organized for the purpose of promoting and financially supporting an orchestral organization. Became popular in nineteenth-century Europe as well as in the United States. Many orchestras originally funded by such a group continue to use the term in their name, such as the New York Philharmonic.

Piano   A string instrument that is played in a percussive manner by employing a series of hammers inside the body of the instrument that hit the strings to produce sound.

Piccolo Trumpet   A smaller and extremely high-pitched version of the trumpet common in music from the 17th and early 18th centuries.

Pie Jesu   "Merciful Lord Jesus . . .," a traditional Roman Catholic Church text asking Jesus to grant eternal rest to the souls of the departed. This text is sometimes included in requiem masses.

Pitch   The relative highness or lowness of a musical sound based on the frequency of vibration.

Polyphonic   A kind of texture that consists of two or more melodic lines.

Polyphony   A polyphonic texture.

Polyrhythmic   Music that contains two or more rhythmic meters occurring simultaneously.

Ponticello   A performance technique unique to bowed stringed instruments where the bow is placed extremely close to the bridge resulting in squeaky, scratchy sounds, and a tone lacking in fundamentals.

Pop music   Popular music.

Popular music   Any kind of music written primarily for mass consumption through the selling of sheet music or recordings.

Popular song   Songs written for the purpose of mass consumption by the general public.

Prelude   A piece of music that precedes another piece of music, such as the introduction to an act of an opera.

Prelude   A short, improvisatory-sounding keyboard composition sometimes paired with a highly-structured work such as a fugue.

Prima ballerina   In ballet, the lead female dancer.

Primitivism   Twentieth-century musical style associated with harsh unresolved dissonance, unpredictable but strong rhythmic qualities, and short motivic melodies. Used to describe the style of *The Rite of Spring*.

Program music   Term used to describe music, usually instrumental music, that represents something extra-musical such as a story, a place, an idea, or an emotion.

Programmatic   Term used to describe music, usually instrumental music, that represents something extra-musical such as a story, a place, an idea, or an emotion.

Proper   Texts appropriate for specific masses such as the texts commonly included in requiem masses.

Protestant Reformation   Sixteenth-century attempt, lead by Martin Luther, to reform corrupt practices within the Catholic Church which resulted in the establishment of other Christian denominations such as Lutheranism.

Psalms   Ancient Biblical songs, poems, or chants of praise.

Publisher   A person or company that prints and sells sheet music.

Publishing house   A company that purchases the rights from a composer or his heirs to print, distribute, and sell his music.

Punk rock   Style of rock music from the 1970s characterized by a primitive, bare-bones sound that was devoid of musical sophistication.

Q

Quadruple meter   Type of meter with four beats to a bar.

Quarter notes   Notes that usually receive one beat each.

Question and answer melodies   Classical period melodic ideal in which a melody consists of two equal parts, the first ascending, the second descending.

R

R&B   Rhythm and blues.

Raga   In Indian music a raga is an improvisatory piece of music based on a series of pitches, similar to, but much more complex than a simple scale, from which melodies are derived. Ragas are remnants of ancient Vedic melodic chants.

Ragtime   A style of music in the late nineteenth and early twentieth century in the United States, primarily for piano, incorporating syncopated rhythms as a prominent characteristic.

Rap music   Vocal component of hip hop culture where spoken rhyming lyrics are rhythmically enunciated over a percussive accompaniment.

Ratchet   Non-pitched percussion instrument that makes a continuous, clicking sound.

Rebec   Forerunner of the modern violin.

Recapitulation The section near the end of a movement in sonata form where both of the two main themes are restated in the tonic key.

Recital A music concert that features one performer with piano or small-ensemble accompaniment.

Recitative A vocal piece that follows closely the inflections of the text, changing dramatically in mood, tempo, and dynamics. Common in operas, oratorios, and cantatas.

Reel A Celtic set dance for four couples.

Renaissance Historical period of music dating from 1450–1600.

Repertoire The combined body of work in a particular genre or the group of compositions prepared for performance by an individual performer.

Repertory The combined body of work in a particular genre or the group of compositions prepared for performance by an individual performer.

Repetition and Contrast The two considerations that need to be balanced by the formal structure of a composition.

Requiem A mass for the dead.

Requiem Aeternam (Introit) "Eternal rest grant unto them, Oh Lord . . .," a traditional Roman Catholic Church text asking that the departed soul be granted eternal rest. This text is frequently used as the first movement in requiem masses.

Responsorial singing Style of singing common in much world music and church music in which a group of singers responds to something sung by a solo singer.

Revue A type of stage production common during the early twentieth century on Broadway consisting of songs, dances, comedy skits, and other acts centered around a unifying theme.

Rhapsody A free-form composition of an effusive nature often with some nationalistic connotation.

Rhythm The element of music that animates it, gives it a feeling of moving through time. Contains the pulse, beat of the music, and the various emphases associated with it such as meter and syncopation.

Ricercar A Renaissance period instrumental composition usually employing imitative polyphony.

Ripieno In a concerto grosso, the full complement of performers including orchestra, soloists, and basso continuo.

Ritardando To gradually slow down the tempo in a piece of music.

Ritornello form A Baroque period single-movement form consisting of repeated sections of music containing the main melody interspersed with contrasting sections with different melodic material.

Rock and roll A style of popular music that developed in the 1950s employing amplified instruments, simple chords and forms, and a rhythmic backbeat.

Romantic Historical period of music dating from 1825–1900.

Rondo form A Classical period single-movement form consisting of repeated sections of music containing the main melody interspersed with contrasting sections with different melodic material.

Royalties Fees paid to the holder of a copyright on a musical composition or other intellectual property.

Rubato A very flexible approach to the rhythmic element of music characterized by speeding up and slowing down of the tempo. Common in Romantic period piano music.

S

Sacred Music that is religious in nature.

Saltarello A fast-paced Italian dance in triple meter felt in one.

Sampling The process of converting analog sounds into digital data that can be downloaded into, and reproduced by, electronic instruments such as synthesizers.

Sarabanda A Spanish dance in a slow 3/4 time.

Saxophone A single-reed woodwind instrument made out of brass but using a single-reed mouthpiece similar to the clarinet.

Scale A series of pitches in ascending or descending order that is used as the basis of a musical piece.

Scat singing Improvisation in jazz songs by a vocalist.

Score The written notation of a piece of music, including all of the individual instrumental and/or vocal parts. Also refers to the music that accompanies a film.

Sea chantey A type of folk song associated with seafaring work.

Secular Music not of a religious nature.

Segue(s) A seamless transition from one piece of music, or part of a piece of music, to another.

Sequence A type of poetic Medieval chant of the Roman Catholic Church. The sequence written by Thomas of Celano, ca. 1200, has often been used in requiem masses.

Serialism A twentieth-century compositional style first applied to the melodic element of music, and later applied to other elements as well, that organized pitches in a random sounding "series" instead of the traditional scale, resulting in very dissonant music.

Set dance A type of dance that employs groups of couples performing sets of dance moves. The reel and the square dance are types of set dances.

Sheet music Printed music for a song intended for sale to the general public.

Sitar An Indian plucked, stringed instrument with two sets of strings, one melodic and another resonating set that provides an unchanging "harmonic" background drone. The "frets" under the melodic strings are raised off of the neck of the instrument in a curved shape which produces a unique twangy, metallic timbre.

Slendro A five-note Balinese scale. The tones don't match the divisions of the octave common in Western music resulting in an out-of-tune sound to Western ears.

Solo Instrumental Dance Suite   Genre of music popular in the Baroque period employing stylized versions of popular dances of the time.

Sonata   An instrumental genre of the Baroque period onward for one instrument with a complementary piano part or for a solo piano.

Sonata form   Single-movement form of the Classical period onward based on thematic development within a prescribed sequence of changing tonal episodes. Consists of three main sections: exposition, development, and recapitulation.

Song cycle   A groups of songs centered around a common theme.

Soprano   The higher-register female voice.

Soul music   A type of music derived from R&B and popular in the 1960s and 1970s.

Source music   Music that comes from something that you actually see on the screen such as a band, a radio, or some other thing that you would normally expect to make music.

Spiritual   A type of song developed in the black slave culture of the American south, often based on biblical stories and expressing hope of deliverance from bondage.

Square dance   Type of set dance for four couples that found exceptional popularity in the United States. A unique feature of this dance is the inclusion of a "caller" who calls out the next set of dance steps throughout the dance.

Stabat Mater   Fourteenth-century hymn dealing with the sorrow of Mary at the crucifixion of Jesus. The text became the basis of many later compositions of the same name.

Staccato   Short and separated as in musical notes played in that manner.

Stanza   A section of a musical composition characterized by a particular melody.

Step dance   A type of Celtic dance emphasizing the lower body with the movements of the upper body and hands deemphasized.

String Quartet   The standard performing ensemble for the stringed instruments, which consists of two violins, a viola, and a cello. There is no bass in a string quartet.

Strophic form   A song form based on verses of text sung to the same music or verses and choruses.

Stylized   Refers to an adaptation of dance music for concert performances through modification of rhythmic elements and performance considerations such as the sequence of dances, inclusion of non-dance movements, and the location of the performance.

Subdominant   A tonal center based on the fourth note of the scale.

Subject   The main theme in a fugue.

Suite   A collection of dance movements played as a unified composition.

Supertitles   A system of projecting the text of an opera on a narrow screen above the stage. Also called surtitles.

Surtitles   A system of projecting the text of an opera on a narrow screen above the stage. Also called supertitles.

Swing   Type of popular jazz-influenced music of the late 1930s and 1940s for a large ensemble consisting of a rhythm section plus sections of trumpets, trombones, and saxophones. Also called "big band" music.

Symphonic poem   Also known as a Tone Poem. A single-movement orchestral composition that is programmatic.

Symphony   An orchestral composition usually in four movements employing significant thematic development and a unified approach to the entire composition.

Synchronized sound   Term used to describe the first successful incorporation of sound into films whereby the sounds were synchronized to the timing of the film.

Syncopated   Rhythmic quality where the emphasis is placed on unexpected beats or off beats.

Synthesizer   An electronic instrument that often uses a keyboard similar to a piano, which produces sound based on digitally stored and manipulated files. These sounds can either be recreated sounds of acoustic instruments or new sounds created by digitally manipulating the stored files.

T

Tabla   An Indian percussion instrument, similar in appearance to, but larger than, a set of bongos.

Tala   The rhythmic element in Indian music.

Tabor   A Medieval period percussion instrument.

Tamboura   An Indian stringed instrument, usually having three strings, that does not play any melodic notes, just a drone harmony in the background to the sitar.

Tarantella   A fast-paced Italian dance in 6/8 time. The dance is based on the legend of the need for continuously faster movement of the people bitten by the tarantula spider in Taranto, Italy in the sixteenth century.

Tempo   The speed of the music.

Tenor   The higher-register male voice.

Ternary form   Refers to any piece with an overall three-part structure. Also known as three-part form or A-B-A form.

Terraced dynamics   Baroque period dynamic ideal in which the volume level changes abruptly rather than gradually.

Texture   The relative melodic complexity of the music usually based on how many or few melodic ideas are prominent.

Thematic development   The compositional process whereby melodies are changed in any number of ways in order to explore the variety of interest inherent in them. Common in the Classical period, especially in movements in sonata form.

Theme   A melodic idea used as the basis of a musical composition.

Theme and variations   Single-movement form consisting of a theme followed by a series of variations based on that theme.

Theremin   Early electronic instrument named after its inventor Léon Theremin.

Three-part form   Refers to any piece with an overall three-part structure. Also known as ternary form or A-B-A form.

Threnody　A "song of lamentation" or a "song of mourning."

Through composed　A song form that really has no form but rather unfolds in an unpredictable manner as the story of the song is told.

Timbral　Refers to the aspect of music involving timbre, or tone color.

Timbre　The "tone color" of a musical sound. The distinct quality of sound that differentiates one instrument or voice from another.

Time signature　The indicator of the meter of a piece of music, usually expressed as a fraction, such as 2/4, 3/4, 4/4, or 6/8, at the beginning of a piece of music.

Tin Pan Alley　Name given to a group of publishing companies that were based in and around W. 28th St. in New York City from the late nineteenth century until about 1940.

Toccata　A free-form improvisatory-sounding keyboard genre of the Baroque period, usually paired with a fugue.

Tonal center　A pitch around which scales and resultant harmonies are derived.

Tonality　Refers to music based on tonal centers.

Tone clusters　Close spaced groupings of pitches that create an extremely dissonant sound in some twentieth-century compositions. Used as an alternative to traditional harmony.

Tone color　The element of music regarding the quality, or distinctiveness of sound.

Tone poem　Also known as a symphonic poem. A single-movement orchestral composition that is programmatic.

Tone row　In serial music, the ordering of the 12 pitches within an octave in order to create a kind of scale that can be manipulated by a composer in a fairly traditional manner.

Tonic　In tonal music, the first pitch of a scale and the chord based on that pitch.

Total serialism　Twentieth-century compositional style that extended Schoenberg's concept of serialism to all aspects of the music such as the rhythm, tone, color, and form.

Transition　In a sonata form movement, a section that "bridges" one part of the movement to the next, especially common between the statements of the two themes in the exposition, and between the development and the recapitulation.

Triangle　Non-pitched, metallic, triangular-shaped percussion instrument played by hitting it with a small metal rod.

Trill　A Baroque period melodic ornament executed by a rapid alternation between the printed pitch and the next highest note in the scale.

Trio　A section in a musical composition characterized by a contrasting mood and melody, usually softer, smoother, and calmer than the music that preceded it.

Trio sonata　A four-movement Baroque period instrumental genre for two high-pitched instruments such as the violin or the flute with basso continuo. Developed by the Italian composer Arcangelo Corelli.

Triple meter　Meter with three beats in each measure.

Trombone　This brass instrument is larger and lower pitched than the trumpet and French horn and does not use valves to change notes like the other brass instruments. Instead, it uses a movable slide to change the length of the tubing, and thereby the pitch.

Troubadours　Noblemen from southern France who wrote poetry and sang during the Medieval period.

Trouveres　Noblemen from northern France who wrote poetry and sang during the Medieval period.

Trumpet　This is the smallest and therefore the highest-pitched instrument in the brass family.

Tuba　The tuba is the largest and lowest-pitched brass instrument.

Turn　A Baroque period melodic ornament executed by playing the printed pitch and then, in rapid succession, the next highest pitch, the printed pitch, the next lowest pitch, finally returning to the printed pitch.

Tutti　Section in a concerto grosso movement in ritornello form when all the performing forces are playing. Also called the ripieno.

Tuvan throat singing　A type of vocalization, from the Republic of Tuva, that produces two pitches simultaneously. Also known as multiphonics.

Twelve-bar blues　Song form associated with the blues consisting of twelve bars (measures) of a specific chord progression utilizing just three chords.

1234	**2**234	**3**234	**4**234	**5**234	**6**234
/ / / /	/ / / /	/ / / /	/ / / /	/ / / /	/ / / /
I	(IV)	(I)		IV	

7234	**8**234	**9**234	**10**234	**11**234	**12**234
/ / / /	/ / / /	/ / / /	/ / / /	/ / / /	/ / / /
I		V	IV	I	I(V)

Twelve-tone music　Compositional style developed by early twentieth-century composer Arnold Schoenberg in an attempt to find compositional techniques equivalent to traditional tonal music while retaining the element of atonality.

Twentieth/Twenty-First Century　Historical period of music dating from 1900–the present.

Tympani　Large, tunable, kettle drums.

U

Unison　The singing or playing of a melodic line by two or more voices.

Unresolved dissonance　A dissonant harmony that is not followed by a consonant harmony, resulting in an extended feeling of unsettledness and unrest. Common in twentieth-century music.

Urban folk　A type of music popular in the 1960s and 1970s consisting of traditional folk songs in updated versions and new songs dealing with protesting of the Vietnam War and songs of social commentary.

V

Vaudeville   A type of stage production common during the early twentieth century on Broadway consisting of songs, dances, comedy skits, and other acts without a unifying theme.

Vedas   Religious texts of the ancient Vedic culture of India dating from between 1500–500 BC.

Vedic   Refers to the ancient culture of India from 1500–500 BC.

Verismo   A late nineteenth-century Italian literary style adapted to operatic writing based on everyday people in real-life situations often emphasizing passion and violence.

Verse   Part of a song that uses the same music with different words each time it is sung. Also called a stanza.

Viola   A bowed string instrument that is a slightly larger, and lower-pitched version of the violin.

Violin   The smallest and highest pitched of the bowed string instruments, which is held under the chin while it is played.

Virtuosity   Extraordinary performing ability of either an instrumentalist or a singer.

W

Walt Disney Studios   Movie studio that became known for its full-length animated films with a strong musical content, such as *Fantasia*.

Waltz   A type of dance in 3/4 time popularized in and around Vienna, Austria in the early nineteenth century. The name is derived from the German word "waltzen," which means to turn.

Warner Brothers   Movie studio that became known for its cartoon shorts featuring characters such as Bugs Bunny, Daffy Duck, etc.

Western swing   A type of country music characterized by an upbeat, easy going feel.

Woodwind Quintet   The standard performing ensemble for the woodwind family, consisting of one flute, one oboe, one clarinet, one bassoon, and a member borrowed from the brass family, the French horn.

Work song   A type of folk song sung by laborers while they worked.

X

Xylophone   A pitched percussion instrument made of different-sized metallic blocks played with mallets.

Glossary of Key People and Compositions

1812 Overture A concert overture premiered in 1882 by Russian composer Peter Ilyich Tchaikovsky in commemoration of Napoleon's retreat from Russia.

A

A Midsummer Night's Dream Incidental music to the Shakespeare play written in 1842 by Felix Mendelssohn.

Adagio for Strings The name of a composition by twentieth-century American composer Samuel Barber. Due to its poignant nature it is often played at memorial services for the deceased.

Adams, John b. 1947. American composer often associated with the minimalist style.

Alexander Nevsky 1939 Russian propaganda film directed by Sergei Eisenstein with music by Sergei Prokofiev. Noted for being the first film with a true melding of music and images.

Anastasio, Trey b. 1964. Guitarist, composer, and "leader" of the popular "jam band" Phish.

Appalachian Spring One of the American-themed ballets by Aaron Copland about a simple Shaker religious sect in the Appalachian mountains.

Arlen, Harold 1905–1986. Composer of *Somewhere, Over the Rainbow* from the movie *The Wizard of Oz*.

Armstrong, Louis 1901–1971. American cornet and trumpet player instrumental in the development and popularization of jazz.

Auld Lang Syne Scottish song, words attributed to Robert Burns, usually sung on New Year's Eve.

B

Bach, Johann Sebastian 1685–1750. Baroque period German composer. Especially noted for his command of writing in a highly polyphonic style and for his cantatas, suites, passions, concertos, and concerto grossos.

Balakirev, Mili 1837–1910. Russian nationalist composer. One of "The Five."

Balakrishnan, David Contemporary American composer and violinist with the Turtle Island String Quartet known for his compositions incorporating both jazz and Indian improvisatory elements.

Barber, Samuel 1910–1981. Twentieth-century American composer whose music combined Romantic era lyrical qualities with judicious use of dissonance and rhythmic complexity. His style is often referred to as neoromantic.

Barron, Louis and Bebe Composers who created the completely electronic score to the 1956 sci-fi movie *Forbidden Planet*.

Barry, John b. 1933. Prolific composer of film music who created the distinctive sound of the scores to the James Bond movies.

Bartok, Béla 1881–1945. Twentieth-century Hungarian composer who incorporated folk tunes and rhythms into his compositions.

Beatles, The One of the iconic English rock and roll bands prominent from the early 1960s to the 1970s.

Beethoven, Ludwig van 1770–1827. Classical period German composer who is regarded as the bridge figure to the Romantic period. Beethoven's music, while based on the formal structures of the Classical period, has an emotional and dramatic quality more in tune with the Romantic period.

Benjamin, Arthur 1893–1960. Composer who wrote *The Storm Cloud Cantata* for Alfred Hitchcock's film *The Man Who Knew Too Much*.

Berlin, Irving 1888–1989 (Really!). Popular songwriter of such hits as *White Christmas, Easter Parade, Blue Skies*, and *Puttin' on the Ritz*. Many of his songs were brought to prominence by being featured in movies.

Berlioz, Hector 1803–1869. Romantic period French composer, conductor, and music critic. His compositions were often very large in scope and employed unique instrumental combinations.

Bernstein, Elmer 1922–2004. Composer of the scores to such varied films as *The Ten Commandments, The Magnificent Seven, The Blues Brothers*, and *Ghostbusters*.

Bernstein, Leonard 1918–1990. American composer and Conductor/Music Director of the New York Philharmonic Orchestra. Wrote compositions in both the edgy classical style of the twentieth century and in a more popular vein for musical theatre, such as in *West Side Story*.

Bethune, Conon de ca. 1160–1220. French nobleman, poet, and musician.

Birth of a Nation One of the first, 1915, feature-length movies to feature a complete musical score.

Bizet, Georges 1838–1875. Nineteenth-century French composer. Known for the opera *Carmen* and the incidental music to *L'Arlésienne*.

Blue Man Group Innovative stage troupe presenting a modern version of vaudeville to rock music.

Bolcom, William b. 1938. American composer of operas, symphonies, concertos, and sonatas.

Borodin, Alexander 1833–1887. Russian nationalist composer. One of "The Five."

Boulez, Pierre b. 1925. Twentieth-century French composer and conductor noted for his writing utilizing total serialism.

Brahms, Johannes 1833–1897. Romantic period German composer whose music emphasized the compositional concepts of the Classical period, such as thematic development and adherence to traditional forms, while sounding thoroughly Romantic in regard to the lyrical quality of the melody and thickness of orchestration.

Britten, Benjamin 1913–1976. Twentieth-century English composer most noted for *The Young Person's Guide to the Orchestra* and the *War Requiem*.

Brubeck, Dave 1920–2012. Jazz pianist prominent in the "cool jazz" style.

Burns, Robert 1759–1796. Scottish poet to whom the lyrics of *Auld Lang Syne* are attributed.

C

Cage, John 1912–1992. Avant-garde twentieth-century composer noted for incorporating aleatoric (chance) qualities into his works.

Carmen An opera composed by French composer Georges Bizet (1838–1875).

Carmen Jones An adaptation of Georges Bizet's opera *Carmen*, first for the Broadway stage and then for film, featuring an all-black cast and set in the southern United States.

Celtic Woman 2004 stage show featuring Celtic songs and fiddling performed by an all-female lead cast.

Chopin, Frederic 1810–1847. Romantic period Polish composer known primarily for music for the piano. He invented or redesigned many small-scale genres for the instrument including the etude, prelude, nocturne, mazurka, polonaisse, and ballade.

Cirque du Soleil Extraordinarily successful stage presentation featuring gymnastics-inspired movement, fantastic settings, and a world music inspired musical score. Conceived by Canadians Guy Laliberté and Daniel Gauthier.

Clapton, Eric b. 1945. Popular English guitarist and singer associated with the resurgence of interest in blues-based rock and roll.

Cohan, George M. 1878–1942. Tin Pan Alley composer of *I'm a Yankee Doodle Dandy, Give My Regards to Broadway*, among other hits. His life story was told in the movie *I'm a Yankee Doodle Dandy*.

Coltrane, John 1926–1967. Jazz saxophonist prominent in modal jazz.

Concerto Suite for Electric Guitar and Orchestra Crossover composition by Yngwie Malmsteen with David Rosenthal.

Copland, Aaron 1900–1990. American composer especially noted for establishing a recognizably American style of music and for his ballet music based on American themes.

Coppola, Francis Ford b. 1939. American movie director noted for the creative use of music in his films.

Corelli, Arcangelo 1653–1713. Baroque period Italian composer noted for developing violin performance technique and the developing of the concerto grosso, sonata, and trio sonata forms of that time.

Cowell, Henry 1897–1965. Twentieth-century American composer.

Cream A three-man band, popular in the 1960s, consisting of a guitar, bass, and drums, whose music was an homage to the blues-based foundation of rock and roll.

Cui, Cesar 1835–1918. Russian nationalist composer and music critic. One of "The Five."

D

Davis, Miles 1926–1991. Jazz trumpeter prominent in the "cool jazz" style, fusion, and modal jazz.

Day the Earth Stood Still Sci-fi movie from 1951, with a musical score by Bernard Herrmann, that included an electronic instrument called the theremin.

Debussy, Claude 1862–1918. French impressionist composer noted for his ballets, orchestral works, and chamber music.

des Prez, Josquin ca. 1440–1521. Renaissance period Flemish composer of liturgical music, most known for the writing of masses and motets.

Diaghilev, Serge 1872–1929. Impresario and manager of Paris' Ballet Russes. Diaghilev was instrumental in fostering collaborations among composers, choreographers, and writers of his time, especially in the creation of new forms of ballet.

Duke, George b. 1946. Contemporary American composer, pianist, and record producer whose compositions have incorporated improvisatory jazz elements into otherwise fully composed works.

Dupéré, René French-Canadian composer known for his music for Cirque du Soleil including the shows *Alegria, Mystere,* and *KA*.

Duruflé, Maurice 1902–1986. Twentieth-century French composer most noted for his writing of a requiem mass.

Dvořák, Antonin 1841–1904. Czech composer noted for his symphonies and Slavonic nationalist dances.

E

Eisenstein, Sergei 1878–1948. Russian film director whose ideas on the indispensable role of music in film were revolutionary and influential on subsequent film directors and composers.

Ellisor, Conni b. 1957. American composer, arranger, and violinist noted for combining folk styles with traditional classical writing.

F

Fauré, Gabriel 1845–1924. Romantic period French composer of primarily small-scale works but most noted for his *Requiem in D minor*. This work, by eliminating the Dies Irae and Tuba Mirum texts, has a more tranquil and reassuring demeanor than most other requiems.

Forbidden Planet 1956 sci-fi movie that featured an all-electronic score by Louis and Bebe Barron.

Ford, Henry Inventor of the automobile who was a great supporter of square dancing.

Foster, Stephen 1826–1864. American composer of popular songs.

Franck, Cesar 1822–1890. Belgian composer who spent most of his life in France.

G

Gabrieli, Giovanni 1548–1613. Italian Renaissance period composer noted for composing in an antiphonal style.

Garcia, Jerry 1942–1995. Guitarist and "leader" of the popular "jam band" the Grateful Dead.

Gauthier, Daniel Along with Guy Laliberté, one of the creators of Cirque du Soleil.

Gershwin, George 1898–1937. Twentieth-century American composer noted for the blending of jazz and classical styles.

Getz, Stan 1927–1991. Jazz saxophonist prominent in the "cool jazz" style.

Gilbert and Sullivan Late nineteenth-century English operetta (light opera) writing team of William Gilbert and Arthur Sullivan.

Gillespie, Dizzy 1917–1993. Jazz trumpeter and one of the influential composer/performers in the bebop style.

Glass, Philip b. 1937. Contemporary, American, minimalist composer. The most successful composer using minimalist techniques having written in many genres including music for movie scores, operas, symphonies, etc.

God Save The Tsar Russian national anthem from 1833–1917 written by Alexei Lvov. Featured prominently in Tchaikovsky's *1812 Overture*.

Goethe, Johann Wolfgang von 1748–1832. German poet.

Gogol, Nicolai 1809–1852. Russian author whose work, *St. John's Night on the Bald Mountain*, was the basis of Mussorgsky's tone poem *Night on Bald Mountain*.

Goldman, Matt Along with Phil Stanton and Chris Wink, one of the founders of Blue Man Group.

Goldsmith, Jerry 1929–2004. Best known for writing the music for five of the *Star Trek* series of films, *Planet of the Apes, The Omen, Alien*, and *Poltergeist*.

Grande Messe des morts Requiem The name of the requiem mass composed by Hector Berlioz.

Grateful Dead Popular "jam band" that performed from 1965–1995 and specialized in extended improvisations.

Gregorian Chant Medieval period, sacred, monophonic, vocal music of the Catholic Church.

Grieg, Edvard 1843–1907. Norwegian composer of nationalistic music.

H

Handel, George Frideric 1685–1759. German-born composer who worked primarily in England. Best known today for his oratorios, operas, and dance suites, particularly the *Water Music* and *The Music for the Royal Fireworks*.

Hava Nagila A popular traditional Jewish dance music composition.

Haydn, Franz Joseph 1732–1809. Classical period composer frequently said to be "The Father of the Symphony" for his contributions to that genre. The court composer to the Esterhazy family for over 30 years, Haydn was one of the most influential composers of his time.

Herrmann, Bernard 1911–1975. Film composer best known for collaborations with Alfred Hitchcock on the movies *Vertigo, North by Northwest*, and *Psycho* and also *Citizen Kane* in 1941 directed by Orson Welles.

Hildegard of Bingen 1098–1179. Abbess of the convent at Rupertsburg near Bingen, Germany, and a prolific composer and writer.

Hill, Mildred and Patti Sisters who wrote "Happy Birthday."

Hitchcock, Alfred 1899–1980. Film director of many suspense films including *Vertigo, North by Northwest*, and *Psycho*.

Hovhannes, Alan 1911–2000. American composer whose works were greatly influenced by non-Western musical concepts.

Hupfield, Herman 1894–1951. Composer of the song *As Time Goes By* which became famous when it played a prominent role in the movie *Casablanca* starring Humphrey Bogart and Ingrid Bergman.

I

Italian Symphony The subtitle of the *Symphony #4* by Felix Mendelssohn, inspired by the music he heard on a trip to Italy in 1829.

Ivanov, Lev Co-choreographer of *Swan Lake*. Originally Marius Petipa's assistant.

J

Jolson, Al 1886–1950. Popular stage entertainer of the 1920s and 1930s who starred in the first feature-length "talkie" movie, *The Jazz Singer*.

Jutras, Benoit Canadian composer known for his music for Cirque du Soleil including the shows *"O," Quidam*, and *La Nouba*.

K

Key, Francis Scott 1779–1843. American lawyer known for penning the words to "The Star Spangled Banner" upon seeing the American flag still flying over Fort McHenry in Baltimore after a 25-hour bombardment by the British.

Kindertotenlieder "Songs on the Death of Children," the name of a song cycle by Gustav Mahler based on poems by Friedrich Rückert.

Kol Nidre An ancient Jewish prayer of atonement, usually sung on the holiest day of the Jewish year, Yom Kippur.

Korngold, Erich Wolfgang 1897–1957. Prominent early film composer, he was one of the figures who established the practice of employing the Romantic period orchestral style in films.

Kubrick, Stanley 1928–1999. Prominent film director who employed music in creative ways in his films including classical compositions re-interpreted through electronic media.

L

Laliberté, Guy b. 1959. Along with Daniel Gauthier, one of the creators of Cirque du Soleil.

La Marseillaise The French national anthem featured prominently in Tchaikovsky's *1812 Overture*.

La Sylphide The first full-length ballet.

Leoncavallo, Ruggiero 1858–1919. Italian composer of operas, such as *Pagliacci*, in the verismo style.

Leone, Sergio Film director noted for his "Spaghetti Westerns" including *For a Fistful of Dollars, For a Few Dollars More*, and *The Good, The Bad, and The Ugly*.

Leonin ca. 1163–1190. Medieval composer noted for organum.

Lerner and Loewe Frederick Lerner and Alan Jay Loewe, a musical songwriting team who wrote *My Fair Lady*.

Liszt, Franz 1811–1886. Virtuoso pianist of the Romantic period and the composer generally credited with the invention of the tone (symphonic) poem.

Lohengrin An opera by Romantic period German composer Richard Wagner based on the old Germanic legend of the Swan Knight. The opening of Act III features the melody that would eventually become *Here Comes the Bride*.

Lovett, Benjamin Dancing master who worked with Henry Ford in popularizing the square dance.

Lucas, George b. 1944. Director of the *Star Wars* films and frequent collaborator with the film composer John Williams.

M

Machaut, Guillaume de 1300–1377. Medieval composer noted for his masses and motets.

Mahler, Gustav 1860–1911. Austrian Romantic composer known for the writing of symphonies and song cycles with orchestral accompaniment.

Mallarmé, Stéphane 1842–1898. French symbolist poet and author of *L'Après-midi d'un faun* (*The Afternoon of a Faun*) upon which Claude Debussy based his famous tone poem of the same name.

Malmsteen, Yngwie b. 1963. Swedish guitarist and composer.

Manzoni Requiem A name frequently used for the requiem mass written by Giuseppe Verdi in memory of Alessandro Manzoni, Italian poet, author, and friend of Verdi's.

Mendelssohn, Felix 1809–1847. Romantic period German composer noted for his orchestral music, oratorios, and incidental music and for reviving interest in the music of the Baroque composer Johann Sebastian Bach.

Messa da Requiem The name of the Requiem Mass written by Giuseppe Verdi.

Modern Jazz Quartet Jazz ensemble prominent in the "cool jazz" style.

Monet, Claude 1840–1926. French impressionist painter.

Monk, Thelonious 1917–1982. Jazz pianist prominent in the bebop style.

Monteverdi, Claudio 1567–1643. Baroque period composer noted for his operas.

Morricone, Ennio b. 1928. Composer known for the scores to "Spaghetti Westerns" in collaboration with director Sergio Leone. Also, for the score to *The Mission*.

Mouret, Jean Joseph 1682–1738. Baroque period French composer primarily known for his operas, sacred works, and fanfares.

Mozart, Wolfgang Amadeus 1756–1791. Classical period Austrian composer noted for his writing of operas, concertos, and symphonies. Especially noted for inventing the operatic sub-genre the dramma giocoso. Wrote an incomplete requiem mass that was completed by one of his students.

Music For The Royal Fireworks A large orchestral suite by Handel.

Mussorgsky, Modest 1839–1881. Romantic period Russian nationalist composer noted for his operas and tone poems. One of "The Five."

N

New World Symphony, The Commonly-used name for the *Symphony #9 in E minor*, by Antonin Dvořák.

Nijinsky, Vaclav 1890–1950. Early twentieth-century Russian choreographer, dancer, and protégé of Serge Diaghilev at the Ballet Russes. Choreographer of both *The Rite of Spring* and *The Afternoon of a Faun*.

Nirvana Alternative rock group prominent from the late 1980s to the mid-1990s.

Nixon, Marni b. 1930. Singer famous for frequently having her singing dubbed over the voice of the featured female stars in filmed adaptations of musicals.

O

Overture Solennelle (Solemn Overture) The original title of the *1812 Overture* by Tchaikovsky.

P

Palestrina, Giovanni Perluigi da 1525–1594. Renaissance period composer of sacred vocal works noted for the clarity of the text and the emotional impact his music evoked while writing in a highly polyphonic style.

Parker, Charlie 1920–1955. Jazz saxophonist prominent in the bebop style.

Pearl Jam Alternative rock band prominent from the early 1990s.

Penderecki, Krzysztof b. 1933. Twentieth-century Polish composer noted for non-traditional performance techniques on traditional instruments. Most noted for his memorial composition, *Threnody to the Victims of Hiroshima*.

Petipa, Marius Co-choreographer of *Swan Lake*.

Phish Popular "jam band" that performed between 1983 and 2004 and specialized in extended improvisatory compositions.

Presley, Elvis 1935–1977. Most successful rock and roll artist of the 1950s. Often referred to as "The King" of rock and roll.

Prokofiev, Sergei 1891–1953. Russian composer noted for his symphonies, film music, operas, and ballets as well as the children's piece, *Peter and the Wolf*.

Puccini, Giacomo 1858–1924. Italian Romantic period composer of operas. Known for the "verismo" style of realism in operatic writing in works such as *La Boheme*, *Tosca*, and *Madame Butterfly*.

Purcell, Henry 1659–1695. English composer of sacred and secular vocal works.

Q

Quantum of Solace The 2008 James Bond film directed by Marc Forster that features a pivotal scene using music as a key component.

R

Rachmaninoff, Sergei 1873–1943. Russian composer, in the Romantic style, of orchestral and piano works. Also noted as one of the great pianists of his time.

Ravel, Maurice 1875–1937. French composer associated with the impressionistic style, noted for his ballets, operas, and chamber music, also for orchestrating Mussorgsky's *Pictures at an Exhibition*.

Reich, Steve b. 1936. One of the pioneering twentieth-century composers in the minimalist style.

R.E.M. Alternative rock band prominent from the 1980s.

Requiem in D minor The name of the requiem mass written by Gabriel Fauré.

Riley, Terry b. 1935. One of the pioneering twentieth-century composers in the minimalist style.

Rimsky-Korsakov, Nicolai 1844–1908. Romantic period Russian nationalist composer. One of "The Five."

Rite of Spring, The A ballet composed by Igor Stravinsky. Noted as an example of musical Primitivism, the piece employs harsh dissonances, unpredictable and irregular rhythmic qualities, and short, motivic melodies.

Riverdance Irish dance-based production featuring songs from Ireland, Spain, and the U.S. Musical score by Bill Whelan.

Rodeo One of the American-themed ballets of Aaron Copland about a cowgirl and her search for love among the cowboys on a ranch.

Rodgers and Hammerstein Richard Rodgers and Oscar Hammerstein, a musical songwriting team. Wrote *The Sound of Music, Oklahoma, The King and I,* and *South Pacific.*

Rolling Stones, The Iconic English rock and roll band prominent from the mid-1960s to the present.

Rorem, Ned b. 1923. American composer noted especially for his songs.

Rossini, Gioacchino 1792–1868. Italian composer noted for his operas.

Rozsa, Miklos 1907–1995. Film composer known for epics such as *Quo Vadis?, Ben Hur,* and *King of Kings.*

Rubio, Jesús Nineteenth-century Mexican composer credited with creating the Mexican Hat Dance musical composition.

Rückert, Friedrich 1788–1866. German poet whose tragic poems, written upon the deaths of two of his children, were used by Gustav Mahler as the basis of his *Kindertotenlieder.*

Rutter, John b. 1945. English composer.

S

Schoenberg, Arnold 1874–1951. Austrian-born composer who developed both atonal and serial (twelve tone) compositional techniques.

Schönberg, Claude Michel b. 1944. French composer of the musical/opera *Les Misérables.*

Schubert, Franz 1797–1828. Austrian Classical/Romantic period composer known for the writing of art songs (lieder), symphonies, and chamber music.

Schuman, Robert 1810–1856. Romantic period composer noted for his symphonies, concertos, and chamber music.

Scott, Raymond 1908–1994. Bandleader and composer prominent in the 1930s whose music eventually was used extensively in Warner Brothers Studios cartoons.

Seeger, Pete b. 1919. American folk singer and political activist notable for the modern version of the song *We Shall Overcome* among others.

Shaw, Lloyd Colorado school superintendent who helped popularize the square dance throughout the western United States through writing books, holding summer classes, and generally being an advocate for the square dance.

Shore, Howard b. 1946. Composer of the music for the *Lord of the Rings* trilogy.

Shostakovich, Dmitri 1906–1975. Twentieth-century Russian composer noted for his symphonies, operas, chamber music, and concert overtures.

Smetana, Bedrich 1824–1884. Romantic period Bohemian composer noted for his tone poems and operas of a nationalistic nature.

Sousa, John Philip 1854–1932. American composer of military-band style marches.

Spielberg, Stephen b. 1946. Director of numerous hit movies such as *Jaws, E.T. The Extra-Terrestrial, Raiders of the Lost Ark,* and *Jurassic Park.* Collaborated with composer John Williams on the music for virtually all of his films.

Springsteen, Bruce b. 1949. American rock and folk singer/ songwriter. His version of *We Shall Overcome* became associated with the 9/11 attacks on America after it was used as the background music for a video compilation by *NBC News.*

Stalling, Carl 1892–1972. Known for his compositions and arrangements that accompanied Warner Brothers Studios cartoons.

Stanton, Phil Along with Chris Wink and Matt Goldman, one of the founders of Blue Man Group.

Steiner, Max 1888–1971. Composer of such film scores as *King Kong* (the original from 1933), *Gone with the Wind,* and *Casablanca.*

Still, William Grant 1895–1978. First prominent black American composer, noted for his symphonies, movie music, and songs.

Stokowski, Leopold 1882–1977. Conductor of the Philadelphia Orchestra. Noted for his collaboration with the Disney Studios in the creation of the animated feature film *Fantasia.*

Storm Cloud Cantata, The Musical composition by Arthur Benjamin that is the underpinning of the climactic scene in the film, *The Man Who Knew Too Much.*

Strauss II, Johann 1825–1899. Austrian composer known as "The Waltz King" for his many compositions in that genre and also for his operettas.

Strauss, Richard 1864–1949. German composer noted for his tone poems and operas.

Stravinsky, Igor 1882–1971. Russian-born composer who later resided in France and the United States and was very influential in the development of primitivism and neoclassicism. Composer of *The Rite of Spring,* one of the most influential musical compositions of the twentieth century, known for being an example of musical primitivism.

Suppé, Franz von 1819–1895. Romantic era composer of operettas and other staged musical compositions. Remembered mostly for two popular overtures, the *Light Cavalry Overture* and the *Poet and Peasant Overture,* both of which have been used prominently as cartoon music.

Süssmayr, Franz Xaver A student of Mozart's credited with completing his *Requiem Mass in D minor.*

Swan Lake A ballet, the music of which was written by Tchaikovsky, often considered the epitome of the full-length Romantic ballet.

T

Tchaikovsky, Peter Ilyich 1840–1893. Russian Romantic period composer known for his symphonies, ballet music, including *Swan Lake, Sleeping Beauty,* and *The Nutcracker,* and concert overtures such as the *1812 Overture* and *Romeo and Juliet.*

The Five A group of five Romantic period Russian nationalist composers, Mili Balakirev, Alexander Borodin, César Cui, Modest Mussorgsky, and Nicolai Rimsky-Korsakov, who favored creating a distinctly Russian style of composition.

The Jazz Singer The first feature-length film to incorporate synchronized songs and dialogue.

The Mighty Five See "The Five."

The Russian Five See "The Five."

The Star Spangled Banner The national anthem of the United States of America with words written by Francis Scott Key and music based on the melody of *To Anacreon in Heaven,* by British composer John Stafford Smith.

Three Tenors, The Stage show from 1990 featuring the voices of tenors Placido Domingo, Jose Carreras and Luciano Pavarotti.

Threnody to the Victims of Hiroshima A memorial composition written by Polish composer Krzysztof Penderecki that employs non-traditional performance techniques on traditional stringed instruments.

Tosca An opera composed by Giacomo Puccini that was featured in the 2008 James Bond film *Quantum of Solace.*

V

Vangelis b. 1943. Composer of electronic scores for the films *Chariots of Fire* and *Blade Runner.* Vangelis is the adopted name of Evangelos Odysseas Papathanassiou.

Varése, Edgard 1883–1965. Avant-garde French composer most noted for developing "musique concrete," music created by manipulating recorded real-world sounds in an electronic studio.

Verdi, Giuseppe 1813–1901. Romantic period Italian composer known primarily for his operas. His *Messa da Requiem,* also known as the *Manzoni Requiem,* is an operatically inspired requiem mass.

Vivaldi, Antonio 1678–1741. Baroque period Italian composer noted for his writing for stringed instruments.

W

Wagner, Richard 1813–1883. Romantic period German composer of operas.

Waltz King, The Johann Strauss II—1825–1899. Renowned composer of waltzes.

We Shall Overcome A protest song associated with labor struggles in the American south and the Civil Rights movement. The song has also become closely associated with the 9/11 attacks on the United States.

Webber, Andrew Lloyd b. 1948. Extraordinarily successful English composer most noted for the writing of musicals such as *Phantom of the Opera, Cats, Evita, Jesus Christ Superstar,* and *Joseph and the Amazing Technicolor Dreamcoat,* as well as a requiem mass.

Webern, Anton von 1883–1945. Early twentieth-century composer and follower of Arnold Schoenberg. Noted for "klangfarbenmelodie," tone color melody.

Whelan, Bill b. 1950. Irish composer of the music for *Riverdance.*

Williams, John b. 1932. American composer and conductor known primarily for the writing of movie music. Some of the movies he has written the scores for include: *Jaws, Close Encounters of the Third Kind, E.T. The Extra-Terrestrial, Jurassic Park, Star Wars, Indiana Jones, Home Alone,* and *Schindler's List.*

Wink, Chris Along with Phil Stanton and Matt Goldman, one of the founders of Blue Man Group.

Y

Young, La Monte b. 1935. One of the pioneering twentieth-century composers in the minimalist style.

Z

Zwilich, Ellen Taaffe b. 1939. Contemporary composer noted for "quotation music" and a neoclassical style.

Appendix

Erlkönig—Modern Translation

Original German

Wer reitet so spät durch Nacht und Wind?
Es ist der Vater mit seinem Kind;
Er hat den Knaben wohl in dem Arm,
Er faßt ihn sicher, er hält ihn warm.

"Mein Sohn, was birgst du so bang dein Gesicht?"
"Siehst, Vater, du den Erlkönig nicht?
Den Erlenkönig mit Kron und Schweif?"
"Mein Sohn, es ist ein Nebelstreif."

"Du liebes Kind, komm, geh mit mir!
Gar schöne Spiele spiel' ich mit dir;
Manch' bunte Blumen sind an dem Strand,
Meine Mutter hat manch gülden Gewand."

"Mein Vater, mein Vater, und hörest du nicht,
Was Erlenkönig mir leise verspricht?"
"Sei ruhig, bleibe ruhig, mein Kind;
In dürren Blättern säuselt der Wind."

"Willst, feiner Knabe, du mit mir gehen?
Meine Töchter sollen dich warten schön;
Meine Töchter führen den nächtlichen Reihn,
Und wiegen und tanzen und singen dich ein."

"Mein Vater, mein Vater, und siehst du nicht dort
Erlkönigs Töchter am düstern Ort?"
"Mein Sohn, mein Sohn, ich seh es genau:
Es scheinen die alten Weiden so grau."

"Ich liebe dich, mich reizt deine schöne Gestalt;
Und bist du nicht willig, so brauch ich Gewalt."
"Mein Vater, mein Vater, jetzt faßt er mich an!
Erlkönig hat mir ein Leids getan!"

Dem Vater grauset's, er reitet geschwind,
Er hält in Armen das ächzende Kind,
Erreicht den Hof mit Müh' und Not;
In seinen Armen das Kind war tot.

Literal Translation

Who rides, so late, through night and wind?
It is the father with his child.
He has the boy well in his arm
He holds him safely, he keeps him warm.

"My son, why do you hide your face so anxiously?"
"Father, do you not see the Erl king?
The Erl king with crown and tail?"
"My son, it's a wisp of fog."

"You dear child, come, go with me!
Very lovely games I'll play with you;
Many colourful flowers are on the shore,
My mother has many golden robes."

"My father, my father, and don't you hear
What Erl king quietly promises me?"
"Be calm, stay calm, my child;
The wind is rustling through withered leaves."

"Do you want to come with me, pretty boy?
My daughters shall wait on you finely;
My daughters will lead the nightly dance,
And rock and dance and sing you to sleep."

"My father, my father, and don't you see there
Erl king's daughters in the gloomy place?"
"My son, my son, I see it clearly:
There shimmer the old willows so grey."

"I love you, your beautiful form entices me;
And if you're not willing, then I need force."
"My father, my father, he's grabbing me now!
Erl king has done me some harm!"

It horrifies the father; he swiftly rides on,
He holds the moaning child in his arms,
Reaches the farm with trouble and hardship;
In his arms, the child was dead.

Index of Key Terms

NOTE: Page numbers in **bold** refer to definitions in text.

A-B-A form, 5, 95, 214
a cappella, **9**
absolute music, **213**
accordion, 207
adagio for strings, 164–166
African folk songs
    motif, **121**
    responsorial singing, 121
Afro-American symphony, 235–236
airs, **95**
aleatoric music, **234**
Alexander Nevsky, 249–250
alternative rock, **145**–147
alto, 71
alto sax, 94
American ballet, 103–105
    intervals, **104**
    orchestrations, **104**
    rodeo, 104–105
American folk songs
    accompany work, 125–126
    born of slavery, 124–125
    inspired by war, 123–124
American square dance, 111
    caller, **111**
    fiddle, **111**
animated movies, 258–260
appoggiatura, **203**
Arabic improvisatory music, 286–287
arpeggiated, **120**
art songs, **118**–119, 127–134
    classical art song, 130–133
    crusades, **127**
    lieder, **128**
    lute, **128**
    lute songs, 127, **129**
    Medieval Troubadour song, 128–129
    motives, **130**
    orchestral accompaniment, 133–134
    rebecs, **128**
    Renaissance lute song, 129–130
    repertory, **127**
    romantic art song, 130–133

song cycle, **130**
strophic form, 130
through composed, 130
with orchestral accompaniment,
    133–134
asymmetrical meter, **80**
atonal music, **17**, 231
atonality, **231**
Auld Lang Syne, 177–178
avant-garde, 233–234
    aleatoric music, **234**
    musique concrete, **233**–234
    total serialism, **234**
avant-garde concert hall music
    aleatoric music, **234**
    musique concrete, **233**–234
    total serialism, **234**

backbeat, **140**
background music, **252**
Balinese gamelan music, 105–106
ballade, **223**
ballet music, **97**, 100–105
    asymmetrical, **103**
    Ballets Russes, 100
    concert performance, **103**
    dissonant, 102
    impresario, **102**
    Nijinsky, Vaclav, 102
    primitivism, **102**
    score, **100**
    staccato, **102**
    The Rite of Spring, 100–103
    unresolved dissonances, **102**
Ballets Russes, 100
band, 6
banjo, 287
baritone, 123
baritone sax, 94
Baroque dance suite, 92–93
    A-B-A form, **95**
    airs, **95**
    hornpipe, **95**

menuet, **95**
meter, 91
orchestral dance suite, 93–96
overture, **95**
stylized, **93**
syncopated, **95**
ternary form, **95**
three-part form, **95**
timbral, **95**
water music, 95
Baroque instrumental genres, 205–206
    concertino, **206**
    concerto grossos, **205**
    concertos, 205
    orchestral dance suites, **205**
    ripieno, **206**
    ritornello form, **206**
Baroque instruments, 204–205
Baroque period, 10–11, 30–34, 203–211
    bassadance, **92**
    "basso continuo", 10
    dancing master, 92
    galliard, **92**
    homophonic, **10**
    improvisation, **10**
    opera, **10**
    pavane, **92**
bass, 51, 123
    pizzicato, 51
bass clarinet, 94
bass fiddle, 51
bassadance, **92**
"basso continuo", 10
basso continuo, 205, 275
basso profundo, 123
bassoon, 94
beat, **4**
bebop, 279–280
bells, 183
big band, **279**
biopic, **256**, 256–258
Birth of a Nation, 246
Blue Man Group, 80

blue notes, **139**, 276
bluegrass, **144**
blues, **137**–138
   chord names, 138
   chord progression, **137**
   improvisation, 137
   twelve-bar blues, **137**
blues/rock, **143**–144
bop, **279**
bow string family
   bass, 51
   bass fiddle, 51
   cello, 51
   contra bass, 51
   double bass, 51
   viola, 51
   violin, 51
   violoncello, 51
bowed string family
   orchestra, 51
boy soprano, 123
brass family
   French horn, 159
   piccolo trumpet, 159
   trombone, 159
   trumpet, 159
   tuba, 159
Brass Quintet, 159
breakstrain, **184**
bridge, **119**
Buddhist monk dancing, 106–107

cadenza, **275**
call, response, **120**
caller, **111**
Camerata, **65**, 203
canzon, **9**
Carmen, 254–256
Carnatic, 285
cartoon shorts, **258**, 259–260
cartoons, 258–260
castrato, 123
celebration, inspiration,
   commemoration music, 175–200
celebratory music, 176–181
   Auld Lang Syne, 177–178
   Happy Birthday, 176–**177**
   Hava Nagila, 179
   Hora, **179**
   Jewish wedding music, 179–180
   klezmer, **179**–180
   mariachi band, **180**
   Mexican Hat Dance, 180
   rondo form, **178**–179, **214**
   theme, 178–179
   wedding march, 179

cello, 51
Celtic reels, 110–111
   hornpipe, 110
   jig, **110**
   square dance, **110**
   step dance, **110**
Celtic Woman, 81
chamber ensembles, 6
Chamber music, 202
characteristics of historical periods, 6–20
Chicago style jazz, 277
Chinese opera, 83
choir, 6
choral societies, **202**
chord names, 138
chord progressions, **137**, **139**
chordal, **120**
chords, **3**
chorus, 75, 118
Cirque de Soleil (Circus of Sun), 80
clarinet, 94
classical art song, 130–133
classical compositions in movies, 256
classical instrumental genres, 216–220
   concerto, 219
   Esterhazy, 217
   motive, **217**
   sonata, 219–220
   string quartet, 218
   symphony, 216
   theme, variations, **218**
   variations, **218**
classical music, **11**
classical opera, 66–67
classical period, 11, 211–216
   A-B-A form, 214
   absolute music, **213**
   Age of Enlightenment, 215
   Age of Reason, 215
   characteristics, 211–216
   classical music, **11**
   closing, **216**
   coda, **216**
   concertos, **11**
   development, **215**–**216**
   dominant, **216**
   exposition, 215–216
   introduction, **215**
   keys, **215**
      major, **215**
      minor, **215**
   musical elements, 213–214
   question, answer, **213**
   recapitulation, 215–**216**
   rondo form, **214**
   sections in sonata form movement,
      215–216

single-movement forms of classical
   period, 214
   sonata form, **214**, 215–216
   string quartets, **11**
   style, 211–216
   symphony, **11**, 214
   ternary form, 214
   thematic development, **11**, 213, 215
   theme, **214**–**215**
   three-part form, 214
   tonal centers, **215**, 216
   tonic key, **215**
   transition, **215**–216
   variations, **214**
Close Encounters of the Third Kind, 254
closing, **216**
coda, **216**
coloratura, **67**
coloratura soprano, 71
Commedia dell'arte, 233
commemoration music, 185–196
   concert overture, **185**–186
   development section, **193**
   Festive Overture, 185–186
   Lincoln Portrait, 193–194
   Mighty Five, 191
   narration from Aaron Copland's
      Lincoln Portrait, 193–194
   nationalism, 185
   Overture of 1812, 185, 191–192
   Overture Solennelle, 186
   programmatic music, **185**
   The Five, 191
   The Russian Five, 191
commissioned music, **181**
compound meter, **90**
concert hall music, 201–244
   appoggiatura, **203**
   avant-garde, 233–234
   Baroque instrumental genres,
      205–206
   Baroque instruments, 204–205
   Baroque period, 203–211
   Camerata, 203
   Chamber music, 202
   choral societies, **202**
   classical instrumental genres, 216–220
   classical period, 211–216
   Commedia dell'arte, 233
   concert overture, 202
   concerto, **202**, 207
   concerto grosso, 205
   crescendos, **204**
   crossover music, 237–238
   decrescendos, **204**
   development of concert tradition,
      201–203

expressionism, **231–232**
fugue, **207–209**
genres, 202
harmonic rhythm, **204**
imitative polyphony, 203
impressionism, **226–227**
minimalism, **234**
Monet, Claude, 226–227
nationalism, **225–226**
neoclassicism, **232–233**
new world symphony, 227–228
ornaments, **203**
overtures, **202**
philharmonic, **202**
primitivism, 232
program music, 224–227
publishing houses, **202**
Pulcinella, 233
recital, **232**
repertoire, **202**
romantic period, 220–224
romantic symphony, 227
serialism, **231**
sonata, **210–211**
Still, William Grant, 234
string quartet, **202**
symphony, 202
terraced dynamics, **204**
The Basso continuo, 205
tonality, 204
tone poem, **202**
traditionalism, 234–235
trio sonata, **210–211**
turn, **203**
twelve-tone music, **231**
twentieth/twenty-first century music, 228–237
Zwilich, Ellen Taaffe, 235
concert overture, **185–186, 202, 224**
concert performance, **103**
concertino, **206**
concerto grosso, **205**
    Margrave of Brandenburg, 206
concertos, **11, 202**, 207, 219
conductor, 255
consonance, **17**
contra bass, 51
contra bassoon, 94
contralto, 71
contrast, **5**
cool jazz, **280**
counter tenor, 123
countermelody, **208**
country music, **144**–145
Cream, 284
crescendos, **158, 204**
crossover music, 237–238

crusades, **127**
cubism, **230**
cymbals, 183

Dama, **166**
dance music, 89–116
    A-B-A form, 95
    airs, **95**
    American ballet, 103–105
    American square dance, 111
    asymmetrical, **103**
    Balinese gamelan music, 105–106
    ballet, **97**–99
    ballet music, 100–105
    Ballets Russes, 100
    Baroque dance suite, 92–93
    bassadance, **92**
    caller, **111**
    Celtic reels, 110–111
    compound meter, **90**
    concert performance, **103**
    Dance of Skeleton, 106–107
    dancing master, 92
    dissonant, 102
    Duple meter, 89
    fiddle, **111**
    folk dance music, 105–111
    full-length ballet, 97–99
    galliard, **92**
    gamelan, **105**–106
    gamelan angklung, **105**
    gamelan beleganjur, **105**
    gamelan gong, **105**
    hornpipe, **95**, 110
    impresario, **102**
    intervals, **104**
    Italian Symphony, 108
    Italian tarantella, saltarello, 107–108
    jig, **110**
    La Sylphide, 99
    Medieval dance—Estampie, 91–92
    menuet, 95
    meter, 89–90
    multiphonics, 106
    Nijinsky, Vaclav, 102
    nineteenth-century waltzes, 96–97
    on pointe, 99
    orchestral dance suite, 93–96
    orchestrations, **104**
    overture, **95**
    pavane, **92**
    pelog, **106**
    pentatonic, **106**
    polyrhythmic, 108
    prima ballerina, **99**
    primitivism, **102**
    quadruple meter, **90**

rhythm, 89–90
ritardandos, **97**
rodeo, 104–105
saltarello, **108**
score, **100**–102
slendro, **106**
solo instrumental dance suite, 96
square dance, **111**
staccato, **102**
step dance, **110**
stylized, **93**
suites, **91**
Swan Lake, 99
symphony, 96
syncopated, **95**
tarantella, **107**
tempo, **90**
ternary form, **95**
The Rite of Spring, 100
The Waltz King, 97
three-part form, **95**
Tibetan Buddhist monk dancing, 106–107
timbral, **95**
triple meter, **89**
unresolved dissonances, **102**
waltz, **96**–97
water music, 95
West African folk dance music, 108–110
western tradition dance music, 91–96
Dance of Skeleton, 106–107
dancing master, 92
decrescendos, **204**
definition of music, **1–2**
development of concert tradition, 201–203
dialogue, 74–76
Dies Irae, 156–159
    requiem without, 159–160
director, influence of, 264–265
dirges, **167**
dissonant, 102
Dixieland jazz, **276**–277
Dogon funeral music, 166–167
dominant, **216**
Domine Jesu (Offertorium), 154
double bass, 51
double features, **259**
dramma giocoso, **66**
drone, **287**
drums, 183
Duple meter, 89

E-flat clarinet, 94
early dramatic musical composition, 62–64

Hildegard of Bingen, 62–64
morality play, **62**–64
early opera, 65
early rock and roll, 281–284
electronic scores, 260–264
elements of music, 2
frequency of vibration, **2**
melody, **2**
pitches, **2**
scales, **2**
emergence of popular song, 134–137
Foster, Stephen, 134–137
English folk songs, 119–120
arpeggiated, **120**
call, response, **120**
chordal, **120**
responsorial singing, **120**
sea chantey, **120**
work songs, **120**
English horn, 94
ensembles
band, 6
chamber, 6
choir, 6
orchestra, 6
String Quartet, **51**
Woodwind Quintet, 94
episodes, **207**
Esterhazy, 217
exoticism, **13**
exposition, **208**, 215–216
expressionism, **231**–**232**

fanfares, 181–182
fantasia, **207**
Fantasia, 258
female voices
alto, 71
coloratura soprano, 71
contralto, 71
mezzo-soprano, 71
soprano, 71
Festive Overture, 185–186
fiddle, **111**
flute, 94
folk art, **83**
folk dance music, 105–111
Balinese gamelan music, 105–106
gamelan, **105**–106
gamelan angklung, **105**
gamelan beleganjur, **105**
gamelan gong, **105**
pelog, **106**
pentatonic, **106**
slendro, **106**

folk songs, **118**–119
African folk songs, 120–122
American folk songs, 123–127
English folk songs, 119–120
Forbidden Planet, 260
forerunners of musical, 73
form, **2**, 4–5
A-B-A form, **5**
contrast, **5**
repetition, **5**
Foster, Stephen, 134–137
French horn, 159
frequency of vibration, **2**
frets, **286**
fugue, **207**–209
countermelody, **208**
episodes, **208**
exposition, **208**
fantasia, **207**
imitative polyphony, 207
orchestrated, **208**
prelude, **207**
subject, **207**
toccata, **207**
full-length ballet
ballet, **97**–99
La Sylphide, 99
on pointe, **99**
prima ballerina, **99**
Swan Lake, 99
funeral march, **163**–164
funk, **143**
fusion, 281
fusion jazz, **283**

galliard, **92**
gamelan, **105**–106
gamelan angklung, **105**
gamelan beleganjur, **105**
gamelan gong, **105**
gangsta rap, 147
Gauthier, Daniel, 80
genres, **72**, 202
Gianni Schicchi, 68–70
Gloria, 42
Goldman, Matt, 80
gongs, 183
grandioso, **184**
Grateful Dead, 284–285
Gregorian Chant, **7**
guitar, 287

Happy Birthday, 176–177
copyright, **177**
royalties, **177**
harmonic rhythm, **204**

harmony, **2**, 3
chords, **3**
major, **3**
minor, **3**
harp, 287
harpsichord, 207
Hava Nagila, 179
head, **279**
heavy metal, **144**
Hildegard of Bingen, **62**–64
Hindustani, 285
hip-hop, **147**
historical periods, characteristics of, 6–20
homophonic texture, **5**, **10**
Hora, **179**
hornpipe, **95**

idiomatic, **275**
imitative polyphony, **9**, 203, 207
impresario, **102**
impressionism, **226**–227
Nijinsky, Vaclav, 227
tone poem, 227
improvisation, **10**, 137, 139, 273–294
framework, 274
in contemporary classical context, 275–276
in jazz, 276–278
in non-western music, 285–289
in rock music, 281–284
in western art music, 274–275
improvisation in contemporary classical context, idiomatic, 275–276
improvisation in jazz
bebop jazz, **279**–280
big band, **279**
blue notes, 276
bop, **279**–280
Chicago style jazz, 277
cool jazz, **280**
Dixieland jazz, **276**–277
fusion, **281**, 283
head, **279**
modal jazz, 280–281
scat singing, 277
swing, **279**
The Modern Jazz Quartet, 280
improvisation in non-western music
Arabic improvisatory music, 286–287
Carnatic, 285
drone, **287**
frets, **286**
Hindustani, 285
Indian improvisatory music, 287
oud, **286**
raga, **274**, 288

sitar, **287**
tabla, **287**
tamboura, **287**
vedas, **287**
Vedic, 287
improvisation in rock music
early rock and roll, 281–284
Grateful Dead, 284–285
improvisational rock—Cream, 284
jam band, **285**
Phish, 284–285
improvisation in western art music
basso continuo, 275
cadenza, **275**
ornaments, 274
improvisational rock, 281–284
In Paradisum, 154
incidental music, 71–72
suites, 72
Indian improvisatory music, 287
inspirational music, 181–185
breakstrain, **184**
commissioned, **181**
fanfares, **181**–182
grandioso, **184**
marches, **184**–185
national anthems, 182–184
nationalism, 183
obbligato, **184**
stanzas, 184
strophic form, 182
The Star Spangled Banner, 182–184
trio, **184**
instrumental music of mourning,
161–163
intervals, **104**
introduction, **215**
Italian Symphony, 108
Italian tarantella, saltarello, 107–108

jam band, **285**
jazz, **139**–140
cool, 280
jazz songs, 139–140
blue notes, **139**
blues, 139
chord progressions, **139**
improvisation, 139
scat singing, **139**
syncopated, 139
Jewish wedding music, 179–180
Jutras, Benoit, 80

Kabuki theatre, 81–82
keyboards, 207–208
accordion, 207
harpsichord, 207

organ, 207–208
piano, 207
synthesizer, 207–208
keys, **215**
Kindertotenlieder, 161
klezmer, **179**–180

La Sylphide, 99
Lacrimosa, 154
lead sheet, **205**
Libera Me, 154
libretto, **74**
lieder, **128**
Lincoln Portrait, 193–194
lute, **128**, 287
lute songs, **127**, **128**
Lux Aeternam, 154
lyricist, **73**
lyrics, 74–76

major chords, 3
major key, **215**
male voices
baritone, 123
bass, 123
basso profundo, 123
boy soprano, 123
castrato, 123
counter tenor, 123
tenor, 123
mandolin, 287
marches, **184**–185
mariachi band, **180**
marimba, 183
Medieval dance—Estampie, 91–92
medieval period, 7–8
Gregorian Chant, 7
secular music, 7
troubadours, 7
Trouveres, 7
Medieval Troubadour song, 128–129
melody, **2**
menuet, **95**
Messa da Requiem, 157
meter, **4**, 89–90
Mexican Hat Dance, 180
mezzo-soprano, 71
Midsummer Night's Dream wedding
march, 179
Mighty Five, 191
minimalism, **234**, 236–237
minor chords, 3
minor key, **215**
modal jazz, 280–281
modern opera, 70–71

modern stage spectacle, 80–81
asymmetrical meter, **80**
Blue Man Group, 80
Celtic Woman, 81
Cirque de Soleil (Circus of Sun), 80
Gauthier, Daniel, 80
Goldman, Matt, 80
Jutras, Benoit, 80
Riverdance, 81
Stanton, Phil, 80
The Three Tenors, 81
Whelan, Bill, 81
Wink, Chris, 80
Monet, Claude, 226–227
monodic, **65**
monophonic texture, **5**
morality play, **62**–64
motif, **121**
motives, **130**, **217**, 222
Motown, 143
mourning music, 153–174
adagio for strings, 164–166
crescendo, **158**
Dama, **166**
Dies Irae, 156–159
dirges, **167**
Dogon funeral music, 166–167
Domine Jesu (Offertorium), 154
funeral march, **163**–164
In Paradisum, 154
instrumental music of mourning,
161–163
Kindertotenlieder, 161
Lacrimosa, 154
Libera Me, 154
Lux Aeternam, 154
Messa da Requiem, 157–158
Native American funeral music,
168–170
New Orleans Jazz Funeral, 167–168
off-stage, **158**
Pie Jesu, 154
program music, **163**
programmatic, **163**
requiem, **154**
Requiem Aeternam (Introit), 154
sequence, **157**–158
songs of mourning, 160–170
threnody, **164**
movie music, 245–272, **256**
Alexander Nevsky, 249–250
animated movies, 258–260
background music, **252**
biopic, **256**
Birth of a Nation, 246
Carmen, 256

cartoon shorts, **258**, 259–260
cartoons, 258–260
classical compositions in movies, 256
Close Encounters of the Third Kind,
   254
composers, 265–269
composition, **256**
director, influence of, 264–265
double features, **259**
early years of movie music, 246–237
electronic scores, 260–264
Fantasia, 258
Forbidden Planet, 260–263
movie, **256**
music biopics, 256–258
musical performances as scenes,
   253–254
musical supervisors, **256**
Nidre, Kol, 247
ponticello, 249
sampling, **263**
scores, **247**
songs in film, 249–250
source music, **252**
Spielberg, Steven, 266
staged musical adaptations, 254–256
Steiner, Max, 248
Stokowski, Leopold, 258
synthesizers, **263**–264
The Jazz Singer, 246–247
The Storm Cloud Cantata, 253
theremin, **260**–263
Tin Pan Alley, 251
Vangelis, 263–264
Walt Disney Studios, 258
Warner Brothers, 259–260
Mozart, 66–67
multiphonics, 106
music
   celebration, inspiration,
     commemoration, 175–200
music biopics, 256–258
Music Director, 255
musical elements, 213–214
musical overture, 76
musical performances as movie scenes,
   253–254
musical songwriting teams, 73
musical supervisors, **256**
musicals, **72**–80
   chorus, 75
   dances, 74–76
   dialogue, 74–76
   evolution, 74
   evolving musical, 76
   forerunners of musical, 73
   genres, **72**

libretto, **74**
lyricist, **73**
lyrics, 74–76
musical overture, 76
musical songwriting teams, 73
opera, 73
opera buffa, 73
operatic *vs.* musical vocal style, 73–74
operetta, 73
Phantom of Opera, 79
revue, 73
supertitles, **74**
surtitles, **74**
tunes, 74–76
vaudeville, **73**
verse, 75
West Side Story, 75–76
musique concrete, **233**
Mussorgsky, Modest, 226
Mysterious mountain, 236

narration from Aaron Copland's *Lincoln
   Portrait*, 193–194
national anthems, 182–184
nationalism, **16**, 183, 185, 225–226
   Mussorgsky, Modest, 226
   Nicolai, 226
   The Five, 226
   tone poem, 226
Native American funeral music, 168–170
neoclassicism, 232–**233**
new musical language-re-evaluating
   common practices, 230–231
New Orleans/Dixieland jazz, 276–277
New Orleans Jazz Funeral, 167–168
new world symphony, 227–228
Nicolai, 226
Nidre, Kol, 247
Nijinsky, Vaclav, 102, 227
nineteenth-century waltzes, 96–97
   ritardandos, **97**
   symphony, 96
   The Waltz King, 97
   waltz, **96**–97

obbligato, **184**
oboe, 94
off-stage, **158**
on pointe, **99**
opera, **10**, 64–71, 73
   Camerata, **65**
   classical opera, 66–67
   coloratura, **67**
   dramma giocoso, **66**
   early opera, 65
   Gianni Schicchi, 68–70
   modern opera, 70–71

   monodic, **65**
   Mozart, 66–67
   opera buffa, **65**
   opera seria, **65**
   Pagliacci, 67–68
   patrons, **65**
   romantic opera, 67–70
   The Magic Flute, 66–67
   verismo, **67**
   virtuosity, **67**
opera buffa, **65**, 73
opera seria, **65**
operatic *vs.* musical vocal style, 73–74
operetta, **73**
oratorio, modern, 40–41
orchestra, 6
   Brass Quintet, 159
orchestra music
   conductor, 255
   Music Director, 255
orchestral accompaniment, art songs
   with, 133–134
orchestral dance suites, 93–96, **205**
orchestrated, **208**
orchestrations, **104**
organ, 207–208
ornaments, **203**, 274
oud, **286**
overture, **95**, 202
Overture of 1812, 185–196
Overture Solennelle, 186
overtures, **202**

Pagliacci, 67–68
patrons, **65**
pavane, **92**
pelog, **106**
pentatonic, **106**
percussion, 183
   non-pitched, 183
     cymbals, 183
     drums, 183
     gongs, 183
     ratchet, 183
     triangle, 183
   pitched, 183
     bells, 183
     marimba, 183
     tympani, 183
     xylophone, 183
percussion
   ensemble, 183
   family, 183
   orchestra, 183
Phantom of Opera, 79
philharmonic, **202**
Phish, 284–285

piano, 207
piccolo, 94
piccolo trumpet, 159
Pie Jesu, 154
pitches, **2**
pizzicato
    bass, 51
plucked strings
    banjo, 287
    guitar, 287
    harp, 287
    lute, 287
    mandolin, 287
    ukulele, 287
polyphonic texture, 5
polyrhythmic, 108
ponticello, 249
pop music, **145**
popular songs, **118**–119
prelude, **207**
prima ballerina, **99**
primitivism, **102**, 232
    unresolved dissonances, 232
program music, **163**, 224–227
programmatic music, **163**, **185**
proper, 154
publishers, **138**
publishing houses, **202**
Pulcinella, 233
punk rock, **145**

quadruple meter, **90**
question, answer, **213**

raga, **274**, 288
ragtime, **139**
rap music, **147**
ratchet, 183
R&B, **143**
rebecs, **128**
recapitulation, **215**–216
recital, **232**
reels, Celtic, 110–111
    hornpipe, 110
    jig, **110**
    square dance, **110**
    step dance, **110**
religious music, 25–60
    altos, **39**, 42
    arias, **39**, 42
    Baroque period, 31, 37
    bass, **42**
    basses, **39**
    basso continuo, **32**
    beat, 26
    cantata, **41**–42
    characteristics of, 39–40

chords, 27
chorus, **28**, 42, 44–45
choruses, **39**, 42
Christian pop music, 50–51
Christian rock music, 50, 52
Christmas carol, 43
classical music, **32**
classical style, 32–34
consonant, **27**, 30
countertenors, **41**
dissonance, **30**
dissonant, **27**
early monophonic style, 30
El Niño, 40–41
gospel music, **44**–46
Gregorian chant, 28–29
Gregorian Chant, 48
harmony, 27–28
hymnals, **42**
hymns, **42**–44
imitative polyphony, 31
interval, **30**
Ketjak, 46–47
magnificat, 54
major, 27
mass, 29–36
mass in b minor, 31–32
Medieval period, 28, 30
melismatic, **48**
melody, 27
meter, 26
microtones, **44**
minimalist, **41**
minor, 27
monophonic, **28**
motet, 52
movement, **30**
movements, **30**
mulitiphonic, 49–50
multiphonics, **48**
Muslim call to prayer, 48–49
oratorio, **37**, 39–41, 42
oratorios, **42**
ordinary, **29**
organum, 54
pitches, 27
polyphonic, **30**
polyphonic style, 30–34
polyphony, **30**
polyrhythmic, **46**
Prez, Josquin des, 31
proper, **29**
psalms, **36**–37
recitatives, **39**, 42
Renaissance, 31
rhythm, 26–27
romantic style, 34–36

scales, 27
secular music, 50
soprano, **39**, 42
spirituals, **44**–46
Stabat Mater, 54
stanzas, **42**
strophic form, **42**
tenor, **39**, 42
texture, 31
Tibetan Buddhist monk chant, 47–48
timbre, 28
Tuvan throat singing, 49–50
unison, **45**
verse, **28**, 42, 44–45
world worship music, 46–50
worship music texts, 56–57
Renaissance lute song, 129–130
Renaissance period, 8–10, 30–34
    a cappella, 9
    bassadance, **92**
    canzon, 9
    dancing master, 92
    galliard, **92**
    imitative polyphony, **9**
    pavane, **92**
    ricercar, **9**
repertoire, **202**
repertory, **127**
repetition, 5
requiem, **154**
Requiem Aeternam (Introit), 154
responsorial singing, **120**, 121
revue, **73**
rhapsody, **235**
rhapsody in blue, 235
rhythm, **2**, 4, 89–90
    beat, **4**
    meter, **4**
ricercar, **9**
ripieno, **206**
ritardandos, **97**
ritornello form, **206**
Riverdance, 81
rock and roll, **140**–142
    backbeat, **140**
    impact of, 141–142
rodeo, 104–105
romantic art song, 130–133
romantic opera, 67–70
Romantic period, 13, 220–224
    ballade, **223**
    characteristics, 220–224
    concert overture, 224
    exoticism, **13**
    instrumental genres, 224
    motives, 222
    musical elements, 222–223

nationalism, **16**
romantic piano, 223–224
rubato, **222**
style, 220–224
symphonic poem, **224**
tone poem, 224
romantic piano, 223–224
romantic symphony, 227
rondo form, 178–179, 214
rubato, **222**

saltarello, **107**–108
sampling, **263**
saxophones, 94
scales, **2**
scat singing, **139**, 277
sci fi movie, 254
    Spielberg, Steven, 266
        scores, 100–102, **247**
sea chantey, **120**
sections in sonata form movement,
    215–216
secular music, **7**
sequence, 157–158
serialism, **231**
    atonal music, 231
    atonality, **231**
    tone rows, **231**
single-movement forms of classical
    period, 214
sitar, **287**
slavery, folk song born of, 124–125
slendro, **106**
solo instrumental dance suite, 96
sonata, **210**–211, 219–220
sonata form, **214**, 215–216
song cycle, **130**
songs, 117–149
    African folk songs, 120–122
    alternative rock, **145**–147
    American folk songs, 123–127
    arpeggiated, **120**
    art songs, **118**–119
    art songs in western historical periods,
        127–134
    backbeat, **140**
    blue notes, **139**
    bluegrass, **144**
    blues, **137**–138
    blues/rock, **143**–144
    bridge, **119**
    call, response, **120**
    chord names, 138
    chord progression, 137, **139**
    chordal, **120**
    chorus, 118

    classical art song, 130–133
    country music, **144**–145
    crusades, **127**
    emergence of popular song, 134–137
    English folk songs, 119–120
    folk songs, **118**–119
    Foster, Stephen, 134–137
    funk, **143**
    gangsta rap, 147
    heavy metal, **144**
    hip-hop, **147**
    impact of, 141–142
    improvisation, 137, 139
    jazz, **139**
    jazz songs, 139–140
    lieder, **128**
    lute, **128**
    lute songs, 127, **128**
    Medieval Troubadour song, 128–129
    motif, **121**
    motives, **130**
    Motown, 143
    pop music, **145**
    popular songs, **118**–119
    publishers, **138**
    punk rock, **145**
    ragtime, **139**
    rap/hip-hop, 147
    rap music, **147**
    R&B, **143**
    rebecs, **128**
    Renaissance lute song, 129–130
    repertory, **127**
    responsorial singing, **120**, 121
    rock and roll, **140**–142
    romantic art song, 130–133
    scat singing, **139**
    sea chantey, **120**
    slavery, folk song born of, 124–125
    song cycle, **130**
    soul music, **143**
    strophic form, 130
    syncopated, 139
    through composed, **118**, 130
    Tin Pan Alley, 138–139
    twelve-bar blues, **137**
    twelve-bar blues chord progression,
        137
    urban folk, 142–**143**
    war, folk song inspired by, 123–124
    Western sing, 144
    with orchestral accompaniment,
        133–134
    work, folk song to accompany,
        125–126
    work songs, **120**, 125–126

songs in film, 249–250
songs of mourning, 160–170
    adagio for strings, 164–166
    Dama, **166**
    dirges, **167**
    Dogon funeral music, 166–167
    funeral march, **163**–164
    instrumental music of mourning,
        161–163
    Kindertotenlieder, 161
    Native American funeral music,
        168–170
    New Orleans Jazz Funeral, 167–168
    program music, **163**
    programmatic, **163**
    threnody, **164**
soprano, 71
soprano sax, 94
soul music, **143**
source music, **252**
square dance, 111
    caller, **111**
    fiddle, **111**
staccato, **102**
stage music, 61–88
    asymmetrical meter, **80**
    Blue Man Group, 80
    Camerata, **65**
    Celtic Woman, 81
    Chinese opera, 83
    chorus, 75
    Cirque de Soleil (Circus of Sun), 80
    classical opera, 66–67
    coloratura, **67**
    dances, 74–76
    dialogue, 74–76
    dramma giocoso, **65**
    early dramatic musical composition,
        62–64
    early opera, 65
    evolution, 74
    evolving musical, 76
    folk art, **83**
    forerunners of musical, 73
    Gauthier, Daniel, 80
    genres, **72**
    Gianni Schicchi, 68–70
    Goldman, Matt, 80
    Hildegard of Bingen, 62–64
    incidental music, 71–72
    Jutras, Benoit, 80
    Kabuki theatre, 81–82
    libretto, **74**
    lyricist, **73**
    lyrics, 74–76
    modern opera, 70–71

modern stage spectacle, 80–81
monodic, **65**
morality play, **62–64**
Mozart, 66–67
musical overture, 76
musical songwriting teams, 73
musicals, **72–80**
opera, 64–71, 73
opera buffa, **65**, 73
opera seria, **65**
operatic *vs.* musical vocal style, 73–74
operetta, **73**
Pagliacci, 67–68
patrons, **65**
Phantom of Opera, 76
revue, **73**
Riverdance, 81
romantic opera, 67–70
Stanton, Phil, 80
suites, 72
supertitles, **74**
surtitles, **74**
The Magic Flute, 66–67
The Three Tenors, 81
tunes, 74–76
vaudeville, **73**
verismo, **67**
verse, 75
virtuosity, **67**
West Side Story, 75–76
Whelan, Bill, 81
Wink, Chris, 80
world musical theatre genres, 81–83
staged musical movie adaptations,
    254–256
Stanton, Phil, 80
stanzas, 184
Steiner, Max, 248
Still, William Grant, 234
Stokowski, Leopold, 258
string quartets, **11**, 51, **202**, 218
strophic form, 130, 182
stylized music, **93**
subject, **207**
suites, 72, **91**
supertitles, **74**
surtitles, **74**
Swan Lake, 99
swing, **279**
symphonic poem, **224**
symphony, **11**, 96, 202, 214, 216
syncopated, **95**, 139
synthesizer, 207–208, 263–264

tabla, **287**
tamboura, **287**

tarantella, **107**–108
tempo, **90**
tenor, 123
tenor sax, 94
ternary form, **95**, 214
terraced dynamics, **204**
texture, **2**, 5
    homophonic texture, **5**
    monophonic texture, **5**
    polyphonic texture, **5**
The Basso continuo, 205
    basso continuo, 205
    lead sheet, 205
The Five, 191, 226
The Jazz Singer, 246–247
The Magic Flute, 66–67
The Modern Jazz Quartet, 280
The Rite of Spring, 100–103
The Russian Five, 191
The Star Spangled Banner, 182–184
The Storm Cloud Cantata, 253
The Three Tenors, 81
The Waltz King, 97
thematic development, **11**, 213, 215
theme, 178–179, **214–215**
    variations, **218**
theremin, **260**–263
three-part form, **95**, 214
threnody, **164**
through composed, **118**, 130
Tibetan Buddhist monk dancing,
    106–107
    Dance of Skeleton, 106–107
    multiphonics, 106
timbral, **95**
timbre, **2**, 5
    tone color, 5
Tin Pan Alley, 138–139, 251
    jazz, **139**
    publishers, **138**
    ragtime, **139**
toccata, **207**
tonal centers, **215**, 216
tonality, **204**
tone color, 5
tone poem, **202**, 224, 226–227
tone rows, **231**
tonic key, **215**
total serialism, **234**
traditionalism, 234–235
transition, **215**–216
triangle, 183
trio, **184**
trio sonata, **210**–211
triple meter, **90**
trombone, 159

troubadours, **7**
Trouveres, 7
trumpet, 159
tuba, 159
tunes, 74–76
turn, **203**
twelve-bar blues, **137**
twelve-tone music, **231**
twentieth/twenty-first century music,
    17–20, 228–235
    Afro-American symphony, 235–236
    atonal music, **17**
    characteristics, 228–230
    consonance, **17**
    cubism, **230**
    in C, 236–237
    minimalism, 236–237
    Mysterious Mountain, 236
    rhapsody, **235**
    rhapsody in blue, 235
    style, 228–230
    symphony No. 002, 236
    tonality-based composition, 235–237
tympani, 183

ukulele, 287
unresolved dissonances, **102**, 232
urban folk, 142–**143**

Vangelis, 263–264
vaudeville, **73**
vedas, **287**
Vedic, 287
verismo, **67**
verse, 75
viola, 51
violin, 51
violoncello, 51
virtuosity, **67**

Walt Disney Studios, 258
waltz, **96**–97
    nineteenth-century, 96–97
war, folk song inspired by, 123–124
Warner Brothers, 259–260
water music, 95
wedding march, *Midsummer Night's
    Dream*, 178–179
West African folk dance music, 108–110
    polyrhythmic, 108
West Side Story, 75–76
Western sing, 144
western tradition dance music, 91–96
    Medieval dance—Estampie, 91–92
    suites, **91**–96

What Makes Music
    bow string family, 51
    brass family, 159
    conductor, the, 255
    ensembles, 6
    keyboards, 207–208
    percussion family, 183
    plucked strings, 287
    woodwind family, 94
    voices, 71, 123
Whelan, Bill, 81
Wink, Chris, 80

woodwind family
    alto sax, 94
    baritone sax, 94
    bass clarinet, 94
    bassoon, 94
    clarinet, 94
    contra bassoon, 94
    E-flat clarinet, 94
    English horn, 94
    flute, 94
    oboe, 94
    piccolo, 94

    saxophones, 94
    soprano sax, 94
    tenor sax, 94
Woodwind Quintet, 94
work, folk song to accompany, 125–126
work songs, **120**
world musical theatre genres, 81–83
    Chinese opera, 83
    folk art, **83**
    Kabuki theatre, 81–82

xylophone, 183

Index of Key People and Compositions

1812 Overture, 191–192

A Clockwork Orange, 166
A Collection of Hymns for the use of the People Called Methodists, 42
A Little Night Music, 12
A Midsummer Night's Dream, 178–179
A Mighty Fortress is our God, 42
A Night in Tunisia, 280
A View from the Bridge, 70
Acrobatic Dance of the Youths, 109
Adagio for Strings, 164, 166, 234, 256
Adams, John, 35, 40–41, 53, 70, 162
Afro-American Symphony, 235–236
Agnus Dei, 34
Ahi Amours (Alas Love), 128–129
Aida, 155
Alas Love, 128–129
Alegria, 80
Alexander Nevsky, 249–250, 263–264
Alive, 52
All Creatures of our God and King, 43
All the Pretty Little Horses, 124–125
Allan, Lewis, 139–140
"Allegro vivace", 42
An der Schönen Blauen Donau (On the Beautiful Blue Danube), 97
Anastasio, Trey, 238, 285
Appalachian Spring, 104
Arlen, Harold, 250–251, 268
Armstrong, Louis, 277–278, 289
Arnaud, Leo, 181
As Thousands Cheer, 176
Auld Lang Syne, 176–178
Ave Maria, 9, 259
Baba Yetu, 263

Bach, Johann Sebastian, 10, 18, 32, 35, 41, 53–55, 95–96, 98, 112, 205–210, 236, 239, 258, 289

Baker, Ginger, 284
Balakirev, Mili, 191, 226
Balakrishnan, David, 275–276
Ballade in G minor, 223
Barber, Samuel, 17, 164–166, 169, 234, 256
Barron, Bebe, 260, 263, 268
Barron, Louis, 260, 263, 268
Barry, John, 266, 268
Bartok, Bela, 17, 256
Basie, Count, 279
Benediktbeuern, 7
Benjamin, Arthur, 253, 268
Berlin, Irving, 139, 146, 176, 251
Berlioz, Hector, 16, 154, 156, 165, 222, 227
Bernstein, Elmer, 266, 268
Bernstein, Leonard, 17, 35–37, 38, 53, 75–76, 234
Berry, Chuck, 140–141, 281, 289
Bill Haley and the Comets, 140–141, 284
Billy the Kid, 104
Birth of a Nation, 246
Bitches Brew, 281
Bizet, Georges, 72, 254–256, 268
Black Sabbath, 144
Blackberry Winter, 237–238
Blake, William, 135
Blow, John, 127
Blow the Man Down, 120
Blue Man Group, 80–81
Blue Skies, 139, 251
Blue Suede Shoes, 141–142
Bluesbreakers, 284
Bob Wills and His Texas Playboys, 111
Bob Wills Square Dance #001, 111
Bolcom, William, 70, 135
Bolero, 256
Borodin, Alexander, 191, 226
Boublil, Claude, 79–80

Boulez, Pierre, 231, 234
Brahms, Johannes, 16–19, 156, 165
Brandenburg Concertos #2, 206
Brigadoon, 73
Bring Him Home, 80
Britten, Benjamin, 135, 156, 165
Brother Mosely Crossed (Smote) the Water, 125
Brown, James, 143
Brubeck, Dave, 280
Bruce, Jack, 284
Bugler's Dream, 181
Burns, Robert, 177, 187, 195

Cage, John, 231, 234
Camelot, 73
Campion, Thomas, 129–130, 146
Camptown Races and *Beautiful Dreamer*, 134
Candide, 76
Candle in the Wind, 145
Canon a tre in D major, 11
Canzon XVII, 10
Carawan, Guy, 194, 196
Carbone, Eddie, 70
Carmen, 255
Carmina Burana, 7, 20
Carreras, Jose, 81
Casablanca, 251, 253
Cash, Johnny, 144–145
Cats, 79
Celtic Woman, 81
Chariots of Fire, 263–264
Chichester Psalms, 36–38
Chopin, Frederic, 16, 163–165, 169, 222–224, 239
Cirque du Soleil, 80
Civilization IV, 263
Clap Your Hands, 45
Clapton, Eric, 143, 161, 165, 169, 284

Cline, Patsy, 145
Close Encounters of the Third Kind, 254
Cohan, George M., 139, 251
Collins, Judy, 143
Come Let Us Be Glad, 179
Concerto for Trumpet and Orchestra, 219
Concerto for Violin and Orchestra, 2
Concerto Suite for Electric Guitar and Orchestra, 238
Copland, Aaron, 17–18, 98, 103–105, 112, 128, 135, 182, 187, 193–195, 231, 234, 251–253, 268
Coppola, Francis Ford, 264
Corelli, Arcangelo, 205, 211, 239
Count Basie Band, 289
Cowboy Dances, 111
Cowell, Henry, 234, 239
Cream, 143, 146, 284, 289
Crelley, Robert, 135
Crossroads, 143–144, 284
Cui, Cesar, 191, 226

Da Palestrina, Giovanni Perluigi, 9
Dance of the Hours, 258
Dance of the Skeleton (Skeleton Dance), 106–107
Darwin, Charles, 230
Das Knaben Wunderhorn (The Young Boy's Magic Horn), 133
Das Leid Von Der Erde (The Song of the Earth), 133
Dat's Love, 256
Daudet, Alphonse, 72
Dave Brubeck Quintet, 4
Davis, Miles, 280–281, 289
Day of Wrath text, 156
de Bethune, Conon, 128–129, 146
de Machaut, Guillaume, 7
Debussy, Claude, 16, 18, 223, 227–228, 239
Deep Purple, 238
Delaunay, Sonia, 230
DeMille, Agnes, 104
Derek and the Dominoes, 143
Des Prez, Josquin, 9–10, 18–19, 31, 35, 53
Desmond, Paul, 4
Diaghilev, Serge, 100–102, 227
Dickinson, Emily, 135
Die Fledermaus (The Bat), 97
Die Wacht am Rhein/La Marseillaise, 253
Die Zauberflöte, 66–67
Dies Irae (Day of Wrath) text, 156–158
Dion, Celine, 145
Dixon, Willie, 284
Doctor Atomic, 70
Domingo, Placido, 81

Don Giovanni, 66, 69
Dorsey, Jimmy, 279
Dorsey, Tommy, 279
Dowland, John, 129
Dr. No ("James Bond Theme"), 266
Dreamgirls, 76
"Drumbone", 81
Dubussy, Claude, 225
Duke Ellington Band, 289
Duke, George, 276, 289
Dvořák, Antonin, 54, 223, 227–228, 239
Dylan, Bob, 135, 142–143, 146

Easter Parade, 139, 251
Eine Kleine Nachtmusik (A Little Night Music), 12
Einstein on the Beach, 70
Eisenstein, Sergei, 249
El Niño (The Child), 40–41
El Shaddai (God Almighty), 51
Electric Light Orchestra, 238
Elephant Man, 166
Ellington, Duke, 279
Ellisor, Conni, 235, 237–239
Eminem, 146–147
Enya, 81
Erdman, Ernie, 247
Erlkönig (The Erlking), 132
Evata, 79
Every Day (I Have the Blues), 138

Fanfare for the Common Man, 104, 182, 234
Festive Overture, 186
Finlandia, 256
First Mass for Christmas, 30
Fischer, William Arms, 228
Five Piano Pieces, 232
Folsom Prison Blues, 145
Forbidden Planet, 260, 263
Foster, Stephen, 134, 137, 139, 146
Franck, Cesar, 227
Franklin, Aretha, 143
Funeral Song, 168

Gabrieli, Giovanni, 9–10, 18–19, 35
Gabriel's Oboe from *Mission*, 265
Gamelan Angklung, 106
Garcia, Jerry, 285
Gauthier, Daniel, 80
Gaye, Marvin, 2
Gershwin, George, 139, 231, 234–235, 237, 239, 276
Getz, Stan, 280, 289
Gianni Schicchi, 68–70
Gilbert, William Schwenck, 73

Gillespie, Dizzy, 275–276, 279–280, 289
Give My Regards to Broadway, 139, 251
Glass, Philip, 17–18, 70, 231, 236–237, 239
Glenn Miller Band, 289
Gloria, 42
Gloria from Missa Pange Lingua, 31
"God, Preserve Thy People", 191
Goethe, Johann Wolfgang, 135
Gogol, Nicolai, 226
Goin' Home, 228
Goldsmith, Jerry, 266
Gone with the Wind, 248
Good Golly Miss Molly, 140, 281
Goodman, Benny, 279
Goosens, Eugene, 182
Graham, Martha, 104
Grant, Amy, 50–51, 53
Grateful Dead, 284–285
Greensleeves, 119–120
Grieg, Edvard, 246
Gumbukumbu, 121
Guthrie, Woody, 118

Haggard, Merle, 145
Hail to the Chief, 181
Haley, Bill, 140, 284, 289
Hallelujah Chorus, 11
Hamilton, Frank, 194, 196
Hammerstein, Oscar, 73, 256, 268
Handel, George Frideric, 10–11, 18–19, 35, 37–39, 41, 53, 95, 98, 112, 205–206
Happy Birthday, 176–177
Harburg, E.Y., 251
Hard Times, 147
Harris Jr., Clifford Joseph, 147
Harrison, George, 142
Hava Nagila (Come Let Us Be Glad), 179
Haydn, Franz Joseph, 12, 54, 214, 216–217, 219, 227, 239
Heine, Heinrich, 135
Henry VIII, 146
Here Comes the Bride, 179
Herrmann, Bernard, 245, 252–253, 260–261, 264–265, 268
Higher Ground, 147
Hildegard of Bingen, 7–8, 18–19, 35, 41, 62–64
Hill, Jessica, 177
Hill, Mildred, 176
Hill, Patti, 176
Hoedown from Rodeo, 17
House Hunting Mice, 259
Houston, Whitney, 145
Hovhannes, Alan, 231, 236, 239

Hunter, Alberta, 138
Hupfield, Herman, 251

I Can Only Imagine, 52
I Can't Get No Satisfaction, 142
I Care Not for These Ladies, 129–130
I Could Have Danced All Night, 75
I Got Rhythm, 139
I Have the Blues, 138
I Heard it Through the Grapevine, 2
I'm a Yankee Doodle Dandy, 139, 251
In C, 234–235
In the Mood, 279
Initiation Dance, 110
Intermezzo in A major, 17
Ivanov, Lev, 99

Jackson, Michael, 145
Jagger, Mick, 142
Jam, Pearl, 147
"James Bond Theme", 266
James, Rick, 143
Jarabe Tapatio, 180–181
Jaws, 269
Jay-Z, 146–148
Jeanie with the Light Brown Hair, 134, 137
Jennens, Charles, 38
Jennings, Waylon, 145
Jeremy, 145
Jesus Christ Superstar, 76, 79
Jewish Prayer, 268
John, Elton, 145
John Henry, 125
John Mayall's Blues Breakers, 143
Johnson, Robert, 138, 143
Jolson, Al, 246
Joseph and the Amazing Technicolor Dreamcoat, 76, 79
Just a Closer Walk with Thee, 168
Jutras, Benoit, 80

Kahn, Gus, 247, 268
Kanjincho, 82
Kee, John P., 45, 53
Key, Francis Scott, 182, 187, 195
Kh mei, 50
Kindertotenlieder (Songs on the Death of Children), 133, 161
King, B.B., 138, 146
King Kong, 248
Korngold, Erich Wolfgang, 247–248, 268
Kumbaya, 122
Kyrie, 8

La Boheme, 34, 68–69
La Traviata (The Fallen Woman), 155
Le Sacre du Printemps (The Rite of Spring), 100, 232
Lennon, John, 142
Leoncavallo, Ruggiero, 67–68
Leonin, 7
Lerner and Loewe, 73–75
Lewis, Jerry Lee, 140
Lieder eines fahrenden Gesellen (Songs of a Wayfarer), 133
L'il Wayne, 146–148
Lincoln Portrait, 104, 193–194
Liszt, Franz, 222–223
Little Bird, 127
Little Fugue in G minor, 209
Little Organ Fugue in G minor, 208
Loewe, Frederick, 73–74
Lohengrin, 3
Lorenzo's Oil, 166
Lose Yourself, 147
Lute Concerto in D major, 207, 275
Luther, Martin, 42

Madame Butterfly, 34, 68
Magnificat Anima Mea Dominum, 54, 56
Mahler, Gustav, 16, 128, 133, 146, 161, 165, 169, 223
Malmsteen, Yngwie, 238–239
Mambozooka, 4
Manzoni Requiem, 157
Maqam Kurd, 287
Margrave of Brandenburg, 206
Mass in B minor, 32
Mathers, Marshal, 147
Mayall, John, 284
McCartney, Paul, 142
McDaniels, Darryl, 147
Meeropol, Abel, 139–140, 146
Mendelssohn, Felix, 16, 108, 112, 178–179, 187, 222
Messa da Requiem, 157–158
Messi di Gloria (Mass of Glory), 34
Messiah, 11, 37–39, 41
Metal Meltdown, 144
Metallica, 144
Mexican Hat Dance, 180
Millard, Bart, 52
Miller, Glenn, 279
Minnie, Memphis, 138
Miss Saigon, 68
Mizell, Jason, 147
Monet, Claude, 226
Monk, Thelonious, 279–280, 289
Monteverdi, Claudio, 10

Morricone, Ennio, 265, 268
Mosely, Andy, 53
Mouret, Jean Joseph, 187
Mozart, Wolfgang Amadeus, 12, 18–19, 32–35, 53–54, 66–67, 154, 156–157, 159–160, 165, 169, 214, 256
Muir Woods Suite, 276
Munch, Edvard, 232
Murder, 265
Music for Strings Percussion and Celeste, 256
Music for the Royal Fireworks, 95
Muslim Call to Prayer, 41–42
Mussorgsky, Modest, 191, 223, 226, 239, 259
My Fair Lady, 73–75

Nabucco, 155, 157
Natya Shastra, 100
Nelly Was a Lady, 134
Night In Tunisia, 275–276
Night on Bald Mountain, 226, 258
Nijinsky, Vaclav, 102, 227
Nirvana, 145
Nixon in China, 70
Notorious B.I.G., 147

O Fortuna from Carmina Burana (Songs from Benediktbeurn), 7–8, 20
Of Mice and Men, 251
Oh! Susanna, 134
Old Folks at Home, 134
On the Beautiful Blue Danube, 97
On the Transmigration of Souls, 162
One O'Clock Jump, 279
Orchestral Suite in D major, 95
Ordo Virtutum (Play of the Virtues), 63–64
Orff, Carl, 19–20
"Orinoco Flow", 81
Othello, 157
Our Town, 251
"Over the Bog Road", 111
Ozatsuma, 82

Pachelbel, Johann, 11, 19
Pagliacci (The Clowns), 67–68
Paint Your Wagon, 73
Palestrina, Giovanni, 54
Papathanassiou, Evangelos Odysseas, 263
Parker, Charlie, 279
Pavarotti, Luciano, 81
Pearl Jam, 145
Peer Gynt Suite, 246
Penderecki, Krzysztof, 164–165, 169

Pergolesi, Giovanni Battista, 233
Perotin, 7
Petipa, Marius, 99
Peul's Dance, 109
Phantom of the Opera, 79
Phillips, Sam, 141
Phish, 284–285, 289
Piano Concerto No. 001 in C major, 275
Piano Concerto No. 003, 256
Piano Concerto No. 021, Andante, 256
Piano Sonata No. 002 in B-flat minor, 163
Piano Sonata, Opus 013, 220
Pilentze Pee (Little Bird), 127
Play of the Virtues, 63–64
Poet and Peasant Overture, 246
Ponchielli, Amilcare, 258
Poulenc, Francis, 38
Powerhouse, 259
Presley, Elvis, 141–142
Priest, Judas, 144, 146
Prokofiev, Sergei, 249–250, 268
Puccini, Giacomo, 16, 34–35, 53, 61, 68–70, 223, 247
Puente, Tito, 4
Pulcinella, 233
Purcell, Henry, 127
Puttin' on the Ritz, 139, 251
Pygmalion, 74

Quiet City, 104

Rachmaninoff, Sergei, 256
Raga: Tilik Shayam, 288
Rain Dance Mega Raga, 285
Ravel, Maurice, 16, 223, 231, 256
Reich, Steve, 236
Rellstab, Ludwig, 135
R.E.M., 145
Renoir, Pierre-August, 226
Requiem Mass in D minor, 155–157, 159
Rhapsody in Blue, 235
Rhapsody on a Theme of Paganinni, Variation #018, 256
Rice, Tim, 76, 79
Richard, Little, 140, 146, 281, 289
Richards, Keith, 142
Ride of the Valkyries, 256
Rigoletto, Il Trovatore (The Troubadour), 155, 157
Riley, Terry, 231, 234–237, 239
Rimsky-Korsakov, Nicolai, 191, 223, 226
Riverdance, 81
Rock Around the Clock, 141, 284
Rodeo, 104–105, 234
Rodgers, Richard, 73

Rogers, Richard, 255
Roll Over Beethoven, 141, 281
Rorem, Ned, 128
Rosenthal, David, 238
Rosseter, Phillip, 129
Rossini, Gioacchino, 222, 260–261
Rubio, Jesús, 180–181, 195
Ruckert, Friedrich, 161, 165
Run-D.M.C., 146–147
Russo, Dan, 247
Rutter, John, 156

Saltarello, 108
Sanctus from Requiem Mass, 34
Sanderson, James, 195
Satisfaction, 142
Schoenberg, Arnold, 17–18, 231–232, 239
Schubert, Franz Peter, 16, 18, 54, 127, 130–132, 135, 146, 165, 214, 218, 222, 239, 259
Schumann, Robert, 222
Scott, Raymond, 259, 268
Seeger, Pete, 118, 187, 194–196
"Sgt. Pepper's Lonely Hearts Club Band" album, 142
Shakur, Tupac, 147
Shankar, Ravi, 288
Shaw, George Bernard, 74–76
Shaw, Lloyd, 111
Shore, Howard, 266
Shostakovich, Dmitri, 17, 186, 187, 195, 231
Sibelius, Jean, 256
Simmons, Joseph, 147
Simple Gifts, 104
Sinatra, Frank, 142
Skeleton Dance, 106
Smith, Bessie, 138
Smith, John Stafford, 182
So What, 280–281
Sohönberg, Claude-Michel, 79–80
Somewhere, Over the Rainbow, 250–251
Sonata, Opus 001 #003, Presto, 211
Songs and Proverbs, 135
Songs from Benediktbeurn, 7–8, 20
Songs of a Wayfarer, 133
Songs of Innocence and Experience, 135
Songs on the Death of Children, 133, 161
Sousa, John Phillip, 184–185, 187, 195
South Pacific, 73
Spears, Britney, 145
Spoonful, 284
St. John's Night on the Bald Mountain, 226
Stabat Mater, 54, 56–57

Stafford, John, 195
Stalling, Carl, 259
Star Wars, 61, 269
Starr, Ringo, 142
Steiner, Max, 248, 268
Still, William Grant, 231, 234–237, 239
Straight No Chaser, 280
Straikovsky, Igor, 112
Strange Fruit, 139–140
Strauss II, Johann, 97–98, 112
Strauss, Johann, 256
Strauss, Richard, 3, 223–225, 231, 234, 236, 239, 256
Stravinsky, Igor, 17–20, 98, 100–104, 231–233, 239, 258
Strayhorn, Billy, 279
String Quartet in D minor, 218
Strong, Barrett, 2
Sullivan, Arthur, 73
Sunset Boulevard, 79
Swagga Like Us, 148
Swallow, Steve, 135
Swan Lake, 97–100, 103, 256
Swanee, 139
Symphony No. 003 in E-flat major, 164
Symphony No. 002, Mysterious Mountain, 236
Symphony No. 003, 237
Symphony No. 004, 108
Symphony No. 004 in F minor, 17
Symphony No. 005 in C minor, 12, 217–218, 230
Symphony No. 009, 228, 256
Symphony No. 009, 002nd movement, Largo, 228

Take Five, 4
Take the "A" Train, 279
Taupin, Bernie, 145
Tchaikovsky, Peter Ilyich, 5, 16–19, 98–99, 112, 186–187, 190–192, 195, 223, 246, 256
Tears in Heaven, 161
The Animals, 284
The Band Wagon, 176
The Banshee, 234
The Bat, 97
The Beatles, 142
The Blue Danube Waltz, 256
"The Boys of the Lough", 111
The Child, 40–41
The Clash, 145
The Clowns, 67–68
The Cruel War, 124
The Day the Earth Stood Still, 260, 264
The Divine Comedy, 68

The Emperor Waltz, 256
The Firebird, 100–102
The Freewheelin' Bob Dylan, 135
The Good, The Bad and the Ugly, 265
The Heiress, 251
The Jazz Singer, 246–247
The King and I, 73
The Lord's Prayer, 263
The Lost One, 157
The Magic Flute (Die Zauberflöte), 66–67
"The Merry Harriers", 111
The Modern Jazz Quartet, 280
The Moody Blues, 238
The Nutcracker Ballet, 5
The Nutcracker Suite, 258
The Pastoral Symphony, 258
The Phantom of the Opera, 79
The Ramayana Monkey Chant, 46–47
The Ramones, 145
The Red Hot Chili Peppers, 145, 147
The Red Pony, 251–253
The Rite of Spring, 17, 100–103, 232, 258
The Rolling Stones, 142
The Sea Hawk, 248
The Sex Pistols, 145
The Song of the Earth, 133
The Sorcerer's Apprentice, 258
The Sound of Music, 73
The Star Spangled Banner, 176, 182
The Stars and Stripes Forever, 184–185
The Storm Cloud Cantata, 253
The Story of the White Snake, 83
The Supremes, 143
The Temptations, 143, 146
The Three Tenors, 81
The Times They Are a Changin', 143
The Troubadour, 155

The White Album, 142
The Wizard of Oz, 250–251, 253
The Yardbirds, 143
The Young Boy's Magic Horn, 133
Theocracy, 52
Threnody to the Victims of Hiroshima, 164
Thus Spake Zarathustra, 3, 256
T.I., 146–148
Tibetan Buddhist Monks, 53
Til Eulenspiegel's Lustige Streiche, 224–225
Til Eulenspiegel's Merry Pranks, 234
Time Turns Elastic, 238
Tin Christopher, 263
T.I.'s Road to Redemption, 147
Toccata and Fugue in D minor, 209, 258
Toot, Toot, Tootsie, Goodbye, 247
Tosca, 34, 68
Tower of Ashes, 52
Traditional Arabic Improvisation, 287, 289
Traditional Indian music, 289
Turandot, 61
Turtle Island String Quartet, 276, 289

van Beethoven, Ludwig, 12–13, 18–19, 153, 163–165, 169, 214, 220, 230, 232, 236, 239, 246, 256, 258, 275
van Brachel, Peter, 53
Vangelis, 263–264, 268
Veni, veni, Emmanuel, 43–44
Verdi, Giuseppe, 16, 54, 154–159, 165, 169, 222
Vivaldi, Antonio, 2, 10, 38, 205–207, 239, 275, 289
von Eybler, Joseph, 156

von Goethe, Johann Wolfgang, 130
von Suppe, Franz, 246

Wagner, Richard, 3, 16, 179, 187, 222, 228, 247, 256, 260, 264, 268
Wallace, Alfred Russel, 230
Warrior Death Song (for Sitting Bull), 168–170
Water Music, 95
We Shall Overcome, 194, 196
Webber, Andrew Lloyd, 76, 79, 156, 165
Webern, Anton, 231
Wedding March, 178–179
Wesley, John, 42
West End Blues, 277
West Side Story, 75–76, 234, 254
Whelan, Bill, 81
When the Saints Go Marching In, 168, 277
White Christmas, 139, 251
Whitfield, Norman, 2
William Tell Overture, 260, 261
Williams, Hank, 145
Williams, John, 181–182, 187, 195, 254, 266–269
"Winter" *(Concerto for Violin and Orchestra)*, 2
Wintereisse (A Winter's Journey), 130

Yardbirds, 284
You Enjoy Myself, 285
Young, La Monte, 236
Yvette, 280

Zwilich, Ellen Taaffe, 231, 235